EXPLORING THE BRIDLEWAYS
OF SUSSEX

G000253459

BY THE SAME AUTHOR

The Selsey Tram
Six Of The Best!
The Jennings Companion
Financial Penalties
Around Chichester In Old Photographs
Here's A Pretty Mess!
Magisterial Lore
*The Beaten Track (republished as The Big Walks Of Great Britain
    and subsequently Best Walks Of The North and Best Walks Of
    The South)*
Poetic Justice
Walking The Coastline Of Sussex
Best Sussex Walks
That's My Girl (a play)
Let's Take It From The Top
*Walking The Disused Railways Of Sussex (republished as
    Walking The Disused Railways Of Sussex And Surrey)*
Once More From The Top
Sussex Top Tens
Walking The Kent Coast From End To End
Walking The Riversides Of Sussex
Walking The South Coast Of England
Anyone For Tenors?
Walking The Triangulation Points Of Sussex
Walking The Disused Railways Of Kent
Walking The Sussex Border Path
Walking The County High Points Of England
Sussex Station Walks
The Joy Of Walking (republished as Walk)
The Walker's Year
Stumbling On Mountains
The Muddlesfield Messiah
The Great Walks Of Sussex
Walkabulary
Memory Guy
Laughing Stock

EXPLORING THE BRIDLEWAYS
OF SUSSEX

By David Bathurst

to Ben

with very best wishes

Nov. 2022

First published in 2022 by
Walk & Write Publications
41 Park Road
Yapton
Arundel
West Sussex BN18 0JE

Cover and typesetting by The Better Book Company,
5 Lime Close, Chichester, West Sussex PO19 6SW

Printed in the UK by Imprint Digital, Seychelles Farm,
Upton Pyne, Devon EX5 5HY

British Library Cataloguing-in-Publication Data.
A catalogue record for this book is available from the British
Library.

ISBN 978-0-9933241-4-7

COVER ILLUSTRATION: A well-signed bridleway junction
between Falmer and Lewes.

INTRODUCTION

As we become increasingly reliant on technology and automation in our daily lives, and spend more and more of our time staring at screens, it is often easy for us to forget that there is a world outside our front door, a world of fascinating landscapes and history waiting to be explored. What better way to enhance our mental and physical health and well-being than exploring this world for ourselves – not behind the wheel of a car but enjoying it at first-hand through walking, cycling and horse-riding. The health benefits of being out in the open air, exercising and exploring under your own steam are inestimable. This book is all about tempting you to do this in beautiful Sussex.

Sussex (which for the purpose of this book includes not only West and East Sussex but also Brighton & Hove) offers a magnificent variety of landscapes, from elevated chalk downland to tranquil riverside embankments, from lush green forests to heather-clad common land, and from flat windswept marshlands to rugged coastal cliffs. It also boasts innumerable historic structures, from cathedrals to stately homes, from castles to opulent town houses, and from quaint timber-framed cottages to sturdy brick farmhouses that might be a perfect setting for a period drama.

While many books and pamphlets have been published, both in traditional paper form and online, which describe journeys through Sussex, there is no guide devoted specifically to the exploration of Sussex through travel along routes designated as public bridleways (which from now on I'll just refer to as bridleways), as opposed to roads or public footpaths. And there certainly are plenty of bridleways in Sussex. At a very rough estimate, there are some 2000 kilometres (km) of bridleways in Sussex as a whole, including Brighton & Hove – just over 1250 miles. If you follow them all, you'll have done the approximate equivalent of travelling from Brighton to Inverness and back!

I use the word "bridleway" or "bridleways" here, and throughout the book, to include not only public bridleways but also (unless otherwise stated) restricted byways. In the first substantive section of this book I shall explain the very fine distinction between bridleways and restricted byways, but the distinction is so slim as to enable me to treat restricted byways as bridleways for the purpose of what follows. This book is about exploring both bridleways and restricted byways.

So, what are the attractions of bridleways as opposed to other types of route? I would say there are four principal aspects which make bridleways unique attractions for the outdoor explorer.

Firstly, bridleways aren't open to motorised transport including e-scooters (save for access for property owners). As a result, they're not only so much safer to travel on than pavement-less public roads and public byways, but they will also be free from traffic noise and the stink of exhaust fumes.

Secondly, bridleways provide often breathtakingly beautiful and always fascinating scenery and surroundings, far more so than most public roads do. Even if you're a seasoned Sussex explorer you may, in the course of your bridleway travels, discover many beautiful corners of Sussex you never knew existed; the 90 routes described in the main body of this book will get you to the very best of them. The countryside certainly doesn't need to be spectacular for a bridleway traverse to be hugely enjoyable. This was my diary entry for a walk across unremarkable countryside between Henfield and Hickstead on 13th May 2019: "Just perfect... nice clear wide track, beautiful spring flowers, the shade of trees, birdsong, and attractive countryside beyond." Days like that, even though the surroundings aren't particularly special, just seem to make the whole idea of bridleway bagging worthwhile on their own.

I used the word "fascinating" above to describe the scenery and surroundings you will find on bridleways.

2

But the bridleways themselves are also fascinating. As you begin exploring bridleways for yourself, you'll quickly get to know, as I did on my explorations, how extraordinarily diverse not only the variety of terrain will be, but also the character of each bridleway. Part of the fun of exploring bridleways is seeing how they will negotiate their way through the surrounding landscape, and indeed what is special about exploring a bridleway, as opposed to a metalled road, for the first time is that you never quite know what you're going to get. You might in fact find yourself on a metalled track or driveway, but equally you could be following a field-edge path, a farm access road, an enclosed path between fields, a wide forest track or a narrow path snaking its way through the trees. There may be no defined path at all, the route itself simply traversing an area of grass. Sometimes the going will be tough; sometimes it'll be very easy. There'll be steep downland climbs and descents (many providing links between the South Downs Way and villages below) on often slippery chalk or grassy surfaces, but bringing rewards of quite fantastic views on the clearer days. By contrast the going may be very straightforward, as you follow waterside paths or travel along lanes that may take you past picturesque country cottages and historic churches. One of my very favourite kinds of bridleway is the firm but not concreted track through shady coniferous woodland which just every so often opens up to provide fine views. I'm a great fan, too, of bridleways passing into and through grassy dry valleys, reminiscent of the Yorkshire Wolds Way, and beside natural amphitheatres such as Devil's Dyke.

History will never be far away. Even if you're walking or riding through remote downland with no historic constructions in sight, you can call to mind the generations of prehistoric settlers and traders who first created and then used the chalk tracks as the M25 and A27 of their day. Woodland walking or riding might bring memories of St Leonard and his battle with the last dragon in England, or the once flourishing iron industry across large parts of West

3

and East Sussex, and the ironmasters who cut down forest trees to heat their forges. Indeed, Sussex boasts countless bridleways which immerse you in history, whether it's the routes themselves, tracing the course of Roman roads or disused railways, or places of historic interest beside or right on the routes, from quaint Norman churches to windmills, from Elizabethan farmhouses to carved hill figures, from elevated follies to ancient burial mounds, from mighty castles to hilltop observatories. It's always particularly rewarding to arrive at a place of special historic interest that is only accessible by bridleway; Charleston Farmhouse, with its Bloomsbury Group connections, is a particularly fine example.

Hand-in-hand with diversity of terrain is diversity of life populating the different types of terrain. Any country walker quickly gets used to inquisitive cattle and frightened sheep, and there are always plenty of those in the Sussex countryside. Waterside bridleways may bring sightings of the heron, kingfisher, oystercatcher, mallard and coot, and many others besides, and you may be treated to the sight of a flock of geese taking off and flying in close formation. I was privileged to see this latter phenomenon beside the river Ouse one wet December morning, and the sight instantly rendered my early start and long train journey worthwhile. Woodland routes sparkle in spring with their profusion of bluebell, wild garlic and wood anemone, and the occasional deer leaping across the path before you. Downland bridleways bring with them butterflies of every size and hue, the joyous carolling of the skylark, and the urgent bounding of rabbit or hare. Any summer excursion is likely to bring with it hosts of dragonflies and damselflies, while July or August exploration of a heath such as Trotton Common promises a sea of dazzling purple. And threading your way through bridle routes in residential West Chiltington Common you should listen out for the roaring engine of the greater-spotted BMW.

As you continue with your bridleway exploration, you'll get to discover contrasts at every turn – contrasts which highlight the need to be properly equipped, an aspect I'll cover in the second substantive section of the book. Bear in mind that progress along some bridleways may not be as straightforward as it will be along others. While many bridleways are clear and unobstructed, others – thanks to areas of mud, fragments of fallen trees and overhanging vegetation – may require skills last honed during primary school obstacle course races. That said, one fabulous payback for chunky vegetation may come in late summer in the form of bushes offering plump and juicy blackberries. By contrast, perhaps the easiest sort of bridleway travel is along disused railway paths such as the Downs Link and the Worth Way, with a firm surface, no route-finding concerns and rapid progress more or less guaranteed; for the distance walkers or riders, this sort of bridleway is ideal for training purposes as well as sponsored activity. Some bridleways are wider than others. There might be bridleways consisting of narrow tracks with stern warnings of death by firing squad for straying half a centimetre from the course of the route, but conversely a bridle route might be across a field with no track to speak of, the only guidance coming from the signposts at their start and finish. I also love the fact that bridleways close to one another may have such a different feel. If you choose the area between Horsham and Crawley for a bridleway bag, you may initially be following rural bridle tracks through the peace and seclusion of St Leonard's Forest, just east of Horsham, but then a few hours later, you could find yourself picking your way along a succession of bridleways in the outskirts of Crawley. I remember how on April Fools' Day in 2019 I spent the morning shinning up and down often inhumanly steep bridleways providing links between the South Downs escarpment and the communities at its foot, then devoted the afternoon to much less undulating heather and pine of nearby Selham and Duncton Commons. And the peace and tranquillity of a bridleway through Benland Wood, near Warnham, one September afternoon could not have contrasted more starkly with the incessant aircraft and traffic noise I encountered on my explorations of bridleways in the vicinity of Gatwick less than ten miles away, a week and a half later. As if to underline the contrasting personalities of bridle routes, it's worth pointing out that a fair few bridleways even have actual names on maps. Within just a few square kilometres north of the A272 between Rogate and Stedham there's a Cumber's Lane (in fact there are two Cumber's Lanes!), a Moorhouse Lane, a Lambourne Lane, a Brier Lane and a Green Lane.

And some bridleways even have the capacity to amuse, albeit unintentionally. Well, in fairness, they may not have amused me too much at the time, but have certainly given me the odd chuckle as I've sat in the comfort of my ancestral semi writing about them. These are what one might call freak bridleways, the ones that help to make up Part 7 in the central section of this book: the ridiculously short bridleways, the bridleways that "die," the bridleways that are devoid of any scenic or aesthetic merit whatsoever, the bridleways that are rudely cut short by the pitiless intervention of a bully-boy dual carriageway, and the bridleway that might have been a perfect location for filming a post-apocalypse drama. It may seem odd that in this introductory section, in which I am anxious to extol the virtues of bridleway exploration, I should be referring to some of the less than lovely bridle routes. But they are only a very small part of the Sussex bridleway package and in any case, there is a certain masochistic pleasure in seeking them out, just as it's fun to watch a selection of TV/You Tube clips from the worst films ever made. The principle's the same.

The third attraction of bridleways is that they are more flexible than public footpaths, being open not only to walkers but pedal cyclists and horse-riders as well. (Note: when I use the words "cycling," "cyclist" or "cyclists" in this book I am referring to pedal cyclists as opposed to motor cyclists or moped riders; when I use the word "rider" I mean pedal cyclist or horse-rider unless otherwise indicated.) You may of course enjoy walking, cycling AND horse-riding in the countryside, and therefore in your exploration of bridleways you can be wholly fluid in the mode of travel you prefer to adopt. Off-road cycling in particular has become extremely popular in the modern age; more and more, cyclists are appreciating that getting off the roads can provide some exciting and highly adventurous travelling, and there's a huge range of cycles on the market that are extremely resilient and can stand up to the battering of even the toughest off-road journey.

Fourthly, bridleways are generally extremely well signed and defined, usually much more so than ordinary public footpaths. I wonder how many times you have ventured into the countryside but felt anxious about straying too far from the road, not knowing how difficult or inhospitable the terrain might be to negotiate without your getting lost. Bridleway travel allows anyone with limited navigational experience or confidence to enjoy the countryside without these worries. More often than not, bridleways follow clear tracks or driveways, and even when they don't, it is most unusual for the identity or course of a bridleway to be obliterated or wholly indistinct. The enjoyment of your journey will therefore be enhanced in the knowledge of your being on the right track.

This book provides the definitive guide to exploring the bridleways of Sussex. You may have heard of the concept of "bagging" in connection with mountain climbing – by "bagging" is simply meant completing the conquest of a mountain. This book is all about "bagging" bridleways – following as many as you wish from end to end. The book is divided into three main sections. In the first section, I provide a brief history and overview of the public bridleway and highlight some of the difficulties, issues and quirks which you as a bridleway explorer will come up against on your travels, and how to cope with them. In the second section, the central part and main body of the book, I divide the bridleways of Sussex into families – bridleways that are official long-distance walking routes, woodland bridleways, waterside bridleways, downland bridleways, common-land/parkland bridleways, and bridleways linking places of historic importance. Under each of these headings I offer a selection of bridleway routes that provide in my view the best experiences of these types of landscape – the best woodland bridleway routes, the best waterside bridleway routes, and so on. There are 90 routes in all. Finally in the central section, I introduce you to the "best of the rest" plus a hotch-potch of bridleways that are unusual, curious and sometimes just plain barmy. Then in the third section, I become more personal and give a description of my own mission to walk every single bridleway in Sussex, a mission that was interrupted by the succession of lockdowns caused by the coronavirus pandemic, but which was finally accomplished in the autumn of 2021, over three years after I began the quest.

I hope by reading the book that firstly, you will come to appreciate more the tremendous variety of scenery and surroundings that bridleway exploration offers you as a walker, cyclist and/or horse-rider; secondly, you'll be tempted out into the countryside to try some of the routes for yourself, and discover scenic or historic delights you might otherwise have missed; and even if you don't feel up for that, I hope you can use this book to enjoy a virtual journey along the routes from the comfort of your armchair.

So lastly, before we move on, what is it that qualifies me to write this book? Well, as stated, I have actually walked every bridleway in Sussex, a feat I am unaware has been achieved by anyone else, so that perhaps will do for a start! Besides that, though, I have loved walking and cycling all my adult life. As well as walking all the name long-distance paths in Sussex, the subject of *The Great Walks Of Sussex*, I have walked all the national trails of England and Wales, walked the whole of the south coast of England, the Gower coast and the coastline of Kent, and walked to the summit of every major Lakeland peak, the highest point of every county of England, and the highest points of all four countries in the UK. I've done a number of sponsored distance walks and to date the longest I have walked over 24 hours is 63 miles, or 101km, walking from my home in

Yapton, near Arundel, to Buckingham Palace in honour of the Platinum Jubilee. Moreover, I have walked extensively in Sussex and written and published a number of Sussex-themed walking guides including not only *The Great Walks Of Sussex* but walks to each triangulation point, along each riverside and along each disused railway in Sussex.

When I am not walking, I work as criminal defence lawyer, acting for clients in the police station, magistrates' court and Crown Court. Besides walking, I enjoy writing, singing and memory challenges, of which my most recent was in July 2022 when I sang all the Beatles songs from memory in a single day.

Finally, and most important, I would like to dedicate this book to Ben Taylor, who has been more of a blessing to my family and to me than words could ever say.

Happy bridleway exploring!

David Bathurst

August 2022

SECTION 1

ABOUT BRIDLEWAYS

The development of rights of way

Let's start our celebration of Sussex bridleways by considering how bridleways fit into the hierarchy of rights of way in this country.

Ever since prehistoric times, and right up to the present day, routes across the country have had to be created to get people from A to B, for various purposes including conveyance of animals and goods, accessing places of work, worship and other community activity, and obtaining supplies of food and medicine. Creating such routes has routinely involved considerable time, expense and ingenuity, particularly where the surrounding terrain is inhospitable and perhaps even dangerous for travellers. Given that all land across the country belonged/belongs to someone, there would also have been, and continues to be, the need to obtain permission from landowners to establish a right of way across the relevant land. It's important at this point to bear in mind that in England or Wales there is not, and never has been, a general presumptive right to travel and roam where you please. It is true that certain areas of England and Wales have been designated as what's called Access Land, where there is a general "right to roam," these areas being clearly marked on maps. However, Access Land accounts for only a very small proportion of land across England and Wales. Outside Access Land, the traveller is restricted to rights of way, that is, routes over which specific rights have been conferred. Note the position is different in Scotland but we need not concern ourselves with Scottish access rights in this book.

It was only towards the end of the 18th and beginning of the 19th centuries that routes across the countryside began to be used for recreational purposes, and indeed in the 1820's the first rambling clubs were established in Great Britain. However, there were still vast areas that were shut off altogether to explorers of the countryside, often as a result of the intransigence of landowners. This led to conflicts between would-be ramblers and landowners, the most famous incident being the so-called Kinder Trespass in 1932 when huge numbers of frustrated walkers deliberately set out into privately-owned land in what's now known as the Peak District. Some trespassers were arrested and five were jailed. The events excited massive public interest, with huge support and sympathy for those imprisoned. Meanwhile, the number of walking clubs and groups that campaigned for walkers' rights had been steadily growing from the mid-19th century to the 1930s. In 1931, six regional federations representing walkers from all over Britain joined to create the National Council Of Ramblers Federations, a body that could advocate on behalf of walkers' rights at a national level. And although not all members of the Ramblers Federations were in favour of the Kinder Trespass, that episode added considerable momentum to the campaign for those rights. The campaign culminated in the formation, on 1 January 1935, of the Ramblers Association, whose objective was to champion the rights of walkers to greater access to the countryside. And it was partially as a result of the work of the Association that the Government during World War 2 laid down a blueprint for greater access to the outdoors. A major breakthrough came in the form of legislation leading to the establishment of National Parks, out of which came an obvious need for the creation of clear rights of way through these areas. Indeed many of the routes described in this book are in the (comparatively new) South Downs National Park. Alongside this legislation, laws were passed in 1949 which imposed on local authorities a duty to compile and publish definitive maps of their areas showing all public paths (footpaths and bridleways) as well as roads. Where there was a dispute as to whether a road or a path was a public right of way or not, the first resort was negotiation and, if that failed to resolve the issue, there would be a public inquiry and a final decision would be made by the Government department concerned. The importance of the definitive maps was huge, because it conclusively proved that something shown as a right of way, whether a road or a path, was indeed a right of way – even if it was included by mistake! – and legislation then imposed a duty on the local authority to keep it open and not to divert or extinguish it except by due legal process. As well as pre-existing rights of way that appeared in the definitive maps, many more new roads and paths have been created as rights of way since the maps were drawn up, these new routes mostly created by agreement without the need for an order. One particularly interesting development in recent decades has been the construction of numerous rights of way along the course of disused railways. There are a number of such routes in Sussex, some of which were actually in use as railways when the definitive maps were prepared! All the while, though, you should remember that the default position in England and Wales is that you can't just walk or ride anywhere without the consent of the relevant landowner; outside of designated Access Land, you must stick to rights of way, whether public roads or paths, as shown in definitive maps and subsequent amendments.

Different Paths For Different Users

The good news is that a glance at any large-scale map, in either paper or electronic form, covering any part of England and Wales will reveal a huge number of rights of way, open to the public, across the countryside as well as in urban areas. However, not all rights of way are open to all types of traveller. Rights of way come in a number of forms, the status of each having their roots in the terms of the permissions granted when the rights were first conferred.

Before going through the different types of rights of way I should explain that as I go through them I shall be referring to Ordnance Survey (OS) maps. We are incredibly fortunate to be blessed with the OS, which has published maps of the whole of Great Britain in astonishing detail and clarity, in both paper form and now online. Though the OS has published maps using a wide variety of scales, I have made an assumption that as a bridleway traveller you will be using the orange-covered OS Explorer maps (scale 1:25,000) either in paper or electronic form. As an alternative you might wish to use the purple-covered OS Landranger maps (1:50,000) which by definition cover much wider areas and therefore give a better overview of places in a given district that you may wish to explore, but because of their smaller scale are really more appropriate for use by motorists or cyclists wishing to stick to roads. So I will stick to reference solely to the OS Explorer maps as the book continues.

Anyway, back to rights of way! At the bottom of the pile, in terms of those who can access them, are **public footpaths**, available only to walkers. These are denoted on standard OS Explorer maps, both in paper and in electronic form, by short green dashes, and in Sussex are signed "on the ground" with yellow arrows but without showing destinations or distances. Public footpaths are very plenteous right across Sussex but the quality of signage varies tremendously, and many footpaths are very poorly defined.

Leaving aside motorways (which in any case have their own significant restrictions on usage), at the top of the pile there are **public roads,** available to all traffic. Public roads will be marked on OS Explorer maps in continuous red (primary routes, i.e. A roads), dark brown (secondary routes, i.e. B roads), lighter brown (minor routes generally more than 4m wide) and yellow (minor routes generally less than 4m wide). Signage on the ground will vary tremendously: modern signage, used on busier roads, is slick, professional and crystal-clear, but the more rural the surroundings, the more delightfully rustic and old-fashioned the signage is likely to be, with black lettering on sturdy white-painted metalled plates and possibly the name of the local authority or council painted on a post above the meeting of the sign plates. You can expect most public road signs to bear distances as well as destinations.

Also available to all traffic are **public byways,** denoted on OS Explorer maps with green crosses and signed on the ground with red arrows (but without showing destinations or distances). There are hardly any public byways in West Sussex or Brighton & Hove, but there are plenty in East Sussex. There is no obvious reason for this discrepancy!

Just to complicate matters, though, there are some roads shown on OS Explorer maps which aren't shaded at all. Many of these are private but, confusingly, some do permit public access, and there is even a separate designation for those that do, namely the so-called **public way.** Again public ways are open to all traffic and are signed on the ground simply with the words "Public Way." In Sussex as a whole, though, public ways are extremely rare birds.

In the middle of the pile, there are those rights of way that are denoted on OS Explorer maps by longer green dashes than public footpaths and generally signed "on the ground" with blue arrows, or white arrows on a blue background – again, though, without showing destinations or distances. They are **public bridleways,** open to walkers, pedal cyclists (as opposed to motor cyclists, currently e-scooter riders, or moped riders) and horse-riders, but not motorised traffic. (Note that I will continue to refer to "public bridleways" as "bridleways" as the book continues.) There has been a further designation following the Countryside and Rights of Way Act 2000, namely **restricted byways**, signed "on the ground" with purple arrows (or white arrows on a purple background), and essentially open to walkers, pedal cyclists, horse-riders, and also any vehicles other than mechanically propelled ones, so for instance a horse and cart would be allowed but a moped or (as the law stands at the time of writing) an e-scooter would not. Not that I've seen a horse and cart on any restricted byway! Restricted byways are denoted on OS Explorer maps by the same longer green dashes but with a small green spur coming out of each dash. It is bridleways and restricted byways that form the subject matter of this book. Because there is really negligible practical difference between classes of people and transport permitted to use bridleways and those permitted to use restricted byways, I have throughout this book, as stated in my introduction, chosen to use "bridleway" or "bridleways" as shorthand for both public bridleways and restricted byways. This book will lead you on an exploration of both types. (Incidentally on the road between Steyning and Sompting in West Sussex I spotted a sign saying "Restricted Bridleway." There is no such designation in law so obviously the sign-writer was having a bad day!)

On top of these bridleways for which rights of way exist, there are (mostly in East Sussex and Brighton & Hove) a number of permissive bridleways (or so-called licensed bridleways, effectively the same things). A permissive route isn't a permanent right of way but is effectively concessionary, ie the landowner has given consent to allow the public to use the route in question but may withdraw such consent either from time to time or permanently. Some permissive/licensed bridleways are marked on OS Explorer maps, with long brown dashes rather than long green ones. However, others are not, and may only become evident from information boards erected locally, meaning that if you want to follow them, you may need to photograph the board on your phone and follow the route from your photos. You need to be particularly careful with permissive routes showing on obviously old information boards where relevant consent may have come and gone a long while ago. But in the case of OS-mapped permissive bridleway routes, the chances of withdrawal of consent to follow such routes are in my experience very slim, and many of them are really very well worth following. In fact I use some of them in the routes described below. Note that some paths are designated both public footpath and permissive bridleway, meaning that access on foot is allowed as of right, whereas there is no automatic right of way for cyclists and horse-riders, and permission for them may be withdrawn. The cliff path between Brighton Marina and Saltdean via Rottingdean, in the Brighton & Hove unitary authority area, and the footpath between Earnley and Selsey via the Medmerry Nature Reserve in West Sussex, are good examples of this. (Both feature later in this book.) Note that there is no such thing as a permissive or licensed restricted byway. Incidentally, one section of bridleway on the Medmerry Nature Reserve is signed as being a public bridleway from south to north, and a permissive bridleway from north to south. Take your pick! (Sadly I am sure the "public" bridleway sign here is erroneous.)

Please note that while bridleways, whether permissive or not, are closed to motorised traffic, it's possible that a bridleway may also serve as a driveway allowing landowners or leaseholders access to their property. This could explain why you may meet motor vehicles along the course of a mapped bridleway, so don't be too quick to remonstrate with drivers who pass you as you follow a bridleway. However, if you're aware of obvious misuse of bridleways by motorists or motorcyclists, you might, if you're sufficiently public-spirited, wish to report the matter to the relevant local authority and leave it to them to take appropriate steps.

All bridleways that are rights of way must effectively live up to their name and be maintained so as to allow passage by horse-riders. All gates on bridleways must be capable of being opened by a horse-rider without dismounting, and the building of stiles across bridleways is prohibited by law. If you find yourself being forced to climb a stile to make progress, you've probably strayed onto a public footpath, or the bridleway has been demoted! Although most bridleways can be easily negotiated by horse-riders, I have come across bridleways which are so narrow as to make it awkward for horses to get through; there are gates which horse-riders will struggle to manoeuvre without dismounting. As far as cyclists are concerned, although the law permits the riding of bicycles on public bridleways, that law "shall not create any obligation to facilitate the use of the bridleway by cyclists." Thus, though the right to cycle exists, it may prove difficult to exercise on occasion. Firstly, the surfaces of some bridleways may mean cyclists among you will need get off and push, or even carry, your machines. Secondly, not only must cyclists using a bridleway give way to other users on foot or horseback, but in Sussex there are a few (generally short urban) routes designated as bridleways where cycling is prohibited, and if you're a cyclist you will have to get off your bike and push! Rest assured that all of the recommended bridleway routes I describe later in this book are open to cyclists.

A word about wheelchairs and mobility scooters. These appear to be permitted on bridleways and restricted byways, even if they are powered (providing a maximum speed of 4mph is maintained), and are therefore an exception to the general rule that powered transport is not allowed on bridleways or restricted byways. However it is an unfortunate fact that a significant number of bridleways are not suitable for wheelchair users: they may be too narrow, too steep or too uneven. If you're contemplating a bridleway expedition by wheelchair or mobility scooter, it may be worth your while contacting the highways department of the relevant local authority who can advise you if your chosen route is suitable.

Mapping of bridleways...or not

So, having decided you wanted to explore some bridleways, perhaps in your locality, you might think it was simply a matter of opening up your map, finding a route denoted on it as a bridleway, and getting yourself there. A little earlier in this section I was extolling the virtues of the OS, and certainly in the vast majority of cases, its mapping of bridleways, with those long green dashes on the Explorer maps, is correct and reliable. All being well, you can plan and then enjoy some great bridleway exploring, simply relying on the maps of your chosen area. And I hope that, duly inspired by this book, you will do just that. There's so much out there to enjoy.

Unfortunately, even those wonderful maps aren't always infallible. On rare occasions, while a route may be stated on an OS map, either in paper or in electronic form, to be a bridleway, things may have changed. In particular some mapped bridleways may have ceased to exist, have been re-routed, and/or have been promoted to a route which is a public right of way for all vehicles, or conversely demoted to a route which is only now a public footpath and therefore unavailable for riders. Re-routing, providing the signage is good enough, is tolerable, and promotion to a public right of way for all vehicles isn't a problem either. But clearly it is irksome in the extreme to be faced with a mapped bridleway that you cannot negotiate at all because (unbeknown to you) it is no longer legally available to bridleway traffic for all or part of its length, or it is simply blocked.

A classic instance of a mapped but very obviously partially defunct bridleway is one mapped as running for 375m just to the north-west of the village of Kingston-near-Lewes, which I visited in 2019 and again in 2021. It is actually shown on an OS Explorer map dated May 2020 as still in existence, albeit "stopping" in the middle of absolutely nowhere. The first 100m or so are walkable/rideable (though not signed as a bridleway) but you then reach a gate with a sign barring further progress. Adjacent to that gate is a notice erected by the Kingston Hill Fields Committee stating they bought the land in 2006 (14 years before the Explorer map in question appeared) to promote biodiversity; the land, a chalk meadow, now boasts a significant population of ground-nesting skylarks, and 500 trees have been planted. Hats off to the Kingston Hill Fields Committee for their enterprise and excellent PR, but if you'd come here wanting to follow the whole 375m-long bridleway as mapped, it would have been a case of close but no cigar. I well remember on another bridleway bag, in April 2021, exploring an OS-mapped bridleway at Hammerwood very close to the Sussex/Kent border between East Grinstead and Ashurst. Near the northern end of it I was challenged, politely but firmly, by a local property owner insisting that the bridleway, which in fairness was quite impossible to discern and negotiate in places, had been extinguished years ago. It would have been a waste of my breath for me to suggest that once a right of way, always a right of way. That is a myth. Any right of way, providing due legal process is followed, may be extinguished, perhaps to allow for the building of a new estate or a new road, and if the map fails to indicate this, it's too bad. Finally, the most recent OS Explorer map number 125 shows a bridleway running from Houghton Lane to Military Road just north-east of Rye. I explored this "bridleway" in September 2021 only to find the middle section had apparently become demoted to a footpath, with footpath signs and, at one point, a succession of steps which cyclists could not safely negotiate without dismounting. The one consolation was that this was early September and there was an abundance of blackberries to enjoy alongside the path as I lugged my bike down the steps!

Of course I realise that if you're out there faced with a bridleway that is mapped but inaccessible to bridleway traffic, you may have no obvious means of knowing whether the bridleway in question has in law actually been extinguished. As the first of the examples given above demonstrates, it may be that that fate has indeed befallen your route of choice. However it could be that the bridleway does still exist in law as a right of way, but is inaccessible either through quirks of nature, eg a fallen tree, or through human intervention such as the erection of, say, a fence or locked gate. It may be that there's somebody around you can ask, who is familiar with the area. But if there's nobody around to ask, one possibility in this situation, assuming you've access to wifi in the spot you find yourself, is to go online and download relevant sections of the rights of way maps supplied online by the relevant local authorities (West Sussex County Council, East Sussex County Council or Brighton & Hove City Council). It is possible that the information on these maps may be more up-to-date than that on OS maps. (But not necessarily: the East Sussex County Council rights of way map still, at the time of writing, suggests that the Houghton Lane-Military Road route mentioned above is a bridleway throughout.) In the absence of any evidence from the resources at your disposal that a blocked bridleway has ceased to exist, it'll be for you to decide whether to attempt to surmount or remove the obstruction. But if you do so decide, you need to be careful not to lay yourself open to allegations of trespass and/or criminal damage, which may theoretically follow if the bridleway in question has indeed ceased to exist and the obstruction is a lawful one. Annoyingly, it may prove to be a lot easier to turn back, and to look on it as part of life's rich pattern.

But don't be too quick to curse the OS (and/or the local authority) for misleading you, forcing you to change your plans, and thereby stopping you from getting home in time for *The One Show*. Remember that OS maps and the local authority rights of way maps can only be as accurate and up-to-date as information given to the map-makers themselves. You could, of course, choose to report any anomalies to the OS and the local authority concerned; one would hope that they would be suitably grateful to you, but whether or not they chose to take action upon your report would be in the lap of the gods, especially given the current huge post-pandemic pressures on human and financial resources.

At the same time, and in a more positive vein, a number of new bridleways have opened up which don't feature on the latest OS maps or local rights of way map, and the existence of which has only become evident through their being included on local information boards or being signposted (about which more below). The problem with an unmapped new bridleway is uncertainty as to how far it will go and where it will emerge, although some bridleway explorers may say that adds to the fun! The position is to a degree complicated by the fact that there are a number of new or comparatively new routes in Sussex that aren't marked on the ground or on maps as bridleways but are signed as "shared-use" routes, open to cyclists and horse-riders as well as walkers. A splendid example of a spanking new shared-use route, not explicitly stated to be a bridleway on signage, is at Combe Haven between Bexhill and Hastings, following closely beside the new A2690. It really is a bridleway in all but name! Another example: a section of pathway parallel with the Lewes-Kingston road in East Sussex is signed as a "public path" and pictorial symbols on the sign indicate that horse-riders and cyclists may use it as well as walkers. Care is needed with some of the newer paths, especially those using the course of disused railways, as there are some baffling inconsistencies which won't always be apparent from OS maps. All of the path sections of the Downs Link, following the old railway between Shoreham and Guildford, are designated as bridleways and therefore available to all bridleway traffic. The Worth Way and Forest Way routes between Three Bridges and Groombridge, again converted railway lines, are also designated as bridleways throughout. However, two other converted railway lines, the Cuckoo Trail, linking Heathfield and Polegate, and the Centurion Way, between Chichester and West Dean, while open to cyclists are either partially or fully closed to horse-riders, even though the surface and width, and indeed ethos, of each, are exactly the same as on the Downs Link. Where new recreational routes are created, it's always worth checking online to seek clarification on whether it is available for all bridleway "traffic."

Bridleway maintenance and negotiation

Generally, bridleways will be wider and better defined than public footpaths, reflecting the need for them to accommodate a wider variety of traffic than just walkers. But that isn't necessarily always the case: it's not easy sometimes to discern why some rights of way have been designated as bridleways rather than footpaths, although there will always be a historical explanation if you choose to look for it. I have encountered some bridleways where both cyclists and horse-riders would have immense difficulty in negotiating the course of the route, not necessarily because the bridleway was badly maintained but simply because of the width of the bridleway and/or the nature of the terrain in which it is situated. As I have stated in my introductory section, one of the joys (and sometimes, paradoxically, one of the headaches!) of bridleway exploration is that you can never be sure what you're going to get, and indeed the character of a bridleway route can change part-way along. One bridleway I walked in August 2021, a short distance to the west of Rye in East Sussex, started as a metalled lane; it then became a metalled driveway; it then turned into a grass track guarded by high hedges; it then became a field edge path heading downhill to a valley; there followed an area of grass, hugging a hedge on one side; then came a narrow pathway through long grass which brought me to a driveway; and it was that driveway that I followed to arrive at the end of the bridleway. Changes can be very abrupt: one moment you're following a clear wide track, and the next you may be struggling along a much rougher path with brambles extending across the way.

Which leads me to path maintenance. Local authorities have a responsibility to maintain rights of way, including bridleways, and, the good news is that overall, bridleways across Sussex are mostly well maintained, well signed and well defined. But sadly, this is not always the case. In these days of limited budgets and as a legacy of the Covid pandemic, resources are continually stretched; as a result there will inevitably be sections of bridleway that are harder to negotiate than one would wish, thanks to, among other things, the incursion of undergrowth or over-hanging vegetation, or the combination of constant usage and poor drainage creating a mud-bath underfoot. It is therefore a real joy to find oneself on a section of bridleway that has obviously been recently improved or even "taken in hand," for want of a better expression, by enthusiastic local volunteers. One band of such volunteers is the Monday Group which operates in mid-Sussex and has done a colossal amount of work to keep paths available to follow and explore. Maybe if you find your passage has been eased by the work of a group like this, you might like to repay them by donating back to them in money or in kind. This kind of work doesn't just happen, but requires a lot of effort, and may necessitate the closure of bridleways at times. But although it will be irksome to be forced to find a way round the closed section, at least you can derive consolation from the knowledge that it will be so much better to walk or ride along in future!

Bridleway signage

In theory, if you are a competent map-reader and/or have infallible technology at your disposal, you should be able to follow any mapped bridleway from start to finish without any assistance "on the ground." Even in the case of an unmapped new or permissive bridleway, a photo on your phone of the relevant local information board displaying the new route may be all you need. However as you set about your bridleway travels you will very soon come to realise the importance of good signage on your routes of choice. You'll find many instances where, even with the help of your mapping or technology, the way ahead is ambiguous, or the bridleway in question has been re-routed, or bad weather has blotted out landmarks on which you're relying to keep you orientated. Numerous bridleways pass through building complexes such as farms, with their barns and outhouses, where it could be very easy to take a wrong turning and face the possibility of unwitting trespass onto private land and the embarrassment of being challenged by landowners or householders, and barked or growled at by their dogs.

How are bridleways signed? When following a public bridleway in Sussex (as distinct, in this paragraph only, from a restricted byway) you'll see a number of different types of sign, sometimes along a single bridleway! There are the old sturdy plinths, stuck in the ground, sadly often obscured by vegetation. There are the older wooden finger posts simply saying PUBLIC BRIDLEWAY with no arrow drawn on it but the end of the "finger" shaped like an arrow. There are also the older metal bridleway signs, usually found leading off public roads, which will boast white lettering on a green background and a white arrow painted at the end of it. Newer signs of both varieties have sprung up in recent years, and you may find these will bear blue arrows painted on the fingers/plates, pictorial signs indicating permitted users of bridleways, and/or a web address! You will also, particularly (but not exclusively) in the neighbourhood of the South Downs, see upright posts with blue arrows etched on them but no mention of the words PUBLIC BRIDLEWAY, and other posts with badges fixed to them consisting of a white arrow on a blue background, again with no words used. Remember the distinction – yellow for public footpath, blue for public bridleway. The clue is in the letter B! East Sussex County Council and Brighton & Hove City Council tend to like to use circular discs nailed either to finger-posts or to simple vertical wooden posts; their more recent bridleway discs have a very pleasing light blue background. Restricted byways are signed in just the same varieties of signage as bridleways except the arrows (or background on the disc-type signage) will ordinarily be in purple. You will never see a restricted byway signed by a plinth; restricted byways did not come into being until 2000, long after plinths stopped being routinely constructed as path signs!

Just a quick word, before I go on, about arrows etched into signposts. I've drawn a distinction between colour arrows used to denote footpaths, bridleways, restricted byways and public byways: remember blue for bridleways and purple for restricted byways. Occasionally on your bridleway travels you may meet arrows of other hues, including darker blue or green, and may wonder what they denote. The answer is probably they are denoting local trails such as nature trails and are likely to be found on common land or within popular tourist territory, where there is already Access Land in existence.

Back to bridleways! My experience is that the standard of bridleway signage in Sussex is generally very high, considerably better in fact than footpath signage, and it's clear that a great deal of work has been done and continues to be done to maintain this standard. Where signage is absent, there will be two possible explanations. One is that signs may have been destroyed or uprooted by bad weather or vandalism. However it may also mean that the route in question has ceased to exist as a bridleway, and I've gone into that earlier in this section. A problem of a different kind arises if the signage appears to be wrong – for instance, what is mapped as a bridleway is signed as a public footpath or vice versa, or if the course of the bridleway as signed is different from that shown on the map. It is possible that in fact the signage may be correct – perhaps since the map was published the bridleway has been demoted to a public footpath (or the public footpath has been promoted to a bridleway!), or the map is simply inaccurate, the inaccuracy based on misinformation being fed to the OS – but it could be a straight signage error. Common sense will usually dictate whether the sign or the map is wrong, but not always. I have also come across signs pointing in a subtly incorrect direction and on occasion it's taken me time and effort to work out what actually is the correct route! If you consider signage to be inadequate or misleading in any way, and it has caused you difficulty, then again you could consider reporting the matter, to the relevant local authority in the first instance. Local authorities are very aware of their responsibilities to keep their paths well signed – it is just as much, if not more so, in the interests of landowners as visitors that signage is clear and unambiguous. Even though your reporting an omission or ambiguity won't compensate for the inconvenience you may have suffered by being delayed or losing the route, it may mean that resultant action taken by the authorities will avoid the same thing happening to others. In my experience, local authorities are extremely helpful in dealing with such issues. If you do find that a sign has been uprooted and/or placed in such a position as to render it unhelpful or, worse, misleading, you could do your good deed for the day, as I have done on occasion, and do your best to reposition it correctly. Even if there's no suitable or obvious hole in the ground for it to go, you can always prop it up against a convenient tree. Just make sure you prop it up so the fingers are pointing the right way. On one occasion on a bridleway near Heathfield I found that an important re-route had not been signed properly. I found a discarded piece of board and took great satisfaction in creating my own brand-new bridleway sign, using a distinctly old school black biro!

But don't worry unduly about signage/mapping discrepancies. The vast majority of bridleways in Sussex will be easy to follow, the mapping and signage clearly accurate and consistent, and you should have few if any problems.

So now it's time to properly explore our wonderful network of Sussex bridleways.

SECTION 2

FOLLOWING THE BRIDLEWAYS

Before you set out – general advice

Introduction

In this section, the main part of this book, I introduce you to bridleways in all their different aspects, in the form of 90 recommended bridleway routes and then a miscellany of bridleways, from the extraordinarily good to just...extraordinary.

First (Part 1, routes 1 to 13), we'll look at bridleways as great Sussex linear trails, namely the South Downs Way, the Downs Link and the Worth/Forest Way. Secondly (Part 2, routes 14 to 31), we'll look at woodland bridleways, where paths through, among others, Kingley Vale, St Leonard's Forest and Friston Forest provide some glorious tree-shaded trails. Thirdly (Part 3, routes 32 to 45), we'll explore waterside bridleways, whether they be alongside lakes, waterways or reservoirs, through river valleys, or running close to the coast. Our fourth category (Part 4, routes 46 to 67), is downland bridleways, providing superb open bracing exploration with tremendous views. Fifthly (Part 5, routes 68 to 74), we look at what I call "parks and recreation" bridleways through areas of common land, open space or parkland; this includes highly enjoyable explorations of commons including those of Ambersham and Ditchling, Stanmer Park, and Ashdown Forest which fits more naturally into this category than any other. Then we turn to what I call bridleways with history (Part 6, routes 75 to 90), where the routes in question will provide you with safe and scenic access to a range of fascinating historical landmarks in Sussex. Last but not least, in Part

7, I'll consider not only the best of the rest, but bizarre and unusual bridleways – some ridiculously short, some ending abruptly and seemingly incongruously, one or two with no discernible purpose whatsoever.

Do bear in mind that some bridleways described below may have more than one attribute and, for instance, a bridleway with history might also provide some terrific downland exploration. Whatever the attributes of the bridleways, I will take you by the hand and provide all the information you need to enjoy them to the full.

I like to feel that if you follow all the recommended routes in this book, you will in fact have covered all the very best bridleway exploration in Sussex. In other words, every section of bridleway that I consider is really worth following in Sussex is incorporated into the routes below. You may of course have experience of following bridleways in Sussex and you may disagree with my choice based on that experience. If you do, let me know! And assuming you are sufficiently inspired by this book to create "bridleway bagging" expeditions of your own, following bridleways that are NOT included in this book, and you find some you like better than the ones I've recommended, please again get in touch. I know for a fact that there are some lovely bridleways that I've had to leave out, but there will be good reasons for that: for instance, the bridleway in question may be too remote from other bridleways to create a satisfying and worthwhile route, or there is another bridleway close by which offers an equally good, if not better, bridleway experience. So please forgive me if your own personal favourite is missing from what follows.

Anyway, onwards and upwards. Before we get properly going, though, we need to deal with some preliminaries, beginning with the question of planning and equipment.

Planning and equipment

I do advise you, as you plan your bagging expeditions, to be aware of your own limitations: it's not a good idea to plan to walk a 20km bridleway route in a single day if you've never walked more than 5km in a day before. But whatever your state of fitness, I would also suggest you allow a little more time than you think you'll need when planning your itinerary. You will of course want to linger in places of particular scenic or historic interest, but, on a less positive note, you may need to deal with issues such as route-finding difficulties and unforeseeable hazards, such as those described in the previous section. To those hazards you can add effects of adverse weather. Following a ridiculously wet February in 2020, just before Covid took over our lives, I found myself on no less than three occasions, in the course of exploring bridleways, wading through what had become lakes; in each case I had no idea how deep they might get. You may also need to build in some time at the start and/or end of your expedition in order to link with public transport. The last thing you want at the end of a long day's bagging is to miss that last bus or train. And on the subject of buses and trains, if you are reliant on public transport you must plan that carefully as well, particularly on Sundays when bus services are often scarce and rail lines are frequently closed for engineering works, with those lovely replacement buses that are not able to accommodate bikes.

Planning a bridleway journey can be fun but also frustrating. Remember that bridleways are dotted very randomly round the countryside. There is no tidy pattern to them – many are clearly accidents of history – and while my 90 recommended routes below try to avoid intervening tarmac crunching or backtracking as much as possible, you will indeed be very fortunate if you manage to concoct an expedition of your own where every bridleway or restricted byway dovetails naturally and neatly into the next. In fact sometimes you may find yourself cynically asking if the routes of bridleways are designed to maximise logistical problems for the explorer! As a result, there may well be occasions when on a "bagging" expedition you will have to use roads or backtrack along a bridleway in order to access the next, and you should be aware of that as you plan your journey, having regard to the distances involved.

Please note that if you are following a bridleway mapped as permissive, you may want to contact the relevant authority in advance for confirmation that permission still exists.

Let's now consider the question of equipment. Whether you're on a horse, on your bike or on foot, the most important thing to get right is what is in contact with the ground. If you're on **horseback,** your horse should be appropriately shod, and you will of course need your own riding shoes or boots. If you're **cycling,** you'll need robust tyres and inner tubes and your machine as a whole will need to be suitable for rough terrain. A folding cycle that you might use for a commute to work, a ramshackle machine you picked up at the car boot for a tenner, or even that trusty steed with 3-speed gears (or fewer) that's been handed down by your loving grandparents, simply won't do. Ideally, seek advice from your local cycle shop about the suitability of your machine for rough country, and upgrade your machine if necessary. A decent cycle repair kit, including one or maybe more replacement inner tubes, is of course essential. If you're **walking,** you'll need comfortable and resilient footwear. Heavy walking boots aren't necessary – the terrain is never as severe as that – and you may find the ideal footwear to be a pair of light walking boots with walking socks, preferably anti-blister ones. That said, in dry conditions, trainers are perfectly adequate, and you may even get away with Converses. When conditions are particularly wet or muddy, wellies are a surprisingly good option; some people say you can't or shouldn't walk too far in wellies but a good quality pair, plus walking socks, may see you cover many miles without discomfort and I have certainly covered vast distances in my own wellies!

As for clothing, this will be dependent on the prevailing weather. You certainly don't want to be overdressed in hot dry weather, although if you decide to leave arms and legs exposed, make sure you use sun block, and in hot weather you should wear a hat. Wearing shorts may feel like a cool (in both senses) option in summer, but renders you vulnerable to nettle stings and insect or tick bites. In colder wetter weather you need to be properly protected from the elements, so get yourself a waterproof jacket, scarf, hat (or hood) and gloves; under your jacket a number of thin layers is preferable to just one or two thick ones. In wet conditions, you can more or less guarantee to get muddy, so clothe yourself accordingly and be prepared for a lot of cleaning up afterwards. Cyclists will, of course, also need cycle helmets and horse-riders will need riding hats.

Whichever mode of transport you're using, you, and your horse if you're a horse-rider, need to be properly sustained. Sadly the days have long passed when on arrival in a village you could expect, in the best traditions of Enid Blyton, to find a well-stocked shop, café and/or pub. If you're lucky enough to find one on your travels, consider it a bonus but avoid disappointment by having with you a supply of high-energy food and (non-alcoholic) drink. A flask for coffee or tea is an excellent investment, while a water bottle is also desirable and indeed essential in hot weather when to avoid thirst and to stay hydrated you should drink frequently from the very start of your journey. It is actually amazing how more positive and energised you'll feel after a stop for food and drink, and by contrast, how demoralising it is to feel hungry or thirsty. So stock up beforehand and if anything, pack a little more than you think you'll need.

Without wanting to sound like a prophet of doom, I suggest it may also be advisable to have with you some basic first aid equipment, although the need to use it could be avoided if you just follow basic rules of safety. While it may be exhilarating to cycle down a steep hill at lightning speed, a single exposed tree root could throw you from your saddle and cause potentially serious injury as well as damage to your machine. So curb your enthusiasm and keep a careful eye on what may lurk beneath your wheels!

My personal bete-noire as a walker is exposed flints which can and do create trip hazards; just watch where you're putting your feet down, or risk a tumble which is not only undignified but could again cause nasty injuries including fractures.

Obviously accidents or other emergencies can befall even the best-prepared and most careful explorer of the countryside; accordingly, it's highly advisable to have a fully-charged phone with you in case It happens, whatever It may be. The Sussex countryside is hardly dangerous or remote, and providing you're properly equipped and follow my guidance set out above, you're unlikely ever to get into serious difficulties. But don't be complacent! Do in particular consider the wisdom of setting out in extreme weather, remembering that spells of such weather are generally very short and the countryside will still be there for you another day.

Mapping

Save for basic location maps showing the situation of the start point of each route described, I have chosen not to include full route maps in this book, on the grounds of cost and also the fact that maps are so readily available both in paper form and online. I hope you will forgive me, therefore, for leaving you to obtain the mapping you think you will need for reach bridleway expedition. I have, however, included hand-drawn location maps at the start of each section of routes, so you can see where in Sussex each route is situated.

It is of course your decision whether to use paper or electronic mapping but remember you can't always guarantee getting a good signal or wifi connection when you're out in the middle of nowhere. You may therefore wish to have a paper map on hand just in case you lose access to your technology.

Throughout this book I have used the traditional OS grid referencing system to identify the start and finish points of routes being described, and also to pinpoint important locations within the described routes. Some readers, especially those who remember geography lessons in their distant youth, may wonder if grid referencing is rather "old school" but it is a system that's been tried and trusted for generations and it is very easy to use. For anyone who hasn't used the system, I set out how to give a grid reference – information which you can then use to locate every route described below.

Every OS Explorer map (scale 1:25,000) is set on a grid of squares 1km (kilometre) x 1km based on the National Grid, these each forming larger 100km x 100km lettered squares. The border of each 1km x 1km square within the lettered squares is numbered vertically and horizontally, the numbers running from 00 to 99. These numbers are shown at regular intervals across the map, vertical from left to right (eastings), and horizontal from bottom to top (northings).

Using the OS Explorer sheet OL10 (Arundel & Pulborough) as an example, the vertical, left to right (eastings), squares begin with the number 90 and end with the number 17, while the horizontal, bottom to top (northings) squares begin with the number 98 and end with the number 20.

The first part of the grid reference will be the two letters denoting the larger 100km x 100km lettered square in which the location in question is found. This will, in Sussex, be the squares SU, TQ, SZ, TV and (exceptionally) TR. The letters are to be found at the top and bottom, left and right corners of the OS map in question.

The second part of the grid reference relates to how far east the particular location is (known technically as "eastings"). Locate the vertical grid line to the left of the point in question, ascertain the 00-99 number applicable to that vertical grid line, then estimate tenths eastwards from that grid line and put that number on the end of the vertical grid line number. That will give you three digits – the number of the vertical grid line then the estimated tenth eastward of it.

The third and final part of the grid reference relates to how far north the particular location is (known technically as "northings"). Locate the horizontal grid line below the point in question, again ascertain the 00-99 number applicable to that horizontal grid line, then estimate tenths northwards from that grid line and put that number on the end of the horizontal grid line number. You thus have three more digits – the number of the horizontal grid line then the estimated tenth northward of it.

Remember, east first, then north – as they are alphabetically!

You should therefore have a grid reference consisting of 8 characters – two letters, then the "east" numbers then the "north" numbers.

By way of example, the grid reference for Woodshill Farm on the Arundel & Pulborough map is found thus:

This location is, as you will see from the top left corner of the map sheet, in the TQ 100km x 100km square. So the first part of the reference is TQ.

Then how far eastwards? The vertical grid line immediately to the left of Woodshill Farm is 09 – estimated tenths east of this line to Woodshill Farm is 4. Putting that number on the end of 09, this part of the grid reference is therefore 094.

Going on to how far northwards, the horizontal grid line immediately below Woodshill Farm is 19 – estimated tenths north of this line to Woodshill Farm is 8. Putting that number on the end of 19, this part of the grid reference is therefore 198.

The complete reference for Woodshill Farm is therefore TQ094198.

Incidentally it is because of my recourse to the grid referencing system, which is entirely metric, that I have used metric measurements throughout this book. Apologies to traditionalists but thanks to modern technology it only needs a few buttons on your phones to translate metres and kilometres to feet, yards and miles should those be your preference.

Recommended routes

We can now turn to my choice of 90 numbered bridleway routes, broken down into routes along six different types of bridleway: trail bridleways (Part 1), woodland bridleways (Part 2), waterside bridleways (Part 3), downland bridleways (Part 4), common land bridleways (Part 5), and bridleways with history (Part 6). This is then followed by Part 7, devoted to not only the "best of the rest" but to bizarre and unusual bridleways, to which I've not allocated route numbers. My choice of routes is obviously subjective but, as stated above, I like to feel that the routes as set out below provide you with the best (and, in the final section, the worst!) bridleway experiences you'll get in Sussex. Ideally I would have liked to concoct routes that involved sticking to bridleways and nothing but bridleways, but in some instances, particularly in East Sussex, that simply has not been practicable, and some tarmac crunching is necessary. I have however tried to keep that to a minimum and sought to ensure that as much of each route as possible, preferably all of it, sticks to bridleways; where recourse to roads is necessary the road sections will be safe for bridleway users to follow.

Before we lace up our boots or mount our trusty steeds, I need to go into a little more detail about route lengths and access to the routes in Parts 1 to 6.

Route preambles and descriptions

I have provided maps to make it easier for you to locate the routes and facilitate your undertaking more than one route in a single expedition should you so wish. Some routes are so close together as to make such endeavours possible and indeed desirable, but again this will depend on how far you're prepared to walk, cycle or ride "between" routes. The West Sussex routes within each Part are listed first, followed by Brighton & Hove and East Sussex routes.

Each route description has a preamble which will include:

1 On the top line of the preamble, the route number for the purposes of this book. Simply refer to the relevant location map to ascertain the location of the start of the route. Please note there are occasional cross-references to other routes in the course of a particular description.

2 On the next line/lines of the preamble, information on locating the route.

Firstly I give the grid reference of the start and finish of the route; where there's a single grid reference with the words "start and finish," it denotes a circular route. (Note that where necessary I have, within the route description itself, added grid references of points along the route to assist in relation to navigation and location.)

This is then followed by the code for the relevant location map within this book on which the route can be found. This should assist you in seeing whereabouts in Sussex any given route is, in particular its proximity to nearby towns and large villages, and, as stated, the feasibility of doing more than one route in a single expedition. The location maps are coded as follows:

W1 is West Sussex map 1; W2 is West Sussex map 2; W3 is West Sussex map 3; W4 is West Sussex map 4: W5 is West Sussex map 5; W6 is West Sussex map 6.

E1 is East Sussex map 1; E2 is East Sussex map 2; E3 is East Sussex map 3; E4 is East Sussex map 4; E5 is East Sussex map 5; E6 is East Sussex map 6. The relevant route number is circled on the relevant map. Note that bridleways within Brighton & Hove will feature on the East Sussex maps.

You'll see that on each map I have grouped together bridleway routes sharing the same theme, eg W2 and E2 contain woodland bridleway routes (as set out in Part 2 below) and W4 and E4 contain downland bridleway routes (as set out in Part 4 below). So if, for instance, you've a particular liking for downland routes in West Sussex, you can see them all together on the one location map, W4.

After that comes the number of the relevant OS Explorer map or maps on which the route is to be found. I'll say again here that even if you're determined to access maps electronically while following the route, you may wish to have a paper map with you in case of failure of phone signal or wifi.

Lastly on this line I grade each route, using an initial letter E for easy, M for moderate and S for strenuous. I realise this is a subjective assessment and what might be very easy for some may prove a lot tougher for others, especially if the weather is bad. I do however advise you not to attempt any route graded as S for strenuous in adverse conditions. Sadly a good number of these routes are not suitable for users of wheelchairs or mobility scooters whatever the weather; as stated in the first section, if you are a user of these amenities and you want to tackle the route in question, you may wish to contact the highways department of the local authority for further information.

3 On the third line is the approximate length of the route, in metric measurements. Remember there are 1000 metres (m) in a kilometre (km) and a kilometre is roughly 0.625 of a mile.

In terms of route length, none of the routes should require more than a day to complete. Each route featured in Parts 1 to 6 will range from a minimum of 5km (3.1 miles) to a maximum of 20km (12.5 miles) in length. I realise these limits are somewhat arbitrary but I am anxious to cater for walkers and riders of all ages and abilities. A 5km route will seem very modest for some, but may prove sufficient, or more than sufficient, for those with disabilities or families with small children. A 20km route, by contrast, may seem far too demanding for the novice walker, but will offer a reasonable and doable challenge for those of greater ability. Indeed for some, even 20km may feel rather modest, but remember that these routes are to be enjoyed and you can't enjoy them if you're in a rush. In any case there's no reason why riders and more energetic walkers couldn't tackle more than one route during a single day out. Some routes can be shortened by omission of recommended detours.

There is however a practical issue which may mean more than the stated route distance is necessarily covered on a single expedition, and I need to go into this a little.

With the exception of the trail bridleways section, where different considerations apply, the designated start of each route will be the place where, on that route, the first section of bridleway begins, and the end of the route will be the place where, on that route, the final section of bridleway ends. Occasionally, the start/finish point may be just across the Sussex border in Hampshire, Surrey or Kent. The stated length of the route is that from its designated start to its designated finish. So in other words, if you're able to be driven to the designated start and then transported home from the designated finish, the distance specified is the distance you will cover. The first section of bridleway on each route will indeed be accessible by car, and the final section of bridleway on each route will end at a spot that's accessible by car.

I have to accept the reality that it is likely to be a great deal easier and more convenient to access the routes by car, either a private car or a taxi (although this is hardly economical!). Indeed it is perfectly possible, and sensible, if two or more vehicles are available, to park one at each end of the route, thus avoiding the need to retrace your steps all the way back to the only car, and the consequent doubling of the overall route distance. Some of the routes set out below are (or can be treated as) circular, ending where you started, but not all of them are; while it would be ideal to have been able to construct exclusively circular routes, that would in many cases not be possible to achieve without creating routes that really were excessively long or involved a great deal of tarmac crunching. So a number of routes described below are linear (non-circular). If only one car is available, you may be fortunate to know someone who is happy to drop you off at one end and pick you up at the other. Bear in mind, if you're seeking to leave a car at the start and/or end of a described route, that parking may not always be available in the immediate vicinity of the route you're seeking to follow. It should go without saying that if no convenient parking area is available, you must take care **never** to obstruct gates or other entrances to fields, lanes, driveways etc, and of course **never** park in designated passing places on narrow roads. Don't confuse passing places and lay-by's! I accept that adequacy of parking space is a particular headache for horse-riders with horse boxes, so it may be worth enquiring as to availability of suitable parking for horse boxes in advance of setting out.

So far so good, if you've access to a car. But if you're getting to (and/or travelling back from) the route under your own steam, extra legwork will often be needed. Mindful of environmental considerations, I am very anxious to ensure that the start and end points of all the routes described in this book are within reasonable reach of practicable public transport. (By "practicable," I mean a reasonably frequent or regular service as opposed to just the odd bus or two each week!) Many of you will not be drivers in any event, but we all have a duty to keep our carbon footprint to an absolute minimum. In order to encourage access to the routes by public transport, therefore, I've ensured that no route described should require more than 5km additional travelling in total from and to practicable public transport. In practice the extra travelling involved will generally be far less than 5km. Sometimes there'll be no extra travelling at all! The text will indicate the location of the public transport in question, how to access the route from it, and/or how to access public transport at the other end. (I deal with this in more detail in paragraph 5 below.) Remember that even if you're wishing to walk rather than cycle the routes, you could, if you've access to a bicycle, put your bike on the train and then cycle to the route or routes to be followed, although you'll somehow need to get back to your bike again afterwards which may, in the case of linear (non-circular) routes, mean retracing your steps and again effectively doubling the overall route distance. Of course you've the option of keeping your bike with you as you follow the route, maybe cycling some and walking some.

Please note that all recommended detours – and there are quite a few! – are incorporated into the overall route distances, so if you decide not to undertake them you can save a bit of time. Note however that where there are places of interest to see outside the start and finish points of the route, these are NOT so incorporated. There are some "out-and-back" sections within the routes that are so integral to the routes in question that I simply include these as part of the routes without according them the status of recommended detours!

4 On the next line/lines, I list the highlights of the route. Note that some of these may require a detour. If this is so I will provide necessary directions.

5 Following on from route highlights, the next line/ lines will give public transport availability, using the abbreviation PT. Here I state the place served by public transport from which you can access the start of the route, and the place served by public transport which public transport users need to access after finishing the route. An asterisk is used to denote rail transport and a B to

denote bus transport. So for instance "Christ's Hospital (* start), Cranleigh (B finish)" means that you need to get a train to Christ's Hospital to start your route, and you can catch a bus from Cranleigh at the end. In the description following the preamble to each route, I will describe how to reach the start of the route from nearest public transport, how to get back to the public transport at the end, and the distances involved. Please note that sometimes it may be necessary to use a particular town as a "base," travelling out to the route from that base by one form of public transport and then returning to base by either another form of public transport or by using a different bus/train service/line. The text will always make clear if and when a "base" is needed.

There are a few buses for which, at the time of writing, prebooking is necessary for certain destinations or pick-ups, these being on the flexible route between Chichester and Petworth operated by Compass Bus. Where prebooking is necessary this is denoted by the initials PB in the relevant preamble.

Please note that on Sundays, scheduled bus services are extremely limited and at times non-existent, and railway services on Sundays are often disrupted by engineering works which means the need to resort to those dreaded rail replacement buses. Sadly bus services are sometimes withdrawn and, particularly in the light of the Covid pandemic, I can't rule out the possibility that between my writing this book and your reading it, one or more services referred to in the text do suffer that fate. It's therefore essential you check online before making your plans.

6 On the last line before the route description starts, I give details of any places on or tolerably close to the route (including on public transport links to/from the route) where refreshments are available, using the letter R. Note that the route itself may not necessarily go past the door of the pub, shop or café in question, and in many

cases it's only at or around the start or end of a route that refreshments can be obtained. I should point out that most of the routes pass through remote countryside with few if any places of habitation, let alone facilities for hungry travellers. Nevertheless, it's one of the great joys of going out and about in the countryside to discover a nice pub or tea room on one's journeyings. That said, as stated above, you should always have some food and drink in your backpack in case the place you've earmarked has decided to shut on the day of your visit. Again, it may be that, whether Covid-related or not, some establishments shut their doors permanently between my writing this book and your reading it. Check ahead to avoid disappointment. If you do find a nice pub, and fancy a drink, just don't drink too much alcohol, for all the obvious reasons!

The route description then follows. I have ensured that for each and every section of route I give the distance of that section. This will assist in planning, in particular whether you choose to undertake recommended detours off the continuous route. I've supplemented the route directions with brief descriptions of places and sights of interest.

So, here goes, then – bridleways grouped under their essential character, incorporating recommended routes.

Part 1 – Bridleways as Great Trails of Sussex

Sussex is blessed with a number of "name" trails. In 2018 in my book *The Great Walks Of Sussex* I identified a total of 19 "name" waymarked trails with more than 12 miles of their length within Sussex. They are largely intended for walkers rather than cyclists or horse-riders. However four of them are bridleways or restricted byways throughout their course, in Sussex at any rate: the Downs Link, the South Downs Way, and the Worth Way/Forest Way (treated as a combined route in my earlier book).

These trails are intended to be followed from end to end. It is for this reason that you will find the routes described in this Part provide, effectively, an end-to-end journey along each of the three trails as they proceed through Sussex, plus links with public transport at the start and finish of each route. In terms of route length, I have chosen to be pragmatic and for this Part only, assuming that you will wish to tackle each route from end to end, will depart from my usual rule of stating the overall length of each route is to be measured from the start of the first piece of mapped bridleway to the end of the last piece. Instead, it will be measured from the point at which you join the trail in question at the start of each route, and to the point at which you leave it at the end of that route. In any case the road sections will be safe and quiet – bridleways in all but name! It's up to you to decide whether to do a whole trail in one go – with, obviously, stops for refreshment and accommodation! – or in a series of day trips. There is of course nothing to stop you stringing a number of routes together on a single expedition.

DOWNS LINK

The Downs Link is a 59km 500m trek from Shoreham-by-Sea in West Sussex to St Martha's Hill near Guildford in Surrey; the majority of the Downs Link is in West Sussex. For most of its route, it follows the course of two disused

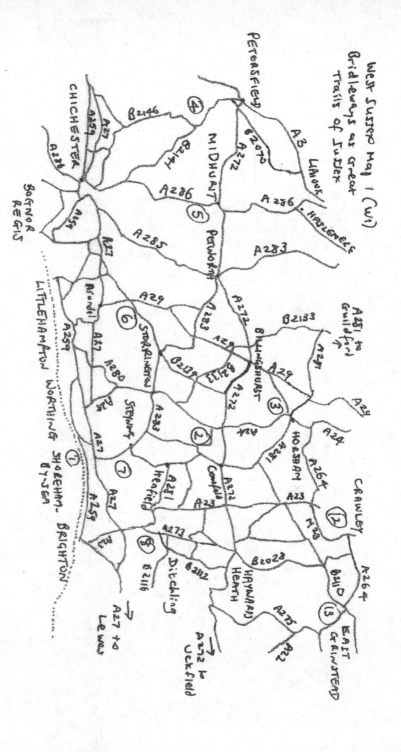

WEST SUSSEX Map 1 (w1)
Bridleways as Great
Trails of Sussex

Scale on all maps - 3.25cm - 10 km

East Sussex Map 1 (E1)

Bridleways as Great Trails of Sussex

EAST GRINSTEAD

ROYAL TUNBRIDGE WELLS

A21 to Tonbridge

A28 to TENTERDEN

B2092 to Tenterden

→ to New Romney

→ to Lydd

RYE

Winchelsea

Camber

HASTINGS

BEXHILL

EASTBOURNE

BEACHY

SEAFORD

NEWHAVEN

BRIGHTON

Ditchling

North Chailey

HAYWARDS HEATH

Forest Row

Crowborough

Wadhurst

Mayfield

Hurst Green

Burwash

Heathfield

HAILSHAM

Polegate

Alfriston

LEWES

Ringmer

UCKFIELD

A264
A22
A275
A272
A26
A21
A267
A265
A272
A26
A21
A268
A28
A262
A259
A271
A271
A259
A27
A26
A27
A259
A22
A22
B2099
B2102
B2026
B2100
B2110
B2192
B2124
B2116
B2123
B2104
B2096
B2192
B2100

⑬ ⑪ ⑩ ⑨

railways, the first linking Shoreham-by-Sea with Christ's Hospital (although all trains in practice continued into Horsham) which opened in 1861 and shut in 1966, and the second linking Christ's Hospital (although all trains in practice started from Horsham) and Guildford, this opening in 1865 and closing in 1965. The going is extremely easy, as might be expected, and signage is excellent. Public transport links are plentiful and it is very easy to break the journey into chunks. All of the Downs Link in Sussex is open to all bridleway traffic; in that respect it differs from other "railway paths" such as the Cuckoo Trail, where horse-riding is forbidden along certain sections, and the Centurion Way, where horse-riding isn't allowed at all. The Downs Link is certainly suitable for wheelchair and mobility scooter users.

ROUTE 1

TQ207059-TQ190190 – Location Map W1 – OS OL11 – E

16km 700m

Old Shoreham, River Adur, Bramber, Stretham Manor, Betley Bridge

PT Shoreham (*, B start), Partridge Green (B finish)

R Shoreham, Bramber, Steyning, Henfield, Partridge Green

It's extremely easy to access the route and the start of the Downs Link from Shoreham-by-Sea town centre (about which I write a little more in route 79). I suggest you make your way to the Ropetackle complex at the western end of the main street, from which a path, working inland beside the Adur river estuary, begins and takes you to the well-signed start of the Downs Link (the sign indicating Guildford is 37 miles away!) at TQ207059, where this route starts. However, you shouldn't proceed further without visiting the lovely mid-Norman (and part-Saxon) church of St Nicholas, **Old Shoreham**, just beyond the Amsterdam

Inn on the eastern side of the A283; among its highlights are its long narrow Saxon nave and superb ornately carved Norman arches. Immediately west of the start of the Downs Link, spanning the river Adur, is Old Shoreham Bridge, a bridleway bridge which became a focus for mourners and wreath-layers following the Shoreham Airshow disaster in August 2015 when a Hawker Hunter plane crashed onto the A27 just to the west of the bridge. There are views further afield from here across the Adur estuary to the magnificent Lancing College Chapel, while ahead of you is the A27 flyover, and although some might regard it as an eyesore it is indisputably a fine piece of road engineering.

You now head northwards along the Downs Link, soon passing under the flyover (500m from the start) and then veering north-westwards through pleasant countryside; although it is marred a little, actually rather more than a little, by the old Beeding cement works to your right, the lovely **River Adur** is always close by to your left. You arrive at the bank of the Adur (described a little more fully in route 37) and, leaving temporarily the course of the old railway, follow the riverbank to a bridge crossing at TQ196093, 3km from the flyover. You cross the river by this bridge, now overlapping with the South Downs Way, and then head westwards for 300m, to a path junction at TQ193094, the South Downs Way going straight on and your route going right with the Downs Link. By following the South Downs Way to the road and bearing left you reach, in just 125m, the village of Botolphs, although this is visited in route 79 so not an officially recommended detour here. As stated the Downs Link, and your continuous route, bears right, north-westwards, at TQ193094, and rejoins the course of the old railway line, following an excellent tree-shaded bridleway north-westwards almost to the A283 crossing at a path junction at TQ189101 (A), roughly 1km from where you parted with the South Downs Way.

The official route of the Downs Link used to go straight on at (A) to cross the A283 then very shortly reach a T-junction of bridleways (B); here you would bear left, parallel with the road along a bridleway, to meet, in some 500m, the roundabout junction at TQ185105 where the A283 meets roads coming from Steyning and Bramber. If you're walking or cycling and in a hurry that option is still available and will save you 1km (the length of the detour) but you need to take immense care when crossing the A283. The official, recommended and much safer route, and the one which should always be taken by horse-riders, turns right at (A) and follows a bridleway almost back to the Adur, veering left to pass under the road at TQ194100 and left again as bridleway-signed, simply following the path past point (B) all the way to the roundabout at TQ185105. By turning right at the roundabout along The Street you shortly reach **Bramber** which boasts a number of features of interest. The first, above The Street to the left, is the spectacular ruin of the Norman-built Bramber Castle, destroyed during the Civil War, while just beyond the ruin is the Norman church of St Nicholas, singled out in the *Pevsner Architectural Guide* for its late 11th century Caen stonework. Then a little further along the road on the right is St Mary's House, a superb timber-framed house dating from around 1470. Among its fine rooms are the Monk's Parlour, notable for its huge "dragon" beam and 17th century inglenook.

The Downs Link used to continue north-westwards from the roundabout at TQ185105 up Castle Lane (between the Bramber turning and the A283), but has now been re-routed to provide much safer progress. Look just to the left of Castle Lane and you'll see what is a new Downs Link-signed path, in fact running alongside the A283 and keeping Castle Lane to your right. Follow this path which initially runs parallel with the A283 then veers right, almost immediately reaching a minor road. Join the road, keeping in the same direction, and bear left at the end along Roman Road then (some 400m beyond the roundabout) bear right as signed up King's Stone Avenue, in 500m meeting a T-junction with King's Barn Lane at TQ187114. The Downs Link turns right here. However, if you wish to explore the most attractive town of Steyning, turn left along King's

Barn Lane, going forward along Jarvis Lane to reach the south end of the High Street, 875m or so from TQ187114. Steyning is in fact visited at the end of route 54 so is not an officially recommended detour on this bridleway route.

However as stated the Downs Link turns right at TQ187114. In 75m or so beyond that spot you veer left, northwards, the lane in due course turning from metalled road to track/bridleway. Continue along the track with the Downs Link, proceeding initially north-westwards then north-eastwards, heading pleasantly for Wyckham Farm. Beyond the farm buildings the ground rises steeply – it's really the only time on this route when your lungs may be tested to any extent – to reach a signed sharp right turn. Take that turn, eastwards, downhill, enjoying a fabulous view along the Downs escarpment from here, to join the course of the old Shoreham-Horsham railway, some 2km 500m from the junction of King's Stone Avenue and King's Barn Lane.

You now head north-eastwards along the course of the old line. The surrounding scenery is most attractive with beautiful meadows bordering the old line and fine views to the South Downs. There is one particularly scenic spot, at the crossing of the Adur, with the beautiful grounds of the tile-hung and timbered **Stretham Manor** – a 17th century building on the site of Henfield's 13th century manor – immediately beyond. In times of very wet weather the fields hereabouts may flood, and you'll be glad of your firm trusty track. You continue along the course of the old line, veering north-westwards, and reach the outskirts of Henfield. Here, at TQ206160, 3km 125m from joining the old line, there is a brief (200m) bridleway break, your having to follow Station Road with the Downs Link, reaching Upper Station Road. Here you could break your journey by detouring right along this road for 875m into Henfield, described briefly in route 37 and therefore not an officially recommended detour here. Keeping to the Downs Link beyond Upper Station Road, you stick to the course of the old railway. Initially the path is in the shade of vegetation, but does open out; shortly after it does so, there is another attractive crossing of the Adur at **Betley Bridge**, 1km 500m from Upper Station Road, with lovely views from here to the South Downs. I always think Betley Bridge sounds more like a North Yorkshire market town than a southern England river crossing! In 1km 250m from Betley Bridge, you leave the course of the old line (but stay with the Downs Link) as you approach Partridge Green; you in fact veer away westwards to reach, in 375m, the B2135, joining it at the village's south end, at TQ190185. This is the end of the bridleway section of this route. Turn right to proceed northwards beside the B2135 for 550m to reach the Downs Link turning off to the left (north-westwards) at TQ190190, which is the start of Route 2. To reach the centre of Partridge Green, continue beside the road, Bines Road, for 100m then bear right along the main street, the B2116 High Street, from where there are buses to Brighton and Horsham.

ROUTE 2

TQ190190-TQ148292 – Location Map W1 – OS OL11, OL34 – E

11km 875m

Furzefield Wood, West Grinstead Station, Southwater, Bax Castle, Christ's Hospital School

PT Partridge Green (B start), Christ's Hospital (* finish)

R Partridge Green, Southwater, Bax Castle

To reach the start of this route from the centre of Partridge Green, served by buses on the Horsham-Brighton service, proceed to the west end of the village street (B2116 High Street), turn left at the end down the B2135 Bines Road and arrive in some 100m at TQ190190, this being the start of this route. Simply turn hard right here to join the Downs Link as signed and head north-westwards from the road. Once you've left the village, the surroundings become delightfully rural and unspoilt. You veer northwards and follow a straightforward northward course with pleasant pasture on both sides although, as you approach West Grinstead, there is the very pretty **Furzefield Wood** to the right. It is just after passing under a substantial bridge carrying the A272 that you arrive at the site of **West Grinstead Station**, 3km 625m from the start. The station has been restored to look very much as it would have done when the old line was still functioning, with platform, signal and station board, and even an old railway carriage on a piece of old railway line; there is a seat on the platform where you can sit, enjoy a snack or a picnic, and pretend to be waiting for a train!

Beyond the old station head north-westwards, sticking to the Downs Link. Initially the surroundings remain very rural; it's such easy going that you can indulge your imagination a little, perhaps to the extent of visualising yourself driving a train along this stretch, enjoying views "real" drivers would have had for roughly a century. You pass, 2km 750m from the old station, the little village of Copsale beyond which there follows a quite beautiful stretch which is best seen in the spring where the surrounding woodland is crammed with bluebells and wild garlic. Slight anticlimax follows with the negotiation of the A24 by means of a modern underpass, beyond which you pass Southwater Country Park and go forward to pass the centre of **Southwater** which is just a few yards away to the right, 2km from Copsale. While Southwater's quite a sprawling place, its centre has been rejuvenated in recent years and you should take the opportunity to view its magnificent modern iguanodon sculpture, created by local sculptor Hannah Stewart and completed in 2006.

Continuing from the most conspicuous red-brick bridge in the centre of Southwater at TQ156262, head north-westwards from the village along the clearly-signed Downs Link. Watch the signposting carefully as you head through a new housing estate, but once clear of that you'll find your Downs Link journey easy and most enjoyable, particularly when in 1km 250m from Southwater you reach **Bax Castle** with its pub and special entrance for Downs Link users!

There's no castle – so, historians, don't get too excited – the pub's name being derived from a weaver called Bax who lived locally. In a further 1km from Bax Castle, following very easy straightforward going along the course of the old railway, you're joined by the existing Arun Valley railway line coming in from your left; continue along the Downs Link parallel with it, now veering north-eastwards, and reaching the road. Aim for King Edward Road heading straight on north-eastwards, going forward to join a brand new Downs Link-signed path parallel with and just to the right of the road. Follow this path which returns you to the road, then as the road bends sharply right, you need to fork left down Station Road. Before taking the fork, however, you should enjoy, to your right, the view of the buildings of **Christ's Hospital School.** The school was founded in London in 1553 and moved here in the 19th century, some ornamental sections being re-used from the original buildings; the present buildings are impressive in their scale, size and ambience but they are private so you'll have to be content just to view them from a distance rather than detouring.

As stated, though, the continuous route forks left down Station Road to reach Christ's Hospital Station, sticking to the (recently re-routed) Downs Link and reaching the end of this route at the station car park, at TQ148292, 2km 250m from Bax Castle.

ROUTE 3

TQ148292-TQ057390 – Location Map W1 – OS OL34 – E

15km 375m

Slinfold, Double Bridge, Rudgwick, Baynards Tunnel, Baynards Station

PT Christ's Hospital (* start), Cranleigh (B finish)

R Slinfold, Rudgwick, Cranleigh

Please note that the latter part of this route takes you well over the county border, to Cranleigh in Surrey, but to continue to Cranleigh makes perfect sense from a logistical point of view. The continuation beyond the border also provides a taste of the delights of bridleways outside Sussex.

If you're starting from Christ's Hospital having driven or taken the train, your route starts almost immediately on leaving Christ's Hospital Station car park! As you exit the car park you'll see the Downs Link signed right and left. This is the start of this route at TQ148292; if you're now only just joining the Downs Link from the station car park, bear left here. Otherwise, just go straight on. Now continue along what is a public bridleway, almost at once passing a Downs Link/bridleway sign, your excellent path dipping down and veering left to pass under the railway, then shortly bearing left again and arriving at the old platform of Christ's Hospital Station from which Guildford-bound trains once departed. It has been quite magnificently restored very recently, the restoration extending to the station name board, and there is an excellent information board as well. Beyond the platform, you simply continue along the course of the old line, which you will continue to do all the way to Rudgwick. It is now plain sailing north-westwards as you proceed along or immediately adjacent to the old line on an excellent well-signed path, with mileposts continuing to provide indicators of progress (in good old-fashioned miles, note, not kilometres!). Initially the surroundings are pleasantly rural, but even when you pass the housing and industrial development of Slinfold – there was a station here, with a private siding to brickworks – the going remains agreeable and very easy.

Your route, keeping to the old line/Downs Link, stays to the south of the centre of **Slinfold**; the pretty village centre is easily accessible from the Downs Link at TQ118308 in roughly 500m via Hayes Lane, the junction of the Downs Link with Hayes Lane 3km 500m from the start of this route. I thoroughly recommend your making the detour! Slinfold is a most attractive village with a gently curving village street and houses of a variety of styles, including a number of 16th and 17th century cottages and some fine Georgian buildings. The church of St Peter is 19th century but contains some much earlier memorials, including an alabaster monument of Katherine Blount from the early 17th century and a brass of Richard Bradbrydge from the early 16th century, and – church trivia buffs please note – there is not one but two lychgates, each with a stone roof. Notable houses on the village's main street include the half-timbered Little Hammers and Slinfold House, both part-16th century.

Back on the Downs Link, in another 875m from Hayes Lane you go under the A29 and then embark on the loveliest section of this bridleway journey, passing really fine unspoilt woodland interspersed with picturesque stretches of open pasture, perhaps the climax coming with the impressive underbridge crossing of the river Arun, the so-called **Double Bridge**. You need to go down the steps at TQ094327 (actually signed "View Point!") to see it properly. The river crossing became perforce a double bridge because the original brick railway bridge was not acceptable to the Board of Trade; the gradient required for the line to drop down to it would have been too great, hence the additional metal bridge built above the brick one. The scene is extremely attractive, particularly if the Arun is swollen during times of heavy rain.

Sadly, not far beyond the Double Bridge, the tranquillity is broken with the crossing of the busy A281, 2km 750m beyond the A29, and having crossed you'll notice the surroundings become more suburban as you approach **Rudgwick**. The large overbridge you reach 500m beyond the A281 carries the village street. Look out for the Medical Centre car park to your right immediately beyond the overbridge, and here you can detour shortly up the road leading from the car park to Rudgwick's village street. Rudgwick is a very attractive village with a number of tile-hung, timber-framed and weatherboarded cottages. A good 1km up the village street from where you'll have joined it is the church of the Holy Trinity, with a 13th century tower, a probably Norman nave wall, and 12th century font made of Sussex marble. (Note that the 2km round trip to the church is NOT incorporated into the overall route distance.)

Your route follows the Downs Link away from Rudgwick north-westwards, keeping to the course of the old Horsham-Guildford railway. In roughly 1km 250m after leaving Rudgwick, the Downs Link leaves the old line to get round the (closed) **Baynards Tunnel**, forking left, and going attractively but quite steeply uphill in the shade of trees. Baynards Tunnel was 348m long and coincided with the highest point of the former railway line at 76m above sea level; it was also the point where the old line moved from Sussex into Surrey. Keeping with the Downs Link you veer left, then at TQ079345, some 250m after leaving the course of the old line, you reach a signed right turn. Hereabouts the Downs Link crosses the border into Surrey.

Having taken the right turn, you descend steeply through attractive woodland to reach a road in 500m; you turn right very briefly along it and then hard right again to rejoin the old line. Continue forward along the old line to within sight of the old **Baynards Station**, named after the nearby Baynards Park. Access to the station is fenced round so when you reach the fence, 250m after rejoining the old line, you need to bear left then almost immediately right. You pass just to the left of the private but beautifully preserved station complex, its buildings and advertising hoardings looking very much as they would have done when the line was last operational in June 1965 – minus actual trains, of course! – and there is also a nicely sited pub just here.

From here, the going really couldn't be easier, it being a straight run of some 4km 500m from Baynards in a north-westerly direction along the course of the old railway line. The surroundings are very pleasantly rural and feel quite remote for a long while, but then in 3km 500m or so they begin to get more urban; you enter the outskirts of Cranleigh and, sticking to the Downs Link, arrive at a junction with Knowle Lane at TQ057390, the end of the route. Turn right to reach Cranleigh's charming village street in just 75m. Buses are available from here to Horsham and Guildford. Or of course you could carry on along the Downs Link to the far-from-bitter end, at St Martha's Hill, not far from Guildford in Surrey.

SOUTH DOWNS WAY

Without question, the South Downs Way (SDW), which starts in Winchester in Hampshire and ends in Eastbourne in East Sussex, is the finest long-distance trail in Sussex. While there are occasional road interruptions, it could be said to be the longest end-to-end bridleway in Sussex; indeed the section of South Downs Way between the crossing of the B2141 near South Harting and the crossing of the A286 above Cocking, at over 11km, is the longest uninterrupted stretch of bridleway in Sussex. In marked contrast to the Downs Link, the SDW provides mostly remote, high-level travel with a great many climbs and descents. Many guide-books to the route are available; the route descriptions below provide an overview only, although signage on the ground is so good that you may not need much more than what is written here.

Although the SDW as a whole is 160km long, part of its length is, as stated, in Hampshire and that does not concern us in this book. Additionally, the final miles of the SDW from Alfriston offer alternative footpath and bridleway routes, the bridleway route somewhat shorter, and again we need not concern ourselves with the footpath section. I have split the bridleway journey along the SDW in Sussex into eight separate routes, none of them longer than 20km. This may seem an unambitious schedule and both riders and hardier walkers may be happy to combine two routes or possibly even more than two on a single expedition, but if you want to really get the best out of the SDW, and you are reliant on public transport, you may prefer to spin out your SDW journey in Sussex over the full 8 days. The South Downs Way is not an endurance test or speed test; take your time and enjoy every minute of it.

When I say "enjoy" I don't just mean the magnificent scenery and the views from the tops of splendid lofty green ridges that are so characteristic of the South Downs – the legacy of geological activity some 60 million years ago. The SDW, part of the South Downs National Park, supports a huge range of flora and fauna. There are of course the ubiquitous sheep, but if you look carefully you'll see many species of butterfly including the silver-spotted skipper and adonis blue, as well as the grasshopper, skylark, kestrel and pheasant; drainage ditches and rivers may bring sight of the heron or cormorant; and rooks may be seen in ash and beech woodland. Among a great variety of plants you may see the salad burnet, squinancywort, round-headed rampion, scabious and cowslip. Look out also for the dewponds, very characteristic features of the South Downs landscape, these created by shepherds to water the flocks of sheep that grazed there. So take your time to stand and stare, and don't forget your binoculars.

Note that routes later on in this book do overlap with sections of South Downs Way. This is the inevitable result of my wishing to cover as many scenic bridleways as I can, the South Downs Way often providing the most convenient way of linking them together. I can assure you it will be no hardship to visit sections of the South Downs Way more than once in the course of your exploration. Like a really good film, it all benefits from being seen more than once anyway.

ROUTE 4

SU749195-SU875166 – Location Map W1 – OS OL8 – S

19km 125m (longer route), 17km 875m (shorter route via Beacon Hill)

Uppark, Harting Down, Beacon Hill, Pen Hill, Devil's Jumps, Didling, Cocking Down

PT Uppark (B start), Cocking (B finish)

R South Harting, Cocking

Unfortunately the point where the SDW enters West Sussex isn't easily accessible by public transport. It may be of course that you've decided to follow the route from its start at Winchester. However if you have not, and you wish to say you have tackled the entire SDW bridleway route in Sussex, you can do one of two things. One is to start from the B2146 crossing of the SDW, this crossing served by buses from Chichester and Petersfield; having left the bus here, work first back to the start (following my instructions below in reverse) then forwards. The other possibility is to get yourself somehow to Buriton, Hampshire – you may be lucky with a bus from Petersfield, some 4km 500m from Buriton – and head for the church at the south end of the village. Proceed north-eastwards from the church along North Lane, then in some 750m bear right along Pitcroft Lane. In 125m turn right up a public byway, heading initially just west of south for 550m then veering sharply south-eastwards and continuing for 625m to meet the SDW at SU749195, where this route begins, still in Hampshire, a little to the west of the border with West Sussex. The SDW strikes out in a south-easterly direction from here. So here goes – your SDW bridleway journey.

Your journey begins with an unremarkable, although undeniably very pleasant, ridge section with good views towards the grounds of **Uppark**. The first 1km or so from SU749195 as far as Sunwood Farm follows a metalled lane but then at Sunwood Farm, just after the lane veers sharp left, you bear right as SDW-signed, initially along a public byway. In 250m from Sunwood Farm your path becomes a bridleway and at this point you enter West Sussex. Now proceed confidently just south of east for 1km or so, reaching a crossing of the Sussex Border Path. The Sussex Border Path, as the name implies, follows, very approximately, the border of Sussex with its neighbouring counties of Hampshire, Surrey and Kent, from Emsworth in the west to Rye in the east, covering 225km. There is also a spur route following, very roughly, the border of West Sussex with East Sussex and Brighton & Hove, starting at

Fishersgate and ending at East Grinstead – a distance of 55km. Beyond the Sussex Border Path crossing, head in a more south-easterly direction for 1km 250m, high above the pretty village of South Harting, to arrive at the B2146 crossing. By detouring 375m or so to the right down the B2146 (and it's a detour I recommend), you reach the turning to the superb red-brick Uppark House, built in around 1690 and turned into a treasure-house of rare carpets, furniture and paintings from overseas. Severely damaged by fire in 1989, it's been beautifully restored and many of its previous glories remain including an 18th century doll's house with original contents. H.G. Wells, whose mother was housekeeper at Uppark, spent part of his childhood at the house. South Harting, reached by detouring 750m left at the B2146 crossing, is also worth exploring if you have the time; see route 46 for a bit more information about the village. Because it's explored there, it's not an officially recommended detour off this route.

Now, whether you've detoured or not, head south-eastwards away from the B2146. Beyond the B2146 you continue uphill, south-eastwards, through the woods, roughly parallel with then over the B2141 (750m from the B2146 crossing), now on the 750ft high **Harting Down**; there follows a very straightforward easterly journey along the clearly signed SDW with quite superb views to the left. You then drop down through woods to the foot of Beacon Hill (1km 375m from the B2141) and a signed path junction (A). From here the SDW describes a large V round Beacon Hill but it's possible to cut the V, saving roughly 1km 250m, by proceeding along the bridleway over Beacon Hill. To do so, go straight over at (A) and ascend along the obvious path to the top of **Beacon Hill**, the site of a late Bronze Age or early Iron Age hill fort, the earthwork enclosing some 25 acres. The area also once housed the Shutter Telegraph Station, built around the end of the 18th century as part of a line of stations that linked

Portsmouth Dockyard with the Admiralty Office in London. The views are fantastic, stretching all the way to the Solent and Isle of Wight. You then continue on the path, soon being reassured by a bridleway sign, and follow the path steeply downhill, turning left at the end back onto the SDW at SU810183. However the official SDW turns south-eastwards from (A), and, keeping Beacon Hill to the left, rises gently up the hillside before then turning hard left, northwards to descend to the valley separating Beacon Hill and Pen Hill, meeting the path coming down from Beacon Hill at SU810183 as stated. If you've stuck to the SDW throughout, this meeting point is 3km 250m from the B2141.

Now the SDW veers eastwards over the delightful **Pen Hill**, skirting woodland and veering south-eastwards, passing just to the north-east of Buriton Farm, beyond which there's quite an arduous climb into West Dean Woods. The path levels out and continues through the woods, passing a memorial to a wartime pilot, Hauptmann Josef Oestermann. By coincidence I found myself walking this part of the SDW at around 11am on Armistice Day in 2014 and stopped here to keep the Silence; it really was silent, apart from the very faint rustle of the trees in the fine drizzle that fell from a leaden sky. Veering north-eastwards shortly beyond the memorial, the SDW soon passes the **Devil's Jumps,** a remarkable line of five Bronze Age burial mounds, 3km from SU810183. Continuing through the woods, veering eastwards, you now pass Monkton House, once lived in by the art collector Edward James. You emerge from the woods and proceed along a straight path between fences for 300m or so until a signed bridleway goes away left at SU837174, 1km 500m from the Devil's Jumps. By following this signed bridleway downhill for 1km to the road, turning right along it and then in 125m turning right again, you reach in another 125m the church at **Didling.** Known as the Shepherd's Church, it boasts a Saxon font but the rest is deliciously simple early 13th century with unusual bench ends containing candleholders. Simply return to the SDW the same way. I strongly recommend this detour!

Beyond the Didling detour point as you continue eastwards on the SDW, you can clearly see the 243m hilltop trig (triangulation) point of Linch Ball, but don't get too excited as there's no right of access to it. Instead the SDW passes just to the right of this hill, and shortly beyond the hill, 1km 250m from the Didling detour point, goes over a bridleway crossroads at SU850172; the masts of The Trundle hilltop above Chichester are now visible ahead. The going is level for a time, before a long descent from the top of **Cocking Down**, heading just south of east, with magnificent views now opening out ahead. The path bottoms out, arriving at a crossing the A286 just by a car park and bus stop, at SU875166. Your route ends here (some 2km 625m from the bridleway crossroads you passed at SU850172), with buses available from here to Midhurst and Chichester. The village of Cocking, with a good range of amenities, is just under 1km down the hill to your left.

ROUTE 5

SU875166-TQ028122 – Location Map W1 – OS OL8, OL10 – S

18km 875m

Heyshott Down, Graffham Down, Crown Tegleaze, Bignor Hill, Toby's Stone, Westburton Hill

PT Cocking (B start), Amberley (* finish)

R Cocking, Amberley

From the A286 crossing at SU875166 where this route begins, the SDW continues south-eastwards uphill initially along the metalled Hillbarn Lane then along a clear track, climbing onto Manorfarm Down, veering in a more easterly direction and now keeping woodland on your right. Be warned that this is all quite hard going, but the views westwards, the way you've come, improve with each step (or turn of the pedals!). Once the woodland to the right is reached and the path has levelled out, you cross the New Lipchis Way and overlap for a while with the West Sussex Literary Trail. The New Lipchis Way is a walking route linking Liphook and West Wittering, incorporating woodland, downland and waterside exploration – something for everybody – in its 62km. The West Sussex Literary Trail runs for 88km between Horsham and Chichester and follows in the footsteps of a number of authors who have associations with this part of Sussex including Hilaire Belloc and William Cobbett.

It's then lovely straightforward ridgetop travelling over **Heyshott Down, Graffham Down** and Woolavington Down, the views restricted by the trees, but a further climb sees the woods relent to the left and takes you to within less than half a mile of **Crown Tegleaze**, the highest point on the South Downs at 253m; even though the SDW only reaches 234m here the views from your path will be tremendous on a clear day. A described bridleway route incorporating the highest point is to be found in route 48. You swing in a more south-easterly direction to pass over Littleton Down then descend through fields, now enjoying splendid views eastwards towards Chanctonbury Ring, to reach and cross the A285 Chichester-Petworth road at High Littleton Farm, 8km 250m from the start.

Beyond the A285 the SDW climbs again, proceeding south-eastwards onto Sutton Down. It's a steady climb, shaving the left-hand edge of the woodland of Burton Down, and indeed the shade of the woods will be welcome on a hot day as you ascend. However the path then levels out and there is then a superb journey along a field edge with tremendous views to the Isle of Wight and Chichester Cathedral to the west and beyond Littlehampton to the east. To your left here are twin radio masts on a hill, marked on maps as Glatting Beacon; the masts are very prominent and you'll be able to pick them out numerous times not only from other spots along the SDW but indeed on other bridleway trips. Just beyond the masts, at SU971129, 3km

125m from the A285, it's worth detouring left very briefly along a bridleway heading for the masts (and passing just to the right of them) for a really splendid view northwards towards Barlavington Hanger.

The SDW continues in a generally easterly direction over **Bignor Hill**, meeting Stane Street, the old Roman road linking London and Chichester, and passing close by the site of a Neolithic camp. Beyond Bignor Hill the SDW climbs gently then begins to drop, passing **Toby's Stone** – a memorial to a local huntsman – from which there are sensational views to the sea, the Weald, the South Downs and the Arun valley; you should also look southwards to the hilltop Halnaker Windmill. Beyond the stone, the SDW swings very sharply north-eastwards (incidentally, ignore the OS Explorer mapping here which is extremely misleading, showing a segment of bridleway that, like John Cleese's parrot, has ceased to be), dropping steeply downhill to reach a bridleway junction at SU989132, roughly 2km from the recommended brief detour at SU971129. Beyond the bridleway junction the SDW then veers south-eastwards to climb again, passing immediately below and to the left of **Westburton Hill**, and skirting the extensive woodlands of Houghton Forest. (A separate route in this book, route 20, explores Houghton Forest and overlaps with the South Downs Way hereabouts, offering a fine detour from the national trail onto Bury Hill.) There's then a descent to cross the A29, some 2km 250m from the bridleway junction at SU989132.

Beyond the A29 crossing the SDW, heading just north of east, descends to the Arun valley, veering sharply south-eastwards and then north-eastwards to drop down to the valley floor and cross the Arun by a footbridge. The descent provides fine views not only ahead to the Arun valley but northwards to the pretty village of Bury, the sometime home of John Galsworthy. Beyond the crossing of the Arun the SDW goes forward to arrive at the B2139. To visit the village of Amberley (not a recommended detour from here as it's covered in route 49) you'd need to bear left, 750m, at this point beside the B2139. Your continuous route turns right to follow a parallel shared-use route to reach the junction with High Titten going off to the left. At this junction, 3km 250m from the A29 crossing, your route ends, at TQ028122. Amberley Station and the nearby Amberley Museum (again, see route 49) are 375m on down the B2139.

ROUTE 6

TQ028122-TQ197093 – Location Map W1 – OS OL10, OL11 – S

19km 875m – add 1km 500m for safe crossing of A24 (note that this will therefore exceptionally extend the journey to over 20km for those using this safe crossing)

Rackham Hill, Chantry Post, Washington, Chanctonbury Ring, Steyning Round Hill, Steyning Bowl

PT Amberley (* start), Upper Beeding (B finish)

R Amberley, Washington

Head north-eastwards up High Titten from the B2139 at TQ028122, where route 5 finished. Follow High Titten uphill for 625m to reach Mill Lane coming in from the left; continue beyond this junction for another 125m to TQ034125. Here bear left off the road to join a South Downs Way-signed bridleway. You ascend very steeply eastwards, the gradient relaxing but then intensifying again as you climb onto Amberley Mount along a clear track beyond the Downs Farm buildings. Watch for cyclists careering down the hill towards you! It's one of the steepest bridleway climbs in this book so pause every so often to get your breath back and enjoy the views which improve with each step or turn of the pedals (though cyclists among you may want to dismount here).

The ascent becomes gentler as you approach and pass the trig point of **Rackham Hill;** though this is off the route and on private land, the view as you pass it is still tremendous, particularly westwards to the Arun valley and also northwards, with the fine Parham House and Parham Park clearly visible just to the north-east. Now continue just south of east, passing a wooded area and then, on emerging, dropping down onto Springhead Hill, where there's a car park 4km from the start of the bridleway section of this route. Despite the slight descent to the car park, you're still very much on top of the escarpment. You continue between areas of pasture, keeping Kithurst Hill to your left, rising to a car park with signpost known as **Chantry Post** on Sullington Hill. Now enjoying fine views south-eastwards towards the distinctive hillside beyond Longfurlong and its busy road, you veer left to proceed over Barnsfarm Hill and drop down to the A24, which you need to cross with extreme care to arrive at a road on the far side of the crossing, at TQ120120, 5km from Springhead car park. To access the picturesque village of Washington, including its popular pub, you can simply follow the road beyond (Washington Bostal) downhill, reaching the village in roughly 1km.

Note that from Barnsfarm Hill at TQ105119, 3km 500m from the Springhead Hill car park, there's an official alternative SDW route. This provides a safe bridge crossing of the A24, much to be preferred for horse-riders, and allows you to visit Washington without detouring. To take this alternative, turn left off the SDW at TQ094117 and head north-eastwards downhill to Home Farm Cottages, where you bear eastwards across a bridge over the A24 into **Washington** then past the pretty flint-built church of St Mary, which contains arches dating from around 1200. Continue on up The Street, through the attractive village centre, and right at the road T-junction to ascend via Washington Bostal to the main route. This will add 1km 500m to your journey.

Beyond the road at TQ120120, go forward along the SDW-signed bridleway. The bridleway, heading eastwards, enters and ascends through a car park and then continues to climb, passing a disused quarry that's to the left; ignoring two left forks, the SDW bridleway then ascends increasingly steeply through woodland before emerging and bearing left at a T-junction, 1km 250m from the A24, at TQ130117. Now, after the hard graft, comes the reward; turning left here, you head confidently north-eastwards, veering eastwards, aiming for the cluster of trees around the famous Chanctonbury Ring hillfort. You pass immediately below and just to the right of the Chanctonbury dewpond, one of a number of such ponds you'll see on the SDW, being man-made shallow hilltop ponds intended for watering livestock and kept supplied with water by dew and condensation. A very brief detour just beyond the dewpond to the left up the modest hillside takes you to the **Chanctonbury Ring** trig point from which there are quite stupendous views that on a clear day may extend southwards to Brighton and as far as the Isle of Wight, while to the north you can enjoy a view to a massive expanse of Sussex countryside and as far north as Leith Hill, the highest point in Surrey. Returning to the SDW, you continue on to the cluster of trees that make up Chanctonbury Ring itself, arguably the most famous natural landmark on the South Downs. A large number of the beech trees that made up the cluster were blown down during the Great Storm of 16 October 1987, but an impressive number of trees remain and below them are the rampart and ditch of an Iron Age camp. Legend has it that if you run seven times backwards round the Ring, you'll conjure up the devil.

The SDW now swings sharply south-eastwards, the views hereabouts still really excellent, with another Iron Age hillfort, Cissbury Ring, clearly visible to the south, while just below you to the north are the grounds and church of Wiston House. In 1km 875m from TQ130117, at TQ145113, you reach a bridleway crossroads, going straight over, still heading confidently south-eastwards across the plateau. As you continue across the plateau your views are restricted by trees, but soon things open out again and you can look ahead to the Adur valley, Truleigh Hill and the escarpment leading to the Devil's Dyke beyond. You skirt the summit of **Steyning Round Hill** and at TQ162100 you meet another

Sussex name trail, the Monarch's Way, 2km 250m from the bridleway crossroads referred to at TQ145113 above. The Monarch's Way, at 982km currently the longest waymarked inland trail in Great Britain, traces as faithfully as possible the journey made by the future King Charles II after the Battle of Worcester in 1651, following which he was forced to flee for his life; he finally embarked for France from Shoreham-by-Sea, returning to reign as the Merry Monarch in 1660.

From TQ162100 you begin to descend, heading southwards to reach the Sompting-Steyning road and following a bridleway running parallel with it, south-eastwards, until at TQ164090, 1km from TQ162100, you strike out eastwards, now separated from the Monarch's Way, enjoying fine views to your left to **Steyning Bowl**. This is a steep semi-circular hillside guarding a dry valley and creating a green bowl-like effect from a distance. So don't forget to look back to it as you begin the next stage of your journey! Now veering just north of east, you have a long descent into the Adur valley over Annington Hill, passing a pig farm. Beyond the pig farm you veer south-eastwards and drop steeply, turning northwards and entering an area of trees, then continuing downhill to the buildings of Annington at the valley bottom. You reach Botolphs Road and turn right to follow it south-eastwards into Botolphs (a parallel roadside bridleway covers part of this route), within sight of the pretty church at Botolphs, visited in route 79. However the SDW turns left just a short distance before the church and, overlapping briefly with the Downs Link, goes forward to a bridge crossing of the River Adur. The SDW then leaves the Downs Link, bearing left beyond the bridge to arrive at the busy A283 at TQ197093, 3km 750m from TQ164090, just south of Upper Beeding; your route ends here. Buses run from here to both Steyning and Shoreham.

ROUTE 7

TQ197093-TQ293127 – Location Map W1 – OS OL11 – S

12km 250m

Edburton Hill, Fulking Escarpment, Devil's Dyke, Saddlescombe, West Hill, Pyecombe

PT Upper Beeding (B start), Pyecombe (B finish)

R Truleigh Hill, Devil's Dyke, Pyecombe

From the start at TQ197093 the SDW follows parallel with the A283 northwards briefly, before crossing it and heading eastwards then north-eastwards uphill, firstly along a path then along a metalled road followed by a wide stony driveway. The climb is long and tiring, but it is at least steady and not unbearably steep, and as you climb there are excellent views back to the Adur valley and the stunning and unmistakeable Gothic-style Lancing College Chapel. Once on the driveway you pass the Truleigh Hill Youth Hostel at Tottington Barn, 3km from the start; refreshments may be available here. Beyond the hostel the driveway rises quite sharply to reach the most prominent of a number of masts decorating the hilltop area. From here you drop steeply north-eastwards to the very edge of the escarpment at **Edburton Hill**, beyond which you veer south-eastwards and rise to proceed in a predominantly easterly direction along the top of the **Fulking Escarpment**. The views northwards all along this section are stunning.

You descend again before climbing extremely steeply, then after a short drop you embark on a longer steadier ascent towards the viewpoint above Devil's Dyke. You can tell you're approaching the Dyke, with its very popular hilltop restaurant, by the number of sightseers and kite-fliers. Signage isn't hugely clear and it's important to keep to the right of the grassy bank topped by a trig point, rather than being tempted to keep to the escarpment edge towards the pub. The SDW continues over the plateau, crossing the metalled approach road (TQ258107), 4km 250m from the youth hostel; I recommend you detour left at the road crossing for 250m or so along the road to visit the hugely popular viewpoint and pub, a stile to your left en route providing easy access via a muddy path to the trig point. Both the trig point and the viewpoint offer excellent views: from the trig point you have sight of Brighton and the South Downs as far as Firle Beacon, miles to the east, and from the viewpoint you'll see a vast expanse of Weald countryside. Beyond the road crossing the SDW proceeds along the right-hand side of that extraordinary phenomenon, **Devil's Dyke** itself. This is a deep dry valley with Ice Age origins. Legend says that it was cut by the Devil in an unsuccessful bid to flood the churches of the Weald where Christianity had taken hold, but when he saw a candle being held by a watching woman, he fled, leaving his work unfinished, believing the candle to be the rising sun. Seasoned bridleway baggers will be aware there are a number of similar features across Sussex but this one is assuredly the best known and best loved. It is undoubtedly one of the natural highlights of the SDW, the lush green of the valley floor a strange oasis between the uncompromisingly stark steep hills rising on each side, randomly furnished with hardy vegetation.

There's now a fine descent north-eastwards high above the Dyke, with views extending to the village and church at Poynings, and indeed as you make progress beside the Dyke, the views to the Weald just get better and better. There's a sharp descent to cross the busy Brighton-Poynings road at TQ271104, 1km 500m from the Devil's Dyke approach road, and immediately beyond the crossing you pass through the picturesque hamlet of **Saddlescombe**, with its small rural life display and (at the time of writing) a farmyard café, with food and drink being served from a caravan. A signed path to the right takes you within sight of the 17th century Donkey Wheel, a wheel turned by a donkey to supply water, housed in a mid-19th century wheelhouse. Continuing north-eastwards, you climb again, firstly through the trees then steeply through open grassland onto **West Hill**. As the ground levels out at TQ279116 you reach a gate and here you can enjoy one of the most stunning and yet unsung views on the entire journey, extending back to the South Downs escarpment in the direction of Chanctonbury Ring and forward to Brighton and the South Downs beyond. You can pick out three windmills from here, namely Jack and Jill above Clayton which you'll reach shortly, and Oldland near Ditchling.

The SDW now drops steeply downhill to a lane which shortly turns 90 degrees to the left to run parallel with the A23; you cross this road by a footbridge, 2km 500m from Saddlescombe, then begin a predominantly easterly course, bearing right and ascending to **Pyecombe**. On the right as you enter the village is its church, almost your archetypal Sussex downland country church, built of sturdy flint and boasting a 13th century tower. Very shortly beyond the church there's a crossroads where a right turn brings you into the village centre in 250m, but the SDW goes straight on, dropping to reach the A273 where this route ends, 500m from the A23 footbridge crossing, at TQ293127. Buses are available from here into Brighton.

ROUTE 8

TQ293127-TQ370092 – Location Map W1 – OS OL11 – S

14km 375m

Jack and Jill, Clayton, Keymer Post, Ditchling Beacon, Balmer Down

PT Pyecombe (B start), Housedean (B finish), Falmer (* finish)

R Pyecombe, Ditchling, Falmer

From the end of the previous route at your arrival at the A273, you begin this one by proceeding for 200m northwards beside the A273, then strike out eastwards, heading steadily uphill past a golf course. In 1km 250m from the start of the route, you reach a bridleway junction at TQ305129, turning left, northwards, here past New Barn Farm and in 375m arriving at a path junction; you turn hard right here to continue along the SDW but I recommend you detour left and then shortly right along a signed bridleway to reach, in 125m on your left, one (or should I say two) of the best-loved features of the South Downs, the twin windmills **Jack and Jill**. Both date from 1821 and were hauled here in 1850 by oxen. You first pass the tower mill Jack, who poor fellow has no sails, then soon reach the entrance and parking area giving access to the white-painted post mill Jill, who is complete with sails. Incidentally the bridleway leads on down in another 750m to **Clayton** and its pretty church of St John the Baptist which dates back to just after the Norman Conquest and boasts a mainly 13th century chancel. Its outstanding feature is its collection of wall paintings consisting of depictions of the Second Coming of Christ; the paintings date back to the early decades of the 12th century and are remarkably well preserved. I do recommend this detour if you've time – try and make the time!

Back on the SDW, you now embark on a straightforward very enjoyable march or ride, initially just south of east, veering just north of east, along the ridgetop, passing a couple more dewponds close to **Keymer Post** and enjoying magnificent views throughout. A stiff climb culminates in your arrival at **Ditchling Beacon**, at 248m the highest point actually on the SDW and indeed the whole of East Sussex, some 2km 750m beyond the Jack and Jill detour point. The beacon was one of a chain of big fires which was lit in 1588 to warn of the approach of the Spanish Armada. The Ditchling Beacon trig point is easily found just to the right of the SDW and provides a tremendous panorama not only to the South Downs but also the Weald and the sea around Brighton.

Returning again to the SDW, you proceed past a car park (which is always busy in good weather!) to shortly arrive at and cross Ditchling Road (250m beyond the beacon). You then continue on a resolute easterly course above Westmeston and Plumpton, passing numerous prehistoric earthworks at Western Brow, Streat Hill and Plumpton

Plain, while if you look south-eastwards you'll see the magnificent Amex stadium, the new (well, now not quite so new) home of Brighton & Hove Albion Football Club.

At TQ370125, 3km 750m east of Ditchling Road and just shy of the tree-covered Blackcap summit ahead, the SDW turns abruptly south-westwards, following a clear track towards **Balmer Down**, with particularly good views eastwards to Mount Caburn and Cliffe Hill behind Lewes. You reach a path junction in 1km 125m at TQ365115 and here turn off left, south-eastwards. Keeping Balmer Down to your right, you now enjoy some glorious open walking or riding, with a great view ahead to the lush green of the next line of hills, while nearer at hand is the remarkable six-sailed Ashcombe Windmill. Despite the nearness of Lewes and the A27, the surroundings are remarkably remote and rural. There's a steady descent and then at a path junction at TQ375102, 1km 750m from TQ365115, you turn sharply right, south-westwards, passing through the trees of the Bunkershill Plantation; it's your first woodland for many kilometres, albeit very brief, and there's a stiff climb in the shade of the trees. On emerging from the plantation you look down to the A27 and there's now a rapid descent to reach this road by Housedean Farm, the end of this route at TQ370092, 1km 375m from TQ375102. Buses are available to Lewes from the immediately adjacent bus stop alongside the main road. Otherwise bear right up the road past the farm. The SDW shortly forks left to cross the A27 by a bridge, and on the far side you reach a bus stop providing buses to Brighton, but by continuing on the path to the right of the road (rather than crossing the bridge), and following the path for 2km, you reach the University of Sussex and an underpass bringing you to Falmer Station.

ROUTE 9

TQ370092-TQ431055 – Location Map E1 – OS OL11 – S

12km 750m

Swanborough Hill, Rodmell, Southease

PT Housedean (B start), Falmer (* start), Southease
(* finish)

R Falmer, Kingston-near-Lewes, Southease

The route starts at Housedean Farm at TQ370092 and begins with your almost immediately crossing the A27 via the bridge; if you've chosen to catch a bus towards Brighton at the end of route 8, you'll already have done that bit! Beyond the A27 crossing, you follow parallel with this road eastwards briefly then turn right, south-westwards, passing under the Brighton-Lewes railway. Now, having lost so much height since Blackcap, you start ascending again, climbing south-westwards towards the line of hills you admired as you passed Balmer Down. It's a tough exposed climb into the prevailing wind, and presents as a huge contrast to the thickly wooded Heyshott Down and Graffham Down many kilometres back.

Just past the trees of the Newmarket Plantation, 2km 500m from the start, you reach a bridleway junction at TQ368078. You take the left-hand path, uphill, for 375m, now heading south-eastwards; to the west you can, from here, clearly see the village of Falmer and the cars on the busy Falmer-Woodingdean road. At the next bridleway junction at TQ370075 you bear left, north-eastwards, to follow, initially, the so-called Jugg's Road north-eastwards, Jugg's Road being an ancient route that was used to carry fish to the market at Lewes. Leaving Jugg's Road after 1km 125m at TQ379079 you veer right with the SDW, to proceed south-eastwards over **Swanborough Hill**, high above Kingston-near-Lewes and the town of Lewes itself. This is absolutely tremendous ridgetop travelling: immediately below you can see both Ashcombe Windmill and the pretty church at Kingston-near-Lewes (visited in route 57), while the views further afield to Lewes, Cliffe Hill, Mount Caburn, the Ouse valley, Firle Beacon, the Beddingham masts and Seaford Head are simply unforgettable. You're signed slightly further away from the edge of the escarpment and join a metalled farm lane along which, heading south-eastwards, you now begin a long, long descent past Iford Hill and Front Hill towards the Ouse valley. The descent is harder and more demanding than it looks: the concrete surface is tiring on the feet (so have those blister plasters on standby), and there's no shelter from what could be biting winds.

As you continue to lose height you also lose the concrete and actually cross from the western to the eastern hemisphere, the moment marked by a fingerpost and an impressive cairn! You're overlapping briefly here with the Greenwich Meridian Trail which runs for 439km from Peacehaven, East Sussex, to East Yorkshire, and endeavours to follow, as closely as possible, the divide between the western and eastern hemisphere. It runs through Sussex for roughly 53km. Back on the SDW, you go forward beyond the cairn to enjoy a very short wooded interlude round the buildings of Mill Hill, 4km 500m from TQ379079, then you plunge steeply into a dry valley. Here you turn hard left, north-eastwards, to follow the valley bottom to just short of the Lewes-Rodmell-Newhaven road at TQ421055, 1km 500m from Mill Hill. By going forward to this road and turning left alongside it you shortly reach **Rodmell**, the highlight of which is the white weatherboarded 16th century Monk's House, home of Virginia Woolf between 1919 and her death in 1941. It's a 750m each-way detour but I certainly recommend you follow it; the house is furnished in similar style to Charleston Farmhouse (which we meet in route 84 below) and is owned by the National Trust. At the time of writing, any visits need to be prebooked. The SDW however bears right at TQ421055, just before the road, to follow uphill, parallel with it, then crosses the road and joins a quieter road going downhill, eastwards, through the village of **Southease**. Shortly you reach its delightful flint church with a round Saxon tower, one of only three in the whole of Sussex. The church's original chancel and aisles have gone although some Norman work remains; the present church contains Jacobean box pews, a fine 15th century chancel arch of wood, lath and plaster, and 13th century wall paintings depicting scenes from the life of Christ, while remains of Reformation texts can be made out between the arches. You continue along the road down to the Ouse valley, soon crossing the River Ouse. Shortly beyond the river you cross the Lewes-Seaford railway just by Southease Station; the railway crossing at TQ431055, 1km 250m from TQ421055, marks the end of this route. There is, at the time of writing, the possibility of refreshment a short way beyond the railway crossing.

ROUTE 10

TQ431055-TQ520032 – Location Map E1 – OS OL25 – S

11km

Itford Hill, Beddingham Masts, Firle Beacon

PT Southease (* start), Alfriston (B finish)

R Southease, Alfriston

This is navigationally one of the easiest sections of SDW and indeed bridleway stretches in this book!

Beyond Southease Station, the start of this route at TQ431055, you follow a gravel track then soon are signed right to cross the busy A26 by means of a bridge. You then start climbing again, and it's a long old haul out of the valley as you proceed southwards then north-eastwards onto Itford Hill, climbing all the while. You then veer eastwards, still ascending, and in 2km from the start you pass just to the right of the **Itford Hill** trig point and the adjacent Red Lion Pond. It's worth detouring from the path to the trig point to enjoy the views which are sensational, particularly to the Ouse valley which you can follow with your eyes all the way from Lewes to the sea. Now having reached the top of the escarpment you can enjoy easy progress north-eastwards then eastwards, passing (at 1km 250m from the Itford Hill trig point) the splendidly sited **Beddingham Masts** and going forward to a car park at the top end of a road, Firle Bostal. A bostal, incidentally, a term specific to Sussex, is a road rising steeply onto the South Downs. You're high above Firle, which we'll visit in route 84.

The SDW continues eastwards beyond the Firle Bostal-end car park along the top of the escarpment, passing the woodland of Firle Plantation, and a gentle climb brings you to the climax of this route, the 217m **Firle Beacon** marked by a large earthwork. This, 2km 750m from Beddingham masts, is a quite magnificent viewpoint and one of the highlights of the SDW with glorious views in all directions, including a splendid panorama to the north and north-west as well as a huge coastal strip. From here the SDW now swings south-eastwards towards Alfriston, dropping initially to the car park at Bopeep Bostal. We now know what a bostal is; as to how Bopeep got its name, there are a number of explanations. The author Mary Delorme makes the point that as this is sheep country, "surely Bopeep was a natural choice," but a more prosaic possibility is a reference to the zealous and watchful eyes of an unpopular soul manning a local turnpike.

You then rise again onto Bostal Hill and now keep a straight and unerring south-easterly course, enjoying fantastic views forward to Windover Hill and left to Alciston, Berwick and the Arlington Reservoir. Soon the village of Alfriston, and its magnificent church, also comes into view. Taking care to follow SDW signage at path junctions, you swing eastwards to reach a metalled road and now descend to Alfriston, one of the loveliest villages in Sussex. You arrive at the High Street, 5km from Firle Beacon, by the 16th century Star inn. This route ends at TQ520032 at the point where the SDW meets the High Street, the SDW turning left up the High Street. It's astonishing to think that Alfriston is the first village you'll have passed through during your SDW pilgrimage. There are ample refreshments available: a splendid delicatessen, which does an excellent takeaway coffee as well as delicious snacks, is actually on the route. The luxury! Alfriston is more fully described in route 86, a rather shorter journey than the whole of the SDW in Sussex, so you may prefer to wait to tackle that route to enjoy the historic attractions it has to offer. Buses serve Alfriston on the so-called Bloomsbury Route between Lewes and Eastbourne, while Cuckmere Buses operate a regular Sunday service from here to Seaford and Eastbourne.

ROUTE 11

TQ520032-TV600971 – Location Map E1 – OS OL25 – S

12km 875m

Windover Hill, Jevington, Willingdon Hill, Warren Hill, Eastbourne

PT Alfriston (B start), Eastbourne (*, B finish)

R Alfriston, Jevington, Eastbourne

Having turned left with the SDW up the High Street in Alfriston at TQ520032, the start of this route, you follow it briefly northwards but then bear right, eastwards, away from it along River Lane. The SDW turns right again to follow the delightful Cuckmere River briefly downstream then shortly crosses the river by a footbridge. The SDW now splits in two, and for trail walkers there's a choice between the inland bridleway route and a seaside footpath route. In this book, of course, we must stick to the bridleway route! This proceeds eastwards beyond the footbridge then just before Lullington Road turns left to head through fields alongside this road, arriving at a metalled lane coming in from the left; here you turn right, cross Lullington Road, and ascend along a path to cross the Litlington-Wilmington road, 1km 750m from the start, at TQ532033.

Beyond the road crossing, the SDW, now heading for Windover Hill, continues to climb, heading just north of east then veering southwards, with superb views southwards to the coast and south-westwards to Alfriston. You can also get an excellent view of a carved white horse, created in February 1924 and renovated in 1949; this is situated on the hill known as High And Over (you may also see or hear it referred to as Hindover), towards the coast. The track bends sharp left (north-eastwards) and levels out; as it does so you could detour shortly to the left across rough grass to the tumulus on the summit of **Windover Hill** from which you can clearly see the sea, the port of Newhaven, the South Downs escarpment westwards to Firle Beacon, and, to the north, a huge tract of East Sussex farmland. You're right above the chalk figure known as the Long Man Of Wilmington. You can't see him from where you are here, but you'll get to meet him properly in route 87, so you needn't feel deprived. Staying on the SDW, you go forward to a gate, now veering south-eastwards, your direction of travel for the rest of the bridleway route to Eastbourne. Beyond the gate, you keep Tenantry Ground, a dramatic dry valley, to your right, and at TQ546032, 2km from the Litlington-Wilmington road crossing, you reach a fork junction, veering left here.

You now enjoy a magnificent open high-level journey, the views particularly good towards the coast. In 1km 500m from the fork junction you veer left into the woods, dropping down steeply, then descend more gently between fields to reach **Jevington,** passing its flint-built church which boasts a Saxon west tower and also some Norman and Early English work. You arrive at Jevington Road, which runs through Jevington village centre, 1km from your entry into the woods; you reach the road roughly opposite the former Hungry Monk restaurant, the birthplace of banoffee pie in 1972! By turning left you could follow the road up to the Eight Bells pub, where banoffee pie may or may not be on the menu, but the SDW bears right, then very shortly second left up Eastbourne Lane which soon becomes a track. It's a long uphill trudge but at length, 1km 500m from Jevington, you pass at TQ577009, the trig point marking the summit of **Willingdon Hill**, another magnificent viewpoint. Now maintaining height and overlapping with the Wealdway as well as the Sussex Hospices Trail, your SDW path then proceeds decisively seawards. There's quite a contrast between left and right: familiar open downland to the right, and the sprawling suburbs of Eastbourne to your left, separated from you by very steep wooded slopes. The views are tremendous throughout, especially towards Eastbourne and Hastings.

Passing Eastbourne Downs Golf Club, you reach and cross over the A259, 2km 500m from the Willingdon Hill trig point, then proceed to the trig point on **Warren Hill**. From here, the last great viewpoint on the bridleway route, the SDW (re-routed from its original course), skirts an area of trees separating you from the western fringes of Eastbourne, crosses Beachy Head Road close to its junction with Warren Hill, then ploughs on towards the sea, still high above Eastbourne as though wishing to avoid the town altogether. Ignore a path crossroads 375m or so beyond Beachy Head Road: then, however, at a path crossroads at TV594969, 2km from the A259 crossing, the SDW bears left, just north of east, and plunges downhill towards the town. The OS mapping suggests it unites with the footpath route roughly halfway between this left turn and Duke's Drive, then continues downhill to the Duke's Drive where both alternative routes of the SDW officially end at TV600971, 625m from TV594969. However, presumably to avoid an awkward stepped descent on the footpath route, the bridleway route is now signed down a narrower and less spectacular path, veering to the left of the mapped route through thicker vegetation, and then, close to the bottom of the hill, swinging right to reach the end point. My advice to walkers is to stick to the OS-mapped route. You've anyway now reached the conclusion of the longest bridleway route in Sussex – so congratulations are in order! There are buses from Duke's Drive into the centre of **Eastbourne** with its many attractions. These include the stunning Carpet Gardens, established in the town for more than a century; the 19th century pier, recently restored; the Towner Gallery with its splendid collection of contemporary art; the Grand Hotel, dating from 1875, and whose guests include Winston Churchill and Charlie Chaplin; the massive brick Redoubt, built to combat the menace posed by Napoleon and his army; and Devonshire Park with its theatre and tennis courts which host an important pre-Wimbledon tournament attracting some of the world's best players. If you prefer to arrive in the town under your own steam, the best way is to turn right to follow Duke's Drive down past Helen Gardens, immediately beyond which you turn right along a narrow road signed for the promenade. Follow this down to reach the prom, bearing left to follow it all the way to the pier, roughly 2km 500m from the end of the SDW.

WORTH WAY/FOREST WAY

Although there are two separate trails here, I chose to roll them into one in my book *The Great Walks Of Sussex* – otherwise they would not have qualified as Great Trails on the grounds of length. However, in this book, I can "uncombine" them to create two discrete routes, route 12 following the Worth Way and route 13 following the Forest Way. Taken together, they follow the course of a now disused railway that once linked Three Bridges and Tunbridge Wells via East Grinstead. It is indeed fortunate that the old railway has been converted into two such excellent shared-use routes, available for all bridleway traffic, albeit that much of it is not actually marked on OS maps as such.

Like the Downs Link, there is no hill-climbing to speak of, and signage is excellent. The trail is eminently suitable for wheelchairs and mobility scooters.

ROUTE 12

TQ289365-TQ388382 – Location Map W1 – OS OL34, 135 – E

12km 325m

Worth, Rowfant House, Gullege, Railway Shaw, Bluebell Railway

PT Three Bridges (*, B start), East Grinstead (*, B finish)

R Three Bridges, Crawley Down, East Grinstead

To reach the start of the route from Three Bridges Station, turn right out of the station exit, bear immediately right again at the A2220 (Haslett Avenue East) to pass under the railway, go immediately right once more up Station Hill (which becomes Billinton Drive), and then, 500m from the right turn up Station Hill, turn left as Worth Way-signed at TQ289365. This is the start of your route. (You may here see a sign indicating horse-riding is prohibited along the path ahead. This is clearly incorrect: the whole of the Worth Way is open for all bridleway traffic.) You begin by heading south-eastwards, veering just north of east, along the course of the old Three Bridges-East Grinstead-Tunbridge Wells railway. The section of the railway between Three Bridges and East Grinstead, which is retraced pretty much in its entirety in this route, was opened in July 1855 and at one time was extremely busy, with 17 weekday and 10 Sunday return journeys in 1955. However being a cross-country route rather than a London commuter route it was particularly vulnerable to the Beeching axe and the whole of the Three Bridges-East Grinstead section was shut at the start of 1967. Ironically, Dr Beeching was a resident of East Grinstead!

At TQ298365, some 1km 125m after the start of the route, you pass through a short tunnel under the B2036 Balcombe

Road and almost immediately beyond it you turn hard right, off the old line, following National Cycle Route 21, signed to East Grinstead and Worth. You ascend gently then turn hard left, eastwards, to follow parallel with and above the old line, before bearing right (southwards) along Church Road at TQ301366, some 250m from the tunnel. In 375m down Church Road you turn left, eastwards, along a road-cum-bridleway actually called Worth Way to reach, in 125m, the church of St Nicholas, **Worth**. Founded by Edward the Confessor, it's one of the finest surviving Anglo-Saxon churches in England; moreover, the chancel arch is one of the largest Saxon arches in the country. Other features of note include a 13th century font, early 17th century gallery, and 17th century monuments to the Goodwin family. As you enter the church by the west door look out for two blocked-in Saxon arches opposite each other, facing the nave; they were said to be for knights on horseback to ride through and pay their respects without dismounting!

You continue predominantly eastwards on what is an excellent bridleway over the M23 then proceed north-eastwards past Worth Lodge Farm to arrive at Turners Hill Road at TQ315365, just over 1km 250m from Worth Church. You turn left to follow beside Turners Hill Road, then in 175m turn right, eastwards with the Worth Way, back on the course of the old railway, and the going is now delightfully rural. In just under 1km you reach Wallage Lane beside which is the former station of Rowfant. It seems an odd place for a station; the explanation is that the land through which the old railway line passed was given by an American fur trader and transatlantic phone cable promoter Sir Curtis Lampson, and the station was given to Sir Curtis in return. Although the Worth Way crosses Wallage Lane and continues just north of east beyond the lane, it's a short recommended detour, roughly 375m each way, to the left along Wallage Lane to **Rowfant House**, where Sir Curtis lived. It's not open to the public but certainly worth seeing from the outside: it's a splendid building which was originally constructed in the late 15th century, probably for

Robert Whitfield, an ironmaster, and added to in the late Elizabethan era. Although it was extensively restored in the 19th century it retains a number of late Elizabethan features. Simply retrace along Wallage Lane to return to the Worth Way.

Whether or not you've detoured, head just north of east from Wallage Lane with the Worth Way as stated. You will remain on or immediately adjacent to the course of the old railway line as well as the Worth Way, continuing just north of east, all the way to Crawley Down, a distance of 2km 500m from Wallage Lane. The going is straightforward and really delightful. At TQ342372 you pass under a bridge carrying the B2028 and now keeping Grange Road immediately parallel with you to your right, continue along the course of the old line, going forward along Old Station Close to the junction with Station Road, Crawley Down.

The next bit is unavoidably dull and fiddly, I'm afraid. From the centre of Crawley Down village, follow Burleigh Way north-eastwards from Station Road, bearing right off Burleigh Way in some 250m to follow Woodland Drive for 75m. You then turn left, just north of east, along Hazel Way. In 450m, when Hazel Way veers sharp left, you fork right along Cob Close, going forward along a path, at TQ354377; that, in turn, goes forward to rejoin the course of the old railway. Dull bit over! Now it's a very easy and delightful journey towards East Grinstead through unspoilt countryside, heading just north of east, with a mixture of woodland, including Rushetts Wood and the lovely Gulledge (sic) Wood, and open fields around you. At TQ365382, roughly 1km 250m from where you rejoined the old line, you reach a crossroads of paths with a lake just to the right immediately before the crossroads – it really is a delightful spot. I recommend you detour left here and follow the bridleway for 250m to reach just to the left of the superb partially-timbered mid-16th century **Gullege** farmhouse; it boasts a really fine smooth stone frontage, dating from 1609, and very impressive 16th century chimney stacks. Its isolated rural setting adds greatly to its charm.

If you've detoured, retrace to the crossroads at TQ365382, and whether you've detoured or not, continue eastwards along the Worth Way. You skirt the pretty woodland of **Railway Shaw** which is to your right, and arrive at the Imberhorne Lane crossing at TQ377381, 1km 125m from the crossroads at TQ365382. Now the surroundings become more urban as you enter East Grinstead, but the going is still very pleasant indeed. At TQ388382 you find yourself immediately above East Grinstead Station, and this marks the end of the route, 1km 250m from Imberhorne Lane, as well as the end of the Worth Way. To access the station, cross the existing railway by the footbridge and descend to reach the station forecourt. (Note that trains from East Grinstead don't link with the main London-Brighton line until East Croydon: if you're wanting to get back to Three Bridges or Crawley, the regular buses available from here to those locations are very much quicker!) The town centre, roughly 500m distant, is reached by then crossing straight over the roundabout beyond the station forecourt and following Railway Approach to its end at London Road, the main shopping area. East Grinstead isn't the loveliest town in West Sussex but there are some fine old buildings on the High Street, described in a little more detail in route 13 below; arguably its most popular attraction is the **Bluebell Railway**, a preserved steam railway which runs from a separate station just south-west of the main one, down to Sheffield Park along the former East Grinstead-Lewes line. The line originally opened in 1882 and flourished in its early years but usage declined and it closed in 1958. The section between Sheffield Park and Horsted Keynes re-opened as a preserved line a few years later, and the extension from Horsted Keynes north to East Grinstead was completed in 2013. A ride on the railway would complement your bridleway journey delightfully so make sure the trains are running on the day of your visit. Having enjoyed your ride, you could go straight on to undertake route 13 which starts at the eastern end of East Grinstead.

ROUTE 13

TQ401379-TQ529365 – Location Maps W1 and E1 – OS 135 – E

17km 475m

East Grinstead, Brambletye House, Forest Row, Hartfield, River Medway

PT East Grinstead (*, B start), Groombridge (B finish)

R East Grinstead, Forest Row, Hartfield, Groombridge

To reach the start of this route from the centre of **East Grinstead**, head eastwards along the High Street, passing a number of fine buildings as you proceed. On the right (very close to the junction with London Road) is the splendid timber-framed late 16th century Clarendon House and several attractive shops (including a great bookshop!) as well as Middle Row beyond, followed by the 18th century Dorset Arms then the superb half-timbered 12th century Cromwell House. On the left there's the sandstone church of St Swithun, built two centuries ago and boasting eight bells, the largest peal in Sussex. Then you reach the fine stone-built Sackville College, dating from the early 17th century, and often open to the public. Beyond the college you continue along the same street (now Lewes Road) away from the town, then at TQ401379, immediately beyond a roundabout junction with Beeching Way, your signed Forest Way route begins with a right fork off the main road, roughly 625m from the centre of East Grinstead.

You now head downhill with the Forest Way, joining the course of what was the eastern section of the Three Bridges-East Grinstead-Tunbridge Wells railway line which you'll have met in the previous route. The section between East Grinstead and Tunbridge Wells opened in 1866; the section as far as Groombridge shut in 1967 while the remainder closed in 1985. Your excellent path soon leaves the suburbs of East Grinstead behind and you now head south-eastwards into open countryside, enjoying really lovely views, particularly to the right, where woodland dominates the skyline. You're overlapping here, and will continue to overlap until Forest Row, with the High Weald Landscape Trail, a trail that runs for 151km between Horsham and Rye through beautiful Wealden scenery of Sussex and Kent. Veering eastwards, you enter East Sussex. You also overlap briefly with the spur of the Sussex Border Path (see route 4) although that leaves the Forest Way fairly soon. At TQ419356, some 3km 250m from the start of the route, there's a well-marked crossing of Brambletye Lane. You could simply continue along the Forest Way if short on time, but the recommended route detours right here along a bridleway that in 375m, beyond a sharp right bend, brings you to the ruins of **Brambletye House**, built in Elizabethan-Jacobean style in 1631 but soon afterwards destroyed in the English Civil War. The ruins do make a highly impressive sight and give a clear impression of how the house would have looked externally had it survived. Retrace to TQ419356 and now, back with the Forest Way, resume your journey eastwards to arrive in 750m from rejoining the Forest Way at a crossing with the A22 at TQ425355. The Forest Way goes straight on, but I recommend you detour right alongside the A22 for 375m to reach the pretty village of **Forest Row,** served by buses to Tunbridge Wells and East Grinstead. Forest Row is an unusual village in that the main hostelry – in this case the tile-hung Chequers Inn Hotel, a former coaching inn, established around 1452 – is older than the parish church, which wasn't built till 1836. A stone in the wall of the 19th century village hall commemorates the visit of President Kennedy.

Back to the Forest Way! Beyond the A22 crossing, continue along the signed Forest Way south-eastwards just to the north of Forest Row; for 2km beyond the A22 there is suburban housing to your right, while the scene to your left is more rural. Having got past the built-up area, you begin to head north-eastwards, enjoying excellent views to the fine Ashdown House which lies on the left (north) side of the old line, and indeed we will actually pass Ashdown House in route 24. The countryside on both sides of your route is quite delightful: you can see why the Forest Way gets its name as the fringes of Ashdown Forest are clearly visible to your right, and you also have lovely views to meadows to your left. This section of route is particularly popular with cyclists as well as walkers, so do not expect to be on your own! In 4km beyond the end of the Forest Row built-up area, at TQ479362, you pass underneath the B2026 Maresfield-Edenbridge road, but by joining this road (reached via the slipway to the right, just beyond the bridge, and then the station approach road) you can (and I recommend you do) detour 400m or so southwards to the delightful village of **Hartfield**. The station building, just to the left down the station approach road, survives and boasts an impressive frontage; despite the modest size of the community it served, the old station at Hartfield boasted a goods yard loop that could hold 13 wagons. Hartfield itself boasts a number of beautiful weatherboarded and timber-framed houses, and the church of St Mary has a superb lychgate which incorporates the upper floor of an adjacent 16th century timber-framed cottage. The village has strong associations with A.A. Milne and Winnie the Pooh, whose stories were set in the surrounding area, and indeed Poohsticks Bridge is near Hartfield and reachable by a Sunday stroll described in Part 7 of this section.

Beyond Hartfield your Forest Way journey is delightfully fast and easy in lovely surroundings. You soon cross the Wealdway, a 134km route linking Tonbridge and Eastbourne, incorporating fine downland and Wealden scenery. You continue past the rather inelegantly named village of Balls Green and the site of the old station at Withyham, which also boasted a goods yard during its lifetime. Very roughly parallel and to your left is the delightful infant **River Medway**, which rises between Crawley and East Grinstead and goes on to become a major river in Kent, emptying into the Thames and being crossed by impressive motorway and rail bridges. There's little hint of that just here! You veer in a more north-easterly direction for a while, but then turn south-eastwards, crossing the B2110 (3km 675m beyond the B2026 crossing) and noting the extant London-Uckfield railway coming in from the left. You veer right to cross the B2188, 1km beyond the B2110 crossing, and continue on beside the extant railway, then veer left to pass under the railway and right, eastwards, to go forward to Corseley Road where the Forest Way (and this route) ends at TQ529365, 500m from the B2188 crossing. To reach the centre of Groombridge, and its bus connections to Tunbridge Wells and Crawley, turn left to follow the road for roughly 1km.

Part 2 – Woodland bridleways

Woodland exploration has its own distinct joys. There may be a lack of constant open views, although often there are great views to be seen through the trees, but the trees themselves are constantly fascinating. Evergreens provide colour all the year round, the rich greenery of pines contrasting beautifully with the bare deciduous branches and the white of snow and frost, while deciduous trees offer vibrant fresh greens in spring and an infinite variety of golden and red hues in autumn. And in April and May there are the joys of carpets of bluebells and white flowers of wild garlic plants across the woodland floor. Woodland can and does support a huge diversity of wildlife as well as plants and shrubs, and can provide welcome shelter from summer heat and colourful relief from the parched fields and downs.

Sussex as a whole has many fine areas of forest, including, in West Sussex, St Leonard's Forest, Houghton Forest and dense areas of woodland round Liphook and Haslemere, while in East Sussex Friston Forest and Dallington Forest are two further outstanding examples. All offer many fine bridleway routes. Note that bridleways on or around Ashdown Forest, where open spaces rather than trees predominate, are explored elsewhere in this book.

So, if you go down to the woods today…what will you find?

ROUTE 14

SU843300-SU837306 – Location Map W2 – OS OL33 – M

11km 425m

Milland Place, Maysleith, Maysleith Hanger/Wood, Milland, Chapel Common

PT Liphook (*, B start and finish)

R Liphook

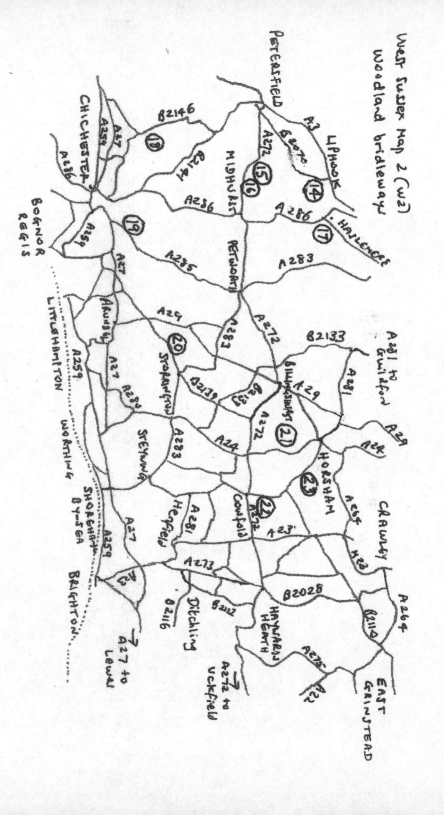

West Sussex Map 2 (W2)
Woodland bridleway

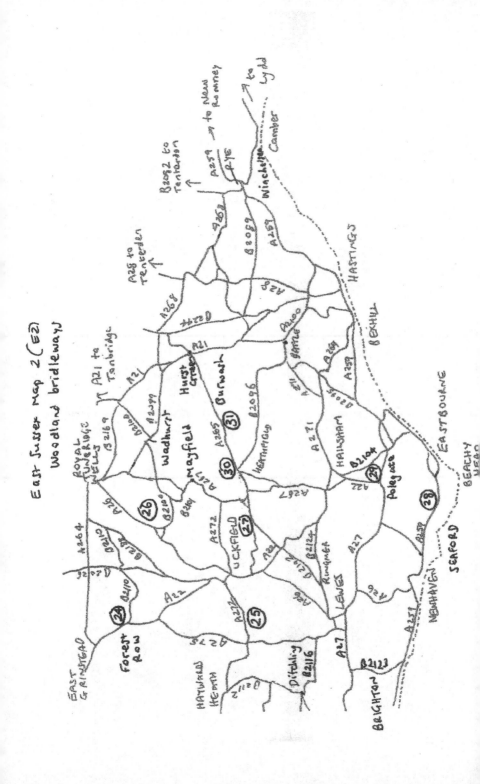

East Sussex Map 2 (E2)
Woodland bridleways

This is a predominantly wooded route but with some fine views and some interesting surprises! To all intents and purposes this is a round trip based at Liphook Station. To access the start of this route from that station, follow the Midhurst road (which crosses the railway by the bridge immediately east of the station) south-eastwards for 700m to the road junction with Highfield Lane which comes in here from the left. Here turn right, south-westwards, along a public byway which here overlaps with two name footpath routes, the Serpent Trail and the Sussex Border Path. You will meet them again, more than once, in the course of your bridleway explorations in Sussex. We met the Sussex Border Path in route 4; the Serpent Trail follows an S-shaped course from Haslemere to Petersfield, crossing a succession of commons with lovely mixed (though largely coniferous) woodland, gorse and heather, superb views and firm sandy tracks, with a total distance of 104km.

Back on this bridleway route (which we still haven't started), follow the public byway for some 625m to the start of the route at SU843300, simply in fact continuing south-westwards along what is now a restricted byway, still with the Serpent Trail and Sussex Border Path. In 1km 125m from the start of the route, at SU834294, turn left, southwards, up a signed bridleway, leaving both the named long-distance routes...for now. Your bridleway proceeds through the trees, keeping a most picturesque short hole of Liphook Golf Club to your right; doubtless such golfers as there are on this hole won't thank you for following their progress from tee to rough to bunker to green. You arrive in 250m at a bridleway T-junction at SU834292. Turn left here and proceed eastwards through Hatch Fir woodland, then as a footpath comes in from the left in some 450m you veer right, south-eastwards. In another 150m or so, just south-west of Hatch Farm, you veer right again, now heading south-westwards, emerging from the woods. Having exited the woods you veer westwards, enjoying a splendid high-level bridleway with excellent views, most notably south-eastwards to the Bexleyhill masts high above Midhurst.

There's then a steady descent to Milland House where you reach Milland Lane at SU831285, roughly 1km 750m from SU834292.

Turn left along the road for 75m or so and as the road veers slightly right you fork left, south-eastwards, for 375m along a bridleway which heads downhill past **Milland Place**; there was once a 17th century house here, but it burnt down in the 1890's and was rebuilt, to quote the *Pevsner Architectural Guide*, as an "exuberant, multi-gabled, balconied, bargeboarded house with a spirelet over the highest gable, in the manner of a Bavarian spa hotel." You reach a bridleway T-junction at SU833282. Turn right here and follow the track south-westwards for 200m down to a T-junction with Milland Lane at SU831281. Turn right up Milland Lane for 200m then at SU830283 fork left off the road along a lane which shortly becomes a bridleway heading south-westwards to a path junction at SU828280, 375m from Milland Lane. Go straight over, past the buildings of **Maysleith**, an attractive stone-built house dating back to 1580, and now follow a really lovely bridleway southwards through **Maysleith Hanger** and **Maysleith Wood**; it's not clear when the former finishes and the latter starts, but they're as attractive as each other. You emerge from the trees and now proceed uphill along a quite delightful open hillside, close to the right-hand edge of the open land. You cross a clear track and now continue along a bridleway track downhill, still south-westwards, passing a charming lake which is to your left. Just beyond this lake, at SU818275, 1km 125m from Maysleith (the house), you veer sharp left as bridleway-signed, then, in some 75m, you veer sharp right into the trees, following a clear woodland path. You emerge at Combeland Farm and continue south-westwards to the end of the bridleway at Canhouse Lane at SU814270, 550m from the sharp right turn into the woods.

Turn right along Canhouse Lane for 100m then bear right along a restricted byway heading just east of north then just west of north through woodland, climbing steadily. It's not clear from the map if you're in Coldharbour Wood or

Maysleith Wood but it's not worth losing too much sleep over. You veer north-eastwards and as you continue to gain height, you should detour up the bank to your right for quite magnificent views to the south and east. You then veer gently left then right, enjoying what is a really lovely woodland track, until you reach the side of the B2070 at SU820281, 1km 500m or so from Canhouse Lane. Before the building of the spanking new A3 to the west of here, this B2070 road WAS the A3, the main road from London to Portsmouth. That explains why this B road is here a dual carriageway. It still conveys a fair bit of traffic but the noise of it, and pollution from it, isn't as bad as it used to be! Don't cross the B2070, not yet anyway, but turn right along the verge – it is quite safe – going forward in just a few metres to follow a bridleway eastwards, and reaching a junction with a crossing track at SU824282, 500m from where the track from Canhouse Lane arrived at the B2070. Your continuous route turns left, north-westwards, up the track here, but you should detour very briefly eastwards along the bridleway to visit the charming 19th century church of St Luke, **Milland**, built in 14th century style, its finest features being two windows made in 1899 and 1904 by Christopher Whall and boasting what the *Pevsner Architectural Guide* describes as "strong jewel-like colours." Behind the church is the old church, known as the Tuxlith Chapel, dating from the 11th century, abandoned in the 1930's but repaired in 1993. It possesses what the *Pevsner Architectural Guide* describes as "the moving simplicity of an ancient and remote local church." Remote is right: neither the chapel nor the more recent church are anywhere near Milland village, separated from you here by 1km of footpath and 1km of tarmac.

Onwards and upwards. As stated your continuous route proceeds north-westwards along the track from SU824282 to cross the B2070 (carefully of course); go straight on along the bridleway beyond, veering north, soon being joined by the Serpent Trail. Continue northwards with the Serpent Trail, here following the eastern edge of the beautiful landscape that is **Chapel Common**. Designated as an Area of Outstanding Natural Beauty, Chapel Common boasts fine mixed woodland, open heaths providing superb views, and plant life which includes a variety of orchids. You veer sharply right, north-eastwards with the Serpent Trail, to a path crossroads at SU825290, roughly 1km from SU824282. Go straight over the crossroads, immediately veering northwards along the bridleway beyond. Although at the crossroads you bade a final farewell (on this route anyhow) to the Serpent Trail, beyond the crossroads you overlap very briefly with the Sussex Border Path again. Then, in 125m bear right, leaving the Sussex Border Path, and follow the signed bridleway for 750m, past the Ripsley Farm buildings and then north-eastwards to arrive at the B2070 at SU832295.

Turn left to very briefly follow the B2070 but then in barely 50m turn left along a bridleway north-westwards, crossing a fairway of Liphook golf course. You cross the railway and veer sharp left to arrive at a bridleway junction at SU831298, 300m from the B2070. Bear right here along a bridleway which soon emerges from the trees and proceeds northwards, downhill, on a clear track, crossing a plank bridge and then veering right, north-eastwards, beside the golf course. You cross the Foley Manor approach road and continue to the B2070 and the end of the route at SU837306, 1km from SU831298. Turn left beside the road for 375m and then right along Station Road for 250m to reach Liphook Station.

ROUTE 15

SU818246-SU814245 – Location Map W2 – OS OL33 – E

8km 175m

Fyning Hill, Cairn Wood

PT Rogate (B start and finish)

R Rogate

This route provides nice contrasts of woodland and open walking/riding in gloriously unspoilt countryside, well away from traditional honeypot destinations – and some might say it is all the better for it. Again this can be treated as a circular route. To reach the start of this route from Rogate (served by buses from Petersfield and Midhurst) follow the A272 eastwards from Rogate for 500m, turning left at Fyning at SU813239 along Fyning Lane which heads north and in 500m bends sharply right, north-eastwards, to enter the village of Terwick Common. Ignoring a bridleway (A) going off to the left 250m beyond the bend, carry on for another 375m beyond that one to reach the start of this route at SU818246. Note that the meeting of bridleway (A) with Fyning Lane marks the end of the route so you can create a circular route by simply following Fyning Lane back to the start.

Turn left at SU818246 along a bridleway heading just west of north for 500m, ascending through the woodland of Fyning Common to an unnamed road. Cross straight over, following a driveway/bridleway briefly north-eastwards with the Serpent Trail (which we met in route 14 and which has come in along the road from the left), but after 125m at SU817251 you reach a fork junction of bridleways. Leaving the Serpent Trail, fork left here across a field north-westwards, going forward in the same direction along a lovely woodland bridleway path on **Fyning Hill**. Keep on this path, veering in a more northerly direction, then at SU815259, 750m from SU817251, you reach a signed bridleway junction. Turn hard right here, heading south-eastwards through the trees. You emerge at the corner of a very large field; don't strike out into the field as the signage suggests, but continue in a south-easterly direction along the right-hand field edge, climbing steeply on what is a reasonably clear path. You reach the top and continue in the same direction along the path, enjoying smashing views northwards to the lovely countryside between Milland and Rake. Note that this obvious path does NOT follow the route shown on the most recent OS Explorer map!

At SU822255, some 700m from SU815259, you reach a bridleway junction and here turn left to head north-eastwards along a very pleasant well-defined path for some 750m, reaching, at SU825262, a signed T-junction of paths. Turn right to follow a clear bridleway track south-eastwards for 375m, to reach another T-junction at SU829261. Turn right again, south-westwards, to follow, for 1km, a really gorgeous restricted byway, dead straight, superbly defined and comfortable to walk/ride on with lovely views to the surrounding countryside including Cairn Wood which you'll be exploring soon. Your bridleway here does have the feel of a piece of disused railway – although no railway company was ever brave enough to construct a line hereabouts! At SU825252 you reach a T-junction with a lane/bridleway just south-east of the buildings of Trotton Marsh. Turn left, south-eastwards, along this lane, in 150m reaching a right-hand bridleway turn at SU825251.

The direct route bears hard right, north-westwards, here, but I do recommend your detouring to visit the lovely Cairn Wood. To do the detour, go straight on along the lane at SU825251, reaching, in 150m, a hairpin road bend immediately ahead. Just before this, at SU825250, is a 90-degree left turn along a signed bridleway. Take this bridleway which heads north-eastwards through **Cairn Wood**, ascending; there's then a really delightful woodland descent along a superb path with a most attractive view at the end of the wood at SU829255, some 700m from SU825250. From here, simply then return exactly the same way to SU825250 and then turn right to further retrace to the bridleway junction at SU825251.

Now, whether you've detoured or not, head north-westwards along the bridleway from SU825251: this is a particularly attractive woodland-edge bridleway. Ignore a bridleway going left after 300m, but continue to a bridleway crossroads, 500m from SU825251, at SU820253. Turn left here and now climb steeply south-westwards through Rondle Wood for 325m to arrive back at the bridleway junction at SU817251, having now come full circle. Now retrace from earlier, following the driveway (and indeed Serpent Trail!) for 125m south-westwards down to the road. This time, however, don't cross over but turn right along the road for 425m, then turn left, at SU812251, following a bridleway through the woods of Fyning Common; you descend along the bridleway, just east of south to Fyning Lane at SU814245, where the route ends, 750m from SU812251. To return to Rogate, bear right along Fyning Lane for 750m down to the A272 at Fyning, then turn right beside the A272 for 500m to reach Rogate.

ROUTE 16

SU843238-SU856237 – Location Map W2 – OS OL33 – M

9km 225m

Chithurst, Tentworth, Lambourne Copse, Oakham Common, Stedham

PT Trotton (B start, optional B finish), Stedham (B finish)

R Trotton, Stedham

This route explores some of the remotest and most peaceful green lanes and tracks in Sussex. Both the start and end of the route are served by buses from Petersfield and Midhurst; to reach the start of the route from the A272 just east of Trotton, make your way to the Chithurst Lane junction at SU840223. Follow Chithurst Lane northwards away from the A272 through **Chithurst**. In 750m from the A272 you reach the simple but delightful 11th century church of St Mary, the church containing a crude Saxon chancel arch. West of the church is the part-15th century Chithurst Manor, while to the north of the village is a Buddhist monastery, and indeed you may see Buddhist monks taking walks hereabouts. In 375m beyond the church, your road takes a sharp right bend and then almost at once reaches a road junction where you turn left. Follow this very narrow road for a further 375m to a sharp left bend; this is the start of the route, at SU843238. Here you leave the road, going effectively straight on, to follow, predominantly northwards, a restricted byway, Moorhouse Lane.

Moorhouse Lane is a quite delightful path through woodland, initially the beautiful Hammer Wood; at one point a flight of steps has been created to assist walkers! You veer north-eastwards, moving from Hammer Wood to Pond Copse, going forward to arrive at Milland Road at SU847251, some 1km 500m from the start. You turn right along the road but then turn almost immediately left, just south of east, up another restricted byway, climbing steeply into and through woodland. There's a very sharp veer to the right, south-eastwards, and at the edge of the wood you reach, at SU850250, a signed path fork. Take the right fork and aim for the Stubbs Farm buildings across the field, enjoying fine views beyond the farm. Just short of the farm (SU851249, 500m from SU847251) you turn right to follow the restricted byway, southwards, downhill. Make the most of the views as you soon lose them, your path, Sharver's Lane, becoming a sunken track. Follow it all the way to Iping Lane at the bottom, SU851243, 650m from Stubbs Farm. Turn left along Iping Lane which almost immediately veers right; just beyond this sharp right turn, bear left along an unnamed lane.

In just 250m this lane becomes a bridleway. Go straight on for a few metres to a signed path junction at SU854242; here turn left, just east of north, along what is initially a clear driveway/bridleway past the fine buildings of **Tentworth**, with lovely parkland to your right. Beyond Tentworth you veer gently left, north-westwards, keeping really beautiful woodland to your right. You then veer northwards, ascending gently, and now enjoy a fine open bridleway track to Bowley Farm. Beyond the farm you descend, entering woodland and arriving at a path T-junction at SU855255, 1km 375m from SU854242. The continuous route bears right, just east of south, here. However I recommend a detour to visit the lovely woodland of **Lambourne Copse**. It is a 1km 500m detour each way – a 3km round trip. To do this, turn left, northwards, at SU855255 and follow a wide restricted byway track to the buildings of Titty Hill at SU855257, meeting and very briefly overlapping with the Serpent Trail which we met in route 14. Go straight on along the restricted byway, ignoring the road going off to your left. Shortly the Serpent Trail is signed off to your right but you continue along the restricted byway, veering north-westwards and following Lambourne Lane through Lambourne Copse. This is a gorgeous track through beautiful woodland – perfect for a picnic in good weather. I walked it in glorious sunshine but not two hours later I was sheltering from a thunderstorm! I suggest you follow the path all the way through the copse; you veer in a more northerly direction, before emerging from the woods and following a super path just west of north between fields to reach the bottom of the tarmac section of Lambourne Lane at SU851268, the path ending here. Then simply retrace all the way to SU855255.

Now, whether you've detoured or not, head just east of south from this point as stated, along an excellent track, a restricted byway, through fine woodland. You veer right, westwards, briefly, then veer left, south-eastwards, and ignoring a left fork (which leads back to the bridleway you followed past Tentworth) you continue through the lovely woods of **Oakham Common**. From here you now descend and veer just west of south to reach a path junction at a parking area at SU856241, some 1km 500m from SU855255. Bear left here: don't then turn immediately right along what seems like the obvious track, but, following the signed New Lipchis Way (see route 5), go straight on for just 50m up a very steep bridleway path to a T-junction of bridleways at SU857241. At this T-junction, you leave the New Lipchis Way, turning right along a track which shortly bends left to a path junction. Don't take the footpath heading effectively straight on, eastwards, but rather veer right with the bridleway. This soon veers southwards and descends through the trees to a junction with a lane at SU856237 roughly 400m from SU857241. At this point the bridleway route ends.

I suggest you turn left down the lane; at the end, in 125m, you reach a T-junction with Stanwater Lane (A). Here you have a choice. If you wish to return to Chithurst, creating effectively a circular route, turn right to follow the road which becomes Hammer Lane. In 2km or so you reach the church at Chithurst; from the church it's another 750m back down the road to the A272. Alternatively, at (A) turn left along Stanwater Lane past Crouchhouse Farm and, 375m after joining the road, turn right down Stedham Lane, reaching the centre of Stedham in 1km – 1km 500m from the end of the route. **Stedham** itself, served by buses to Petersfield and Midhurst, is a very pretty village of brick and sandstone; its architectural highlights are the church of St James with Saxon tombstones and a Gothic-style 17th century tower, and the impressive partially-timbered 17th century Stedham Hall, lying to the north of the church.

ROUTE 17

SU903317 (start and finish) – Location Map W2 – OS OL33 – S

7km 725m

Black Down

PT Haslemere (*, B start and finish)

R Haslemere

This circular route takes you to the roof of West Sussex, in fact the highest point across all of Sussex. It's one of the tougher routes in this book and can be quite fiddly, with lots of different paths and tracks, but it's hugely rewarding. To reach the start of this route from the attractive Surrey town of Haslemere, served by rail, head for the top (south) side of the main town square, at SU905328, crossing straight over the main road and following College Hill, south of the main road, uphill, south-westwards, for 250m. At the end bear left into Hill Road and, in 125m, turn right into Old Haslemere Road. At the end of this road, in 375m, turn left along Scotland Lane then in 175m bear right for 500m along a public byway, which heads south-westwards and, entering West Sussex, descends to Bell Vale Lane by Stedlands Farm, the start of the route, at SU903317.

Cross Bell Vale Lane (which effectively ends just here), and turn left, heading south-eastwards along a signed bridleway. In 125m you veer right, just east of south; here you pass the fine 15th century Valewood Farm House, timber-framed but faced with Wealden sandstone and tile-hanging. Some 150m from the point at which you veer right, you reach a signed bridleway junction at SU905315. Turn hard left along the signed bridleway but in a few metres bear right, eastwards, as Sussex Border Path-signed; climb very steeply up this bridleway, arriving in 125m at a bridleway T-junction. Turn right here, south-eastwards, to follow a bridleway which carries both the Sussex Border Path (see route 4) and the Serpent Trail (see route 14). You proceed through a field then veer left and right to enter woodland; continue along the bridleway south-eastwards through the wood, forking left at a signed bridleway junction at SU911306 (1km from the top of the very steep rise referred to above). In 250m from here you go straight over at a signed bridleway crossroads, and, continuing to gain height, you stay on the Sussex Border Path/Serpent Trail for a further 625m to reach a multi-track junction at SU918302. Here turn left as Sussex Border Path-signed – NOT hard left! – and now head north-eastwards with the Sussex Border Path, here a bridleway.

This is lovely going, along the broad heather plateau of **Black Down**. Black Down is the highest ground in the whole of Sussex, some 280m above sea level, the only pity being that the views are restricted by the density of the woodland. There is a trig point but it is all but buried in the surrounding woodland and some way off the bridle route. You would have hoped for something more panoramic from the roof of Sussex! The area has strong associations with Alfred, Lord Tennyson, who had a summer retreat at Aldworth House on the eastern slopes of Black Down, but again this is some distance away from the bridle route. In 275m from the multi-track junction, at SU920304, you reach a bridleway junction, just short of a T-junction. Turn right at SU920304, leaving the Sussex Border Path, and in just 25m or so you reach another bridleway T-junction, turning right onto what is the Serpent Trail. Now follow the Serpent Trail as signed southwards for some 1km 125m to a path junction at SU920294. This is quite glorious – a wide path, fabulous views and gorgeous woodland. Just perfect!

Unfortunately OS Explorer mapping now becomes misleading. The important thing to note is that at SU920294 the Serpent Trail bends hard right, westwards, and that is how your continuous route proceeds. However you should detour just a few metres as signed at this point to visit the Temple of the Winds. There's no temple – just a shelter, of no real architectural significance, but there's a topograph and a quite astonishing view that on a clear day stretches all the way to the Devil's Dyke and beyond. It is arguably only when you arrive here that you get the sense of how high up you are. The hill itself is described by Nikolaus Pevsner as a "great whale-backed sandstone hill" while Keith Spence referred to it as the "nearest approach to a mountain in these parts...shaggily coated in trees like one of the foothills of the Jura."

Return to SU920294 and now follow the Serpent Trail, which here is still a bridleway, westwards as stated, again sticking to signs rather than the possibly misleading mapping. You descend to a fork junction at SU919294, roughly 125m from SU920294. Here you lose the Serpent Trail which forks right; you take the left fork, continuing along the signed bridleway. You now plunge down along an excellent track to the buildings of Cotchet Farm at SU914295, 500m from the point where you lost the Serpent Trail. Pass through the gate and then bear left as bridleway-signed, in 250m reaching Fernden Lane. Turn left along the lane but in 125m turn right as bridleway-signed at SU912293; head south-westwards along the bridleway for 200m to reach a signed bridleway junction at SU912292.

Turn right, north-westwards, to follow a lovely woodland path, which in roughly 1km 125m arrives at a junction with a metalled driveway at SU906301.

At this junction turn right, north-eastwards, to follow the driveway, mapped as a restricted byway, back to Fernden Lane, a distance of 250m. Turn left along Fernden Lane for 250m then at SU906305, at Wadesmarsh Farmhouse, turn right as bridleway-signed and head just west of north on a superb wide green track which in 625m arrives at a metalled lane/bridleway, at SU905312. Turn left along it and in 300m you'll find yourself back at the signed bridleway junction at SU905315. You've come full circle. From here retrace past Valewood Farm House to SU903317 at Stedlands Farm, the start and now the end of the route. Simply now return to Haslemere the same way, via the byway, Scotland Lane, Old Haslemere Road, Hill Road and College Hill.

ROUTE 18

SU793105-SU782109 – Location Map W2 – OS OL8 – S

17km 650m

Walderton Down, Adsdean Down, Hounsom Firs, Devil's Humps, Kingley Vale, Chilgrove Hill, Stoughton Down, Stoughton, Haslett Copse, Watergate Hanger

PT Walderton (B start and finish)

R Walderton, Stoughton

This is a glorious journey across some of the most unspoilt and peaceful terrain in West Sussex, along excellent clearly defined bridleways. Navigationally it's very easy too; it's the bridleway traveller's dream! The journey can be treated as a circular route based at Walderton. To reach the start of the route from the B2146 at Walderton, served by buses from Chichester and Petersfield, head north-eastwards from the B2146 along the Stoughton road. After 500m, at the very eastern edge of Walderton at SU792107, turn right, south-eastwards, along a lane which leads in 250m to the start of the route at SU793105, your bridleway heading directly left (eastwards) from the end of the lane. You ascend steadily eastwards along the bridleway through woodland onto the picturesque **Walderton Down**, kinking right-left at SU800105, 625m from the start of the route. You then enjoy a stunning high-level march or ride eastwards with great views across a swathe of coastline, continuing to rise onto **Adsdean Down** and into the charming woods of **Hounsom Firs**. In some 1km 500m from the right-left kink you emerge from the woods, your track now skirting the north edge of the woodland. At SU814103 you reach a track fork (A); OS mapping and bridleway signage directs you straight on, plunging back into the woods and descending. If you are being a purist, follow the signed bridleway into the woods and then in 125m or so reach a bridleway junction, turning hard left here and climbing quite steeply for another 125m to a path junction (B) at SU814104. In fact, by forking left at (A) you reach (B) in just a few metres!

From (B) follow the track (a bona fide bridleway!) north-westwards along the woodland edge then in 250m from (B) at SU813105 turn right at a bridleway junction to follow a signed bridleway north-eastwards. Initially you continue through woodland but then emerge to pass just to the right of the **Devil's Humps**, which are among the most impressive Bronze Age round barrows (burial mounds) to survive on the South Downs. The views from the top of the mounds towards Chichester, the Manhood Peninsula and the sea are exceptional. You're now in the heart of the **Kingley Vale** Nature Reserve; the woodlands are particularly noteworthy for their yew trees, the chalk grassland hereabouts is home to nearly 40 species of butterfly as well as numerous orchids, and bird life includes sparrowhawks, tawny owls and woodpeckers. Beyond the Devil's Humps continue along the track past the Bow Hill trig point to reach a bridleway crossroads at SU825113, roughly 1km 500m from the bridleway junction at SU813105. Cross straight over, continuing just east of north along a fine, clear woodland bridleway, crossing the Monarch's Way (see route 6) at

SU828125 and, ignoring turnings off, veering northwards to reach a bridleway crossroads at SU828139, some 2km 500m from the bridleway crossroads at SU825113. The continuous route bears left here, but I recommend your detouring 500m or so straight ahead, north-westwards, along a bridleway onto **Chilgrove Hill** from which there are some really great views. Whether you've detoured or not, head south-westwards along the bridleway from SU828139 for 1km 250m to a bridleway junction at SU819129. Turn hard left here and follow the bridleway for 1km, initially eastwards then south-eastwards to a crossroads bridleway junction with the Monarch's Way at SU824121, now on **Stoughton Down**. Bear right here onto the Monarch's Way and, emerging from the woodland, you can enjoy a really fine view south-westwards towards Portsmouth.

Keep following the Monarch's Way, here a bridleway, south-westwards for 1km to SU814117. At this point, for reasons best known to itself, the Monarch's Way turns into a public footpath; here, therefore, you must temporarily leave the Monarch's Way, turning right, briefly north-westwards. In 125m you veer sharp left and follow the bridleway on for another 750m, initially westwards then veering fractionally north of west to reach the road at SU807118. Turn left along the road into **Stoughton**, being rejoined by the Monarch's Way at Old Bartons. Stoughton boasts a popular pub and an 11th century church, St Mary's, with a particularly fine lofty 11th century Saxon chancel arch, an east window dating from about 1200, and a low massive slate-roofed tower. The *Pevsner Architectural Guide* also gives a special mention to a magnificent stretch of herringbone stonework along the south wall of the nave.

In the village, at SU801114, 750m from joining the road, turn right off the road with the Monarch's Way; keeping the church to your right, go forward to join a bridleway heading westwards, uphill, arriving at a T-junction of tracks at SU796115, 625m from Stoughton. This is a gorgeous viewpoint with the added curiosity of a cairn, a most unusual phenomenon in Sussex. Here you leave the Monarch's Way, turning right, north-westwards, and descending steeply to a road linking Walderton with Up Marden, 375m from the cairn. Cross straight over, continuing north-westwards along a bridleway and (ignoring a bridleway going off shortly left) ascending through the lovely woodland of **Haslett Copse**, emerging and reaching a path junction at SU788126, 875m from the road. Here bear left, westwards, along the bridleway that in 375m arrives at another road, Locksash Lane; turn right along the lane then almost immediately left along a lovely bridleway that heads westwards for 875m with glorious views, descending to the B2146 at SU775127. Cross straight over along Oldhouse Lane, following it for 150m, then turn left along a bridleway that heads initially south-westwards then veers south-eastwards, ascending once more through the lovely woods of **Watergate Hanger**. At SU775119 you reach a multi-track junction at the edge of the wood, 750m from Oldhouse Lane. Turn left (NOT hard left) to follow a glorious bridleway south-eastwards along the woodland edge with really great views down towards the coast. It's a great finale to a superb bridleway experience. In 1km 125m from the multi-track junction, at SU782109, you reach the end of the route at Woodlands Lane. To return to Walderton, thereby creating effectively a circular route, turn left down the lane to arrive back at the B2146 in Walderton in 500m.

ROUTE 19

SU907083-SU899174 – Location Map W2 – OS OL10, OL8 – M

10km 625m

Boxgrove, Halnaker House, Halnaker Park, East Dean, Charlton Forest, Heyshott

PT Halnaker (B start), Cocking (B finish)

R Boxgrove, Halnaker, East Dean, Heyshott, Cocking

This route, incorporating some history as well as great woodland scenery, is a linear one and if you're reliant on public transport you need to base yourself at Chichester, getting a bus from Chichester to Halnaker to start, and then getting a bus from Cocking back to Chichester at the end.

To access the start of the route, you need to get yourself to the junction of The Street, Boxgrove, with the A285 at Halnaker, at SU907081; this junction is well served by buses plying the Chichester-Boxgrove-Tangmere route. Before getting going, you should detour southwards some 500m down The Street to visit **Boxgrove** and its really splendid Priory Church and ruins. The church of St Mary and St Blaise, dating back to the early 12th century, is regarded as the most important Early English building in Sussex after Chichester Cathedral; among its many highlights are the sumptuous De La Warr Chantry chapel, dating back to the 16th century with quite exquisite carvings, and the early 16th century ceiling painting that consists of a rococo floral pattern including Tudor roses and De La Warr heraldry. Adjoining the church are the ruins of the monastic buildings, arguably the most impressive of which is the late 13th century flint-built Prior's Lodging, doubling as a Guest House. Having visited the Priory, you can enjoy refreshment at the excellent village store on The Street, before returning to SU907081, passing the Countess of Derby's Almshouses which date back to the mid-18th century. On your returning to SU907081 there's a further opportunity for refreshment, this time at the Anglesey Arms, Halnaker, immediately adjacent to the junction of The Street and the A285.

Now it really is time to get going! Starting from SU907081, you head fractionally west of north from the A285 up Park Lane, arriving in around 175m at the start of the route at SU907083, going forward from here along the bridleway in the same direction. As you proceed from the start, look to your right for views of the imposing ruins of **Halnaker House**. Halnaker House was a medieval house that was given a thorough remodelling in the 16th century in Renaissance style, but became ruined around the start of the 19th century. It's now described in the *Pevsner Architectural Guide* as "a pretty, picturesque group of walls," with pieces of the hall, 13th century chapel and 14th century gatehouse still standing. Your bridleway, still heading north, passes to the left of the Halnaker House ruins and the adjacent modern Little Halnaker and, 750m from the start of the route, enters woodland, following a clear wide track; to the east, well beyond the woodland, is **Halnaker Park** and its house, one of the last country houses to be built by Sir Edwin Lutyens, and dating back to the 1930's. Roughly 750m from the entry into woodland, your bridleway veers north-eastwards and proceeds in a dead straight line through the woodland of Halnaker Park and Ladys Winkins, past exceedingly tall trees, gaining height steadily. Having proceeded north-eastwards for 1km 625m, the bridleway then veers north-westwards to arrive, in 375m, at Selhurstpark Road at SU911116. Turn right very briefly alongside the road then in some 75m turn left as bridleway-signed north-westwards. Following what is a clear bridleway track, well signed and easy to navigate, you head north-westwards through beautiful woodland, your path overlapping for some 500m with the Monarch's Way (see route 6) and offering gorgeous views through the trees. The Monarch's Way goes off to the left at SU907121 at which point you veer gently right, northwards, through the woodland of Bubholts. Take great care here to leave the main track at a bridleway-signed right fork, this turning being easy to miss. You now descend significantly; emerging from the woods, the bridleway drops to the Lavant valley to arrive just east of the village of East Dean at a minor road, Butcher's Lane, some 1km 500m from Selhurstpark Road.

Turn left along Butcher's Lane to reach a junction with Main Road in the village of East Dean in just 250m. (Note that there's also an East Dean in East Sussex, itself a very fertile area for bridleways. Don't get your East Deans mixed up!) **East Dean** back here, in West Sussex, contains some lovely flint cottages, a pub called the Star & Garter, the hillside church of All Saints with a particularly fine south doorway dating back to 1200 and a mid-12th century tower, and a green with a pond. The pond is effectively the source of the River Lavant, which we'll get to know rather better in route 32.

Your continuous route however bears right along Main Road from Butcher's Lane and then in 250m forks left up Newhouse Lane, past the church. As Newhouse Lane bends right, 125m after your joining it, turn left along a bridleway which heads initially north-westwards then veers sharply right, northwards, uphill. You pass a beautifully-positioned seat – you can allow yourself a rest and a sit-down here! – then proceed in the shade of trees and along a right-hand field edge. You then enter the extensive and extremely beautiful woodlands of **Charlton Forest** as you veer north-westwards again, then veer north-eastwards. This is a glorious section of woodland bridleway on an excellent track. You're then joined by the West Sussex Literary Trail (WSLT – see route 5), coming in from your left, at SU905149, 1km 875m from the start of the bridleway. Continue with the WSLT north-eastwards through the forest, ignoring crossing tracks, ascending increasingly steeply, until you arrive at the South Downs Way at SU910164, 1km 500m after you were joined by the WSLT.

Turn left along the South Downs Way for 500m then at SU904165 turn right onto a bridleway heading away from the South Downs Way north-westwards, initially across grass then steeply downhill through woodland to arrive in 1km 250m from the South Downs Way, at SU899174, at a lane. This marks the end of your bridleway route. If reliant on public transport, you would turn left, westwards, along the lane to arrive, in 2km, at the A286 in Cocking, which we'll have a slightly closer look at in route 47; there are regular buses from here back to Chichester. However, whether or not you're needing to proceed to Cocking, you should bear right at SU899174 along the lane to reach, in just 250m or so, the village of **Heyshott**. This is a most attractive village, boasting the 13th century church of St

James which contains an unusual 13th century font; the striking 18th century Royal Arms; and a memorial to the 19th century free trader Richard Cobden. Other buildings of note in the village are the 16th century Heyshott Farmhouse and the timber-framed Laurel Cottage, described in the *Pevsner Architectural Guide* as "delectable!" Having enjoyed the village, retrace to SU899174 and then follow the lane westwards from there to Cocking.

ROUTE 20

TQ017115-TQ026088 – Location Map W2 – OS OL10 – S

14km 475m

Houghton, Houghton Forest, Westburton Hill, Bury Hill, River Arun, South Stoke, Arundel

PT Amberley (* start), Arundel (*, B finish)

R Houghton, Whiteways Lodge, Arundel

This route explores the lovely Houghton Forest and there's a splendid riverside finale; it's nice and easy to access too, with both start and finish points within easy reach of stations on the Arun Valley railway line. What's not to like! To reach the start from Amberley Station, simply follow the B2139 south-westwards for 1km to **Houghton,** with its George & Dragon pub, where a plaque commemorates the visit of the future Charles II on his way to France. Here (TQ017115), just by the pub, is the start of your route, as you fork onto a bridleway (part of the Monarch's Way – see route 6) which you follow uphill for 750m to reach and pass a car park/ viewpoint at TQ010112. From the car park/viewpoint, continue with the Monarch's Way ascending westwards, veering south-westwards, then curving westwards to cross the A29, some 750m from the car park/viewpoint. Head initially westwards beyond the A29 but in 100m bear left with the Monarch's Way – this left turn could be easily missed – then in 75m reach a T-junction of bridleways at TQ001111 where you bear right. (If you were to turn left here you'd reach, in some 200m, Whiteways Lodge with its café, exceedingly popular with motor bikers – so expect some noise and fumes to mingle in with your chosen refreshment!) Having made the right turn at TQ001111 you now proceed on a clear path, staying with the Monarch's Way, continuing just north of west through the delightful woodland of **Houghton Forest**, with its mixture of trees including ash, yew, maple and beech. It's very popular with walkers and cyclists and some of the well-used tracks can get rather muddy.

At SU988113, 1km 250m beyond the T-junction at TQ001111, you reach another T-junction, here turning right, north-westwards, staying with the Monarch's Way. Remain on this clear track through the forest for another 1km, heading north-westwards, but at SU982122 you bear right, away from the Monarch's Way, along a bridleway heading north-eastwards through Barkhale Wood. There follows a steady field ascent, your bridleway veering more eastwards before veering back north-eastwards. The views are magnificent. You pass through another strip of woodland then descend steadily to meet the South Downs Way at SU989132, 1km 375m from leaving the Monarch's Way. At SU989132 you turn right to continue south-eastwards along the South Downs Way, ascending onto **Westburton Hill**, skirting the extensive woodlands of Houghton Forest and enjoying further tremendous views. In 1km 750m from SU989132 you arrive at a bridleway junction at TQ001120. The continuous route turns right, southwards, here, but a 250m-each-way detour along the bridleway going left here onto the very top of the **Bury Hill** plateau provides a quite fantastic view, and I really recommend it.

However as stated the continuous route takes the bridleway heading southwards from TQ001120, leaving the South Downs Way, and following a woodland edge; in 875m your bridleway turns sharp left to meet, in 75m, a right turn (A) along the Monarch's Way you were following earlier. You have now come full circle. If you wished to avail yourself of refreshments at Whiteways Lodge, motorbikes and all, you could turn right here for 75m then left for 200m as stated above. However your continuous route retraces back to Houghton; for this, don't take the right turn at (A) but carry on eastwards for 100m, crossing the A29 and then following the Monarch's Way downhill for 1km 500m back to where you started, by the George & Dragon at TQ017115.

At this point, having covered 10km 100m, and arrived back at where you began, you may be happy to call it a day and, if reliant on public transport, simply return to Amberley Station. However you could decide, and I strongly recommend, that you continue to Arundel; this journey offers a lovely mix of woodland and waterside bridleways. (There is, of course, no reason why you shouldn't return and continue to Arundel another day – this continuation can easily be accomplished as a linear or straight out-and-back route.) From the pub continue briefly back towards Amberley Station but then in some 125m turn right, south-eastwards off the B2139 along South Lane. Follow South Lane then in 225m veer right at TQ019113 to join and follow a bridleway which is also the route of the Monarch's Way. Follow the bridleway south-westwards, then veer south-eastwards, enjoying the sight of the parallel **River Arun** close by to your left. The Arun is one of the great rivers of Sussex, historically having seen a significant amount of container shipping: it rises in the outskirts of Horsham and continues via Pulborough and Amberley to reach the sea at Littlehampton. Although its container shipping has gone, it remains very popular for river cruising and pleasure craft, while much of the riverside is followable (though chiefly only on foot), and is immensely attractive.

At TQ015104, 1km 250m from leaving South Lane, the Monarch's Way goes off to the right. You however remain on the bridleway continuing south-eastwards, the Arun never far away to your left, initially through woodland and then in more open country, away from the woods, as far as a junction with the road at **South Stoke** (TQ026099), another 1km 250m from TQ015104. By detouring left along the road at TQ026099, you reach, in just 200m or so, the church of St

Leonard, and, just beyond that, an attractive bridge crossing of the Arun. I recommend you look at both! The bridge crossing is very picturesque – a nice place to linger on a hot day – while the church, which dates back to the latter part of the 11th century, boasts a tall wide nave and chancel and an impressive 13th century south porch. However your continuous route crosses more or less straight over the road at TQ026099 along a bridleway heading initially south-eastwards but quickly veering south-westwards. You're in delightful water meadows, again close to the Arun, following firstly a wide grassy track and then a narrower muddier path in vegetation close to the woodland edge. You veer south-eastwards and then south, passing a cottage which is to your left and rising through trees. This last piece of woodland on this route is particularly attractive, with gorgeous flowering wild garlic here in spring. I walked this on a gloriously sunny Monday afternoon during the first lockdown in April 2020 and there was a lovely sense of tranquil timelessness – here, anyway, all seemed right with the world! Continue to ascend to reach the end of the bridleway at TQ026088, 1km 125m from the road at South Stoke. This spot, just above the little village of Offham, also marks the end of your route. To reach Arundel, some 2km distant, turn left along the road here, bearing right in 75m and following the road downhill past the Black Rabbit pub, and then further on, Arundel Wetland Centre and Swanbourne Lake. You continue past the castle grounds, bowling green and museum into the centre of **Arundel**.

Arundel is a great destination however you have got here. Architecturally its highlights are its superbly photogenic castle, rebuilt in the 18th and 19th centuries but retaining some 12th and 13th century features; its Roman Catholic cathedral, built in Gothic style in the 1870's; its 14th century parish church of St Nicholas, partitioned into separate Anglican and Roman Catholic areas (the Catholic area, the Fitzalan Chapel, being the final resting place of former Dukes of Norfolk and Earls of Arundel), and its flint-built Priory which today incorporates a theatre. Along Mill Road at the bottom of the town there's the lovely Swanbourne Lake and the Arundel Wetland Centre with its profusion of swans, geese and ducks. Or you can simply enjoy pottering amongst the shops and have tea at one of the town's many pubs and cafes! To reach the railway station, 750m from the town centre, you need to make your way down to, and cross, the bridge over the River Arun in the town centre. Carry on south-eastwards along Queen Street, going forward along The Causeway and beside the A27 south-eastwards, following the signed shared-use route under the bridge to the station.

ROUTE 21

TQ149264 (start and finish) – Location Map W2 – OS OL34 - E

14km 300m

Middle Wood, Newbuildings Place, Madgeland Wood, Sharpenhurst Hill, Itchingfield, Marlpost Wood

PT Southwater (B start and finish)

R Southwater, Barns Green

This is a rather long but easy and enjoyable circular woodland expedition, with a little bit of climbing added to the mix, but there is necessarily some tarmac crunching.

To access this route from Southwater, very well served by buses from Horsham, head just north of west along Church Lane from the village centre at TQ156262. In 625m the road bends sharp left and then in 125m sharp right. At this right bend, you reach the start of the route at TQ149264, bearing left off the road along a bridleway and heading initially south-eastwards then veering south-westwards to reach the buildings of Birchwood Farm. Continuing south-westwards beyond the farm along the bridleway you enter the very pretty **Middle Wood**, and at TQ148254 you reach a bridleway junction, roughly 1km from the start. Continue along the bridleway heading south-westwards through the wood, kinking left and right at a footbridge and then following the woodland edge to Trawler's Farm. At the farm buildings at TQ145247 you reach a path junction, turning left, southwards, with the bridleway to a path crossroads at TQ145245, 1km 125m from TQ148254. This is a lovely, peaceful spot. Turn right and follow the bridleway just north of west for 375m to Dragons Green Road, here turning left down the road for 250m to see the very impressive stone-built **Newbuildings Place** to the right. The house dates back to 1683, and was once the home of a writer and traveller rejoicing in the wonderful name of Wilfred Scawen Blunt.

Having admired Newbuildings Place, retrace up the road northwards but this time continue past the bridleway that took you here, following the road northwards then north-westwards to a road junction at TQ140251, 875m from Newbuildings Place. Turn left at the junction onto Marlpost Road then in 100m leave the road, turning right, northwards, up a woodland bridleway for 250m to reach junctions with bridleways going left and right. Turn left here, TQ139254, to follow a bridleway just north of west for 800m through the attractive **Madgeland Wood**. You arrive at the metalled Trout Lane at TQ131257. Turn right, northwards along the lane for 1km 125m to a T-junction. By turning left here you would reach, in 750m, the amenities of Barns Green, which include a pub and an excellent general stores. However your continuous route turns right at the T-junction. In 125m at TQ134268 turn left to follow a bridleway that heads off in a predominantly northerly direction; although the mapping doesn't necessarily make this clear, the bridleway is for most of its course in the shade of trees, and very attractive woodland it is as well. You cross the railway in some 500m from leaving the road then climb up on to **Sharpenhurst Hill**. Sadly the bridleway doesn't go to the trig point at the very top, nor is there a right of way to it – attempt it at your own risk or seek permission! From the trig point there are lovely views to the buildings of Christ's Hospital (which we visited on our Downs Link journey in routes 2 and

3), the church at Itchingfield (see below) and the town of Horsham. The views from the shoulder, however, are still excellent, the bridleway skirting the right-hand edge of the woods and reaching its highest point as it gets level with the trig point. The bridleway then veers north-westwards downhill at TQ134282, 875m from the railway.

Now you have a choice. The continuous route turns back at TQ134282 and retraces via the railway crossing to the road. However I strongly recommend you carry on downhill, north-westwards, for 125m to Westons Hill, turn right along the road for 450m and then turn left along Itchingfield Road that in 375m takes you to the pretty village of **Itchingfield.** The village boasts attractive timber-framed houses and a Norman church of St Nicholas, dating from around 1125. The church's most remarkable feature is its 600-year-old belfry tower made entirely of huge beams held together by oak pegs, while in the churchyard is the tiny half-timbered Priest's House, dating from the 15th century and intended to serve as overnight lodging for a priest who rode over from Upper Beeding to collect church dues. Then retrace to TQ134282.

Whether you've detoured to Itchingfield or not, retrace southwards as stated all the way to the road at TQ134268 via the railway crossing. Turn left along the road for 750m then at TQ141266 turn right, southwards, along a delightful bridleway that initially ascends gently through the woods. You emerge from the woods to pass Crookhorn Farm then re-enter woodland to arrive, at TQ139254 (1km after leaving the road), at the bridleway junctions you met earlier just before entering Madgeland Wood. This is a really delightful spot, and a good place for a picnic if you've not indulged at Barns Green – or even if you have! This time turn left, fractionally south of east, through another lovely stretch of woodland, **Marlpost Wood,** along an excellent bridle track, going straight over Marlpost Road in 150m. Look out for a sharp bend (after 500m from TQ139254) just before a footbridge crossing. You arrive, some 875m from the junctions at TQ139254, at a bridleway T-junction, the same junction you met earlier at TQ148254. You've come full circle! Turn left to retrace for roughly 1km to the road at TQ149264. This is the end of the route. Turn right along the road to reach Southwater in 625m.

ROUTE 22

TQ227251-TQ202276 – Location Map W2 – OS OL34 - M

16km 450m – but this route can easily be split at Crabtree after 9km 375m

Minepits Wood, Furnace Pond, New Pond, Freechase Hill, Warninglid, Rout Farm, Lodgesale Wood, Nuthurst, Sedgwick Park, Home Wood, Finche's Wood

PT Crabtree (B start) Monk's Gate (B finish)

R Crabtree, Warninglid, Nuthurst, Monk's Gate

This route, passing through lovely woodland and past a number of sites of historical interest, is a linear route but at both ends there are bus connections to Horsham and Brighton. As stated above you can easily split this route if you wish. To access the start of this route from the A281 at Crabtree, served by the Horsham-Brighton bus route, follow Mill Lane south-eastwards from the A281 (at TQ220253) for 750m to its end. Here, the start of the route at TQ227251, you fork left, north-eastwards, onto a bridleway which soon veers northwards through the charming **Minepits Wood** and then right, eastwards, passing between two attractive lakes, **Furnace Pond** and **New Pond**. The name Furnace Pond would indicate that that this was a so-called hammer pond. These considerable stretches of water, now extremely beautiful and peaceful, were first created some 500 years ago to make water power sufficiently strong to forge iron, a major Sussex industry at that time. For a long time, water mills had been used for the relatively simple process of grinding corn between millstones; the hammer pond made it possible to generate sufficient power to work the machinery of blast furnaces and forges.

Continue eastwards to a path junction at TQ232254, 750m from the start, here going left with the bridleway, predominantly north-eastwards through very pretty woodland on the side of **Freechase Hill**, on an excellent track. Going forward through William's Wood, you cross a path crossroads at TQ239260 and now continue north-eastwards uphill, arriving just short of the B2115 Warninglid Road, roughly 1km 625m from TQ232254. Turn right along the bridleway, parallel with the road, and continue parallel with it for 375m, keeping to a most pleasant tree-shaded path, which eventually drops to the road at TQ247262. Turn right along the road, in 250m arriving at the top end of **Warninglid** village street. The village's most interesting feature is arguably its village sign which depicts a spear-brandishing Saxon with the words "Werna Gelad" meaning "Werna's path" inscribed over his head. The village also has a pub. Turn right to follow the village street for 400m, but as the road bends right at TQ250257 you go straight on southwards along the bridleway. You will after a stiff 750m ascent reach **Rout Farm** where you'll get a magnificent view ahead to the South Downs. Having kinked left and right with the bridleway at the farm, continue along the bridleway southwards, with orchards either side, reaching Colwood Park; on getting to the park, your bridleway veers sharp right and left to reach Colwood Lane at TQ249239, 1km 100m from Rout Farm. Turn right along the lane for some 750m, reaching a very steep ascent. Just here (TQ241242), at a sharp left bend/road junction, bear hard right onto a bridleway known delightfully as Earwig Lane, proceeding northwards through woodland for roughly 875m. At the end of the bridleway you arrive at the splendidly-named Spronketts Lane, turning left down this lane for 250m, then turn hard right, north-westwards, at TQ241249 onto another bridleway. You then enjoy a very pleasant woodland bridleway journey in a predominantly westerly direction, turning sharp right at a path junction in 1km 375m from Spronketts Lane and arriving in a further 125m back at the east end of Mill Lane at TQ227251. You've come full circle; now turn left to follow Mill Lane for 750m back to the A281 at Crabtree.

You may be happy to leave it there, having completed 9km 375m. To continue, however, cross the A281 with care and turn right beside it for roughly 175m to reach a bridleway going off to the left at TQ220255. Turn left along this bridleway, heading south-westwards away from the A281 through woodland. At a bridleway junction at TQ213254, 750m from the A281, you turn right, north-westwards, continuing in a virtually straight line through the woods for 1km 125m from the junction to reach Prings Lane. You cross more or less straight over (kinking left then right) then continue along the bridleway through the delightful **Lodgesale Wood.** You head initially south-westwards then veer north-westwards before turning south-westwards again and then westwards (following the signage carefully) past a number of impressive buildings to reach, at TQ193262, the centre of the village of **Nuthurst,** 1km 500m from Prings Lane. Nuthurst is a small village but boasts the pleasing combination of a historic church and a pub. The church of St Andrew dates back to the late 11th century and has been much added to and restored since; among its features of interest are a superbly painted chancel and rood screen. On the south wall is a tablet to Sir Nevile Henderson, the British ambassador to Berlin during the Hitler years; he lived at Sedgwick Park (which we visit shortly) and achieved notoriety as an out-and-out appeaser of Hitler. Meanwhile, the early 19th century monument to John Aldridge comes complete with what the *Pevsner Architectural Guide* describes as a "lumpy cherub!"

Turn right up Nuthurst village street for 100m then at TQ193263 turn left along a bridleway lane that heads just north of west past Nuthurst Farm, climbing to reach a bridleway junction at TQ185265, 875m from Nuthurst village street. At this junction turn right, just east of north, and follow the bridleway/driveway through **Sedgwick Park**, just south of the remains of Sedgwick Castle. The castle dates back to the 12th and 13th centuries, while the main house over to your left, not open to the public, originated in the early 17th century and was greatly altered and enlarged in the late 19th and early 20th century. In 375m from TQ185265 take great care to turn right as signed with the bridleway; this turning is signed but is surprisingly easily missed. It is now a really lovely bridleway journey north-eastwards through **Home Wood** and **Finche's Wood**, with beautiful views. At length your bridleway emerges from the woods and some 125m after doing so, at TQ200279, reaches a junction with a footpath, 1km 875m from the easily-missed right turn. Here you veer sharp right, south-eastwards, with the bridleway and now follow the bridleway on for a further 300m to its end, at Nuthurst Road, at TQ202276. This is the end of the route. Turn left along the road to reach, in just 75m, the A281 at Monk's Gate. Regular buses to Horsham and Brighton stop here.

ROUTE 23

TQ214293-TQ245365 – Location Map W2 – OS OL34 – E

9km 500m

Hawkins Pond, St Leonard's Forest, Buchan Country Park, Ifield Mill, Horsham

PT Mannings Heath (B start), Ifield (*, B finish)

R Mannings Heath, Colgate, Ifield

This route, passing through beautiful historic woodland, is a linear route but with good transport connections from/ to Horsham at both ends. To reach the start of this route from Mannings Heath, served by frequent buses on the Horsham-Brighton service, follow Golding Lane north/ north-eastwards from the crossroads junction in the middle of the village. This brings you in 1km to a T-junction with Hammerpond Road. Turn right to follow Hammerpond Road for 450m to TQ214293, where a bridleway heads away left, just east of north. This is the start of your route. Before you get under way, though, I recommend you carry on along Hammerpond Road for another 175m or so to view **Hawkins Pond**, one of a number of so-called "hammer ponds" created to service the iron industry which prospered in this area (see also route 22 above). Its woodland setting is extremely attractive. If you've detoured, retrace to TQ214293 to get going properly.

Follow the bridleway just east of north from TQ214293 for 1km; at TQ218302 you turn sharp left then in a further 125m you reach a path T-junction. Turn right, northwards, to follow a superb track through the forest. For 1km 675m, as far as TQ216319, you continue resolutely in a northerly direction, ignoring crossing tracks. You're now in the heart of **St Leonard's Forest**, and will remain in or around the forest all the way to the A264 crossing later on on this route. St Leonard's Forest is so called because legend says that here St Leonard killed the last dragon in England (so you should be quite safe); the forest once supported a flourishing iron-smelting industry, and mounds called pillow mounds were created to provide accommodation for rabbits who were valued for their fur and as food. Another legend says that the absence of nightingales in the forest is attributable to a bad-tempered hermit who banished them for disturbing his meditations. For the first 750m or so of this northward bridleway you share your route with the High Weald Landscape Trail (see route 13). At TQ216319 your bridleway bends right, north-eastwards, the going remaining most pleasant. In 1km 125m from the right bend you reach Forest Road. Turn right along this road, passing through Colgate with its pub, then, in 1km 125m from where you joined Forest Road, you reach a bridleway left turn at TQ235330. Turn left here to now follow the bridleway northwards from this point.

Your bridleway proceeds very enjoyably through the woodlands of part of St Leonard's Forest known as **Buchan Country Park**, veering a little east of north. The Country Park offers a great variety of wildlife: birds to be found here include grebes and nightjars, and you should also look out for dragonflies and adders. The going is very easy but watch carefully for (at the time of my research, unsigned) right path fork at TQ236338. You need to take this right fork but once you've done that, the going is straightforward all the way down to the A264, which you reach in 1km 625m from Forest Road. Maps would appear to indicate you simply cross the A264 to continue on towards Ifield, but don't attempt to cross the road here. Rather, turn left as bridleway-signed and proceed beside the A264 up to the new safe crossing across this very busy road; having crossed, bear right – again as bridleway-signed – along an excellent metalled track which rises initially then winds its way downhill past the new housing estate which is to your left. At the bottom of the hill, you reach a junction of paths at TQ239347, roughly 700m from reaching the A264. Now you're back on the mapped route and can continue towards Ifield as per the OS map.

Turn left at TQ239347 and follow an excellent path just east of north, keeping a new housing development to your left. You then veer just west of north beside Spruce Hill Brook to reach a bridleway junction at TQ239357 within sight of the railway bridge, 1km from TQ239347. Here you fork right. Initially you proceed through woodland, with the very active brook to your right, then continue forward past houses to your left, bearing left as signed to cross the railway. Having crossed the railway you turn right, initially parallel with the railway before striking slightly away from it to proceed to **Ifield Mill** and its adjoining pond, at TQ245365, 1km 125m from TQ239357. The pond is a lovely haven for wildlife, including dragonflies, grebes, coots and mallards, while plant life includes willow, alder, reedmace, watermint and yellow iris. The mill, built in 1817, has been impressively restored in recent years and is occasionally open to visitors. If you're keen to visit, check beforehand to avoid disappointment.

At the mill, your bridleway route ends. To reach Ifield Station, served by frequent trains on the main London-Horsham line, continue a very short distance on beyond the mill to Hyde Drive, turning right onto Hyde Drive and following the road for roughly 150m. At the end turn right along Rusper Road for some 375m, then turn right along Tangmere Road for 200m. At the end turn right along Ifield Drive to immediately arrive at Ifield Station for trains on the Horsham-Crawley-London line. If you decide to base yourself in **Horsham** for this route, it's certainly worth a look round the town before you head for home. Its attractions include the 1812 Old Town Hall, which resembles a castle; the 13th century church of St Mary, which boasts a beautiful spire; Talbot Lane with its fine timber-framed buildings; and the street named Causeway and in particular the stunning pink timber-framed no.12 and the 17th century house Flagstones.

ROUTE 24

TQ442347 (start and finish) – Location Map E2 – OS 135 – M

16km 950m – but note this includes two substantial detours; if either or both are not taken, the route will be significantly shortened

Ashdown House, Highams Wood, Cansiron Lane, Holden Wood, Acre Wood, Wet Wood, Hammerwood

PT Forest Row (B start and finish)

R Forest Row

This circular route starts roughly 1km 750m east of the centre of Forest Row; to reach this point from the village centre, follow the B2110 Hartfield Road to TQ442347, where there's a junction with a bridleway lane heading left (northwards) from this road. Your route starts here. If you're arriving by bus (on the East Grinstead-Tunbridge Wells route), don't get off the bus in the village centre but ask the driver to drop you at (or as close as possible to) the junction of Hartfield Road with Forest Road then head eastwards along Hartfield Road for just 125m to TQ442347.

From here, head away northwards along the bridleway lane which descends, crossing over the Forest Way, which we met in route 13, and striking out just east of north through lovely open country. You pass the buildings of Ashdown Farm, opposite which is **Ashdown House**, a school and Grade II listed building which dates from 1794, and which was designed by Sussex-born Benjamin Latrobe. Latrobe also designed nearby Hammerwood House which we'll meet later on this journey, as well as the front portico of the White House in Washington DC – which we won't.

Shortly beyond Ashdown Farm and Ashdown House, at TQ445359, 1km 250m from the start, you reach a T-junction of paths, here turning left. In 200m or so you veer sharp right, passing some very attractive ponds on the left, with warnings not to swim! Heading just west of north along the edge of **Highams Wood**, you ascend steeply; it's quite hard work, so you have every excuse to pause for breath and look back to enjoy superb views to Ashdown Forest. You veer left, west, with the clear bridleway and arrive at a path junction at TQ439363, 1km from the path T-junction just beyond Ashdown Farm. Here (TQ439363) you meet **Cansiron Lane**. This is a really lovely spot with fine views to the east. Don't be tempted onto the path heading hard right (there's a stile in your way in any case) but instead take the bridleway heading more gently right, north-eastwards, actually a continuation of Cansiron Lane. This is fabulous going, along what is a lovely path with superb views. Heading north-eastwards, you enter woodland and start to descend, and in 1km from TQ439363, at TQ442373, you reach a signed bridleway fork. The continuous route forks left, north-westwards, here but I recommend you detour on north-eastwards through **Holden Wood** and **Acre Wood** and on past Cansiron Farm to the metalled road (a further continuation of Cansiron Lane), 1km 250m away. There's no "destination" as such – it's just a lovely piece of woodland bridleway, well away from tourist hotspots, with plenty of good picnic opportunities. Then return the same way to TQ442373.

Whether you've detoured or not, fork north-westwards from here as stated along what is another fine track with beautiful views ahead. You descend to Owlett's Farm, passing through the complex and ascending along a metalled lane to reach, in 1km 125m from the fork, a lane junction with the Vanguard Way, at TQ435380. There is a beautiful tile-hung house, Dog Gate Lodge, just here. The Vanguard Way, which you'll be following for a while now, is a 71km route linking the London suburbs and Sussex coast via the North and South Downs. It was conceived by the Vanguards Rambling Club, their name being derived from an occasion in 1965 when a group of ramblers found themselves in a train so packed they were forced to occupy the guard's van. They began their own rambling club which they therefore decided to call the Vanguards!

The continuous route turns left, south-westwards, at this junction, but by turning right along the bridleway here (TQ435380) and following it northwards, you could visit Hammerwood. I thoroughly recommend your doing so, but just make sure it's open before you set out – unless you're happy simply to view its exterior. To make the detour, turn right as stated at TQ435380, head downhill to cross a stream, then rise steadily, proceeding through the lovely **Wet Wood**. After you emerge from the wood, the Vanguard Way goes off to the left but you keep going straight on, following a left-hand field-edge round, then at TQ436391 bearing left up a potentially muddy path through the trees to arrive at the A264, 1km 500m from TQ435380. To visit **Hammerwood** turn right beside the A264 and then in 125m right again along the approach road for 1km. Built by Benjamin Latrobe around 1793, the house was one of the first in England to be constructed in Grecian Revival style and has been superbly restored in the last 30-35 years. The *Pevsner Architectural Guide* describes it as a masterpiece. You then need to retrace exactly the same way to TQ435380 to progress.

Whether you've detoured or not, you head south-westwards from TQ435380. It's now very easy and pleasant going along the Vanguard Way; you're following a metalled bridleway lane but there is virtually no traffic and the views are excellent. Having headed south-westwards you pass the splendid buildings of Thornhill in 1km, ascending beyond the buildings and veering right; there's then, at TQ430368 (a little under 500m from Thornhill), a left turn which is unsigned and easily missed. Take the left turn, sticking to the Vanguard Way and veering south-eastwards, to arrive, at TQ432364 (875m from Thornhill), at a sharp left bend where the Vanguard Way goes straight on and becomes a public footpath. Veer left, eastwards, here as bridleway-signed along what is Cansiron Lane which we met much earlier on this route. In 325m the High Weald Landscape Trail (see route 13) comes in from the right, and you now overlap with that as you continue eastwards along the lane for another 375m to arrive again at that lovely spot at TQ439363. You've now come full circle but there's still some legwork as you now need to retrace to the start, a distance of 2km 250m. Head eastwards from TQ439363, veering southwards and descending along the edge of Highams Wood, going past the ponds where you're not allowed to swim (a shame on a hot day), and then veering left to the path junction above Ashdown Farm. Here you turn right to follow the bridleway back to Hartfield Road. You arrive at Hartfield Road at TQ442347, from which it's 1km 750m back to the centre of Forest Row. Of course walkers have the option of the bus, there being a number of stops along this road.

ROUTE 25

TQ411201–TQ405155 – Location Map E2 – OS OL11 – E

13km 775m

Newick, Starvecrow Wood, Hurst Barns, Warningore Wood, Folly Wood

PT Newick (B start), Barcombe Cross (B finish)

R Newick, Barcombe Cross

This is a linear route but both Newick, near the start, and Barcombe Cross, near the end, are served by buses to and from Lewes. It visits some lovely unspoilt and unsung countryside which incorporates a number of fine woodland sections.

To get to the start of the route from **Newick,** head south-eastwards away from the A272 at the delightful village green along Church Road. You veer southwards with Church Road, passing the impressively large Norman church of St Mary, with its magnificent sandstone tower; adjacent to it is a very fine timbered house. Carry on along Church Road then at the road fork at Founthill, 1km 125m from the A272, fork right, south-westwards, to reach a road T-junction at Schoolhouse Farm in 375m. Here turn right along a lane, Cornwell's Bank, which arrives in 700m at a junction with a bridleway heading left, southwards, from the lane. This junction marks the start of your route, at TQ411201.

Turn left to follow this very pretty bridleway, marked on maps as Cockfield Lane. You head initially just west of south, then in 750m cross a stream by way of Cockfield Bridge and veer southwards. In 750m from the bridge you veer just east of south, and for 250m you go parallel with and immediately adjacent to the course of the old Lewes-East Grinstead railway, the northern half of which is now the preserved Bluebell Railway (see route 12).

This parallel journey with the old railway takes you, 1km 750m from the start, to a T-junction with Markstakes Lane. Turn right along the lane for 100m or so then turn left along Town Littleworth Road heading southwards. Ignore a footpath going off to the right in 375m but another 300m beyond that, at TQ411176, turn right along a bridleway that follows the charming Balneath Lane, following woodland edges first just north of west then just south of west. In 1km 250m at TQ400177 you make a sharp right turn taking you into the heart of the particularly attractive and unspoilt **Starvecrow Wood**. Just a shame about the name! In 125m from the sharp right turn you turn sharp left with the bridleway and now head westwards along the bridleway which then in 750m from the sharp left turn reaches a crossing of a public byway. Cross straight over and, veering south-westwards, arrive in 250m at the A275 just north of the centre of South Chailey at TQ390176. Sadly, South Chailey lacks any refreshment possibilities; for these you'd need to detour roughly 1km 500m northwards beside the busy A275. Not appealing.

Cross the A275 in South Chailey with care and bear left, following alongside the main road for 125m, then turn right, westwards, along Mill Lane, veering south-westwards along the lane and passing Chailey School. At TQ384173, 625m from the A275, turn left, just east of south, along a bridleway that heads downhill and shortly veers just west of south, passing the buildings of Yokehurst and continuing downhill on a most attractive path through a strip of woodland between fields. Emerge from the wood and continue downhill across pasture, now enjoying lovely views southwards to the South Downs. You ascend to pass the splendid buildings of **Hurst Barns** including a fine redbrick farmhouse, then descend along a farm lane, the views getting better all the time.

You arrive at a road, Chiltington Lane, at TQ383154, 1km 750m from the start of this bridleway, turning right here and following the road for 250m until a sharp right bend. Turn left here at TQ381154 along a bridleway, and having straightaway crossed the railway with care, head southwards to the buildings of Wootton Farm. You reach a junction of lanes by the farm complex at TQ381051 and turn left, but then very shortly veer right with the bridleway and head just west of south, striking away from the buildings and following a field edge. Continue in the same direction along a clear track leading to Warningore Farm. Here, at TQ375137, 1km 750m from TQ381154, you bear left as bridleway-signed, heading in a predominantly easterly direction, going forward along a charming path through a thicket to reach a lake at the south-western tip of **Warningore Wood** at TQ380136. This is a really charming and tranquil spot. Continue along the bridleway to reach, at TQ382136 (750m from Warningore Farm), a bridleway coming in from the left.

Turn left to follow this bridleway heading northwards through the middle of Warningore Wood. Another grisly name for a piece of woodland! The wood is mainly hornbeam coppice, the hard wood being used historically for fuel, cog wheels, charcoal and gunpowder. The woodland supports many wild flowers and butterflies including white admirals, while the clear streams and lake are fed by chalk streams from the foot of the South Downs and are full of aquatic vegetation including watercress. Continue through the wood, veering north-eastwards and emerging from the trees, passing the Spooners Farm complex. You go forward to cross the railway, immediately arriving at a T-junction with Chiltington Lane at Chiltington, at TQ388150, 1km 500m from TQ382137. Now there is an unavoidable road section of 1km 250m. Turn right, south-eastwards, along Chiltington Lane to arrive at a T-junction with Wickham Lane in 500m; turn left here and follow the road north-eastwards for 750m to reach the A275. Cross with care and turn right beside this busy road but almost immediately bear left along a bridleway heading just north of east along the edge of the pretty **Folly Wood**, arriving, in 875m, at a T-junction with a road, Deadmantree Hill. This is the end of your bridleway route at TQ405155. To reach Barcombe Cross, turn very briefly left along Deadmantree Hill and almost immediately right along Cooksbridge Road, heading eastwards, then south-eastwards, reaching a road junction at Pound Corner in 1km 125m. Veer sharp left here to arrive in the centre of Barcombe Cross in a further 500m. Barcombe Cross, unlike its sister villages (that is, plain Barcombe with its historic church, and Barcombe Mills with its lovely riverside setting) has no features of great interest, but it boasts a pub and shop and, as stated, bus connections to Lewes.

ROUTE 26

TQ553324-TQ513321 – Location Map E2 – OS 135 – E

9km 300m

Marchant's Wood, Spa Valley Railway, Marchant Wood, Pocket Birches

PT Boarshead (B start), Crowborough (B finish)

R Boarshead, Eridge, Crowborough

This is an ideal expedition for bluebell time! Though this is a linear route, the start and finish points link conveniently with locations on the Brighton-Tunbridge Wells bus route. To reach the start of the route from the A26 at Boarshead, the nearest bus stop on that route, follow Boars Head Road heading south-eastwards from the pub, past Cherry Tree Farm, veering north-eastwards in 1km 375m and reaching Newhouse Farm in another 750m. Turn right at the road junction opposite Newhouse Farm along Redgate Mill Lane, passing immediately underneath the railway, then in 150m you reach the start of this route at TQ553324, where a bridleway goes off to the left. Turn left as bridleway-signed and head just west of north along a clear track, very soon veering just east of north and entering the pretty **Marchant's Wood**. It's then a delightful path on a clear track, veering just west of north again and emerging from the woods, passing Stitches Farm, dropping to Stonewall Ghyll and arriving at a junction of tracks by Hamsell Manor at TQ553338, roughly 1km 500m from the start. Bear right here as bridleway-signed along a lane heading north-eastwards for 625m to arrive at Sham Farm Road. Turn left to follow it for 1km 125m; although it's a longish piece of road, it is quiet and doubles up as National Cycle Route 21. At TQ555352 you reach a road junction, with Eridge Station and National Cycle Route 21 signed to the left. Bear left here, along National Cycle Route 21, following a lane that runs parallel with the A26 that's on your right, and you continue forward along what is a bridleway, still keeping the A26 to your right. Despite the proximity of the road this is actually very pleasant going indeed, through a nice strip of woodland.

At TQ545345, 1km 125m from TQ555352, your bridleway turns abruptly right to pass under the A26, keeping a stream to your left – pause to admire the superb feat of engineering that makes your route under the A26 possible – and arrive at a road, Groombridge Lane, almost immediately. Turn left along the road, very soon passing Eridge Station. The station is not only on a network line (London to Uckfield) but it is the southern terminus of the preserved **Spa Valley Railway.** In Route 13 we visited the Forest Way, following part of a now disused stretch of railway that ran from East Grinstead to Tunbridge Wells. The Spa Valley Railway follows a section of what is still part of the rail network as far as Groombridge, then continues along the easternmost section of the old East Grinstead to Tunbridge Wells line, this section not actually shutting until 1985. I well recall travelling on that line when it was still part of the British Rail network, with its noisy diesel trains and chunky seats with very squeaky springs! It's certainly worth your while to plan to follow this route on a day when trains are running on the Spa Valley Railway; the scenery is quite delightful especially in the neighbourhood of High Rocks just east of Groombridge.

Having passed the station, and maybe enjoyed a train ride, turn shortly right along Forge Road, the turning some 300m from TQ545345, and follow the road initially on a straight north-westerly course then negotiating a sharp left and a sharp right-hand bend. Just beyond the sharp right-hand bend, as the road bends left again, you reach a signed bridleway going off to your left at TQ538345, roughly 500m from where you joined Forge Road. Turn left to follow this bridleway which you'll follow all the way to the end of your route; the good news is that it's very clearly defined and well signed. There are a number of lovely sections of woodland which are at their best when the bluebells are out, hence the first sentence in this route description! You pass initially through the attractive Holden Wood heading westwards, veer south-westwards through more open farmland and cross the Sussex Border Path (see route 4), then veer south-eastwards through the very pretty **Marchant Wood**.

You emerge from the wood and at TQ531340, 1km 250m from TQ538345, there's a sharp right turn, south-westwards, which will be your predominant direction of travel all the way to the end. It's now an absolutely lovely journey through an area of woodland known as **Pocket Birches**, past Orznash Farm and through Bream Wood, skirting Parkgrove Wood and veering sharply left and sharply right to pass Gildridge Farm, some 1km 750m from TQ531340. In 250m from the farm there's then another sharp left turn and descent into Tyler's Wood. From here you proceed just west of south, uphill, along Gildridge Lane to reach a T-junction with London Road at TQ513321, the end of the route, 875m from the left bend beyond Gildridge Farm. Turn left up London Road for 750m to reach the centre of Crowborough with good bus connections to Brighton and Tunbridge Wells. Crowborough is a sprawling town with little of architectural interest: its principal church, All Saints, dates back to 1744 and has been extensively altered since.

ROUTE 27

TQ518220-TQ517208 – Location Map E2 – OS 135 – E

7km 125m

Warren Farm, Waste Wood, Hadlow Down, Tickerage Mill

PT Blackboys (B start and finish)

R Hadlow Down, Blackboys

Although comparatively short, this is a delightful woodland journey with two pleasing features at the far end and another on the return journey which make the effort extra-worthwhile. Though the start and finish points are different, by basing yourself at Blackboys you can easily create a circle starting at the junction of the B2102 with Gun Road. To reach the start of this route from the main street (B2102) at Blackboys, served by buses running Mondays-Fridays from Uckfield to Etchingham, head northwards away from the B2102 at TQ522207 along Gun Road. Follow this road past Shawford Farm to a T-junction at its end, roughly 1km from Blackboys' main street. Turn left here, and in 175m you reach the start of the route at TQ518220, turning right here to join the plinth-signed bridleway. You now head north-eastwards, following a wide straight track which enters woodland and in just over 500m, as it emerges temporarily from the woods, takes you past **Warren Farm**, with a beautifully situated farmhouse that might come straight out of a film set. Shortly beyond the farm buildings your path narrows a little and you continue north-eastwards in the shade of trees but with excellent views to the east. You then enter **Waste Wood** which despite the name is delightful; your path is unerring, continuing in a north-easterly direction, and the trees provide very welcome shade on a hot day. I well recall following this path one hot languid day in late July, with almost complete absence of birdsong, the only sounds among the trees coming from the buzzing of what seemed like swarms of bees. Fortunately none of them seemed interested in me!

You emerge from the woods, veering northwards, and you can now enjoy a lovely view to your left (south-westwards) which includes the tops of the South Downs. Continue to the end of the bridleway at TQ528242 on the A272 just west of Hadlow Down, here 2km 500m from the start of the route. By turning right beside the road you will see, immediately, the very prominent and photogenic church of St Mark, **Hadlow Down**; walkers can access it by using a footpath just a few metres from the end of the bridleway. The church, with its slender shingled spire, dates from 1836; its most attractive features are its pulpit and its very pretty Lady Chapel with its vignettes of wild flowers. In his book *Sussex*, Arthur Mee makes mention of the church's "fine timbers and an open timber roof supported by corbels." The New Inn is just a little further on along the A272 in what is the centre of Hadlow Down.

Now retrace along the same bridleway through Waste Wood and past Warren Farm all the way to the start of the route, 2km 500m from the A272. If you were pushed for time you could simply retrace along Gun Road to Blackboys, but the continuous route turns right along the road from TQ518220 (where this bridleway route began), in 375m reaching a T-junction with Pound Lane. Turn left to follow Pound Lane southwards for 500m, veering right, south-westwards, for a further 375m to a bridleway going off to the left at TQ512215. Turn left here along this bridleway, heading south-eastwards, following a short section of the Vanguard Way which we met in route 24. You descend through an open landscape but then in 500m from Pound Lane reach Tickerage Wood, and the quite delightful **Tickerage Mill**, a 17th century iron mill which was once the home of actress Vivien Leigh following her divorce from Laurence Olivier. The mill has a stunning setting with a really beautiful waterfall.

You follow the bridleway/Vanguard Way straight on, south-eastwards, beyond the mill through Tickerage Wood, going straight over a crossing public footpath which takes the Vanguard Way with it, and also takes the Wealdway (see route 13) with which you have very briefly overlapped in the vicinity of Tickerage Mill. Carry on along the bridleway to reach, very shortly beyond the crossing footpath, a junction with what is the end of Tickerage Lane on the edge of the woods at TQ517208, the end of the route, 375m from Tickerage Mill. Turn left to follow Tickerage Lane eastwards then southwards to reach the B2102, just west of Blackboys, 250m from the end of the route. Turn left alongside the B2102 to reach the start of Gun Road in Blackboys in 375m or so. Opposite the Gun Road turning, School Lane heads south from the B2102 to shortly reach the popular village pub. The peculiar name of the village is derived from Richard Blakeboy, whose home it was around the end of the 14th century, though local tradition likes to derive the name from the "black boys" or charcoal handlers who after a day at the iron foundries in the area would come to the village inn for a well-earned drink!

ROUTE 28

TV552988 (start and finish) – Location Map E2 – OS OL25 – S

13km 850m

Friston Forest, Lullington Heath Nature Reserve, Winchester's Pond, Litlington, Westdean, Friston

PT Friston Pond (B start and finish)

R Litlington, East Dean

This is a long circular route with a good many climbs and descents, and involves following many unsigned paths. It is essential to follow my instructions carefully! That said, it is an immensely rewarding journey and one of the finest bridleway expeditions in Sussex.

To reach the start of this route from Friston Pond, served by frequent buses on the Brighton-Seaford-Eastbourne route, head north-eastwards away from the A259 along Jevington Road (ignoring the right-forking Willingdon Road), then in 600m from the A259 reach a bridleway signed going off to the left – this is the start (and finish) of the route at TV552988. Turn left, north-westwards, initially along a metalled road through the trees; in about 250m you're signed along a path going parallel with and to the right of the road. The buildings of the originally 16th century Friston Place (not open to the public) are to the left on the far side of the road. Your parallel path reaches a crossroads junction with a track, a barrier just to the right; this is TV548990, 500m from the start. Go straight over the track and now climb quite steeply, just west of north, through the woods, emerging temporarily from the trees to follow the obvious path across Friston Hill in the same direction. In 375m from TV548990 you then plunge into the beautiful unspoilt woodlands of **Friston Forest**.

Friston Forest is one of the most extensive areas of woodland in the southern half of East Sussex, consisting of just over 600 hectares and 4 million trees, mainly beech. In spring look out for varieties of violet including early wood, common dog and hairy, while later in the year you may find the white helleborine and broad-leaved helleborine orchid, as well as the rare yellow bird's nest and pheasant's eye. Butterflies here include small tortoiseshell, speckled wood, meadow brown, grizzled skipper and white admiral, while sightings of blue tit and long-tailed tit are common. I've visited the forest in early spring and in the height of summer, and was captivated by its freshness in spring and then grateful for the shade from the August heat.

Be warned, however – you won't see any bridleway signs in the forest at all so follow these instructions carefully and use your technology when you need. Your bridleway continues in a predominantly north-westerly direction, ignoring crossing tracks 500-600m into the forest, and gaining height to pass over Snap Hill. Your cue to sit up and take notice is a slight descent to what is a bridleway crossroads at TQ545005, 1km 250m from entering the forest. Note a sturdy fir tree just to your left at this crossing. Go straight over and descend very steeply, veering left, going over another bridleway crossroads and arriving at a multipath junction at the valley bottom, at TQ541007, some 450m from TQ545005. There are lots of paths leading away here, NONE of them signed!! Working clockwise, ignore the one heading hard left, and ignore the next two round – the one you want is the next one after that, reached by going through a gate.

Your excellent bridleway track heads initially north-westwards from the gate (if it heads initially north-eastwards you're on the wrong one), then veers north-

A superb sculpture at the very start of the shared-use Downs Link at Shoreham, part of route 1

The Double Bridge, arguably the most iconic feature of the shared-use Downs Link near Rudgwick, part of route 3; the route goes over the upper bridge

A superb stretch of the shared-use South Downs Way at Balmer Down between Falmer and Lewes, part of route 8

A section of the Forest Way shared-use route between East Grinstead and Groombridge, part of route 13

A beautiful spring afternoon on the fine field-edge bridleway just north of Halnaker, traced in route 19

The delightful bridleway through Green Wood between Three Cups Corner and Burwash, part of route 31

A bridleway sign points across the river Lavant, visited in route 32

A beautifully mown stretch of bridleway leading past Rottingdean Windmill, part of a recommended detour in route 39

One of many lovely waterside stretches of the shared-use route round Bewl Water near Wadhurst, part of route 42

A well-signed bridleway/footpath junction by a footbridge at Wainway Wall on Romney Marsh between Camber and Rye, part of route 45

The cairn and adjacent bridleway at Crown Tegleaze, the highest point on the South Downs in West Sussex, part of route 48

The trig point at Blackcap, one of the finest downland summits off the South Downs Way, immediately adjacent to a bridleway and part of route 62

eastwards, still in the forest. You emerge from the trees, veering gently left and then more sharply right, reaching the more open ground of **Lullington Heath Nature Reserve**. Covering an area of some 72 hectares, the Reserve supports two nationally uncommon habitats, chalk heath and chalk grassland, and is rich in flowering plants and bird life, with more than 98 different types of bird having been seen here. The best time to visit is in August, when the heather turns a glorious pink, complementing the yellow of the gorse. Heading eastwards, you go forward to reach a signed bridleway junction at TQ545018, roughly 1km 500m from TQ541007. Turn hard left here to enjoy a really lovely bridleway, ascending through the heart of the Reserve.

Now, and indeed for the rest of this route, the going is very straightforward, without the fiddlyness (if there is such a word) of the last few kilometres. As stated you continue to follow the bridleway westwards, arriving at (and possibly lingering at) the beautifully situated **Winchester's Pond**, 500m from TQ545018 at TQ539019. Go straight over the bridleway crossroads here, then continue westwards, ignoring a right-forking bridleway and dropping all the way down to the **Litlington,** veering sharply left to hit the road (The Street) in the village – 1km 500m from Winchester's Pond.

Turn left onto The Street, heading southwards past the part-Norman church of St Michael; the church has a large font 500 years old, and lancet windows containing glass thought to be 600 years old with figures of an angel, a winged lion and a golden eagle. Continuing along the road, you are joined briefly by the South Downs Way (footpath section) and pass a welcome pub. Then at TQ523016, roughly 400m from where you joined the road, leave it by turning left, initially with the South Downs Way. However rather than then turning immediately right with the South Downs Way, continue on south-eastwards along the bridleway which rises to pass the buildings of Chamber's Court. You veer fractionally west of south then more decisively left, south-eastwards, enjoying a really splendid bridleway stretch,

135

dipping then ascending again, with great views southwards to the High And Over (Hindover) White Horse, which you will have seen in route 11.

You re-enter Friston Forest and, 2km 125m after leaving the road at Litlington, you reach a bridleway junction at TQ540005. Turn right here, shortly emerging from the forest, heading just south of west along Charleston Bottom and reaching a cattle trough at TQ533003, 625m from the junction at TQ540005. Here you need to turn hard left, onto a narrow crudely-stepped dirt bridle track climbing steeply up the hillside to meet a wide green bridle track onto which you turn left. You now continue uphill to reach a wider bridle track running left to right at TQ536001, 375m from TQ533003. Turn right along the track which soon passes through a gate and enters the forest. Continue south-westwards on the obvious track, taking the right fork at TV532997 and arriving at a signed bridleway T-junction at TV530997, 750m from TQ536001.

You could, if short on time, turn hard left here, along the bridleway signed for Friston, but the recommended route bears right, westwards, to arrive in 500m at the very pretty flint village of **Westdean**. Its most interesting features are its Norman church of All Saints, the 13th century flint-built Old Parsonage, the walls of a ruined manor house, and a medieval dovecote. The church, as well as boasting canopied tombs over 600 years old, contains a bronze head by Jacob Epstein in memory of Lord Waverley who, as Sir John Anderson, was Home Secretary during the Second World War and introduced a type of air-raid shelter that bore his name. Having enjoyed Westdean, retrace to TV530997.

Whether you've visited Westdean or not, now follow the bridleway heading just south of east from here, signed, as stated, for Friston. It's an undulating path culminating in a descent to a path T-junction at TV548989, 1km 875m from TV530997. Turn left, north-eastwards, along the track for 125m to arrive back at TV548990 by the barrier. You've come full circle. Simply turn right to retrace along the bridleway for 500m to reach Jevington Road at TV552988 (the end of the route), here turning right to return to the A259 Friston Pond for buses towards Eastbourne or Brighton. Instead, or as well, you have just a 750m descent along the A259 eastwards from Friston Pond to East Dean where refreshments are available (in the form of a pub, a café and a deli), but be warned that the A259 here is narrow, steep and busy. Walkers are advised to use the parallel footpath. Before catching a bus or descending to East Dean (from which you can also pick up a bus) you may wish to explore the pretty church of St Mary the Virgin at **Friston**, by the pond on the south side of the A259. The church has Norman and Saxon features and particularly fine roof timbering believed to date back to 1450; the south door commemorates Frank Bridge, who taught Benjamin Britten and who lived in Friston.

ROUTE 29

TQ593051-TQ566091 – Location Map E2 – OS OL25 – E

8km 100m

Cuckoo Trail, Ogg's Wood, Abbot's Wood, Michelham Priory, Hailsham

PT Polegate (*, B start), Hailsham (B finish)

R Polegate, Caneheath, Michelham Priory, Hailsham

This is a very straightforward undemanding route incorporating lovely woodland and a major visitor attraction. It's a linear route but you can base yourself at Polegate, served by rail, and catch a bus back there from Hailsham.

To access the start of this route from Polegate Station, turn right out of the station approach road and follow Polegate's High Street uphill for 250m or so to its top end, at a junction with Station Road. Turn right to follow Station Road for just under 1km then turn left along Levett Road, part of National Cycle Route 21, and follow it for 300m to the start of the route at TQ593051, with the Cuckoo Trail signed to your left. Now take this left-signed turning to follow an attractive restricted byway through the trees. You're here on the 23km **Cuckoo Trail,** which for most of its length follows sections of disused railway between Heathfield and Eastbourne. This was part of a railway that linked Eastbourne with Tunbridge Wells via Hailsham, Heathfield and Rotherfield; it became fully open in 1880 but most of it shut between 1965 and 1968. The Cuckoo Trail opened as a walkway and cycleway in the 1990's and boasts a fine variety of plant life including lots of seasonal wild flowers. It is a magnificent trail, providing some of the best disused railway exploration in Sussex, but sadly large parts of it are closed to horse-riders. This section, being a restricted byway, is fine for horse-riding, although ironically it is one of the few sections that does NOT follow the course of a disused railway!

In 800m from the start you arrive at a multi-track junction at TQ585053. Go more or less straight over, proceeding pleasantly for 375m north-westwards along a clear restricted byway track with new-build housing to your right, arriving at TQ582057 at the end of the track. Turn right to cross the bridge over the A22, then descend to a junction with a bridleway. Turn westwards, along the clearly-signed bridleway, which runs as a track parallel with roads to your right and the A22 embankment to your left. Sticking to the clearly-signed path you pass under the bridge carrying the A22, then veer right with the track, keeping parallel with a slip road, to arrive at a sharp left-hand path bend at TQ577060, some 625m from the crossing over the A22.

At this spot, bend left with the path and now follow the bridleway north-westwards through the lovely (and deliciously named) **Ogg's Wood**. It's nice to be getting away from the A22 although the noise may linger for a bit. The path is clear and the going is excellent. In 1km 375m you cross a public byway, going straight on north-westwards through the equally delightful woodland of **Abbot's Wood**

138

with the possibility of detouring onto one of the many tracks leading more deeply into the forest. Abbot's Wood is an ancient woodland teeming with wildlife and plant life; it supports around 30 different species of butterfly including the rare pearl-bordered fritillary, in early spring you may hear the nightingale, and on summer evenings you may be rewarded with sightings of bats, glow-worms and nightjars. The whole wood is designated Access Land, meaning you can follow whatever paths and tracks you please! Your bridleway is clear throughout, arriving at the road at Caneheath at TQ556075, 1km 250m from the public byway crossing.

Turn right up the road, in some 375m reaching and perhaps patronising the very attractive 17th century Old Oak Inn. Continue along the road for another 1km beyond the pub to arrive at a T-junction at TQ561087. The continuous route turns very briefly right, eastwards, here, but I recommend you turn left to follow the road for some 875m to reach a very popular Sussex visitor attraction, the house and gardens of **Michelham Priory**. The priory dates back to 1229 when Augustinian canons arrived, taking over the site of a Norman manor house. The priory was dissolved in 1536 and what survives of the priory buildings is masked by the stonework of a Tudor farmhouse. The Tudor rooms are furnished with a superbly presented array of Dutch paintings, old English furniture and Flemish tapestries, while the garden is packed with colour and variety including exotic waterside plants and sweeping herbaceous borders. In the gatehouse there is the reconstruction of a Sussex forge. Retrace to the T-junction at TQ561087 to continue.

Head very briefly eastwards from here as stated but almost immediately fork left along a very charming well-kept bridleway north-eastwards through woodland. Follow it for 550m to reach a path junction at TQ566091 where your bridleway route ends. To continue to Hailsham, go forward in the same north-easterly direction along a woodland-edge public byway, this maturing into a road, Hempstead

Lane. In 1km 500m from the end of the route you reach the A22. Cross with care then head eastwards on along Hempstead Lane for another 750m to reach London Road on the outskirts of Hailsham. Buses can convey you from here all the way to Polegate. Of course you may prefer to continue under your own steam into Hailsham town centre before boarding your Polegate bus; to do this, turn right and follow London Road for some 500m. **Hailsham** isn't the prettiest town in East Sussex but boasts a fine part-flint church, Town House and Manor House in Market Street, and the splendid Pavilion cinema in George Street, dating from 1921.

ROUTE 30

TQ586227-TQ565217 – Location Map E2 – OS 135 – E

5km 375m

Quarry Wood, Oxen's Wood, Herrings Farm, Crawlsdown Wood

PT Heathfield (B start), Cross-in-Hand (optional B finish), Heathfield (optional B finish)

R Heathfield, Cross-in-Hand

This is a short and straightforward linear route but you can easily make it circular by using the centre of Heathfield, with its ample amenities, as your start and finish point. The Tunbridge Wells-Eastbourne bus route may also assist as I explain below. You reach the start of this route in the first instance by proceeding to the junction of the A267 with the B2203 (south) and Marklye Lane (north), 750m east of the centre of Heathfield, this junction served by buses on the Tunbridge Wells-Eastbourne route. Head fractionally west of north from that junction along Marklye Lane, arriving in just under 1km at Marklye Farm at TQ586227, this being the start of the route. Follow the bridleway on in a predominantly northward direction. The going, following National Cycle Route 21, is mostly wooded, the bridle track easy to follow, passing through the delightful and unspoilt **Quarry Wood**; look out for a sharp right-hand bend at TQ585241 and left bend shortly beyond that, passing round the edge of the pretty **Oxen's Wood** and arriving at Newick Lane 1km 875m from the start.

Turn left along the road but then almost immediately, at TQ588244, turn left as signed along a bridleway heading south-westwards, your direction of travel throughout the rest of this journey. Almost immediately you cross the course of the old Tunbridge Wells-Eastbourne railway. Though the southern half of this defunct railway has been converted into a walking/cycle route that makes up a substantial part of the lovely Cuckoo Trail (see route 29), this is part of the northern half which is still private – a great shame, as the scenery all the way along it is absolutely beautiful. (Don't ask me how I know that!) Beyond the railway crossing you follow a clear and unerring path past the fine farm buildings of St Quentins Farm and then **Herrings Farm**, enjoying absolutely super views back towards Mayfield. At Herrings Farm, 1km 500m from Newick Lane, your bridleway crosses the Sussex Diamond Way, a trail conceived in 1995 to mark the diamond anniversary of the formation of the Sussex Ramblers. The trail runs right across Sussex from Midhurst to Heathfield; though signage was for a long time virtually non-existent, it has been greatly improved in recent years, so if you're a walker, this may be one for your to-do list.

Beyond Herrings Farm you ascend, skirting Coalend Wood and entering **Crawlsdown Wood**. This is excellent going in lovely woodland surroundings. You arrive at a T-junction of tracks at TQ568223 and turn left here, soon passing the twin masts of Heathfield transmitting station which opened in 1969; the taller mast is and has for a long time been an extremely conspicuous feature for miles around. It has a certain Marmite quality to it – you can admire its height, (possibly) its elegance and those who constructed it, or you can hate this modern intrusion into previously unspoilt countryside. It's certainly worth a look anyway! Beyond the masts, continue pleasantly on, following the bridleway along the woodland edge to reach the A267, 2km from Herrings Farm, at TQ565217. This is the end of the route. By turning right alongside the A267 you reach Cross-in-Hand in 250m; refreshments and buses to Heathfield, Eastbourne and Tunbridge Wells are available here. Or you could turn left beside the A267, forking left onto the A265 in 500m and then following the A265 for another 1km 500m to reach the centre of Heathfield, which boasts a wider variety of amenities, including buses, but is of no real historical or architectural importance.

ROUTE 31

TQ657225-TQ638225 – Location Map E2 – OS 124 – M

5km 875m

Dallington Forest, Green Wood, River Dudwell

PT Burwash Weald (B start), Burwash Common (B finish)

R Burwash Weald

This lovely, not too long woodland journey is best undertaken when the bluebells are out. It is a linear route but can be treated as a circular based at Burwash Weald, and in any case buses on the Uckfield-Etchingham route (note – there's no service at weekends) serve both places, 1km apart.

To reach the start of this route from the A265 at Burwash Weald, head south-eastwards from the main road along Willingford Lane for 1km to a point where, just beyond Willingford Bridge, a bridleway goes off to the right, just west of south, at TQ657225. This is the start of your route. You turn right off the road to follow this bridleway, shortly passing Willingford Farm, and now veer southwards, ascending steadily and entering a patch of woodland, Blackbrooks, veering gently south-eastwards as you enter it. You pass through the woods and, continuing south-eastwards, ascend through open fields, the views getting better with each step – or turn of the pedals. Hugging an area of woodland that's to your left, you go forward to arrive at a bridleway T-junction at TQ663214, 1km 375m from the start. Here you turn right to follow a bridleway towards **Dallington Forest**, heading just south of west, which will be your general direction of travel all the way through the forest.

Initially you enjoy splendid views to your left, southwards, then enter the forest, arriving at Little Worge Farm 375m after joining the bridleway, and continuing past the farm. The going is straightforward as far as the farm, but having left the farm behind, you'll find it becomes a great deal rougher as you then descend steadily through the trees, the going quite steep in places. Cyclists may need to dismount. The path isn't always well defined but you shouldn't stray. I managed not to! But don't count on people being around to tell you the way; there's a sense of real quietness and remoteness in this area of the woods, adding to its beauty. These ancient woodlands are particularly noteworthy for their majestic beech trees, and these, together with oaks, are the most common out of the 22 different species of tree and shrub found in the forest. At TQ651213, 750m from Little Worge Farm (though somehow it feels longer!) you reach a T-junction with a track, here turning right as signed and almost immediately passing the buildings of Glazier's Forge, temporarily emerging from the forest.

Now things do get a lot easier. Ignoring a footpath forking right, you then proceed uphill, south-westwards, re-entering the forest and now following a clear track, the going straightforward and enjoyable. Finally you emerge from the heart of the forest, the views opening out to the left again, and go on westwards through more open country to arrive at a bridleway crossroads at TQ637208, 1km 625m from Glazier's Forge. Here you turn right, just east of north, and dive into **Green Wood**, then continue in a predominantly northerly direction, descending through what is beautiful woodland to reach (at 1km from the bridleway crossroads) a bridge crossing of one of the lesser known rivers of Sussex, the **River Dudwell**. This river rises only a short distance to the west of here and flows into the River Rother near Etchingham some way to the east, through lovely Wealden scenery. Arguably it is at its most picturesque at the bridge where your bridleway crosses it. The scene is completely timeless – beautiful woodland complementing the waters of the river. And is if that was not enough, the bluebells hereabouts are stunning, so try and do this route when the bluebells are out.

Beyond the crossing your bridleway then ascends, very pleasantly, through a mainly wooded landscape, your enjoying fine views where the trees relent. You reach the official end of the bridleway, and indeed the end of the route, just east of Poundsford Farm at TQ638225, some 750m from the Dudwell crossing. Continue straight on from here along the road, Vicarage Lane, which in 750m or so swings right and then in a further 250m reaches a T-junction with Westdown Lane. Turn left here to almost immediately reach a T-junction with Vicarage Road, your now having reached Burwash Common. As stated, buses serve the village; if you want to create a circular from Burwash Weald, it's a not massively enjoyable 1km to get there, your needing to turn right along Vicarage Road and then forward alongside the busy A265 to the Willingford Lane turn. Those lovely bluebells will seem a long way back!

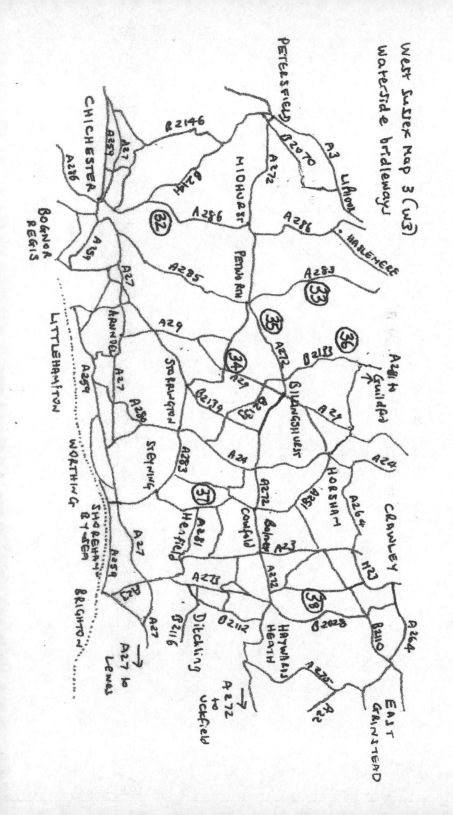

West Sussex Map 3 (w3)
Waterside bridleways

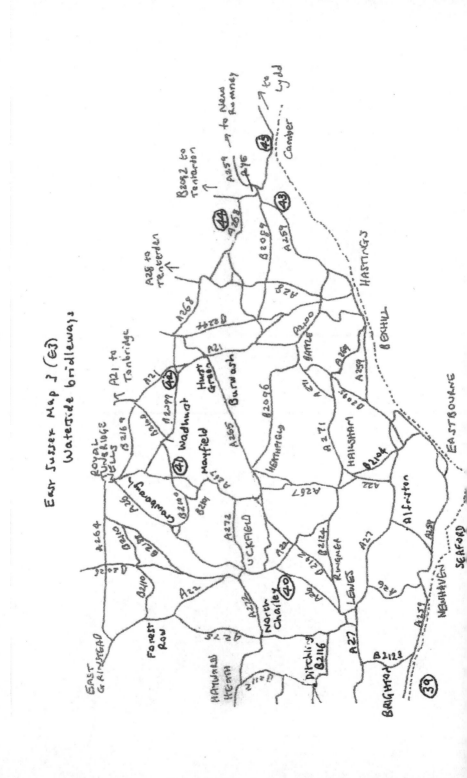

East Sussex Map 2 (E3)
Waterside bridleways

Part 3 – Waterside bridleways

Sussex is blessed not only with a fine coastline but many attractive expanses of water inland, whether rivers, ponds, lakes or reservoirs. There are comparatively few bridleway routes in Sussex that follow beside a stretch of water for significant distances but all of those listed below enjoy close encounters with often very beautiful areas of water, from the exuberant River Lavant near Chichester to the impressive Bewl Water at the far north-eastern end of East Sussex.

You'll notice that one famous West Sussex river, the Arun, is all but missing from the waterside routes described below, my having covered an Arun-side bridleway journey as part of route 20 above. That route can be split so you can confine yourself simply to the Arun-side section if you wish, and mentally transfer it to this part of the book!

ROUTE 32

SU858122-SU878065 – Location Map W3 – OS OL8 – M

9km 850m

River Lavant, West Dean, The Trundle, East Lavant, Chichester

PT West Dean (B start), Chichester (*, B finish)

R West Dean, Lavant, Chichester

This is a linear route but can conveniently be based at Chichester, a bus journey taking you from Chichester to West Dean and buses also being available from the outskirts of the city into the city centre at the end. The route includes some climbing but it is essentially a valley route, following close to and often within sight of the River Lavant.

The **River Lavant** is one of the most remarkable rivers in Sussex. It's a winterbourne river which generally dries

145

up in summer, and when dry the riverbed does look rather sorry for itself, so I do recommend you to undertake this route when the river is flowing even though that may mean donning your winter woollies. It rises at the village of East Dean which as the crow flies is some 4km east of where this route starts, and empties into Chichester Harbour near Fishbourne. One of its particular delights is the many most attractive stone bridge crossings, most notably at West Dean and East Lavant. When the river is flowing normally it is superbly picturesque, but it has been known to flood, most famously in January 1994 when in the course of a very wet winter it burst its banks and caused widespread flooding in Lavant and on the approach to Chichester, leading to road closures and traffic chaos. When the riverbed is dry it is hard to think that could ever have happened!

Buses on the Chichester-Midhurst route serve the A286 immediately above the centre of **West Dean**; I suggest that wherever in the village you choose to start, you make your way to the top (north-east) end of the village, turning south-eastwards off the A286 down Church Lane which shortly veers south-westwards. On the corner here, there's the church of St Andrew, largely rebuilt in 1934 following a fire but boasting some impressive effigies of 17th century origin; immediately south-east of the church is West Dean College, an early 19th century flint house in beautiful grounds.

Continue south-westwards down Church Lane and at the bottom (south-west corner) of the lane, at SU858122 (625m from the top of Church Lane), you arrive at a crossing of the River Lavant, which you'll see plenty of as you progress. Your route starts here and you join the bridleway, striking out south-eastwards from this spot. You're now following the signed Monarch's Way (see route 6). In 400m from the start, at SU860118, you reach a bridleway fork, taking the left fork here and now proceeding uphill, following the edge of the trees then passing through the middle of woodland. You emerge to reach a T-junction of bridle tracks at SU871110, 1km 500m from the fork referred to above; the views from here are great and they're about to get better still. Turn left, still with the Monarch's Way, and in around 75m you reach a signed junction with Chalkpit Lane which heads south-westwards from here. Ahead of you (eastwards) is **The Trundle**, an Iron Age fort and one of the best viewpoints in West Sussex. On a clear day it is possible to see from the top as far as the Seven Sisters in East Sussex! Unfortunately only the first few metres of the path going ahead of you onto The Trundle are on a bridleway; the bridleway then forks right and contours the hillside then disappears into trees, while the route heading for the hilltop is a public footpath. Walkers can of course detour up to The Trundle on the footpath, this necessitating a detour of some 750m for the round trip, but cyclists or horse-riders, to appreciate the fine view from the hillside, will have to use the bridleway, from which the view isn't quite as good! I still recommend it, though; again it requires an extra 750m.

Whatever you choose, you then need to retrace to SU871110 and this time go straight on, just south of west, along a bridleway section which here overlaps with two discrete name paths that run through West Sussex. One is the West Sussex Literary Trail (WSLT), the other is the New Lipchis Way (NLW), and we encountered both in route 5. You descend steadily and very enjoyably with both the WSLT and NLW and arrive at a bridleway crossroads at SU856106, 1km 500m from the meeting with Chalkpit Lane. Leaving the NLW here, you turn left and now follow the WSLT, initially just west of south then just east of south, through the delightful Lavant valley, the River Lavant never far away to your right, to reach Sheepwash Lane, **East Lavant,** at SU860084, some 2km 500m from SU856106. Turn left beside the River Lavant, keeping the beautiful village green to your right, then in 75m turn left again at the T-junction with Pook Lane, immediately crossing the river. This is an absolutely gorgeous river crossing which you really need to see when the river is in full flow.

Continue briefly along Pook Lane; immediately to your left beyond the river crossing is the fine church of St Mary, East Lavant, which boasts a 12th century nave, a charming

Norman doorway, a collection of five oak stalls with carving under the seats and on the arm-rests, and a grand reredos of stone and marble. Opposite the main church path, some 250m from arriving at Sheepwash Lane, turn right along Fordwater Road. Follow beside this for 500m or so, reaching a very sharp left-hand bend. Follow the road, now New Road, for another 125m beyond the bend then at SU866080 turn right as bridleway-signed along a most attractive bridleway, Stocks Lane, that proceeds in a generally south-easterly direction round the edge of Goodwood Airfield. As you progress, look back for what are lovely views towards Kingley Vale.

At SU878065, 2km 250m from SU866080, you reach the end of the bridleway and indeed the route, at a T-junction with a road, Madgwick Lane. Turn right alongside it, arriving at a roundabout in 500m. Take the right-hand exit which leads in 375m to the Portfield Retail Park and a large Sainsbury's on your left, from which buses can take you into the centre of **Chichester**, a brisk 1km 500m away via Westhampnett Road and St Pancras. Chichester's attractions are well documented: the city's focal point is its magnificent 11th century cathedral, with its Norman sculptures, 14th century choirstalls, imposing 15th century Arundel screen, shrine of St Richard, John Piper's altar tapestry, and Marc Chagall's stained glass window. However Chichester has many other attractions including its Market Cross of 1501, right in the city centre; the brick-and-flint Vicar's Hall above a late 12th century crypt; St Mary's Hospital, once occupied by Franciscan monks; the 1731 Council House; the 13th century brick-and-flint Bishop's Palace; and a number of fine historic churches.

ROUTE 33

SU951329 (start and finish) – Location Map W3 – OS OL33 – M

14km 250m

Shillinglee Park, Shillinglee Lake, Frith Wood, Northchapel, Mill Copse, Birchfield Copse, Beanfield Copse, Shillinglee Park House

PT Ramsnest Common (B start and finish)

R Ramsnest Common, Northchapel

This is a lovely circular lowland journey, mostly wooded but with some fine open sections as well, and with a lake as its principal waterside attraction.

If you're reliant on public transport to get to the start of the route you'll need to get a bus to Ramsnest Common, Surrey, the bus stop served by buses from Haslemere and Guildford. Then head south-eastwards at SU950330 from the A283 at Ramsnest Common along Gostrode Lane which in 150m becomes a bridleway at SU951329, this point being the start of your route. Follow the lane for another 375m, reaching a bridleway fork at SU955329. Fork right, south-eastwards, reaching the Sussex Border Path (see route 4) in 250m at SU957328, crossing the border here to enter West Sussex. Continue straight over, heading just east of south steeply downhill, going forward along a grassy path to reach Plaistow Road, 500m from SU957328. Turn left, just south of east, along the road, passing between two lakes, Upper North Pond and Lower North Pond. In 625m after joining the road you bend sharply right with it (A), then in 125m you reach a sharp left bend; here you arrive at a bridleway at SU965320, heading southwards from the road bend.

Follow the bridleway in a predominantly southerly direction through the lovely surroundings of **Shillinglee Park**, looking carefully to your right after 500m or so to the Gothic-style Deer Tower of 18th century origin, later added to and restored in 1995. Ahead of you, you can see **Shillinglee Lake** (named on maps simply as The Lake!) and this provides a delightful prospect. You make your way towards the lake and pass just to the west of it; sadly there's no bridleway access alongside the lake although walkers can make a detour to it a bit later on. On or around the lake you may see the great-crested grebe, heron, tufted duck, mallard and common tern. Moreover, the lake is one of very few places in Sussex where a plant known as the Limosella aquatic grows, it being one of four nationally rare water plants established at this lake.

Almost immediately after passing the lake's west end, at SU965310, 1km from the road, you veer sharply right, south-westwards, with the bridleway towards the fine buildings of Frith Lodge. Just before the house you need to turn sharply left and then, on reaching a parking area by the house (note the beautiful gardens to your right as you approach it) you turn right to resume your south-westward journey. Very shortly, at SU962305, 625m from SU965310, you reach a bridleway junction.

You now have a choice. The continuous route heads left, eastwards, at this point. However I recommend you detour to the pretty village of Northchapel. If you decide to do this, don't turn left at SU962305 but continue south-westwards along the fringes of the delightful Frith Wood. **Frith Wood** is an ancient oak woodland with a variety of trees including alder, birch, hazel and sweet chestnut, while birds to be found here include blackcap warbler, chiffchaff, willow warbler and nightingale, and you may also see the white admiral butterfly. Follow the bridleway all the way to a bridleway T-junction at SU958301, 500m from SU962305. Turn right and in just 75m reach another bridleway junction. Don't fork right but continue westwards with the bridleway through Frith Wood, then in 250m from the second junction veer sharply left, southwards for 625m, emerging from the wood and reaching, at SU955295, a T-junction with a road, Pipers Lane. To visit **Northchapel**, turn right and follow the lane for 300m. The village consists of a nice mix of sandstone, tile-hung and brick-built cottages, while the 14th century church of St Michael boasts an unusual 17th century font of Sussex marble. There's also a timber-framed pub, the Half Moon, dating from the 17th century.

Now retrace along Pipers Lane but this time go straight on along the lane and in 1km from Northchapel village centre you reach a bridleway crossing at SU961294. Turn left here and proceed most pleasantly just west of north to return in 750m along the bridleway to SU958301. You've come full circle. From here, simply retrace the 500m to SU962305 to complete the Northchapel detour.

Whether you've detoured or not, turn eastwards as stated along the bridleway from SU962305, following woodland/field edges. A signed footpath (for walkers only) heads left after 750m from Frith Lodge at SU969305 to reach Shillinglee Lake in 250m and the chance of a brief walk beside the south-eastern shore of the lake, but then walkers will need to retrace and continue eastwards along the bridleway. In some 300m beyond SU969305 there is one particularly delectable patch of woodland, **Mill Copse**, with a fine bridge crossing of a stream; on a hot day this will feel like a little piece of paradise. You then pull away from the woods and continue eastwards across fields to arrive at a bridleway crossroads at the edge of the attractive **Birchfield Copse**, at SU980307, 1km 875m from Frith Lodge.

At SU980307 turn left to proceed north-westwards, veering westwards as you pass (but ignore) a right-forking path to Haymans Farm. At SU975311, 500m from SU980307, you reach another path junction, and here you turn right, north-westwards, along a bridleway through the very pretty **Beanfield Copse** and then a further area of woodland to arrive, in 1km from SU975311, at Shillinglee Road. Turn left to follow the road for 500m to SU965320 to complete a circle. Now retrace exactly the same way back to Ramsnest Common via Plaistow Road past Upper North Pond and Lower North Pond. If, prior to embarking on the full retrace, you've a little extra time, I recommend that, at the sharp bend at (A) above, you fork right along a continuation of Plaistow Road, arriving in 500m at the 18th century **Shillinglee Park House**, the west-facing front described in the *Pevsner Architectural Guide* as "Baroque in intention and Palladian in detail." You would then need to retrace to (A) and head back from there to Ramsnest Common.

ROUTE 34

TQ042210-TQ025190 – Location Map W3 – OS OL10, OL34 – M

5km 650m

Toat Monument, Pallingham Bridge, Wey & Arun Canal, Fittleworth Wood, Stopham

PT Pulborough (*, B start, optional *, B finish), Stopham (optional B finish)

R Pulborough, Stopham

There's tremendous variety in this route, from gentle waterside tracks to steep woodland paths, and there's a good bit of history too. Although it is a linear route, you can create a circle by following beside the A283 from Stopham back to Pulborough.

To reach the start of this route from the roundabout junction of the A29 and the A283 just west of Pulborough (but 250m east of the Pulborough Station approach road) make your way beside the A29 north-eastwards from the roundabout for 250m. Then, just by the church of St Mary – an impressive construction in English Gothic style with fine clerestoried nave, aisles and tower – turn left along Church Place, going forward along Coombelands Lane and in 250m from the A29, crossing over the railway. (If you're a walker coming from Pulborough Station, simply turn left out of the station exit, make for the bike shed and pick up a path from here which heads north-eastwards for 300m, parallel with the railway, to arrive at Coombelands Lane. Turn left here to immediately cross the railway bridge.) Now continue along Coombelands Lane beyond the railway bridge, initially just west of north, then veering in a northerly direction and proceeding past racing stables. The road is narrow, so take care: walkers have the option of following the signed parallel Wey South Path, here a footpath, soon after the road veers northwards, although this footpath then reunites with the road after 750m. The Wey South Path, which we'll meet elsewhere on our bridleway travels, is a delightful long-distance route linking Amberley in West Sussex with Guildford in Surrey, following the river Arun and the Wey & Arun Canal (see below) for much of its length; over 44km of the path runs through Sussex. Much of it, as you might expect, is close to water and after heavy rain can get badly flooded, as I learnt the hard way one soggy December morning when, walking the Wey South Path a little further north, I lost my balance and sank into an enormous accumulation of flood water. Wellies are the best winter footwear option for your Wey South expedition! Anyway, back to the route. Whether following the road or parallel Wey South Path footpath you climb quite steeply and from the top of the rise there's a splendid view ahead to the hilltop **Toat Monument**, 12m high and built in 1823 as a memorial to a Samual Drinkald who, poor fellow, died as a result of falling from his horse. You then descend with the road to arrive at the hamlet of Pickhurst and the start of the route at TQ042210 where a signed bridleway forks left, away from the road, taking the Wey South Path with it. This fork is 2km 500m from the railway bridge on Coombelands Lane.

Sticking to the Wey South Path, with which you'll overlap for a while yet, fork away from TQ042210 with the bridleway just north of west to reach the buildings of Sheepwash, here veering right, northwards. Don't be seduced by the footpath forking left 125m beyond the right bend, but stick to the signed bridleway which, 875m from the start of the route, reaches a bridleway T-junction at TQ039216. Here turn left, westwards, to cross, in 75m, the beautifully restored **Pallingham Bridge** over the **Wey & Arun Canal**. It was hereabouts that a canal route, the northern part of the Arun Navigation, opened in 1787, connecting Pallingham with Newbridge further north, and becoming part of what was to be the complete Wey & Arun Canal, which ran from Pallingham to Shalford near Guildford. The Wey & Arun Canal opened in 1816 but saw little traffic and was abandoned in 1871. While the canal was functioning, the area just south/south-west of Pallingham Bridge was known as Pallingham Docks and created for the building and repair of barges. Since 1970, the members of the Wey & Arun Canal Trust have worked hard to restore parts of the canal to navigable standard, and the restored Pallingham Bridge is a magnificent example of their work. There are other routes in this part of the book that will visit further stretches of the canal.

Keeping to the Wey South Path, you continue westwards beyond the bridge, shortly crossing the River Arun (note – the path could easily flood here after wet weather) and soon reaching, at TQ036216, a junction with a farm lane just north of Pallingham Quay Farm. You turn right with the bridleway along the lane but almost immediately you veer left with the lane and simply follow it westwards until at TQ030218, 1km from Pallingham Bridge, you reach a bridleway junction. Here turn left, leaving the Wey South Path, and follow the wooded bridleway initially just west of south, veering south-eastwards then south-westwards, and ascending to reach, at TQ029212, another bridleway junction, 650m from TQ030218. Here turn right.

From TQ029212 you head just north of west along a field edge, from which there are tremendous views. At the end, in 175m from TQ029212, at TQ027212, you reach a path junction, and here turn left, south-westwards, along a bridleway which initially stays at the field edge with further superb views ahead then after a left-right kink dives into **Fittleworth Wood**, continuing south-westwards. There's a very steep descent leading to a stream crossing, and then a very tough climb, before a further ascent and subsequent steadier descent through what is beautiful woodland. At TQ022202, 1km 250m from TQ027212, you reach a bridleway crossroads. Go straight on, southwards, emerging from the woodland and descending further, veering very gently west of south then southwards again, going forward along a lane past Limbourne Farm. Beyond the farm you enter another area of woodland and reach a path junction at TQ020191, 1km 125m from TQ022202. Turn left, eastwards, along a charming woodland bridleway that veers gently south of east to reach, in 500m, a road at TQ025190, the end of your route. Ignore a lane heading immediately right here but go forward along the road for 50m or so to a T-junction, turning right, just east of south, and following the road southwards past the church at **Stopham**. It's certainly worth looking inside the church as it boasts an impressive early Norman nave and chancel, an Anglo-Saxon doorway, and a fine array of 15th century brasses in memory of the Barttelot family. Just north of the church is the stone-built 15th century manor house, with a number of mullioned windows.

For public transport and/or refreshment, continue just west of south along Church Lane to proceed to the A283, 375m from the end of the route. Buses are available from here to Midhurst and Pulborough. However by turning left alongside the A283 you reach, in some 500m, the riverside White Hart pub, which sits adjacent to a very fine medieval bridge over the Arun and is a very good place to celebrate your completion of the route! To create a circle, you could, as stated, carry on beside the A283 beyond the pub to reach the station approach road at Pulborough in 1km 500m and the A29/A283 roundabout 250m beyond that. Though there is no pavement for much of these 1km 750m, there are reasonably wide verges so the experience should be relatively tolerable.

ROUTE 35

SU978240-TQ073233 – Location Map W3 – OS OL33, OL34 – M

18km 700m

Petworth, Blackbrook Farm, Medhone Copse, Petsalls Copse, River Kird, Wey & Arun Canal, Harsfold Bridge, Wisborough Green

PT Petworth (B start), Adversane (B finish)

R Petworth, Wisborough Green, Adversane

This is a linear route; if you're reliant on public transport your best base is Pulborough (on the rail network), from which there are regular buses to Petworth and to which you can get a bus back from Adversane at the end. The route described below may not be spectacular but it passes through consistently peaceful and unspoilt countryside, with plenty of fine water features, and is a joy from start to finish.

Assuming you start from **Petworth**, served by buses from Chichester and Midhurst as well as Pulborough, you should have a look round this very attractive town before setting off. Its chief glory is Petworth House, which dates back more than six centuries and contains a magnificent collection of paintings including works by Turner, Rembrandt, Gainsborough and Holbein. The house is situated in Petworth Park, which consists of 700 acres of beautiful parkland, ponds and woodland including ancient oaks, and accommodates the largest herd of fallow deer in the county. Other highlights in Petworth are the Cottage Museum, the early 18th century Angel Hotel, the picturesque Lombard Street, and the late 18th century Leconfield Hall.

To reach this bridleway route from Petworth, head northwards beside the A283 Guildford road then go straight over the A272 roundabout (500m from the town centre); in 200m or so beyond the roundabout fork right off the A283 at Hampers Green along Balls Cross Road, signed for Balls

Cross and Kirdford. It's then roughly 1km 500m along the road to Ratford Farm, the start of this route, and 2km 200m for the complete journey from Petworth centre.

Your route starts at the Ratford Farm buildings at SU978240, your heading away right from the road here along a bridleway going just north of east. You head downhill along a field edge then, continuing north-eastwards, you enjoy a lovely woodland bridleway, with good views to Petworth through the trees. You also pass a number of lakes. Ignoring a left bridleway turn at SU987245 you continue briefly in an easterly direction then veer left to reach a bridleway T-junction at SU990245, 1km 500m from the start. Go right, eastwards, here, passing the picturesque half-timbered **Blackbrook Farm**, and in 750m from SU990245, at SU996244, you arrive at a bridleway crossroads. Go straight over and now enjoy a lovely bridleway north-eastwards through the fine woods of **Medhone Copse** and **Petsalls Copse**, reaching a T-junction of bridleways at TQ008254, 1km 675m from the bridleway crossroads at SU996244. The continuous route turns right, eastwards, from here along a bridleway known as Gandersgate Lane; but by detouring left through the trees you can enjoy, in just 300m or so, fine views to your right across the water meadows around the **River Kird.** The Kird is a tributary of the Arun, rising between Ebernoe and Balls Cross to the west, and flowing into the Arun near Wisborough Green. It may not be the widest or longest river in Sussex but it's one of the prettiest, and this detour, which I recommend, gives you a little taster of it. You then need to retrace to TQ008254 to continue.

As stated, the continuous bridleway route heads east from TQ008254 and in 625m your bridleway, Gandersgate Lane, reaches a minor road, Glasshouse Lane. Turn right, south-eastwards, along it; in 375m you bend right, ignoring a bridleway going off left at this bend, and continue south along Glasshouse Lane for another 500m to a road junction at TQ016246. Here you turn left along another minor road, which in 150m bends right. At this point you fork left onto a bridleway, Chicken's Lane, which passes eastwards along the edge of Crouchams Copse, and in 750m reaches and crosses the A272. Cross straight over to follow a pleasant largely level bridleway heading south-eastwards and then veering southwards to reach a T-junction with a road, Crimbourne Lane, at TQ033234, 1km 375m from the A272 crossing. Turn left along the road for 150m to arrive at a T-junction with Fittleworth Road.

Turn right to follow this road south-westwards for 1km – it's a pleasant quiet country road so this will be no imposition! At TQ030225 turn left off the road along a bridleway heading initially eastwards then north-eastwards, following the Wey South Path, and in 1km 750m crossing the **Wey & Arun Canal** which we met in route 34. Continue along the Wey South Path (again see route 34) beyond the canal crossing for 500m to arrive, at TQ047236, at a path T-junction at the buildings of Haybarn. Turn right here, leaving the Wey South Path, and in a further 625m you arrive at a T-junction of bridleways at TQ053235. Turn left here, and in 125m you reach a 4-way bridleway junction just adjacent to Lee Place House, at TQ053236.

At this point you have a choice. The continuous route bears right, eastwards, here, bound for Adversane. However, I strongly recommend you detour to Wisborough Green. To do this, take the bridleway going half-left, north-westwards, at TQ053236, descending to cross the Wey & Arun Canal again at TQ051241, in 500m, using the quite superbly restored **Harsfold Bridge.** Take a moment or two to admire the bridge from the canal side before proceeding. Having crossed the canal at TQ051241 your bridleway continues very pleasantly northwards through delightfully unspoilt meadows, crossing the Arun in 125m, passing Harsfold Hanger and Harsfold Farm and going forward to reach the A272 at **Wisborough Green** at TQ052257, 1km 625m from the canal crossing. Wisborough Green is an attractive village with not only a beautiful green lined with chestnut trees, and houses of brick, timber and tile-hanging, but the very splendid church of St Peter ad Vincula boasting an 11th century nave, fine carved Jacobean pulpit and wall paintings dating from the early 13ᵗʰ century including depictions of Christ's crucifixion and also St James The Great. During the Middle Ages it was an important pilgrimage centre. As far as your own pilgrimage is concerned, having enjoyed the village you will then need to retrace all the way to the 4-way bridleway junction at TQ053236.

Whether you've detoured or not, head eastwards as stated along the bridleway from TQ053236, shortly entering the lovely North Wood, veering in a more south-easterly direction. You emerge from the wood and head eastwards to a junction of tracks at TQ064234, roughly 1km from the 4-way junction. You bear right here to follow a bridleway track that snakes round the south side of Westlands Farm then heads pleasantly eastwards past Well Farm to reach a T-junction with the B2133 at Adversane where the route ends at TQ073233, a further 1km from the junction at TQ064234. By turning right here you almost immediately reach the A29 where there's a pub and there are buses to the railway stations at Billingshurst and Pulborough.

ROUTE 36

TQ029338 (start and finish) – Location Map W3 – OS OL34 – E

11km 475m

Wey & Arun Canal, Brewhurst, Drungewick Aqueduct, Loxwood

PT Alfold Crossways (B start and finish)

R Alfold Crossways, Loxwood

This is a glorious circular canal-side journey with some lovely scenery and what will feel like a trip back to a different age. To reach the start of this route from Alfold Crossways (on the A281 Horsham-Guildford road, served by buses from Guildford and Cranleigh), head southwards along the B2133 to Alfold, a distance of some 1km 250m. Just short of the church in Alfold, turn hard right onto Rosemary

Lane and follow it for some 875m to TQ029338 where the route starts, bridleways going off to the right and left here. You take the bridleway going left, just east of south, from here, kinking right and then left, continuing to a bridleway crossroads at TQ031326, some 1km 250m from the start. Turn right, south-westwards, here to follow what is the Sussex Border Path (here a bridleway – see route 4), then in 325m at TQ028325 you reach a crossroads path junction, meeting the Wey South Path, which I referred to in route 34 above, and the **Wey & Arun Canal**, a brief history of which is again provided in route 34. Here you're able to view the stunningly restored Gennets Bridge Lock, one of a number of lovingly restored locks you'll see on this journey. Turn left, leaving the Sussex Border Path, and now follow the Wey South Path (here a bridleway) just east of south past Southland Lock, veering in a more easterly direction and keeping the canal to your left, passing Devil's Hole Lock and Loxwood Lock. At TQ041312, 2km 250m from your joining the Wey South Path, you reach the B2133 and you've the option of going up to the road and crossing it, perhaps visiting the beautifully situated canal-side Onslow Arms pub, or passing under the road by the tunnel. This tunnel, opened in 2009, is arguably the biggest achievement of the Wey & Arun Canal Trust to date. Continue eastwards on a bridleway alongside the canal beyond the B2133 for 500m past Brewhurst Lock, reaching a right turn at TQ046312. Here turn right to reach, in a few metres, the lovely white weatherboarded Brewhurst Mill – a water-powered corn mill originally built in the 18th century and restored around 1890 after a fire – and the superb tile-hung/timber-framed buildings of **Brewhurst**. Returning to TQ046312, you have the (highly recommended) option now of detouring eastwards on the bridleway alongside the canal beyond Brewhurst, to view the stunning **Drungewick Aqueduct**, some 1km 750m beyond Brewhurst, and rebuilt in 2002. The bridleway route is beautiful, the towpath (which on this detour passes another lock, Baldwin's Knob Lock) is superbly maintained throughout, and the canal waters, complemented by the mainly wooded scenery, are quite delightful and unspoilt.

Whether you've detoured or not, return now to the B2133 at TQ041312 and turn right to follow it for 400m or so into the centre of **Loxwood**, a pretty village of tile-hung and timber-framed cottages and boasting a charming pond. Directly opposite the junction of the B2133 with Station Road (don't be fooled: there's no station here and never has been!) which goes off to the right, turn left at TQ038315 off the B2133 along a bridleway heading north-westwards. It is a delightful easy-to-navigate bridleway, following attractive field-edge, parkland and woodland tracks, reaching the Sussex Border Path in 1km 500m at TQ031326. Here you meet your outward route, and you simply retrace from this point to the start, crossing straight over the Sussex Border Path and following the bridleway for 1km 250m back to Rosemary Lane, and the start point at TQ029338. Turn right along Rosemary Lane to reach Alfold and then left up the B2133 to Alfold Crossways for buses.

ROUTE 37

TQ206160-TQ214159 – Location Map W3 – OS OL11 – E

8km

Henfield, Bineham Bridge, River Adur, Tanyard

PT Henfield (B start and finish)

R Henfield

This is a lovely route that incorporates sections of riverside and old railway. Although it's not strictly circular, you can easily make it so by starting and finishing at Henfield's main street and I indicate below how you can achieve this.

It's worth having a look round **Henfield**, served by buses from Horsham and Brighton, before starting. The village boasts the fine church of St Peter with 13th century nave walls and impressive brasses of the 16th and 17th century, and there are a number of attractive houses both adjoining the church and on the main street, including the 17th century White Hart and red-brick Norton House. To reach the start of this route from Henfield, you need to head westwards from the main street along Church Street. Continue forward along Upper Station Road, then in 875m from the main street turn left down Station Road (part of the Downs Link and incorporated into route 1) for 200m to a road T-junction at the bottom where this route starts at TQ206160.

Turn right here onto a bridleway and head just south of west, away from the Downs Link, going forward along a clear straight track. You quickly leave the suburban feel behind, passing through a delightful tunnel of trees, and soon you're able to enjoy really gorgeous views southwards, with Lancing College Chapel clearly visible as well as the South Downs stretching to well beyond Chanctonbury Ring to the west and Truleigh Hill to the east. Your path becomes a clear firm track between fields, and there's a lovely open feel. You pass the fine buildings of Leeches and, ignoring a number of footpaths leading away from your bridleway, you descend and go forward to the delightful **Bineham Bridge** crossing of the Adur (TQ190152), 1km 750m from the start. This is a particularly picturesque spot, with beautiful views from the vicinity of the river to Chanctonbury Ring.

Cross the bridge and continue south-westwards along the very pleasant signed bridleway; in 500m from the bridge at TQ188148 you veer sharp right and in barely 50m from the right turn you reach a bridleway junction. Turn left here, south-westwards, then in 125m at a path junction turn left, south-eastwards, along a bridleway/farm lane which in 950m reaches the Adur again at TQ195144. The **River Adur** is one of the great rivers of Sussex, its western arm rising at Coolham not far from Billingshurst, and the river flowing into the sea at Shoreham-by-Sea. It effectively serviced the shipbuilding industry at Shoreham, with boatloads of timber from the Weald being conveyed along the river to the port. If you complete route 80 below, you'll become aware of its comparatively humble and inauspicious beginnings near Coolham; it presents as a much more impressive waterway on this route, and will get more impressive still as it nears the coast.

On reaching the river, turn right to enjoy a delightful bridleway south-eastwards alongside it, taking you in 1km to the Downs Link at TQ200136. Here turn left up the Downs Link and follow it, overlapping with route 1, for 2km 625m, to arrive back at TQ206160. Here you leave the Downs Link, turning right and heading eastwards (veering south-eastwards) along Lower Station Road (which becomes Dropping Holms then Nep Town Road) for 750m, going forward to TQ213157. Turn left here up Blackgate Lane, a bridleway, to reach, in 250m, a delightful area of Henfield known as **Tanyard**, with a pond and a superb 17th century timber-framed house, Potwell, once the home of the botanist William Borrer; there is a blue plaque erected in his honour. Your route ends at this point, at TQ214159. Here Cagefoot Lane goes off to the right, and if you're a walker you can simply follow this lane for 200m to reach Henfield's main street, from which there are buses to Horsham and Brighton. If you're a rider (of a horse or bike), Cagefoot Lane is unavailable to you, it being a public footpath; rather than bearing right along that road from Tanyard, you'll need to go straight over along a metalled path, passing first the RC church and then the parish church, going forward along Church Lane to return to Church Street. Turn right along Church Street to return to Henfield's main street, a distance of 750m from Tanyard.

ROUTE 38

TQ313303-TQ361325 – Location Map W3 – OS 135 – E

10km 50m

Ardingly Reservoir, Ardingly, East Wood, Wakehurst Place, West Hoathly

PT Balcombe (* start), West Hoathly (B finish)

R Balcombe, Ardingly, Wakehurst Place, West Hoathly

This route, which might easily qualify as a bridleway with history as well, features water in a number of aspects. It's a linear route and I suggest you use Three Bridges as your base if reliant on public transport, with trains available from Three Bridges to Balcombe, and buses available from West Hoathly back to Three Bridges.

To get to the start from Balcombe Station, served by frequent trains on the London-Brighton line, exit the station by making your way to the immediately adjacent B2036 London Road. Turn left along the road, then almost at once turn hard right along Newlands. In 250m this road bends sharp left and becomes Oldlands Avenue, heading eastwards and arriving at a T-junction with Haywards Heath Road, 700m from that sharp left bend.

Turn left along Haywards Heath Road, in 125m reaching a bridleway leading off to the right, at TQ313303, immediately beyond Barn Meadow. This is the start of your route. Take the bridleway, which heads north-eastwards from here, descending quite steeply through open fields then keeping an area of woodland to your left. At the field corner, 350m from the start, you reach a path junction, turning left to continue along the bridleway through the woods; there's shortly another sharper left bend, your bridleway then going forward to emerge at Mill Lane in some 200m from the field corner. Turn right along Mill Lane which you follow for some 500m, actually crossing a narrow inlet of the reservoir, then at TQ320304 you fork right, off the lane along a signed bridleway. This now follows **Ardingly**

Reservoir, which is to your right, for roughly 1km 750m. The reservoir not only supplies water but is used for water sports and enjoys a fine array of wildlife and plant life; trees to be found here include English oak, silver birch, ash, alder and Scots pine, among birds you may see are the kingfisher, great-crested grebe and green woodpecker, and plants you might find include the oxeye daisy and orchid. All of the reservoir-side part of this route, incidentally, overlaps with the Sussex Hospices Trail, the most recent and also the longest name trail in Sussex. It starts and finishes at Chichester and is a mere walk round the block at 322km! The trail was conceived by the Friends of Sussex Hospices; by buying this book you are helping to fund their vital work in raising money for hospices across Sussex, so thank you.

After 1km 750m of reservoir-side walking or riding, you reach a road bridge crossing at TQ331299. You now have over 2km of road, although most of it is quiet and/ or paved. Turn right onto the road, crossing the bridge, and following the road, Balcombe Lane, uphill to reach, in 875m, the lovely church of St Peter, Ardingly. The church boasts a splendid timber-framed porch, dating from around 1500, a 14th century nave, and an impressive set of brasses depicting the Culpeper family, some of the brasses dating back to the early 16th century. Continue along the road beyond the church, the road now Street Lane, to arrive, in 1km from the church, at the B2028 in the charming centre of the village of **Ardingly**.

Turn hard left along the B2028, High Street, for some 500m then turn right along Cob Lane, very steeply downhill; in 100m you veer sharp left and continue downhill for 125m to arrive at TQ347301, forking left here along a signed bridleway. This heads north-westwards uphill, through woodland, to reach a bridleway T-junction in some 275m at TQ345303. Turn right here and now proceed northwards on what is really delightful bridleway path along a thickly wooded hillside. You emerge into a more open landscape, and at TQ346311, 875m from TQ345303, are joined by the

High Weald Landscape Trail (HWLT – see route 13) coming in from the right.

Continuing on with the bridleway, you then enter **East Wood** and it's a delightful woodland walk/ride in a predominantly northerly direction, the rhododendron flowers (when in bloom!) enhancing the beauty of the surroundings, and the sight or sound of streams and waterfalls never far away. Some 750m after being joined by the HWLT you descend to reach, at TQ345319, a bridleway junction; the continuous route bears right, eastwards here, but by taking the bridleway going left and following it for some 250m uphill to the B2028 and turning left, you reach, in a further 250m, the entrance to **Wakehurst Place.** The gabled stone house was built in 1590 and the gardens, noteworthy for their fine Himalayan collection and Japanese iris, have been managed by the Royal Botanical Gardens, Kew, since 1965. Of particular note is a Millennium Seed Bank that was opened in 2000. On a waterside theme, there are ponds and lakes within the grounds.

Returning to TQ345319 you now proceed eastwards as stated along the HWLT, veering from eastwards to north-eastwards and climbing steadily through the trees, emerging from the woods and at TQ352321 kinking right and left to pass the buildings of Philpots, some 750m from the start of the Wakehurst detour. Beyond Philpots you follow a farm lane, continuing north-eastwards with the HWLT, still here a bridleway, and enjoying extensive views as you keep on climbing. In due course you veer just south of east to reach North Lane where, at TQ361325, the route ends, 1km from Philpots. Join North Lane, effectively continuing in the same direction then veering left, and in 250m or so from the end of the route you arrive in the centre of **West Hoathly.**

West Hoathly, with its pretty tile-hung cottages, boasts two gems to your left: the superb 15th century timber-framed Priest House which is open to the public and contains a small museum and attractive gardens, and the early 17th century stone-built Manor House. The Norman church of

St Margaret contains a gigantic possibly 12th century chest, a marble font dating back possibly also to the 12th century, and early 17th century cast-iron tomb slabs to Richard Infield of Gravetye and his son. Close by the church there's a popular pub, The Cat. For buses to Three Bridges you need to follow North Lane, still with the HWLT, past the left side of the pub (not veering right down Church Hill) and on to a T-junction with Chapel Row where you'll find bus stops. The T-junction is some 625m from the end of the route. Incidentally, a note to walkers: if you followed the HWLT on from here you'd pass, in 1km or so, the magnificent late 16th century Gravetye Manor – another walk for another day and well worth adding to your ever-growing to-do list.

ROUTE 39

TQ335034-TQ383019 – Location Map E3 – OS OL11 – M

7km 725m

Brighton, Brighton Marina, Roedean School, Rottingdean, Saltdean

PT Brighton (*, B start), Saltdean (B finish)

R Brighton, Rottingdean, Saltdean

This route follows a section of the England Coast Path that is designated as a public footpath but also, according to the most recent OS Explorer mapping, a permissive bridleway; as explained earlier in this book, it is possible that permission to ride along any permissive bridleway could be withdrawn, although I suspect that as far as this route is concerned, that is highly unlikely to happen. If you want to make sure of the situation, contact the local authority concerned (in this case Brighton & Hove Council). I am anxious to include this particular bridleway in this book, it being the only truly coastal bridleway in Sussex (as opposed to a bridleway that merely ends by the sea). It's a splendid route, with tremendous views out to the English Channel. I have twice had the privilege of walking it as dawn was breaking, as part, in each case, of a 60+-mile walk from my home near Arundel to Hastings; in each case I'd started at midnight, the sunrise I witnessed on the clifftops here on both occasions proving that I'd made it through the night!

Before setting off, you may want to spend some time in **Brighton**, one of the best known and best loved resorts in the country. Among its long list of attractions there's the sumptuous Royal Pavilion, completed in 1823; the Palace Pier, dating from 1899; the aquarium, now the Sea Life Centre, which opened in 1872; the narrow shopping streets known as the Lanes, also of 19th century origin; the luxurious Grand Hotel, built in Italian Renaissance style; the church of St Bartholomew, Ann Street, once the biggest brick church in England; Volk's Electric Railway which opened in 1883; and, most recently, the tall thin I360 tower, completed in 2016, with its covered viewing platform which rises to provide potentially stunning views along the coast. To reach the start of the route from the Palace Pier, simply follow the wide pavement on the sea side of the A259 coast road and at TQ335034 join the signed coastal path, level with the Brighton Marina but on the clifftop. This is the start of the route. You now simply follow the coastal path, though note that for some stretches there are separate routes for walkers and riders. Initially you have **Brighton Marina** for company on your right: the marina, which was officially opened by Queen Elizabeth II in May 1979, is a fascinating complex of elegant modern housing, often very impressively large boats, and stylish waterfronts. Continuing beyond the marina, you can now look out across the open sea towards France. Meanwhile you can monitor your progress by noting **Roedean School** to your left, about 1km 500m from the start. The school, arguably the most famous girls' independent school in the country, was founded in Brighton in 1885 and moved to its present site at the very end of the 19th century. The buildings, Jacobean in style, include a chapel dating back to 1906. Another 1km 250m beyond that, on the left-hand side, are the buildings of St Dunstan's, home of Blind Veterans

UK since 1938, although Blind Veterans UK are set to leave the site in 2024.

Although your path (whichever you follow) has been undulating from the start, it then descends more decisively to **Rottingdean,** reached in 1km from St Dunstan's. As you descend, look to your left to see Rottingdean Windmill about which more shortly. At the bottom of the hill, as you reach Rottingdean, your permissive bridle path ends just shy of the White Horse Hotel, and you then need to follow make your way to the coast road. The centre of the pretty village of Rottingdean is up High Street to your left just here: you can't miss the busy road junction of the High Street with the coast road.

In fact I recommend you break off your permissive bridleway coastal route here to explore Rottingdean and its windmill. Simply turn inland off the coast road up High Street and in 225m bear left again up Nevill Road for another 225m to the Sheep Walk turning on the right, TQ367023. Bear right here up Sheep Walk, following the blue arrow sign to head along an obvious bridle path north-westwards, soon passing just to the right of Rottingdean Windmill. This is an 18th century smock mill that was formerly used to store contraband goods and owes its preservation to it being an important landmark for sailors at sea. Continue along the path in the same north-westerly direction, soon passing the Beacon Memorial and crossing Beacon Hill with its nature reserve, enjoying fine views from the plateau. It's really up to you how far beyond the Beacon Memorial you want to go as you'll be retracing to it, but the actual end of the bridleway is at TQ363032, at the south-east end of Longhill Road, 1km from the Sheep Walk bridleway turning off Nevill Road. Now, however far you've progressed, retrace to the Beacon Memorial at TQ365026, 625m from Longhill Road. Here turn left by a water tap along a clear (albeit unsigned) bridleway path heading downhill past the tap (keeping it to your right), eastwards, passing through an area of trees to reach the High Street at TQ368026, 250m from the memorial. Turn right down the High Street, soon reaching Prospect Cottage and North End House, sometime home of Edward Burne-Jones, Rudyard Kipling's uncle by marriage. On the nearby village green is The Elms, where Kipling himself lived, and across the green is the flint Saxon church of St Margaret and the imposing Grange, the former vicarage and now a museum with many Kipling-related exhibits. The High Street has many attractive old buildings including a number built of flint, brick and timber; the oldest complete secular building is the early 16th century Black Horse, a popular haunt for smugglers. Having enjoyed Rottingdean, follow the High Street back to the coast road, 500m from where you joined High Street following your descent from the memorial.

Now, whether you've detoured or not, head on along or beside the A259 coast road beyond (south-eastwards of) its junction with the High Street, climbing quite steeply. There is no alternative, as Maggie once famously said, there being no coast path initially. However in roughly 150m beyond High Street, more or less opposite the Newlands Road left turn, you're able to bear right off the road/roadside along the signed England Coast Path. The England Coast Path is our latest national trail, intended to take you by the hand and lead you all the way round the English coast. Sadly large sections remain unsigned, including much of the route through Sussex, at the time of writing. Anyway, signage can't be faulted here and it's now a good straightforward 1km section of permissive bridleway cliff path that takes you across the cliffs and down to meet the A259 at **Saltdean**. Your route ends at the meeting with the A259, at TQ383019. Saltdean is a sprawling dormitory village but does contain two gems. One is the recently restored and reopened Saltdean Lido, an Art Deco building which you can view by doubling back briefly up the A259 and crossing to the land side. The other is the Grand Ocean, another Art Deco construction on Longridge Avenue, visited in route 60. There are frequent buses from Saltdean back to Brighton.

ROUTE 40

TQ449174 (start and finish) – Location Map E3 – OS OL11 – E

7km 975m

Isfield Station, River Ouse, Anchor Inn

PT Isfield (B start and finish)

R Isfield, Barcombe Mills (Anchor Inn)

This circular route qualifies as a waterside bridleway route because of its proximity to the River Ouse, one of the great Sussex rivers, but with its exploration of a section of disused railway could equally be said to be a bridleway with history! To reach the route from the centre of Isfield, served by regular buses on the Tunbridge Wells-Brighton route, head north-westwards from Lewes Road past **Isfield Station** along Station Road. The station lies on the now defunct railway between Lewes and Uckfield, which opened in 1858 and shut in 1969. This could be seen as one of the more short-sighted railway closures of the Beeching era, given how useful it would be to have an alternative route from London to Brighton, and there have been proposals to re-open it in recent years. Well, a short section of the line has been revived, here at Isfield, but it is only very short. The station here was purchased by the Millham family in 1983, the building was restored and the adjacent track was re-laid for up-and-down journeys (in the form of 3km round trips), and called the Lavender Line. Its picturesque name is derived not from any profusion of lavender hereabouts but the coal merchants A.E. Lavender who used to operate from the station yard.

In 500m from Lewes Road as Station Road bends right, fork left at TQ449174, the start of the route, following a signed bridleway in the form of a lane heading north-westwards. You shortly veer south-westwards and cross White Bridge over the **River Ouse**. Having been made navigable in the 19th century, the Ouse was once an important means of transporting goods and materials, the fast-flowing waters

171

invaluable for milling, and the mills themselves assisting in the manufacture of such diverse products as oil, paper, cloth and gunpowder. The Ouse rises near Horsham and flows into the sea at Newhaven, the harbour of which accommodates some impressively sized vessels including the Dieppe ferry. It's difficult to visualise all that, standing on the tranquil rural White Bridge! There is a long-distance walking route, the 70km Sussex Ouse Valley Way, which follows the course of the river as closely as it can, starting near Lower Beeding and ending between Newhaven and Seaford.

Having crossed the river, don't turn hard left beside it but rather half-left as bridleway-signed, across a broad field, just west of south. At the far end, cross a footbridge and go forward through a thicket, emerging and going straight on along the narrow but clear path, keeping a pond to your right and veering briefly just east of south. You drop very gently then at TQ442168 you veer left and now follow a wider better-defined field path, continuing just west of south and then just at the end, veering sharply right to reach Anchor Lane at TQ439162, 1km 750m from the start. Turn left along the lane for 250m. At TQ440160 a narrow unsigned path goes off, south-westwards to your right, and your continuous route follows this, but I recommend you detour on along the road for 150m or so to reach the Ouse and the beautifully situated **Anchor Inn**. The pub has been quenching thirsts since its establishment in 1790; even if you don't want to eat or drink here, it's worth seeing it simply for its setting, and if you fancy messing about on the river, boats may be available for hire.

Whether or not you've detoured to the inn, your route heads south-westwards along the path from TQ440160, immediately passing a house which is to the right. This path is in fact a permissive bridleway following the course of the old Lewes-Uckfield railway. Initially the path is narrow but then widens and you get a greater sense of following an old railway track, the path broad and clear with lovely views to the South Downs. At TQ430149, 1km 625m from TQ440160, you reach Barcombe Mills Road with the old Barcombe Mills station immediately opposite. Turn left along the road, but almost immediately fork left along a lane which is part of the Sussex Ouse Valley Way. Follow it to TQ433149, 300m from TQ430149, where the Sussex Ouse Valley Way turns sharp right. The continuous route turns left, northwards, here but I recommend your detouring right with the Sussex Ouse Valley Way for 125m to arrive at Pikes Bridge, a fine old bridge, grooves in the parapet of which were cut by ropes that were used to haul barges. You may be amused by the table of tolls that are still exhibited by the bridge. Then retrace to TQ433149. Whether you detoured to Pikes Bridge or not, turn northwards from here as stated along the lane leading in 125m to Mill Farm at TQ433150. Turn right along what is a restricted byway, actually a farm lane which heads initially eastwards then veers north-eastwards. It's very pleasant going through meadows, especially so when you cross a tributary of the Ouse and then proceed parallel with an arm of the Ouse, the river having actually split in two hereabouts.

In just under 1km from Mill Farm you reach a junction of paths at TQ439158 where you turn left as restricted byway-signed. Now, taking care to keep to the right of the driveway leading to the house on the left, follow a narrow partially paved path which very soon reunites you with the permissive bridleway on the former railway track you followed earlier, now 1km from Mill Farm. Turn right along the permissive bridleway, returning in 375m to the road at TQ440160. There's another opportunity to detour to the Anchor along the road to the right (see above). However your continuous route turns left along Anchor Lane then in 250m turns right at TQ439162 and retraces for 1km 750m all the way to Isfield, reaching the end of the route at TQ449174. You then need to retrace down Station Road for buses at Lewes Road. Before heading home you should certainly take the opportunity to view the old station and railway paraphernalia around it; you may actually be fortunate enough to get a train ride!

ROUTE 41

TQ603314-TQ654235 – Location Map E3 – OS 136 – M

20km

Sharnden, River Rother, Mayfield, Hawksden Park Wood, Bivelham Forge Farm, Newbridge Wood, Holton Lane

PT Mark Cross (B start), Burwash Weald (B finish)

R Mark Cross, Mayfield, Burwash Weald

This is a long linear route but can conveniently be split at Mayfield, or Stonegate, or both, and can be shortened somewhat by missing out the detour to Mayfield. Note also that at the time of writing, buses do not serve Burwash Weald at weekends so if undertaking this journey on a Saturday or Sunday you may need to retrace to Stonegate. If you are using buses you may find Heathfield to be the best base, with buses available to Mark Cross at the start and from Burwash Weald at the end. Heathfield is in turn served by buses between Tunbridge Wells and Eastbourne.

The start of this route is unfortunately some distance from the nearest public transport at Mark Cross, it being necessary for those arriving at Mark Cross by bus to follow the B2100 Wadhurst road eastwards from the A267 at Mark Cross for just over 2km. However at TQ603314, the start of the route, you reach and join a bridleway heading right, southwards, off the B2100. Your bridleway begins with a straightforward and very pleasant 800m of lane that takes you southwards to the buildings of Bassetts. Just before you reach them, though, you're signed left, south-eastwards, soon veering southwards and heading quite steeply downhill on a rather rough path. You veer gently just west of south, arriving at a T-junction of tracks 375m from Bassetts, kinking left here then shortly right, southwards along a left-hand field edge, keeping a stream to your left. This really is delightful, and gets even better as, veering south-eastwards, you veer briefly right with the field edge, away from the stream, then veer left to enter a lovely combination of woodland and water. Your obvious albeit sometimes narrow path continues south-eastwards with the stream never far away. At TQ609297, 1km 225m from Bassetts, you arrive at a T-junction with a clearer track, turning left, very shortly veering right and ignoring a footpath forking left. Continue along the track to the Tidebrook-Mayfield road at TQ612296, 250m from TQ609297. Turn right, south-westwards, here to follow what is an unavoidable 1km 500m stretch of road through the straggling village of Tidebrook, almost all of it uphill! Fortunately the road isn't usually too busy.

After 1km 500m, at a crossroads lane junction at TQ603284, turn left as bridleway- signed, and in 50m you reach a left bend. DON'T veer left with the bend as you might be tempted to do, but at the bend bear gently right along the bridleway heading south-eastwards through the Sharnden estate. You shortly pass **Sharnden** itself, a brick and tile-hung building dating from 1894. Your bridleway follows an extremely clear track, the way ahead obvious, and the lofty surroundings absolutely magnificent. Classic bridleway-ing! You descend gently, your trusty track veering left then right, but proceeding predominantly south-eastwards, until at TQ607275, 1km from leaving the Tidebrook-Mayfield road, you reach a T-junction of paths. Turn left, eastwards, to reach the buildings of Sharnden Old Manor Farm which date from the 15th century, but then in 250m, just adjacent to the buildings, veer sharp right with the bridleway, just west of south, then veering just east of south. You drop down to arrive in the valley of the **River Rother,** one of the main rivers of Sussex (but not to be confused with the Rother in West Sussex!). The East Sussex Rother rises close to Mayfield, which we will visit shortly, and flows picturesquely via Etchingham, Bodiam and Northiam to reach the sea at Rye Harbour, a much narrower and less busy harbour than at the mouths of other Sussex rivers such as the Arun, Adur and Ouse. At TQ609271, 500m from Sharnden Old Manor Farm, you actually cross the river and immediately reach a bridleway junction.

Now you have a choice. The continuous route turns left here, proceeding eastwards into the lovely **Hawksden Park Wood** in the Rother valley. However you could choose to detour to **Mayfield** here, at TQ609271. To do this, bear right along a bridleway heading just south of west from here for 875m to a road, East Street at TQ601269. Go effectively straight on here for 1km to reach the east end of the main street at Mayfield. Once a flourishing Wealden iron-working centre, this is one of the prettiest villages in East Sussex, with its exceptional variety of brick, timber and sandstone houses. Among its most noteworthy buildings are the oak-beamed late 16th century Middle House, the 15th century sandstone gatehouse which guards the remains of what used to be the palace of the Archbishops of Canterbury, and the partially 13th century church of St Dunstan with Jacobean pulpit and some excellent stone carvings. There are plenty of good pubs and cafes, and buses on the Eastbourne-Heathfield-Tunbridge Wells route. Having enjoyed Mayfield, retrace via East Street and bridleway to TQ609271.

Whether you've chosen to detour to Mayfield or not, head eastwards as stated from TQ609271 along an excellent and very clear bridleway track which in 500m enters Hawksden Park Wood. As you enter the wood there's actually a T-junction with a track where you need to take care to turn right and ascend slightly, then ignore a permissive bridleway signed off to the right, 125m or so after entering the wood. In 375m beyond that, just beyond a track coming in hard from the right, you reach a T-junction with a bridle track where you need to bear right, and 125m from there, at TQ619265, you need to turn left off the more obvious-looking one, onto the bridleway heading east. Thankfully, the signage here is pretty reliable!

In 175m or so from the left turn, at TQ621265, you reach another track T-junction. OS maps suggest you ought to go straight over, but in fact there is a re-routing here, the path beyond the track no longer in existence. Accordingly, turn left at the T-junction along the bridle track which brings you in some 125m to a beautifully situated house. Don't be tempted to follow the track beyond the house, but bear left as signed almost adjacent to the house, to meet a public footpath coming in from the left. Here you bear right, eastwards. The bridleway isn't always clearly defined here as it crosses an area of grass but as you continue eastwards it becomes more obvious, passing through an attractive area of woodland. It then emerges, veering gently right to arrive at a road at TQ632265, at the Pound Bridge river crossing – this 1km 125m from TQ621265.

At Pound Bridge, TQ632265, turn left, eastwards, along the road, but in 400m as the road bends sharp right, fork left, north-eastwards, along a signed bridleway, a clear track bringing you in 375m to the fine buildings of **Bivelham Forge Farm,** the timbered farmhouse thought to date back to the 16th century. As you pass the buildings don't get sucked away to the left, but stay in pretty much the same direction heading eastwards into the woodlands beyond, going forward along a clear track. Take care to veer left round a large clearing, keeping that to your right, but beyond the clearing the going is straightforward and enjoyable along what is a very obvious bridle track through the attractive **Newbridge Wood.** As you approach the far north-east end of the wood you veer right, south-eastwards, with the track to exit the wood, 1km from Bivelham Forge Farm, at TQ649272. You then follow a clear bridleway path south-eastwards across the grass to reach another river bridge crossing. Immediately beyond the bridge you join a bridle farm track heading uphill, eastwards, to reach and pass the buildings of Witherenden Farm, veering sharp right with the track and arriving at the Stonegate-Burwash Common road at TQ655270, some 750m from TQ649272.

Turn left along the road at TQ655270 then in 100m turn right, eastwards, at TQ655271 along the signed bridleway which immediately descends then rises to cross the railway. Veer left as you do this, then continue across the grass, keeping farm buildings to your left and arriving at a T-junction with a track (A), 500m from TQ655271. By turning left along the track and almost immediately left at a path fork, you reach Stonegate Station in some 300m from (A). However at (A) your continuous route turns right along the track, keeping farm buildings to your right, then in 125m you veer sharp right, southwards, along a field edge. In another 175m or so, at TQ663269, bear left as arrow-signed (literally just an arrow; there's no bridleway sign here) to follow the right-hand edge of a large expanse of grass, with a thin strip of trees to your right, descending all the while. At the bottom of the hill you enter woodland and follow a clearly defined bridleway path through the wood, shortly veering sharp right then sharp left beside the railway. At TQ667266, roughly 500m from TQ663269, bear right to cross the railway, taking extreme care. Once over the railway you can enjoy a great view of the delightfully unspoilt Rother valley. This will be a constant feature of the next part of your journey.

Now things do get a little messy! Head in a straight line southwards beyond the railway crossing for 200m or so then at TQ667265 you veer gently left downhill through the field, aiming for the corner. Veering eastwards from the corner, aim for the bridge crossing and having crossed the bridge, aim to the right of the plantation you see ahead of you. There is no path; one option, if you're uneasy, is to follow the right-hand field edge round having executed the bridge crossing. However, the bridle route approaches the plantation and skirts the right-hand edge of it. As you skirt the plantation, look carefully to the right and you will see a bridge crossing of the Rother, known somewhat ominously as Wreckery Bridge. Once you're level with that, turn right onto what is an unsigned bridleway that leads you southwards to cross the bridge, 625m from TQ667265.

From here it gets rather easier – or should do. Carry straight on southwards beyond the bridge for 125m or so to a signed path junction at TQ670259. Here turn right. You need to be careful just here: it would be very tempting to follow the obvious-looking path alongside the left-hand edge of the meadow. I was seduced in this way and paid the penalty. This is NOT your route! You need to aim a little to the right of this seductive path, just south of west and just to the left of a large and picturesquely sited pond. Belatedly a bridleway sign reassures you as you head steadily uphill through the grass, your bridleway not well defined, but things become clearer as you rise, veering to the right and keeping the curving boundary fence for the Italianate mid-Victorian buildings of Franchise Manor your left. All the while make sure you enjoy the increasingly lovely views across the Rother valley. You veer round to the left, picking up a clear farm track that heads briefly southwards then veers south-eastwards to a path T-junction at TQ664256, 1km from TQ670259. Here turn right along a lane that runs south-westwards for 325m to a T-junction with Spring Lane at TQ662252, at the hamlet of Holton Hill.

Turn left onto Spring Lane then almost immediately right as bridleway-signed, south-westwards along **Holton Lane**, taking care to avoid a public footpath heading away to the right, westwards from the bridleway, just at the start. Holton Lane is quintessential bridleway travel: an unmetalled but very clearly defined track, free from motorised traffic, free also from difficulties with navigation, and boasting fine views across Wealden countryside. There are no landmarks to monitor progress, but after 1km 750m you're signed left, south-eastwards, your track continuing for 250m to reach the A265, and the end of this route, at TQ654235. By turning right and following the A265 for 500m you reach the village of Burwash Weald where there are refreshments and bus connections.

ROUTE 42

TQ700321-TQ700319 – Location Map E3 – OS 136 – M

20km

Bewl Water

PT Berner's Hill (B start and finish)

R Bewl Water, Wadhurst

Bewl Water is a reservoir that opened in 1975 at the north-east end of East Sussex, close to the border with Kent. It was constructed as part of a project to increase water supplies to meet demand in Kent and Sussex, and constitutes the largest inland body of water in south-east England. It is also exceedingly picturesque and unspoilt and has become a haven for bird life. Among a huge number of species sighted here are the great-crested grebe, dabchick, kingfisher, tufted duck, Canada goose, barn owl, kestrel, buzzard, sparrowhawk and woodpecker, while animals include deer and vole, and the water itself contains trout, pike and perch. The surroundings of the reservoir are quite delightful, with many areas of attractive woodland bordering the waters. Not only is the reservoir a crucial amenity in terms of its water supply, but it is also a lovely place to come to visit and explore.

A glance at an OS map will suggest that only small sections of the reservoir edge are designated as bridleways. However the good news is that there is a signed circular route all the way round the reservoir, available to walkers throughout the year, and to all other bridleway traffic for much of the year (see next paragraph), and I therefore consider it worthy of inclusion in this book. Signage is very clear throughout, although in fairness you can hardly go wrong for much of the way, as it follows as closely as it can to the water's edge, often negotiating inlets that are very much a feature of the reservoir. As well as that, much of the first half of the route overlaps with the Sussex Border Path (SBP – see route 4) so you'll have SBP signage to help you too. There are also distance markers so you can monitor your progress.

The less good news is that the route is only fully open to cyclists and horse-riders between the beginning of April and the end of October. Small parts of it do stay open all year for those on bikes or horses, but if you want to do it all in one go during the winter months, you'll have to walk it! There is a fair bit of road tramping with one quite long stretch of road in the second half of the journey. The other problem is the lack of convenient "escape routes" for those of you wanting to avail yourselves of public transport and for whom 20km is too much in a day. Nonetheless it can be split as I will demonstrate below.

The easiest way to get to the start of the route by public transport is to catch a bus on the Tunbridge Wells-Hawkhurst route. Leave the bus at Berner's Hill on the B2087 Ticehurst-Flimwell road (1km north-east of Ticehurst and 1km west of Flimwell), and then follow Rosemary Lane northwards from the B2087 for about 1km 875m to reach the bridge crossing of the reservoir at TQ700319. A bridleway comes in here from the left; you'll be following that one later on! For now, carry straight on over the bridge then in 250m from TQ700319 turn left as signed at TQ700321, the start of the route, along what is a clearly signed path that will take you all the way round the reservoir, returning you to just short of the bridge at the end of the circuit. This is, therefore, effectively a circular route even though the grid references for start and finish are just slightly different.

Your route initially sticks to the waterside, following the course of the SBP, all the way to TQ677338, 3km 750m in. You soon get a flavour of the reservoir (not literally I hasten to add!) with three inlets to negotiate in those opening kilometres, and you then have Chingley Wood for company to your right. You leave the wood behind you and follow beside a dam, this taking you to just shy of a complex which includes a parking area and a number of other visitor amenities. You must here, at TQ677338

181

(A), bear right to head away from the reservoir as signed, veering left to arrive at a junction with Bewlbridge Lane at the bottom edge of Wiskett's Wood at TQ676341, 375m or so from leaving the water's edge, adjacent to water treatment works. Still with the SBP you turn left to head south-westwards along the lane, then in 750m, at TQ670337, turn left, just east of south, off the lane, descending along a path. In 250m you veer sharp right with the path and in another 125m return to the water's edge. It's then very straightforward going for the next 2km 750m or so, straightforward in the sense that you stick to the path nearest the waterside throughout, heading in a predominantly south-westerly direction. But there are occasions when the path has to drift a little away from the waterside, and you also have to negotiate another five inlets, some longer than others, between (A) and the westernmost point of the reservoir at TQ655325 (B), a total of 4km 250m from (A). Here, at (B), you'll see a footpath signed to the right (south-westwards) for Wadhurst, and for walkers, this may be a good point to break your journey, it being a case of simply following that path for 1km and then going forward along the road into Wadhurst with its shops, cafes, pubs and train/bus connections. Cyclists and horse-riders, you'll need to wait a little longer to access Wadhurst! Wadhurst is a very pretty village with many tile-hung and weatherboarded cottages, and its church boasts a Norman tower and impressively tall spire. Just a few metres shy of the footpath to Wadhurst, you lose the SBP, which strikes out away from the water towards Cousley Wood. You won't meet it again on this route.

Beyond (B) you start to work your way in a predominantly easterly direction, with two more inlets to negotiate as your path continues to stick reasonably closely to the waterside. It is just as you complete your negotiation of the second inlet that at TQ661324, some 1km 750m from (B), you're signed away from the reservoir, up a steep path, shortly veering left and passing the buildings of Newbarn, arriving at a T-junction with a lane at TQ664325. Turn right up the lane to a T-junction with a road, Ward's Lane, at TQ665324 (C), 2km 400m from (B).

Now you have nearly 5km of tarmac, which may seem a lot, but don't worry as the roads are extremely quiet and safe. Turn right here along the road which you follow for 1km 500m to TQ663315 where there's a road junction. The continuous route goes straight on but riders can, by turning right here along the road for 1km 125m, reach the B2099; Wadhurst is reached by bearing right up the B2099 for 2km 250m. However as stated at TQ663315 the continuous route goes straight on, south-eastwards, along a winding road (Beatles fans might call it a long and winding road!). Follow this road, Birchetts Green Lane, via Birchett's Green and Tolhurst to reach, in 2km 175m, a crossroads junction with Burnt Lodge Lane at TQ677306. Turn left to proceed northwards up the road for 1km 125m. The road, which has become Lower Hazelhurst, ends at TQ679317 (D), 4km 800m from (C) and you now go forward along a path. From here it's paths all the way to the end.

From (D) simply continue initially in the same direction along a track which in 150m or so veers sharply right. Your trusty track immediately embarks on negotiation of an inlet, heading southwards beside the water then bending sharply left to follow the east side of the inlet northwards. You veer right, eastwards, enjoying fine views of the reservoir, and follow the neck of a peninsula past Hazelhurst Farm. You reach the end of the Hazelhurst Farm peninsula in 1km 600m from (D), and from the end of the peninsula (E) you make your way up the right-hand side of an inlet then head south-eastwards beside the reservoir before negotiating one final, substantial inlet. Once that has been negotiated, your route ends most pleasantly, the track staying close to the side of the reservoir and arriving back at Rosemary Lane, 3km 200m from (E), at TQ700319. Unless you physically began at the official start of the route across the bridge, you have completed the circle and thus ends your route! For buses back to Ticehurst or Flimwell and beyond, simply turn right along Rosemary Lane and retrace to Berner's Hill.

ROUTE 43

TQ918175-TQ913203 – Location Map E3 – OS 125 – M

15km 100m

Winchelsea, River Brede, Camber Castle, Rye, River Tillingham, Peasmarsh Church

PT Winchelsea (*, B start), Rye (*, B finish)

R Winchelsea, Rye

This may, on the face of it, seem like yet another long route but in fact it is effectively a short linear route and rather longer circular route rolled into one. The linear part runs from Winchelsea to Rye and the circular part begins and ends at Rye. Note therefore that you can very easily split this route at Rye and I recommend you spend some time in Rye in any event. The linear section from the start to Rye, at 2km 875m, is much shorter than the almost-circular route that follows, and therefore the linear route could easily be treated as a Sunday stroll should you wish!

Although there is a station at Winchelsea, it is much better to access Winchelsea by bus as the railway station is nearly 1km from the centre. You should spend time in **Winchelsea** before you start: it is one of the prettiest towns in Sussex. Highlights include the superb church of St Thomas with its marbled effigies, canopies and pinnacle tombs; the Court Hall, which is now a museum in High Street; the 14th century Armoury in Castle Street; and the Strand Gate, one of Winchelsea's superb medieval town gates.

To reach the start of this route from the centre of Winchelsea, follow the A259 from the town towards Rye, then as the A259 bends sharply left to pull away from the town at TQ909175, turn right along Sea Road. There's a sharp left bend in 750m, and in a further 250m an even sharper right-hand bend at TQ918175, the start of the route. Here you leave Sea Road, going straight on, eastwards, as bridleway-signed and very shortly veering sharp left with the bridleway. You now follow the bridleway in a predominantly northerly direction, keeping the River Brede to your left and enjoying fine views to Camber Castle to your right. The **River Brede**, which rises near Battle and flows into the Rother at Rye, isn't one of the "heavyweight" rivers of Sussex but its valley is absolutely delightful. **Camber Castle** was built in 1539 on orders from Henry VIII and at its peak of activity in 1542 had a garrison of 42 men, but the main fortifications were abandoned and demolished because of the encroachment of the marshland. It makes a superbly photogenic sight and a most helpful landmark in otherwise quite featureless surroundings. As you continue beyond Camber Castle you're joined by the Saxon Shore Way and Royal Military Canal Path, with which you will overlap for the rest of your journey into Rye. The 262km Saxon Shore Way, running from Hastings to Gravesend, follows a line of fortifications built along the coastline during the period of the Roman Empire to deter Saxon invaders, while the 45km Royal Military Canal Path between Cliff End and Hythe follows a canal built in 1804 in response to the military threat posed to England in the Napoleonic Wars. The Brede (as far as Rye) acts as part of a link between separate stretches of canal; in route 44 you can view the canal north-east of the rest of the link, which is provided by the Rother.

At TQ918194, roughly 2km from the start, you reach a gate with a signed bridleway to the right. Go straight on here, keeping the Brede to your left, and going forward through an area of quite dense vegetation to reach a T-junction with a clear track beside a house. Bear left along the bridle track, which continues parallel with the Brede to arrive at a T-junction with Harbour Road at TQ920198, 500m from TQ918194. Turn left to immediately cross the river and almost at once arrive at a T-junction with the A259. Turn right alongside this road which bends sharply to cross another river, the Tillingham, about which more below. Immediately beyond the crossing, 375m from TQ920198, don't veer right with the A259 but go straight on along Wish Street, going forward along Cinque Ports Street.

By detouring to the right up Market Road, opposite Station Approach, you arrive in the centre of **Rye**. Rye is another beautiful town, its principal attractions being the cobbled Mermaid Street with 16th century Mermaid Inn; the 18th century Lamb House in West Street, sometime home of the author Henry James; Rye Castle, also known as Ypres Tower, built in 1249; the 14th century Landgate, the last remaining medieval town gate in Rye; the 15th century timber-framed Fletcher's House; the fine arcaded 18th century Town Hall; and the Norman church of St Mary, particularly famous for its 16th century clock, the oldest working church turret clock in the country. You really need a full day to do justice to all of it.

However the continuous route carries on along Cinque Ports Street, then, 500m after leaving the A259, bears left along Rope Walk. Cross the railway and go on along The Grove then just beyond Rye College turn left along Love Lane. Follow the metalled road which becomes a bridleway at TQ917209, 625m from the start of Rope Walk. Continue north-westwards along the bridleway, a clear track that in another 125m reaches Rolvendene Farm. Care is needed here: don't be tempted to join the footpath striking out southwards (hard left) here, nor the path north-westwards up the hillside, but rather follow the bridleway westwards, joining the High Weald Landscape Trail (HWLT – which we met much further inland in route 13) and which in fact you'll be following for roughly 3km. Initially you proceed beside the **River Tillingham**, another very pretty but unsung Sussex river that rises near Broad Oak not far to the west of here, and empties into the Brede in Rye shortly before the Brede itself meets the Rother.

Anyway, back to this route. As the Tillingham veers southwards, 250m or so from Rolvendene Farm, you fork right, away from it, heading south-westwards, then in 500m from Rolvendene Farm at TQ911208 take great care to veer right, just north of west. You continue in that direction, the path not hugely clear on the ground, but with the Tillingham drawing near to you to the left, and another stream to the right, you shouldn't drift! The way forward becomes a lot clearer as, in the vicinity of a sheepfold in 1km from TQ911208, you begin to ascend from the Tillingham valley bottom. It's worth pausing as you rise, to look back and enjoy lovely views of the valley and the town of Rye. Some 500m beyond the sheepfold you pick up a clear track, then in another 250m you veer right, northwards, at TQ895213, and it's then straightforward going past orchards and then Clayton Farm to your right, your bridleway veering north-westwards. At TQ891217, 750m from TQ895213, the HWLT goes off to the right, following a footpath. You however stick to the bridleway, passing further orchards with very tempting-looking fruit in late summer. Look, but don't touch!

In just 250m from parting with the HWLT, at TQ888217, you reach Church Lane. Turn left along it, passing the Norman **Church Of St Peter & St Paul, Peasmarsh,** which contains a nave dating back to the start of the 12th century, late 11th century animal carvings, and late 12th century arcades. The centre of Peasmarsh village is some distance away and well off this route. Continue along Church Lane to reach a T-junction, 625m from where you joined the road; at the T-junction turn left, south-westwards, to follow Dew Lane.

In 250m you reach, at a sharp right bend at TQ882216, a bridleway (mapped as Dew Lane) forking away, effectively in the same direction as the road you've been following. Follow the bridleway, a metalled driveway, south-westwards, taking great care after 375m to fork right – this junction wasn't properly signed when I walked this – and continue along the driveway (mapped as Tillingham Lane) to reach, in another 500m, the buildings of Pelsham Farm. Your clear bridleway veers left, south-eastwards, to pass the complex, your driveway now becoming a rougher track but still clearly defined. Veering more gently left, you then begin to descend south-eastwards along the right-hand (west) edge of Hooker's Wood. There are now lovely views ahead to the Tillingham valley. Keeping in a straight line, you reach the valley bottom, cross the Tillingham then ascend along a right-hand field edge. At the top of the rise you go forward along a more clearly defined path south-eastwards beside farm buildings to reach a clear T-junction of tracks at TQ885194, 1km 750m from Pelsham Farm. Turn right along a bridle track that ascends, bending round to the left then veering more sharply right to arrive at the B2089, 625m from TQ885194, at TQ887189.

Turn left alongside this road for 1km – take care as it can be quite busy – but then at TQ897194 turn right, off the road along a much narrower road which descends steeply for roughly 600m to a very sharp right bend at TQ900190. Turn left here to join a bridleway that's part of the 1066 Country Walk and National Cycle Route 2. The 1066 Country Walk, incidentally, is a long-distance walking route that commemorates the places and people around the Norman invasion. The main route runs for roughly 50km between Pevensey and Rye but there are link routes starting at Polegate, Bexhill and Hastings. The section you've now arrived at is part of (and indeed right at the end of) the main route. Follow it north-eastwards for 2km, initially just below Cadborough Cliff; it's straightforward easy going on an excellent track, continuing forward along West Undercliff, your bridleway route ending at TQ913203 at a T-junction with Udimore Road, the B2089. To reach the centre of Rye and public transport connections, some 500m away, turn right alongside the B2089 which crosses the Tillingham, becomes Ferry Road and veers right to cross the railway. Turn left immediately beyond the crossing to follow the road to the station; for the centre of Rye, veer right just by the station and continue up Station Approach, cross Cinque Ports Street and carry on up Market Road.

ROUTE 44

TQ885258-TQ936245 OR TQ915254 OR TQ926237 –
Location Map E3 – OS 125 – E

5km 750m OR 8km 250m OR 7km 500m

River Rother, Royal Military Canal

PT Wittersham (B start), Iden (B finish)

R Wittersham, Iden

This easy route is arguably the best piece of riverside bridleway in Sussex. It comes with three alternative endings – if you read on, you'll understand why – and how!

To reach the start of the route from the nearest public transport at Wittersham (in Kent) served by buses between Rye, Iden and Tenterden, follow The Street south-westwards away from the B2082 Poplar Road; buses stop very close to the junction of these two roads. Keep on The Street heading south-westwards past Wittersham House, the village church and the primary school. Continue along this road for 2km 250m beyond the B2082 and all the way to the Blackwall Bridge crossing of the **River Rother** at TQ885258 where your route starts, actually still in Kent. We met the Rother in route 41 and it's certainly a lot wider now than then, with a much greater "presence." You turn left off the road at Blackwall Bridge to enjoy an extremely straightforward, relaxing and enjoyable bridleway beside the Rother, keeping to its left bank, heading eastwards and overlapping with the Sussex Border Path, which we've already met in route 4 and indeed a few more times in our travels! Note that OS mapping between TQ900251 and TQ903251 is misleading; your path sticks to the embankment, and the bridleway doesn't dart away from the river. A line of pylons comes in from the right on the other side of the river at this point, and if you have an OS map you can use those to monitor your progress. You have now imperceptibly entered East Sussex – you would have done so 1km 500m after starting.

In 3km 250m from the start you cross the B2082 at New Bridge (TQ915254) then continue beside the water, initially eastwards then veering south-eastwards. To your right across the river is the particularly fine set of hilltop buildings of Thornsdale Farm, with a splendid oast house, while ahead of you to the left is Stone Cliff, a prominent hillside, perhaps all the more impressive because of the low-lying surroundings. In 2km 500m from New Bridge you arrive at a junction with Military Road, just west of the **Royal Military Canal** which the Rother meets at this point, TQ936245 – the canal coming in from the left. Before you decide on how to continue – you do have a choice – it's worth pausing at this watery T-junction, the meeting of the Rother with the canal, and possibly detouring briefly left up Military Road to view the canal which, together with the Royal Military Canal Path, I mentioned in route 43. As I stated there, the canal was constructed in 1804; despite it being no more than 30ft wide it was capable of carrying both troops and equipment. William Cobbett, author of *Rural Rides*, was extremely disparaging about its effectiveness to deter potential invaders and looking at the canal you can probably see why. Fortunately its effectiveness was never tested.

Now you have these alternative endings:

You could choose to end the route here; to reach Rye, 4km away, riders will need to turn right to follow Military Road south-westwards from here. Walkers can cross the waterway to use the Royal Military Canal footpath which follows the east side of the Rother (the Royal Military Canal breaking at its meeting with the Rother) into Rye. Note that the path floods at high tide on the approach to Rye, so check tide times or risk a wait!

As a second option, it is open to you to retrace to New Bridge (TQ915254) then turn left to follow the B2082 southwards for 1km 500m to reach Iden where buses are available back to Rye.

A third (and if you can do it, the best) option is to follow

Military Road southwards for some 750m to Boonshill Bridge (for walkers there is the parallel Royal Military Canal footpath on the far side of the canal, with bridge crossings at either end). At Boonshill Bridge, TQ936237, turn right, westwards, along a lane. This is now signed as a public footpath but still shows on OS maps as a bridleway and at its western end is signed as a bridleway. However riders may find negotiation of it problematic whatever the legal position. It starts as a nice wide lane, rising to pass between Cliff Farm and Spring Farm. Beyond the farms, though, it narrows and, continuing in the same direction, rises steeply through thick vegetation, with occasional steps and bridge crossings. Cyclists would clearly need to dismount and horses may struggle to get through. Attempt at your own risk! You emerge from the vegetation to immediately reach a T-junction with a clear track. Now the going becomes very easy and suitable for all bridleway traffic. Turn right to follow the track past a beautiful old house and on, westwards, to reach a road, Grove Lane at TQ926237, 1km from TQ936237. This is the end of this particular alternative route. To reach Iden, where there are buses available to Rye, turn right along Grove Lane, arriving in Iden in just under 1km.

ROUTE 45

TQ967188 (start and longer route finish – shorter route finish at TQ938211) – Location Map E3 – OS 125 – E

10km 75m (longer route), 5km 575m (shorter route)

Romney Marsh

PT Camber (B start, optional B finish), East Guldeford (optional B finish)

R Camber, East Guldeford

This route contrasts hugely with the downland and woodland bridleway routes in Sussex, there being no woodland to speak of and certainly no hills on this route.

However there is a real grandeur and beauty in this traverse of the south-west corner of Romney Marsh. The longer route is circular, the shorter route linear but the end point of the linear route is served by regular buses back to the start.

Your route starts at TQ967188 in the centre of Camber, served by regular buses to and from Rye, your start point being specifically on the west side of the Camber Castle pub car park on Lydd Road. OS mapping suggests a bridleway route heading north-westwards from Lydd Road here, but in fact that's now defunct; simply follow the path/bridleway heading away from Lydd Road north-eastwards, keeping the pub car park immediately to your right. You continue along a clear track in the shade of trees then in 250m from the start turn very sharp right to follow the path onwards, eastwards, keeping a large caravan park to your right. At TQ974191, in 500m from the right turn, you reach a bridleway junction. Turn left here, just west of north, past a sheepfold, then in some 250m cross a stream and turn sharp right, heading for 125m towards a fence and gate.

As you approach that fence and gate, though, fork left at TQ975193 along a clear path, effectively a slipway off the embankment you're on, aiming for a gate. Pass through the gate and continue along a rough bridleway path through the grass, past an isolated building known as Chittenden's Cottage, veering north-westwards and keeping another embankment to your right. The path becomes rather unclear but keep the embankment close by you to your right and you'll be fine. The grass becomes smoother and as it does you now make for the embankment, join it (at TQ971197, 625m from TQ975193) and follow it.

Now things get a great deal easier as you continue north-westwards on the bridleway along the low grassy embankment known as Wainway Wall, keeping a channel just to your right. This is all part of **Romney Marsh**, a massive area of grassland interspersed with streams, channels and drainage ditches (you're never far from water anywhere on Romney Marsh), and lots of sheep! The marsh has a huge range of bird and insect life, including godwit, goldfinch, oystercatcher, egret, pied wagtail, grey heron, sparrowhawk, and varieties of butterfly, dragonfly and moth; plants on the marsh include evening primrose, red valerian, viper's bugloss and sea kale; while among mammals you may see on the marsh are fox, stoat and water vole. The surroundings are certainly never dull, with views towards Rye and the cliffs east of Hastings. In roughly 1km 125m from where you joined the embankment you pass a charming bridge to your right taking a public footpath (NOT your route!) with it. This is a most helpful landmark as you will see, and actually a very attractive spot indeed.

Don't cross the bridge but stay on Wainway Wall, veering very gently left, fractionally north of west. In 750m or so from the bridge, DON'T be sucked away to the right along the tempting embankment which goes off at TQ953201. Rather, keep on in a straight line then at TQ950201, 1km from the bridge, you veer right, north-westwards, with the obvious track. In 750m from TQ950201 you reach a pond, just before which you veer left, past various farming paraphernalia, going forward along a farm lane. OS mapping is misleading here, the (now incorrect) mapped bridleway route forking slightly left at TQ943208 beyond the paraphernalia and continuing through rough grass to a dead-end just before a house. It is clear that route has now been superseded. You should rather stick to the farm lane which reaches a T-junction with another farm lane/bridleway at Moneypenny Farm at TQ943210, some 450m from the pond.

Here, Moneypenny Farm, you have a choice. The shorter route turns left along the farm lane/bridleway to reach Camber Road, TQ938211, the end of the shorter route, in 500m; by turning right here you reach East Guldeford in 250m where you can pick up a bus back to Camber or one on into Rye.

The longer, circular route turns right at Moneypenny Farm at TQ943210, heading eastwards along the bridleway, then in 900m striking out south-eastwards beyond Black House Farm. It is a fascinating landscape, the assembly of wind turbines of Little Cheyne Court wind farm a very conspicuous feature to your left, and it is most enjoyable and straightforward going. However, after 1km of heading south-eastwards, care is needed from TQ961204 onwards. At this point you veer left, eastwards, then in 125m sharp left again, to reach in another 25m, at TQ962204, a three-fingered signpost indicating a bridleway heading back the way you've come, a footpath going straight ahead, and another bridleway heading to your right. Turn right as bridleway-signed along a clear track, south-eastwards. You might be tempted to stay with the track, but DON'T – after 250m, at TQ964203, strike out to the right, across the pasture, aiming for a stream crossing in 250m at TQ966200. Here you veer right, southwards, crossing the stream and arriving in a further 200m at Wainway Wall again, at TQ966198. Bridleway signage from TQ964203 to this point is non-existent, so be warned. Assuming you've made TQ966198 safely, you just need to make for the far side of the Wainway Wall embankment and you'll see you've now come full circle. From here you'll simply be retracing to Camber. As it's fiddly, I describe the retrace here.

Your retrace proceeds as follows. Having got to the far (south) side of the Wainway Wall embankment you bear left to follow it, then at TQ971197 – 500m from TQ966198 – you strike out gently along the smooth grass. Go forward along the rougher grass, passing Chittenden's Cottage and the gate, rising up the slipway, bearing right and then shortly left. Cross over the bridge and go on past the sheepfold to reach the bridleway junction by the caravan park; turn right alongside the caravans then bear sharp left along the path back into Camber and your finish point at TQ967188. There are plenty of amenities in Camber including buses back to Rye, Camber being a visitor hotspot with its large holiday camp complexes. So don't expect to have the place or the bus to yourself. Note that there's another, far more formidable, bridleway circuit you can do based in Camber but it's not for the faint-hearted. In fact it's earned a place in the Room 101 of this book.

Part 4 – Downland bridleways

There is so much more to Sussex downland than the South Downs Way, and while the South Downs Way is the classic downland traverse of Sussex, there are many other magnificent downland bridleway routes, offering stunning views and gloriously remote countryside. Welcome to the best of these routes!

ROUTE 46

SU769135-SU777197 – Location Map W4 – OS OL8 – S

9km 925m

Robin Wood, Ladyholt Park, Eckensfield, West Harting Down, South Harting

PT West Marden (B start), South Harting (B finish)

R West Marden, South Harting

This is a very rural route with a wonderfully peaceful and remote feel. It is a linear route but the start and finish points of the route are close to bus stops on the same (Petersfield-Chichester) bus route.

To reach the start of this route from the B2146 at West Marden, served as stated by buses from Chichester and Petersfield, head westwards from the B2146 up the village street (the road for Forestside), then in 375m when the road bends sharply left, you arrive at a bridleway going straight on. This is the start of the route, SU769135. Follow the bridleway which almost immediately bends very sharply left and describes a semi-circle round a driveway, before heading left again and proceeding to a bridleway junction at SU766135. Turn right and follow a clear bridleway track in a generally north-westerly direction. Having passed West Marden Hall, a late 19th century building in Italianate-early Georgian style, you pass the buildings of Horsley

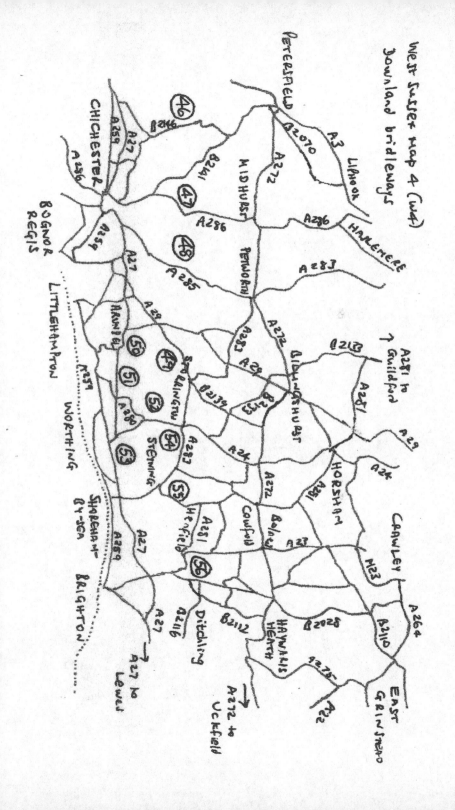

East Sussex Map 4 (E4)
Downland bridleways

Farm (500m from the start), and continue north-westwards beyond the farm through open countryside.

At SU757142, roughly 1km from Horsley Farm, you reach a path fork at the edge of the woods; ignore the footpath forking left but take the right-forking bridleway, reaching another fork in some 100m. This time you fork left and proceed just east of north downhill along a bridleway through the very pretty **Robin Wood**, emerging and veering just west of north to arrive, 500m or so from the second fork described above, at a road linking Finchdean with the B2146 (SU758147). Cross more or less straight over. Beyond the road crossing there's initially a steady climb north-westwards on a clear bridleway track, bringing you (in 750m beyond the road) to the crossing of Cowdown Lane; you then continue predominantly north-westwards along an obvious track for 500m, arriving on a plateau some 140m above sea level. You then, at SU755160, veer north-eastwards, here passing just to the east of a trig point. You're now in **Ladyholt Park**, a lovely unspoilt area with extensive views, but don't waste your time trying to pinpoint the original buildings of Ladyholt Park as these were demolished back in 1770. Landmarks to watch out for from here instead include the buildings of Ditcham Park School to the north-west and Upark to the north-east.

In 375m beyond the turn north-eastwards your path kinks left and right, continuing north-eastwards for another 375m to reach a bridleway T-junction at SU758166. Turn right along the track and in 250m at SU761165 reach **Eckensfield**, a splendid recently extended flint and brick house dated 1710 but in fact a refronting of two 16th century timber-framed cottages. At the path junction here, turn left and head north-eastwards into woods, following a lovely woodland bridle track. You veer eastwards to arrive at a crossroads of paths at SU771171, roughly 1km 250m from Eckensfield; turn left here and follow the bridleway northwards then in 375m at the bridleway junction at SU770175 fork left, north-westwards. Now follow a clear bridleway track through the extensive and beautiful woodland of **West Harting Down**.

This is woodland bridleway going at its best, with a good firm path and clear signage. In 500m or so you cross the Sussex Border Path at SU768180, then beyond the crossing you continue north-westwards; having proceeded for 1km 500m beyond the Sussex Border Path crossing you emerge from the woods, descending and veering right to arrive, 200m beyond the woods, at a T-junction with the South Downs Way at SU762193. Now turn right to follow the South Downs Way, which is here designated a restricted byway, just south of east for exactly 1km, looking down to Old Ditcham Wood to the left.

At SU772191 you reach a crossroads of tracks. Here you leave the South Downs Way, turning left and descending along a bridleway which is part of the Sussex Border Path, initially north-eastwards but veering northwards. Please see route 4 for a little more information about the Sussex Border Path; it isn't the most scenic path in Sussex but does enjoy some delightful stretches, the stretch on this route being one of them. At SU777197, 750m after leaving the South Downs Way, you reach the B2146 again. This is the end of the route, but by turning right alongside the B2146 and following it for some 875m – there's a good wide verge – you reach **South Harting**. This is a very pretty village with thatched, brick and timber-framed cottages and the splendid church of St Mary & St Gabriel, containing nave walls which could be pre-Norman, a fine 16th century chancel, an impressive tower linked to the church by a splendid wooden spiral staircase completed in 1852, and part of a 13th century effigy in the chancel. Among the most attractive secular buildings in the village are the thatched early 17th century Beacon Cottage and Downsend, situated to the south of the church, the 15th century timber-framed Fowler's Bucke to the north of the church, and the 17th century White Hart Inn. Buses are available from the village centre to Petersfield and Chichester.

ROUTE 47

SU858143-SU877136 – Location Map W4 – OS OL8 – S

12km 275m

West Dean Gardens, West Dean Woods, Bepton Down, Stead Combe, Cocking Station, Cocking, Levin Down, Singleton

PT West Dean (B start), Singleton (B finish)

R West Dean, Cocking, Singleton

This route combines glorious downland scenery and some pleasant woodland too – plus a bit of railway history! It's another linear route but both the start and finish points are close to bus stops on the same (Chichester-Midhurst) route and in any case you can create a circle if you don't mind a bit of roadside travelling.

If you're relying on public transport, leave the bus (as stated, the Chichester-Midhurst service) at **West Dean Gardens**, themselves well worth a visit before you set off; they boast a rich variety of plants including hydrangea, clematis and climbing roses, as well as an arboretum and lily pond. From the main entrance to the gardens off the A286, proceed westwards (ie in the Chichester direction) for 250m beside the A286, turning right at SU864129 onto a road which takes you 1km 500m north-westwards to reach the start of the route at Colworth Farm, at SU858143. From Colworth Farm follow the bridleway, effectively a continuation of the road, north-westwards, veering northwards at Colworth Barn and reaching a bridleway T-junction at SU853151, 1km from the start.

Turn right, north-eastwards, proceeding through the heart of the lovely **West Dean Woods** and arriving, in 1km from the T-junction, at SU860158 where there's a junction of bridleways. Here turn left (not hard left) as bridleway-signed, then in 75m or so, fork left and head just west of north along another woodland bridleway for 750m to a T-junction of bridleways at the edge of the woods, at SU858166. Turn left here, then in 125m you reach a bridleway fork. Fork right here, in 75m reaching a junction of tracks. Here bear right again, northwards, along a bridleway to arrive in 350m at a crossroads junction with the South Downs Way, at SU855170.

Cross straight over, northwards, along a restricted byway onto **Bepton Down**, with quite fantastic views ahead; having headed northwards for 625m you veer round to the right, heading eastwards with the fine woodlands of Stead Combe to your right. **Stead Combe** is a hugely impressive natural feature, not dissimilar to Devil's Dyke with its steep sides tumbling down to a narrow central dry valley. Ignore a bridleway heading off left at SU863174 but continue to follow the restricted byway along Henley Lane, veering just south of east, to reach a T-junction of tracks at SU872172, 1km 875m from the South Downs Way crossing. Turn left here, and follow what is a restricted byway north-eastwards for some 625m, veering northwards and passing the fine old **Cocking Station**, one of three splendid old stations built on the Chichester-Midhurst railway line (the others being at Singleton and Lavant), the station buildings boasting extravagant ornamentation and floral patterns in the plasterwork. The railway line, incidentally, opened in July 1881 and closed to passengers in 1935; however, freight services along the full length of the line continued until 1953, and the southern section remained open for non-passenger traffic until as comparatively recently as 1991. Following closure of the line, the southern section was converted into the Centurion Way footpath/cycle route although sadly it can't be called a bridleway as it's not open to horse-riders; if it were, it would definitely feature in this book. Let's hope firstly that the Centurion Way will one day continue all the way along the old line as far as Midhurst, and secondly that the duly extended route will acquire bridleway status.

Immediately beyond the old station building you reach a road, Bell Lane. Turn right along Bell Lane to arrive in the pretty village of **Cocking** at the A286 in 450m at SU878176. Cross straight over but, having crossed, don't go straight on along Mill Lane; rather bear right immediately, heading south-eastwards along a lane away from the A286. You descend past the church of St Catherine Of Siena, a very pretty pebble-dashed church with an 11th century chancel arch, remnants of 13th century wall paintings and a 12th century font. Just beyond the church, the lane bends sharply left (eastwards) but you go straight on, southwards, along a restricted byway that rises to meet the South Downs Way at SU878166, 1km from the centre of Cocking.

Turn left to follow the South Downs Way for 1km 500m: this part of the route is a bit of a slog, though the views improve with each step. Then at SU894165, at a bridleway crossing, turn right onto the signed New Lipchis Way (see route 5). Follow this south-westwards for 500m then southwards for 1km through the woods. You emerge from the woods and go forward for another 450m to a bridleway junction at SU889145. Here turn half-right, (not hard right) and, staying with the New Lipchis Way, follow it south-westwards over the shoulder of Levin Down. **Levin Down** is a chalk hillside covered in natural scrubby grassland, its name thought to be derived from "Leave-alone hill," it being too steep for the plough or intense agriculture. It's a Site of Special Scientific Interest, with a wealth of plant life that includes lady's bedstraw, pyramidal orchid, round-headed rampion and marjoram, and birds you might find here include the yellowhammer, buzzard, garden warbler and kestrel. Despite its treasures, it's certainly not one of the tourist honeypots – and one might say, it is all the better for it! It is certainly a grand climax to this bridleway journey.

Your bridleway descends off Levin Down, veering westwards and dropping down through trees to reach the A286 where the bridleway route ends at SU877136, 1km 500m from SU889145. By turning left alongside the A286 and descending, you arrive in 375m in **Singleton**. It boasts a lovely green, flint cottages, part-Saxon church of St John the Baptist with 11th century tower, and, just south-west of the village centre, the superb Weald & Downland Open Air Museum with its collection of reconstructed buildings from centuries ago and displays of traditional country crafts and industries. Buses are available from Singleton on the Midhurst-Chichester service. Or to return to West Dean Gardens you can simply follow the A286 on towards Chichester from Singleton for just over 1km.

ROUTE 48

SU924128–SU942138 – Location Map W4 – OS OL10 – M

5km 700m

Oxen Down, Crown Tegleaze, Upwaltham

PT Upwaltham (B start and finish – PB)

R none

Although this is a great route for woodland fans, it is downland that makes this journey special, and in particular your conquest of the summit of the South Downs in West Sussex. It is a linear route but you can effectively create a circular by starting at Upwaltham, served by prebooked buses between Chichester and Petworth. You need a fine, clear day for this route: rain, mist, fog and/or haze will really spoil it.

To reach the start of this route, immediately adjacent to the Droke car park, follow the A285 south-westwards from Upwaltham, described below, for 375m, then fork right along a pleasant country road signed for East Dean. The Droke car park is reached in roughly 1km 750m along this road on the left; continue further on the road for just 50m or so and you'll reach a bridleway going off to your right at SU924128. This is where your route starts.

Head just east of north as signed along this bridleway, initially in the valley then ascending quite steeply into pretty woodland on **Oxen Down**; in less than 2km you'll be climbing from 92m to 204m. The bridleway continues most pleasantly through the woods of Oxen Down, just east of north. At SU927140, 1km 250m from the start, there's a signed but easily-missed left fork; having taken this left fork you reach, in 150m, a T-junction, here bearing left and now heading just west of north for 375m to a 5-way junction of tracks at SU926146. Again it would be easy to go wrong here! Take the signed bridleway going off 90 degrees to the right, initially heading fractionally north of east then veering in a more north-easterly direction, your path evolving into a restricted byway and reaching, in some 2km from the 5-way junction, a crossroads of tracks and with it a junction with the South Downs Way at SU943155. From here, you can enjoy magnificent views to the north and west.

Now retrace for no more than 100m to SU942155 where there's a bridleway junction. Turn left to follow the bridleway southwards through the woods, emerging in 500m at **Crown Tegleaze**, the summit of the South Downs in West Sussex at 253m, and actually loftier here than the nearby South Downs Way. (Trivia note: although the summit of the South Downs in East Sussex – Ditchling Beacon – is also the highest point in East Sussex, Crown Tegleaze is NOT the highest point in West Sussex. That honour goes to Black Down which we visited in route 17.) As you emerge from the wood, follow the bridleway round to the right, south-westwards, sticking to the woodland edge. You should pause here for two reasons. Firstly there is here a very moving memorial to the crew of a Lancaster bomber of the Dambuster Squadron which crashed here on 13th February 1944 having just refuelled at Tangmere; the entire crew lost their lives. There is also here an absolutely stunning view, the Isle of Wight clearly visible on a good day. That's why you need to pick a clear day for this journey! I was up here during the lockdown in May 2020 in glorious clear sunshine and it was perhaps my favourite memory of that extraordinary period in our history.

Continue briefly on from here in the same direction until at SU939148, 250m after emerging from the woods, you turn sharp left with the bridleway and now head just east of south along an excellent track over North Down. The views from here are again fantastic, stretching eastwards along the South Downs to Chanctonbury Ring and beyond. Your path descends steadily, never too steeply, and in 1km from SU939148 you reach a bridleway junction at SU943139, just level with **Upwaltham** Church. Turn right here along a bridleway that in 75m brings you down past the church to the end of the route just above the A285 at SU942138; turn left along a track for another 125m to the A285 itself, served here by buses to Chichester and Petworth. The delightful 12th century flint-built church of St Mary the Virgin **is** described in the *Pevsner Architectural Guide* as "simple and lovable;" its finest features are arguably its broad 12th century chancel arch and ornate 12th century piscina. Don't miss also the west window of 2002 with its depiction of local birds and flora, while just west of the church you should look out for another fine building, the part-17th century timber-framed Church Farm.

ROUTE 49

TQ034125 (start and finish) – Location Map W4 – OS OL10 – S

10km 200m

Rackham Banks, Wepham Down, The Burgh, Amberley, Amberley Museum

PT Amberley (* start and finish)

R Amberley

Please note that this is one of the tougher routes in this book – albeit an exceedingly good one – and you need to be prepared for some stiff climbing. A dry clear day is essential!

To reach the start of the circular route from Amberley Station, turn left out of the station exit down the slip road then bear right, beside the B2139 for 375m, turning right up High Titten, now on the course of the South Downs Way. Follow High Titten uphill for 625m to reach Mill Lane coming in from the left; continue beyond this junction for another 125m to TQ034125 where a South Downs Way-signed bridleway goes off to the left in the shade of trees. This is the start of your route. Turn left to follow the South Downs Way eastwards as signed, climbing very steeply initially, although the gradient then eases as you emerge from the trees. In 450m or so from TQ034125 you reach a path junction at TQ038125. Here turn right, away from the South Downs Way, but in some 125m you reach a path fork. Take the path going left and now veer left to enjoy a simply stunning high level journey along a restricted byway in a predominantly easterly direction over what is marked on maps as **Rackham Banks,** along the south edge of the ridge, with the hugely impressive dry valley, a kind of miniature Devil's Dyke, immediately below you to the right. Note that the course of the path along the ridge to this point is NOT as marked on some OS Explorer maps – it has clearly been re-routed further south than as indicated by the maps.

You reach an area of woodland and keep to the path, going to the right of the trees, heading south-eastwards; continuing beyond the woods you arrive at a 4-way junction of tracks at TQ055122, about 1km 750m from TQ038125. Turn left at TQ055122 and follow what is a restricted byway for 500m to arrive at the South Downs Way. Here turn right along the South Downs Way to reach, in 1km, the Springhead Hill car park. Just beyond the car park at TQ071125 a bridleway forks off to the right, south-eastwards, and you leave the South Downs Way to follow this one; DON'T be tempted to take the one just before this going hard right, south-westwards. The bridleway you want heads south-eastwards across fields for some 425m to reach a bridleway crossroads at a thicket, at TQ073121. Turn right, south-westwards, through the thicket and then steadily downhill in a straight line. Your bridleway here is not always well defined, although there is some reassuring signposting. It does however provide magnificent views towards Arundel and the coast, as well as the line of hills – Barpham, Harrow and Blackpatch – separating you from the coastal strip. At TQ062111, 1km 500m from TQ073121, you reach a bridleway T-junction, now on the lovely **Wepham Down**. There is a great feeling of remoteness and space just here. Turn left, just east of south, onto a bridleway which in 125m bends sharp right, just south of west, to pass the edge of the trees and, 100m from the sharp right bend, to reach another bridleway T-junction at TQ061109. (Some OS maps show a bridleway going off south-westwards from this point. This no longer exists.) Turn left, again just east of south, and follow the bridleway for some 250m, arriving at a gate and a bridleway junction at TQ061106. Take the bridleway signed as going hard right from here, and follow what is an excellent track, heading just north of west; it is very undulating and there are good views southwards from the tops of the hills. Listen out for the linnet, look out for the whinchat, a migrant bird from Africa, and look too for plants which include common toadflax, field pansy and scarlet pimpernel.

In roughly 1km 500m from TQ061106, at TQ046111, you reach a T-junction of bridleways. Turn right, north-eastwards, reaching a further track junction in 275m at TQ048113; here you turn left, just north of west, for 375m along a restricted byway across a charming area known as **The Burgh,** to a path junction at TQ044114. Turn right here along a signed bridleway which descends dramatically north-westwards to a dewpond in a dry valley. This whole area, in which there is evidence of Bronze Age and Roman habitation, offers sightings of many types of plant, including wild clematis, hawthorn, dog rose and gorse, while around the dewpond you may see frog orchid, autumn lady's-tresses, carline thistle, felwort, small scabious and harebell.

As you reach the valley bottom you turn sharp right across it, being reassured by a bridleway signpost at the far side and bearing left, uphill. This is a magnificent stuff, with a very dramatic dry valley to your right, not named on even the larger scale OS maps. You now ascend steadily north-westwards, the views to the left (west) absolutely superb; keeping the fence to your left, you continue uphill, still north-westwards, and go forward to reach the junction with the South Downs Way at TQ038125, here roughly 1km 375m from TQ044114. You've come full circle. Turn left to retrace some 450m westwards down the South Downs Way to the top of High Titten, where the route ends, as it started, at TQ034125.

You may wish, instead of going straight on down High Titten for the station, to bear right down Mill Lane, crossing the B2139 and continuing on into the beautiful village of **Amberley**, 750m from the end of route. It boasts a splendid castle (now a hotel) dating from the late 14th century and built on the site of a manor house, and the part-Norman church of St Michael & All Angels, its highlights being its vast nave windows and late 13th/early 14th century wall paintings. In the village there are a number of historic houses of brick, timber and thatch, and at the time of writing there's also a shop and (separate) tearoom. It's then possible for you to follow beside the B2139 for roughly 1km 250m back to Amberley Station. Immediately adjoining the station is the fascinating **Amberley Museum** devoted to crafts and industries of yesteryear such as those of blacksmith, wood turner, claypipe maker, wheelwright and potter. There are also stationary engines, old buses and a working narrow-gauge railway. Those amongst you who are of a certain age will definitely feel it when you see items that were business as usual when you were younger!

ROUTE 50

TQ041069–TQ035075 – Location Map W4 – OS OL10 – M

12 km 125m (longer route), 9km 575m (shorter route)

Barpham Hill, Tenantry Copse, Wepham Wood, Burpham, Warningcamp Hill

PT Arundel (* start and finish)

R Arundel

This is a fine journey to a great viewpoint. It is a linear route but you can create a circular journey by starting and finishing at Arundel's railway station.

To reach the start of this route from Arundel Station, follow the A27 south-eastwards uphill from the station for some 500m to reach a sharp right bend at the top of the rise, turning left here into Crossbush Lane. Go along the lane for 625m then turn left up Clay Lane which you follow for 1km until you reach a bridleway forking left off the lane at TQ041069. This is the start of the route. Head just east of north along this bridleway, climbing steadily but then descending into a lovely dry valley where, 625m from the start of the route, you join a bridleway section of the Monarch's Way which has come in from the left.

Follow the Monarch's Way (see route 6) just north of east for 750m as far as a 4-way bridleway junction at TQ048077; here, DON'T turn right with the Monarch's Way but continue effectively in the same (north-easterly) direction on a bridleway along the valley bottom. Another path joins you from the right at TQ052079 and you now begin to climb, your bridleway parallel with a horse gallop. This is a steady and most enjoyable ascent, north-eastwards, veering northwards, the views getting better all the time. At TQ061101, roughly 3km after leaving the Monarch's Way, you reach a signed path junction, a footpath going left and bridleways being signed straight on and right. Take the bridleway going right, east, here, and in 125m at TQ062012, turn right again along a signed bridleway ascending south-eastwards onto **Barpham Hill**. Initially the course of the bridleway is a little ambiguous but aim for the thicket ahead and you won't go wrong. This is quite superb going with tremendous views. There was actually a Barpham village close by, but it was wiped out by plague in the 15th century and virtually no traces remain.

You pass through the thicket and onto the hilltop, going just to the east of the trig point (though I recommend you detour the short distance to the trig point for the finest views), and arrive at a bridleway junction at TQ067092, roughly 1km 125m from TQ062012. Turn hard right, westwards, here along the bridleway. This again is superbly enjoyable going, with fabulous views particularly to the South Downs west of the Arun valley. In 250m from TQ067092, at TQ065093, your bridleway turns sharp left and now heads south-westwards downhill into **Tenantry Copse**, going on imperceptibly into **Wepham Wood**. A good deal of this beautiful woodland consists of oak, sycamore and Scots pine, but there are areas of spruce and beech also. Bluebells abound here in spring, and you'll also enjoy primrose, lesser celandine and wood anemone. Listen out for the chiffchaff and willow warbler, and watch for fallow deer and also adders. At the end of this bridleway you go forward to arrive at a multi-track junction at TQ051077, 2km from the left bend at TQ065093. Here, take the track heading right, north-westwards, with the Monarch's Way, and drop steeply along the bridleway to the valley floor. You arrive at the point where you previously left the Monarch's Way at the 4-way bridleway junction at TQ048077, 250m from TQ051077.

Now you've a choice. The shorter, more direct route follows the Monarch's Way just south of west from TQ048077 along the valley floor, in 700m reaching a bridleway junction at TQ042076. However there is the (highly recommended) option of a route variation here, incorporating Wepham, Burpham and Warningcamp Hill. To do this, take the bridleway heading effectively straight on, northwards, from TQ048077, veering north-westwards to arrive at the road at Wepham in 750m at TQ044084. By turning right and following the road northwards for 750m or so you reach the village of **Burpham**. This is a lovely quiet village, benefiting from being at the end of a no-through road, and boasts a number of attractive flint and brick cottages. Architecturally Burpham's highlight is its church of St Mary, built chiefly between 1160 and 1220 almost entirely of local flint, though Roman tiles appear in its fabric; arguably the most notable aspect of the interior is the elaborately carved pillars. The village also boasts a very popular pub, the 18th century George & Dragon. Having enjoyed Burpham, retrace to where you joined the road at Wepham but this time carry on for 250m past TQ044084 to TQ043083. Here turn left along a bridleway which climbs pleasantly through woodland known as the Conyers up onto the most picturesque **Warningcamp Hill**. You then descend southwards to TQ042076, 750m from TQ043083, to pick up the Monarch's Way and be reunited with the shorter route.

Now, whichever route you've chosen to this point, simply continue in a generally westerly direction along the Monarch's Way, soon reaching and proceeding through a really delightful and refreshing area of woodland on a lovely bridleway path. It makes a beautiful contrast with the stark hillsides you were following earlier; I walked this route on a scorching June day and the relief of the shade of the trees was immense! At TQ035075, some 750m from the point at which the longer route joins the Monarch's Way, you reach the Arundel-Warningcamp-Burpham road, where this route ends. To return to Arundel Station, turn left and follow this road for 1km 500m; at the end cross the A27 and turn right to follow beside it for 125m to the station entrance. Incidentally, Arundel's town centre is reached by carrying on alongside the A27 to the roundabout and then going straight on along the Causeway and Queen Street, a total of 750m from the station. There'll certainly be no shortage of eateries waiting to welcome you, offering you everything from cream teas to jumbo burgers. A fuller description of the delights of Arundel is given in route 20.

ROUTE 51

TQ071060-TQ084134 – Location Map W4 – OS OL10 – S

12km 875m

Michelgrove Park, Patching, Harrow Hill, Chantry Post, Kithurst Hill

PT Angmering (B start), Storrington (B finish)

R Angmering, Storrington

This is a great route through quite remote countryside, building to a tremendous climax. It is a linear route but you can use Worthing as a base, travelling from there by bus to Angmering and returning to Worthing by bus from Storrington. Or you could use the Arun Valley railway as a base, getting a bus from Arundel (served by rail on that line) to Angmering and a bus from Storrington to Pulborough (also served by rail on that line) at the end. The agony of choice!

To reach the start from the centre of Angmering, a distance of 1km 750m, head north-eastwards from Angmering's village square up Water Lane then, in 500m or so, turn left up Dapper's Lane. You follow it northwards for 1km to pass under the A27 and go straight on up Swillage Lane for 250m to reach the start of the route, where the lane becomes a bridleway. Starting here at TQ071060 at a delightful pond, your bridleway ascends gently northwards, passing the very attractive Norfolk House and keeping woodland to the left. At the bridleway T-junction after 750m at TQ072067 turn right, immediately veering left and, ignoring a bridleway shortly going right, proceed north-eastwards on a lovely bridleway through stunning woodland, notable for its ivy-clad trees. Ignoring a number of paths going off to the right, you veer just west of north along the west end of the woods with fields beyond, then veer right to arrive at a signed bridleway junction, meeting the Monarch's Way (see route 6) at TQ075082, roughly 1km 625m from TQ072067. Turn

211

right, south-eastwards, along the signed Monarch's Way through the trees of lovely **Michelgrove Park,** arriving in 750m at a bridleway junction at TQ082077.

Your continuous route turns left, north, here with the Monarch's Way but there is the option of a detour here to the pretty village of Patching, 1km 500m from here, incorporating a really good viewpoint. To do this detour, go straight on from TQ082077 south-eastwards, following the clear bridleway to the end of the wood, emerging and enjoying a superb green track along a ridge with tremendous views to Longfurlong and Chanctonbury to the left. The bridleway actually subdivides here; keep to the left path for the best views. The two subdividing paths reunite and you continue straight across a bridleway crossroads downhill to meet a metalled road coming from the half-right, just over 1km 125m from the start of the detour. Go forward along this metalled road for 375m to the village of **Patching** with its fine 13th century church of St John the Divine, boasting a particularly impressive tower, 15th century font, and a pulpit with panels of birds and foliage. Now retrace the same way to TQ082077.

Whether you've detoured or not, head north from TQ082077 as stated on a bridleway along the Monarch's Way, descending and emerging from the woods to reach, in 425m or so, a lane onto which you turn left, northwards. To your left, as you proceed up the lane, are the buildings of Michelgrove. This is the site of one of the most renowned Sussex courtyard houses, built for Sir William Shelley in 1534 but demolished in 1828, and only a few walls remain although Michelgrove Cottages were converted from stables that were part of the complex. After some 250m from your joining the lane, the Monarch's Way goes off to the right. You continue northwards along a bridleway for 750m to a sharp bend in the lane at TQ082093. Take care here NOT to continue on the lane, instead joining a signed bridleway heading half-right from the lane (ignoring also the signed footpath going right), and proceeding just north of west round the base of the shapely and imposing

Harrow Hill. The neighbourhood of Harrow Hill was one of the sites occupied by Iron Age Celts; these invaders came from mainland Europe around 500 BC, bringing iron, then a new material, with them, and building huge ramparts on hilltops. You cross first a grassy field then a much muddier one, going forward onto a clearer track and now veering northwards, dropping steeply downhill and following what is a field path along the valley bottom. You'll notice the lane coming in from the left to meet your bridleway 1km 250m from TQ082093, just east of the buildings of Lee Farm.

At this point, TQ078103, you bear right as signed onto a bridleway track which very shortly veers left and heads north-eastwards, veering just east of north, ascending steadily. The views are sensational, extending all the way to the sea, from Cissbury Ring to Bignor Hill and beyond. In around 1km 875m from TQ078103 you arrive at the **Chantry Post** car park on the South Downs Way. Turn left along the South Downs Way (here a restricted byway) for 625m, a very fine 625m with great views to the south, then at TQ081122 turn right, just east of north, away from the South Downs Way along a bridleway which provides even more magnificent views – a breathtaking climax to your journey, making all that climbing worthwhile!

You drop just a little to a bridleway T-junction after 250m at TQ082125; the **Kithurst Hill** trig point is immediately to the left just here. However your route bears right, south-eastwards, in 250m reaching a bridleway junction at TQ084124 at Chantry Hill. Pause here to enjoy the great view, then turn left along what is a spectacular bridleway with tremendous views to the north. Initially you head north-eastwards then veer north-westwards, descending very steeply and entering woodland, veering sharp right and dropping down to a bridleway T-junction at Grey Friars Farm at TQ083131, 750m from TQ084124. Turn right here. The bridleway and indeed your route ends in 325m at TQ084134 but by simply carrying on along Greyfriars Lane you reach the centre of Storrington in 800m. Storrington isn't the most picturesque place in West Sussex but it has plenty of refreshment opportunities and boasts a church (dedicated to St Mary the Virgin), the spire of which was destroyed by lightning in 1731; the church has monuments to two soldiers who fought at the Battle of Waterloo, Sir Henry Bradford and Major Hugh Falconer. Buses are available from Storrington to Pulborough and also Worthing.

ROUTE 52

TQ118090–TQ121082 – Location Map W4 – OS OL10 – S

14km 235m

Highden Beeches, Sullington Hill, Sullington, Blackpatch Hill, Findon

PT Findon (B start and finish)

R Findon

This is a superb route in glorious open countryside which can be treated as a circular route if you choose to begin and end in Findon.

To reach the start of this route from the centre of Findon, well served by buses from Worthing, proceed for 250m or so north-westwards up School Hill to the roundabout junction of the A280 with the A24, and having crossed the A24 with care, bear westwards briefly along the north side of the A280. In just 75m at TQ118090, the start of the route, bear right, north-westwards, up a bridleway that ascends, keeping just to the left edge of woodland. In 1km, at TQ109096, leave this bridleway by turning left onto a link bridleway of some 60m – it must be one of the shortest bridleways in the country! It takes you to a restricted byway onto which you turn right; you continue to steadily gain height, passing just to the left of thick woodland around Muntham Farm. The path is unerring and there is a choice between a rutted track and a smoother grassy track parallel and to the right. A number of bridleways are signed to the right but you ignore these.

Continuing to gain height, you now veer in a more decisively north-westerly direction, along the edge of **Highden Beeches**. The views are fantastic, particularly the way you've come and also to your left, where in the foreground is the mass of Blackpatch Hill and further west you can see the South Downs escarpment including the masts of Glatting Beacon. The going is lovely, open and airy. Some 2km 625m from where you joined the restricted byway, you reach the South Downs Way at TQ095117, and as you do so the view opens out impressively to the north; looking down you can see the lovely church at Sullington.

The continuous route turns left, north-westwards, to follow the South Downs Way from here, but there is the option of a bridleway detour to explore Sullington, and I thoroughly recommend it. To make this detour you join, just east of TQ095117, a bridleway heading a little west of north away from the South Downs Way. To your left is the impressive **Sullington Hill**; there are superb views to the mini-Devil's Dyke to the right as well as northwards to the Weald. Ignore the left-hand fork in 175m but now veer just east of north and drop down steeply, going forward along a track heading due north, to arrive at **Sullington** with its lovely flint church of St Mary, roughly 1km 375m from the South Downs Way. The church has Anglo-Saxon origins; it contains a Norman chancel, a Norman north window, and 13th century tower, and it also boasts what is thought to be the oldest stone monument in Sussex, dating from the 13th century, of a knight in chainmail. There's a lovely view to Chanctonbury Ring from the lychgate. Close by is Sullington Manor Farm, which has its origins in the 13th century; its enormous timbered wheat barn, largely of the 17th century, is described in the *Pevsner Architectural Guide* as having one of the best interiors in Sussex. Now simply return exactly the same way to TQ095177.

Whether you've detoured or not, head north-westwards as stated from here along the South Downs Way, here a restricted byway, for just 250m, enjoying tremendous views to Chanctonbury Ring, Cissbury Ring and the line of hills to the south – Blackpatch Hill, Harrow Hill and Barpham Hill. You then, at TQ093118, turn left, away from the South Downs Way, along a dead straight bridleway heading just east of south for 800m as far as TQ093109 where there's a very sharp right turn. From this right turn you proceed, again in a dead straight line, this time just south of west, for 300m to a bridleway junction at TQ090109. Here turn left. Ignore a right fork in 125m, but continue along a clear bridleway heading south-eastwards, rising and following the shoulder of **Blackpatch Hill**; the views from here are superb. The trig point marking the summit is just a little to the left of your route, not on Access Land, so I couldn't advise you to access it without permission. Standard disclaimer alert: your call and your risk! But if you go for it, you'll enjoy a superb 360-degree view, which incorporates a long coastal strip to the south and Chanctonbury Ring to the north-east. The hill is the site of a Neolithic flint mine and Bronze Age burial place.

Coming off the hill, you veer in a southerly direction and then in fact veer just west of south, descending to Longfurlong Farm, 2km 375m from TQ090109. There's actually a short break in the bridleway by the farm here, at TQ094085, but you continue along the lane downhill for 250m to meet the Monarch's Way (see route 6) at a path crossroads at TQ093082. Turn left here along the Monarch's Way, following the bridleway eastwards, looking up ahead to the very steep-sided valley of Longfurlong and the cars labouring up the valley along the A280. You veer north-eastwards with the bridleway/Monarch's Way and ascend towards this road; note that some OS maps show a bridleway forking right at TQ109087 but this no longer exists and the bridleway has effectively been re-routed along the Monarch's Way which at the top of the rise reaches a T-junction with a restricted byway. Turn right here to arrive, in just a few metres, at the A280 at TQ110088, 2km after joining the Monarch's Way.

Leaving the Monarch's Way here, cross the A280 and join a restricted byway heading southwards from the road, uphill and now looking DOWN on that labouring traffic, for 625m to reach a left-hand bridleway turn at TQ111082. Here turn left with the bridleway and follow it downhill, south-eastwards but veering eastwards to reach, in 1km from TQ111082, a bridleway junction at TQ120080. Here turn left, north-eastwards, along the bridleway, Roger's Lane, to arrive in 200m at the A24, at TQ121082. The route ends here. To return to the centre of Findon, served as stated by buses to Worthing, cross the A24 carefully, and continue up High Street on the far side, reaching the village centre in some 625m. **Findon** is a very pretty village although its finest features, the 18th century Findon Place and flint church with 13th century oak screen and medieval oak pews, are to the west of the village, across the busy A24.

ROUTE 53

TQ144055-TQ125091 – Location Map W4 – OS OL10 – S

10km 525m

Cissbury Ring, Tenants Hill, Pump Bottom, Worthing

PT Worthing (*, B start), Findon (B finish)

R Worthing, Findon

This provides exhilarating exploration of the area around, and including, one of the great hilltops in Sussex. It's a linear route but you can use the Broadwater district of Worthing as a base, with buses available back to Broadwater from Findon.

To access the start of this route at Fifth Avenue in Broadwater, well served by buses from Worthing's town centre (its attractions briefly summed up at the end of this route description) and station, follow First Avenue northwards from the A27 (the junction of these two roads is at TQ145050) , reaching the Fifth Avenue left turn after 500m. Turn left along Fifth Avenue to reach, in 100m, a bridleway heading off to the right, at TQ144055; this is the start of the route, and indeed here you turn right up the bridleway, beginning with a steady wooded ascent north-eastwards. You continue to ascend past a golf course with sensational views which get even better as you climb, with not only a large stretch of coastline but also the Isle of Wight on show. You now veer in a predominantly north-westward direction, and as you reach the top of the rise, the views also extend northwards to the Weald and eastwards to Truleigh Hill and Devil's Dyke.

At TQ144079, 2km 500m from the start, you reach a signed bridleway junction, with a bridleway going off to the left. Don't take this left turn but go straight on, then very shortly a path forks to your half-left, heading for a gate. By taking this path and proceeding through the gate you almost immediately reach the outer ring of **Cissbury Ring**; once here you can either climb onto the ring itself (though cycling is restricted) or head straight on to the trig point (a round trip of 250m from the continuous route and back). The 183m-high hilltop site was occupied prior to the Iron Age, but the fortifications were built by an Iron Age community around 300 BC. The views from the trig point are astonishing, both eastwards towards Brighton and beyond, and westwards across a massive stretch of coast, again as far as the Isle of Wight. Not for the first time, I need to stress you should save this one for a clear day – and be prepared to change your plans if what you believed would be a clear day...isn't. There needs to be word for the refusal to believe that the mist and fog which wasn't forecast is in fact real and prevents your being able to see anything more than your hand in front of your face.

Returning to the continuous route, in 200m beyond the TQ144079 left bridleway turn, at TQ143081, turn right, eastwards, along a bridleway through the trees, arriving in some 700m at a bridleway junction at TQ150080 (A). The continuous route turns hard left, north-westwards here, but it's worth bearing right and almost immediately right again up a bridleway for some 625m to enjoy, on emerging from the trees, a breathtaking view from **Tenants Hill**. Then return to (A) to continue. Head north-westwards from there, as stated, for some 750m to a junction with a track at TQ144084. Turn hard right here along what is a restricted byway and descend along it, heading eastwards and descending to reach, in 750m, a junction with a bridleway at TQ151083. This is a lovely spot with a dewpond and bench.

Turn left here and follow the signed bridleway northwards along the **Pump Bottom** dry valley, veering north-westwards then north-eastwards. This is a terrific path in really remote-feeling surroundings. You arrive, in 1km 500m from TQ151083, at TQ151097, a T-junction with the Monarch's Way (see route 6). Turn left but then immediately fork right, away from the Monarch's Way, up a signed restricted byway predominantly south-westwards, gaining and maintaining height. At TQ139095, roughly 1km 250m from your meeting with the Monarch's Way, you reach a crossroads path junction and go straight over along the restricted byway, enjoying excellent views to Cissbury Ring to your left. Ignoring a path forking right, follow the obvious track just south of west, to arrive at the top of Stable Lane, Findon, at TQ125091, the end of the route, 1km 375m from TQ139095. For buses from Findon to Worthing, follow Stable Lane south-westwards from here for some 375m to the village square. For a little more information about Findon, see route 52 above. **Worthing** itself is worth exploring, its highlights including its fine 1812 church of St Paul, the 1834 Grecian-style Town Hall, the 1910 Dome cinema, the 1933 neo-Georgian Town Hall, the fine Steyne Gardens with its grand Boer War memorial, and the Art Deco-style Connaught Theatre.

ROUTE 54

TQ120120-TQ169107 – Location Map W4 – OS OL10, OL11 – S

13km 50m (longer route), 11km 50m (shorter route)

Chanctonbury Hill/Dewpond, Buddington Bottom, No Man's Land, Steyning Round Hill, Steyning

PT Washington (B start), Steyning (B finish)

R Washington, Steyning

This is a classic downland route. It's a linear route but both Washington, where you start, and Steyning, where you finish, are on the same (Horsham-Burgess Hill) bus route. Some of the early part of this route overlaps with some of route 6. If it feels familiar, that may explain it!

Your route starts immediately east of the A24 on the South Downs Way above Washington, served by buses from Worthing, Horsham and Pulborough, at TQ120120 (reached from the centre of the village by following Washington Bostal uphill for roughly 1km). Follow the South Downs Way bridleway eastwards for 550m from the start point as far as TQ126121, taking the second of the two signed bridleways forking to the left around this point. This climbs very steeply indeed, just south of east, passing through a quarry, and superb views quickly open out both to the north and behind you to the west. Aim for a gate at the top of the quarry, now on **Chanctonbury Hill**, and continue in the same (just south of east) direction, passing just to the right of the **Chanctonbury Dewpond** and arriving back, at TQ134119, at the South Downs Way (875m after leaving it) onto which you turn left. Just north of the join, across the grass, is a trig point from which the best views can be enjoyed, but the view from the South Downs Way, as you now follow it briefly eastwards, is still pretty good; you can actually see as far as Brighton and beyond on a clear day.

You now head towards Chanctonbury Ring but 125m or so before you reach it, and some 400m after rejoining the South Downs Way, turn hard left, north-westwards, off it at TQ138120, aiming for a gate down the hillside. You may wish to detour to visit the trees of the Ring itself but will then need to backtrack – and in any case the Ring is visited in route 6. The continuous route goes off north-westwards at TQ138120 as stated, going down to a gate with a signed bridleway beyond. Now head north-westwards very steeply downhill along this bridleway through the trees, the views through the breaks in the trees absolutely superb. Veering left and then right, you drop to a T-junction of bridleways at TQ132124, 750m after leaving the South Downs Way. You turn right then in about 100m reach another bridleway junction and, bear right onto the bridleway heading eastwards.

You now follow this undulating path eastwards for 1km 250m through woodland or along the edges of woodland, past Owlscroft Barn to the south end of Chanctonbury Ring Road at TQ145124. Turn right here, your route now a dirt track. After 125m you bend right with the track and enter the trees, then, at a bridleway sign some 125m beyond the right bend, at TQ143121, go left up a wide dirt track/bridleway known as Wiston Bostal, ascending through the woods for 750m to reach the South Downs Way at TQ145113.

Cross straight over onto a restricted byway where you now have a choice. The direct, shorter route simply follows this byway just west of south for 1km 250m to the next path junction at TQ142101, beyond which you proceed in the same general direction. The longer but highly recommended route, adding 2km, turns right off the byway in just a few metres from TQ145113 along a bridleway heading south-westwards downhill, passing through **Buddington Bottom,** a gorgeous dry valley; the sense of tranquillity and remoteness is very special, and it feels so different from the lofty, airy surrounds of Chanctonbury Ring. You might very easily be in the Yorkshire Wolds, and if you've walked the Yorkshire Wolds Way you'll definitely be reminded of it here! Your clear bridleway continues through the valley along the right-hand edge of an area of woodland until at

TQ131101, 2km from TQ145114, you reach a track junction. Turn hard left with the bridleway and ascend steadily, heading just north of east but veering south-eastwards to reach the junction with the shorter restricted byway route at TQ142101, 1km 250m from TQ131101.

Whether you've taken the longer or shorter route you now proceed just west of south from TQ142101 along the restricted byway, enjoying quite stupendous views which extend as far as Glatting Beacon (Bignor Hill) to the west and beyond Brighton to the east. In 750m from TQ142101 you reach a path crossroads at TQ139095. Cross straight over and go forward south-westwards for 500m along a bridleway to a crossroads junction with the Monarch's Way at TQ138088. Here turn left to follow the Monarch's Way, here a bridleway, north-eastwards for 2km 625m, passing a delightful area of woodland known as **No Man's Land**, enjoying fine views to Chanctonbury Ring to your left and Cissbury Ring to your right. Beyond No Man's Land, your path becomes a restricted byway.

At TQ162100 you reach a 5-way junction of tracks. Leave the Monarch's Way here and take the bridleway heading half-left (not hard left along the South Downs Way), north-eastwards, in 250m reaching a bridleway junction and a very nicely-placed seat. You're now on **Steyning Round Hill**, a very fine hilltop indeed and a glorious climax to your journey. Turn right here and head north-eastwards with a bridleway that descends steeply to reach (in 750m from the junction with the seat) Newham Lane at TQ169107. This is the end of your route. Turn left along Newham Lane to drop down to reach the centre of **Steyning** in a further 750m.

Steyning is a great place to end your journey. It's well served by shops, pubs and cafes, and there are also plenty of buses, not only on the Horsham-Burgess Hill service but also to Shoreham and Brighton. The town also has many architectural highlights. These include the old Grammar School in Church Street, founded in 1614 but housed in a 15th century building, and further along the same street, the church of St Andrew. This boasts a late Norman nave with 12th century arcades and clerestories, decorated with magnificent carvings depicting the heads of humans and animals; the altar has 48 carved panels, one of which bears the coat of arms of Henry VIII. The town's lovely High Street is dominated by the tile-hung Old Market House and its very prominent clock tower and all along this street there are 14th and 15th century hall houses, and many examples of tile-hanging, timber-framing and weatherboarding. Off the High Street is one of the shortest bridleways in Sussex, as you will see in Part 7 of this section. Make sure you check it out before boarding your bus – I promise it won't take you long!

ROUTE 55

TQ199102-TQ238066 – Location Map W4 – OS OL11 – M

8km 500m

Windmill Hill, Room Bottom, Tottington Mount, Thundersbarrow Hill, Rest And Be Thankful Stone

PT Upper Beeding (B start), Southwick (B finish)

R Upper Beeding, Truleigh Hill, Southwick

This fine and easy-to-follow linear route starts and ends close to locations on the Rottingdean-Steyning bus service. From the Rising Sun at Upper Beeding – buses on this service stop right outside it – head south-eastwards along High Street, immediately reaching a mini-roundabout. Bear left alongside Henfield Road (A2037) and after 375m from the Rising Sun, bear left into Manor Road. Immediately to the right off Manor Road is a signed restricted byway (TQ199102) and the start of the restricted byway is also the start of the route. Follow this restricted byway, heading north-eastwards over **Windmill Hill;** there are fine views as you reach the modest summit. You descend to arrive at the A2037 at TQ207108, 1km from the start.

Cross straight over onto and along a signed bridleway, initially a driveway then a track heading south-eastwards uphill, in 500m reaching a bridleway junction at TQ211104. Turn left at TQ211104 and head north-eastwards, gaining height quickly then contouring the hillside, with fine views to Tottington Mount, this being the hillside ahead of you, and the most attractive dry valley of **Room Bottom** to your left. At TQ217107, 750m from TQ211104, there's a very sharp right-hand turn – don't miss this – and your bridleway now climbs extremely steeply southwards for 125m to a signed bridleway junction at TQ217106. This must be one of the most exposed and bracing bridleway junctions in Sussex – not a place to linger on a very cold or windy day!

The continuous route ploughs on uphill although I recommend that, at that exposed bridleway junction, you detour 375m left along what is a not-very-clear bridleway just east of north to the summit of **Tottington Mount**, with tremendous views down to Room Bottom. Simply retrace to TQ217106 to progress. As stated the continuous route carries on uphill from TQ217106, arriving in 250m at a T-junction with the South Downs Way at TQ219105. Turn left to follow the South Downs Way, passing Truleigh Hill Youth Hostel where refreshments may be available. In 375m you reach, at TQ223106, a bridleway heading right, just east of south, away from the South Downs Way.

Turn right to follow this fine ridgetop path unerringly on, firstly keeping Bushy Bottom to your left then heading south-eastwards over **Thundersbarrow Hill**, named, you will be astonished to learn, after Thunders Barrow. Thunders Barrow is an earthwork that was originally Bronze Age, the subsequent version being early Iron Age; east of Tthe fort was a Romano-British settlement incorporating corn-drying ovens, a well, and large banks known as Thunders' Steps. Sadly the site has been affected by damage caused through ploughing. At any rate the going hereabouts is superb, with wonderful views towards the sea. In roughly 1km 500m from leaving the South Downs Way you're joined by the Monarch's Way (see route 6). You drop slightly to enter an area of rough vegetation and pass the trig point on Southwick Hill, now looking ahead to the sprawling Brighton suburbs of Mile Oak and Portslade, and passing over Southwick Tunnel which carries the A27 under Southwick Hill.

In 3km 875m from TQ223106, at TQ241074, immediately overlooking Mile Oak, you reach a path junction. Signage isn't massively clear but you need to take the restricted byway going half-right, south-westwards, from this junction, leaving the Monarch's Way. (DON'T take the footpath going straight on south-eastwards.) Having now joined the restricted byway, continue south-westwards then veer southwards, passing the so-called **Rest And Be Thankful Stone**, a block of sarsen stone that was once part of Southwick Church and which now makes an excellent seat. Your route ends at TQ238066, at the south end of the restricted byway, 875m after your joining it. For the nearest bus connections, simply continue southwards along Upper Kingston Lane for 500m to the A270 Old Shoreham Road at Southwick where buses to Brighton and Shoreham are plentiful, rather more so than buses serving Upper Beeding!

ROUTE 56

TQ279156 (start and finish) – Location Map W4 – OS OL11 – M

7km 750m (longer route), 7km 125m (shorter route)

Hurstpierpoint, Wolstonbury Hill

PT Hurstpierpoint (B start and finish)

R Hurstpierpoint

This is a tremendous up-and-down circular route, describing a splendid bridleway circle of one of the great hilltops in West Sussex that is NOT on the South Downs Way!

Before starting this route, you should certainly spend some time in Hurstpierpoint, served by buses from Hassocks where there's a station. **Hurstpierpoint** is a delightful village, its centre dominated by the 19th century Gothic-style church of the Holy Trinity, built of dark sandstone. Other buildings of note in the village include the mid-18th century Church House, the early Georgian Mansion House and Wickham House, and the New Inn which was a 15th century Wealden house.

To access the bridleway route from the centre of Hurstpierpoint, head southwards from the mini-roundabout in the village centre by the church, down the B2117 Brighton Road for some 850m. Turn left off this road at TQ279156, the start of the route, onto the bridleway and proceed very pleasantly along the bridleway in a predominantly southerly direction, along a mixture of metalled lanes and tracks, past Randolph's Farm, beyond which there's a delightful lake to the right, and through the most attractive Randolph's Copse.

In 1km 125m from the start, the bridleway veers south-westwards and passes Foxhole Cottages, and in 125m from that south-west turn your bridleway takes an important and easily missed left turn, just east of south, up a hillside looking towards Wolstonbury Hill which you will effectively circle on your journey. In 250m from the left turn you arrive at a bridleway crossroads at TQ278141, here turning left to follow a really lovely tree-shaded path just north of east. In 750m at TQ285142 a bridleway goes off left; don't take this but continue on, eastwards, very shortly veering sharp right and then left, just south of east, through the trees of the lovely Ashen Plantation on an excellent bridleway track.

You emerge from the woods and straight ahead you can see the fine white-painted Jill windmill, which you South Downs Way veterans should easily recognise! Continue on a path just south of east keeping the woods to your left, and arrive just to the right of the far corner of the woods, at a T-junction with a track – TQ291139, 750m from TQ285142. Turn hard right here as bridleway-signed, south-westwards along the edge of the trees, with a splendid

A splendid chalk bridle track high above Newhaven, part of route 63

A narrow but crystal clear bridleway through fields on Heighton Hill above Seaford, part of route 64

A lovely late summer morning on one of the bridleways across Stanley Common, visited in route 68

Beautiful late summer colours as seen from the bridleway ascent onto Ambersham Common near Midhurst, part of route 71

The signpost says it all – a bridle road to Bignor! This bridleway links Bignor Hill and Slindon and is traced in route 77

The trig point on Steep Down high above Lancing, immediately adjacent to a bridleway and visited in route 79

Charleston Farmhouse, a favourite haunt of the Bloomsbury Group; the farmhouse is only accessible by bridleway which you see to the left of the house. It's part of route 84

A fine green bridle track high above Berwick near Alfriston, part of route 86

A glorious summer's afternoon on the bridleway between Salehurst and John's Cross Road near Robertsbridge, part of route 90

A pretty bridleway descent from Cissbury to Findon

A lovely May morning on this quiet bridleway between Aldingbourne and Tangmere near Chichester

A firm bridleway surface in fine unspoilt countryside just east of Mayfield

natural amphitheatre to your right. You then veer sharply left and, taking care to follow the bridleway-signed path to the left of the more obvious track, head uphill, with trees to your right and fine views to your left, to a T-junction of bridleways at TQ293136, 750m from TQ291139. Turn right here and climb further, to reach a bridleway crossroads in 250m at TQ292134.

Turn right, westwards, here and ascend, veering north-westwards as you reach the top of the rise. This is quite magnificent going, with the summit of Wolstonbury Hill clearly visible to the right, and superb views opening out in all directions. In some 875m from TQ292134, at TQ285135, you reach a signed path junction. This provides an opportunity for a detour to the summit of **Wolstonbury Hill**, 250m each way, but it is only available for walkers, so it is not officially part of the bridleway route and not included in the overall distance calculation. To do the detour, turn right along the signed footpath aiming for a metal pole, forking left just before the pole and following the rough path to the trig point at the top of the hill. It has been an important landmark for thousands of years. It was used by Iron Age farmers for grazing animals, there's a Bronze Age enclosure near the summit, and it was visited by David Lloyd George who following the end of the First World War was staying at nearby Danny House where the terms of the German armistice were being planned; he used to take papers up on to Wolstonbury Hill when he wanted to work in peace. From the summit, there is a superb 360-degree panorama, with the whole of the South Downs escarpment visible from Bignor Hill in the west to Ditchling Beacon in the east, and, appropriately enough, you can also see the i360 viewing platform in Brighton! What a shame that the path to get to the hilltop is not designated as a bridleway.

Now return to TQ285135 to resume the bridleway journey, and from TQ285135 follow the bridleway as it continues north-westwards, your track gradually losing height. You should be aware that the obvious track, keeping the hillside earthworks close by to your right, does not, as the current

OS Explorer map suggests, meet the junction of paths shown at TQ279138 (nor do any signs direct you to it), but stays well to the right of that junction, passing closest to it at TQ280138, 500m from the Wolstonbury Hill detour, with the earthwork just to your right. It is all Access Land in any case so there are no issues, but in fact I do offer choices here. Read them and see what you think.

You could simply opt to keep straight on north-westwards along the obvious track, keeping the earthwork close by to your right. The ground then starts to fall away quite suddenly and there is an extremely narrow steep descent; so much so that at TQ279139, you can opt to fork right along a clear V-shaped permissive bridleway which involves negligible extra legwork and takes the gradient more gently, returning you shortly to the main path which in turn goes forward to the bridleway crossroads at TQ278141, 250m from TQ280138.

For a gentler safer descent to TQ278141 from TQ280138, bear left along one of a number of available access land paths to very shortly reach a bridleway running left to right at TQ279138. Turn right along this bridleway, descending rather more gently, north-westwards, along a better track, then in 500m, at TQ275140, turn hard right as bridleway-signed along a very pleasant tree-shaded bridleway just north of east for some 375m to reach the crossroads at TQ278141. This alternative route will add 625m to your journey.

Whichever route you've gone for, when you reach TQ278141 you've now come full circle; from here you simply retrace to Hurstpierpoint the way you started, beginning by heading along the bridleway going just west of north from TQ278141 and then continuing back to Hurstpierpoint via Foxhole Cottages and Randolph's Copse.

ROUTE 57

TQ338065-TQ401092 – Location Map E4 – OS OL11 – S

8km 550m

Bevendean Down, Newmarket Plantation, Jugg's Road, Kingston-near-Lewes, Ashcombe Windmill, Southover

PT Bevendean (B start), Lewes (*, B finish)

R Bevendean, Kingston-near-Lewes, Southover, Lewes

This is a route full of contrasting surroundings and landscapes, but its principal attraction is its spectacular open countryside. It's a linear route but both start and finish points are within easy reach of stops on Brighton & Hove bus services.

The Bevendean School bus stop on Brighton & Hove route 48 is right by the start of this route at TQ338065. Head initially north-westwards away from Heath Hill Avenue (immediately across the road from the primary school) along a bridleway going uphill through trees, soon veering north-eastwards and emerging into open countryside on an excellent track. As you gain height, you pass through **Bevendean Down** Nature Reserve with its wide variety of plants, including pink centaury, autumn gentian, round-headed rampion and horseshoe vetch, and butterflies including Adonis blue, chalkhill blue, small blue and marbled white.

You reach the top of the plateau, now on Falmer Hill, and enjoy really splendid views particularly northwards, with the buildings of Falmer and its Amex Stadium very conspicuous and the attractive Stanmer Park visible beyond that. At TQ348074, 1km 250m from the start, you reach a bridleway junction. Take the bridleway forking right here then in 125m turn sharp left with the bridleway and head just north of east for 1km to reach the Falmer-Woodingdean road. Cross straight over and continue just north of east, keeping Newmarket Hill to your right.

In 1km from the Falmer-Woodingdean road you reach the edge of a spectacularly sited piece of woodland, the so-called **Newmarket Plantation**. You veer right here to arrive immediately at a junction of bridleways at TQ368078. Here you join the clearly-signed South Downs Way, heading straight on uphill, south-eastwards. This climb is quite a trudge, so pause to get your breath back and enjoy the wonderfully exposed surroundings. Make sure you're wrapped up warm in the winter! At the top of the rise, 375m from TQ368078, you reach a path junction at TQ370075. Veer left, now following the South Downs Way north-eastwards along a segment of restricted byway, following what's known as **Jugg's Road**. This is an ancient route that was used to carry fish to the market at Lewes, a "jug" being a Brighton fisherman. From here there are superb views, the best ones to your left.

In 1km 125m from TQ370075, at TQ379079, the South Downs Way bends very obviously right, and at this bend there is a signed fork junction of paths. Leave the South Downs Way here, forking left to join what is a restricted byway heading north-eastwards and dropping down the hillside, providing glorious views to the north. Continuing north-eastwards, you drop down to the valley bottom, going forward to reach **Kingston-near-Lewes**. In 1km from TQ379079, actually at the start of the built-up area, at TQ387085, there's a signed junction of tracks. The continuous route carries straight on north-eastwards along a restricted byway here, but by detouring right here along a bridleway heading south-eastwards for 400m and then veering left for a further 125m, you reach the very pretty 14th century flint church of St Pancras, Kingston-near-Lewes, with an elegant and photogenic tower. I do recommend your detouring to view it.

However the continuous route as stated carries on north-eastwards from TQ387085, passing along the edge of the village to reach a crossing of Ashcombe Lane at TQ390087, 375m from TQ387085. Cross straight over heading north-eastwards along a restricted byway – this is still Jugg's

Road – and soon you'll see the superb six-sailed **Ashcombe Windmill** to your left. The mill was built in 1828 and destroyed in 1916 but has recently been restored; at the time of writing it's not open to the public. The track becomes a bridleway and continues most pleasantly north-eastwards across pasture, but ends as a bridleway at TQ401092, the end of the route, 1km 250m from the Ashcombe Lane crossing.

From TQ401092 you can simply carry on along the track which drops to cross over the A27, veering right to arrive at the west end of **Southover** High Street. To reach Lewes, about 1km 500m from the end of the route, go straight on along this street past the magnificent timber-framed Anne of Cleves House, an early 16th century Wealden hall house given by Henry VIII to his fourth wife Anne of Cleves as part of their divorce settlement. It's now an excellent museum. Beyond the house is the Norman church of St John and splendid Priory Crescent. Go forward along the main street, now Priory Street, bearing left along Station Road. Lewes Station is on the right along Station Road, but for buses back to Brighton, continue along Station Road beyond the station, going forward up Station Street to reach a crossroads with High Street, with bus stops just to the left up the High Street. The attractions of Lewes are well documented, but are summarised briefly in route 62 below.

ROUTE 58

TQ330048-TQ355058 – Location Map E4 – OS OL11 – M

7km 250m

Red Hill, Ovingdean, Mount Pleasant

PT Brighton (B start), Woodingdean (B finish)

R Brighton, Ovingdean, Woodingdean

This is a fine open route exploring some of the attractive downland just a stone's throw from the dense urban sprawl of Brighton. It's a linear route but both start and finish points are served by bus from the city centre.

Starting from Manor Hill by the Brighton Racecourse stands at TQ330048, head north-eastwards along a signed bridleway, staying immediately parallel with the racecourse. Your bridleway veers east; ignore tracks forking away, but keep to the main path running closest to the racecourse. In 1km 250m from the start you cross Wilson Avenue and continue along the obvious path beside the racecourse, veering south-eastwards and passing a car park just across the racecourse. DON'T fork left onto the bridleway heading south-eastwards from the car park. Rather, staying parallel with the racecourse, you veer southwards with the bridleway you've been following. The views are quite dramatic and this is fabulous going; you can clearly see two trig points and Rottingdean Windmill.

At TQ344040, 2km from the Wilson Avenue crossing, you reach a signed bridleway junction, the **Red Hill** trig point situated just south-east of you at this junction. From the trig point there are fine views towards Brighton and the sea, and also the buildings of Roedean School to the south-east. At the bridleway junction turn hard left onto a signed bridleway which heads initially just north of east, crossing East Brighton golf course, then veering eastwards and descending to a bridleway junction at TQ351039, 750m from TQ345040.

Your continuous route turns hard left, north-westwards, here, but I recommend you detour here in order to view the pretty village of **Ovingdean** and in particular its church. To do this, proceed straight on, south-eastwards, from TQ351039 along the bridleway which in 375m reaches Ovingdean at a junction with Ovingdean Road. Go straight on along the road, almost immediately reaching the 11th century flint church of St Wulfran, one of only two English churches so dedicated. (The other, if you want to avoid losing sleep over it, is in Grantham, Lincolnshire.) Features include a 12th century west tower, a Norman chancel arch, an east window possibly of Saxon origin and one of the smallest east windows in any church in England, and painted decoration on the roof, including birds and foliage.

The village itself boasts some lovely flint cottages. Having enjoyed Ovingdean, retrace to TQ351039 to continue.

As stated, from TQ351039, your continuous route turns north-westwards along what is a clear bridle track, keeping the golf course to your left. In some 125m at TQ351041, by the 6th tee, turn right along a bridleway which proceeds most pleasantly north-eastwards through the valley. Then in 625m at TQ352046 you reach a signed path junction. Turn right, eastwards, here, climbing very steeply along the shoulder of **Mount Pleasant**: its white-painted trig point, offering excellent views to the South Downs and the coast, is just off the bridleway to the right of the track, and you'll get level with it some 375m from TQ352046. You then descend along the edge of access land to a bridleway T-junction at TQ357046, 500m from TQ352046. Turn left here, heading north-westwards then veering northwards, following an excellent track to arrive, in 1km 250m from TQ357046, at the route's end, TQ355058 at Woodingdean. This sprawling village has shops and cafes waiting to refresh you after your journey, and is well served by buses to Brighton.

ROUTE 59

TQ356064 (start and finish) – Location Map E4 – OS OL11 – M

6km 575m

Standean Bottom, Bullock Hill

PT Woodingdean (B start and finish)

R Woodingdean

This is a lovely, straightforward, not too long, circular route in glorious downland countryside between Rottingdean and Lewes.

To reach the start of this route from the centre of Woodingdean, well served by buses from/to Brighton, simply head north along the B2123 Falmer Road from its junction with the eastern end of Warren Road, Woodingdean's main street, arriving at TQ356064, the start of the route, in 500m. Head eastwards from there along the signed public bridleway (NOT the public byway going north-eastwards from TQ356064) and follow the bridleway for 1km 750m, initially due eastwards then south-eastwards, ignoring a left fork in 700m from the start. The views back to Brighton and the coast are astonishing; you can in fact see far beyond Brighton to Shoreham, Worthing and a huge expanse of downland.

At TQ370056, 1km 750m from the start of the route, you reach a signed bridleway fork. Ignore the path forking right but carry effectively straight on, south-eastwards. The views from here are tremendous, extending to the cliffs between Rottingdean and Peacehaven. You now begin to descend, veering eastwards and then north-eastwards, on an excellent green bridle track with really fine views. You veer north-westwards to arrive at a wide stony track coming hard in from your right, at TQ378058, 1km 125m from TQ370056. Follow very briefly northwards alongside this track, crossing over (not joining) an unsigned footpath which heads hard left up the hillside. You then almost immediately strike out half-left, south-westwards, along a bridle track following the right-hand edge of the trees with the beautiful grassy **Standean Bottom** just to your right. Your track now veers westwards, then north-westwards, then just south of east, all the time keeping Standean Bottom to your right.

Now at last you leave Standean Bottom, veering away north-eastwards up the hillside, before veering north-westwards. This is quite fantastic: you've an excellent clear green bridleway path and can enjoy wonderful views northwards to Falmer Bottom and the Castle Hill Nature Reserve (see route 60 below). To your left is Bullock Hill, and in roughly 2km 500m from TQ378058, where you first met Standean Bottom, you get level with the **Bullock Hill** trig point which is across the grass to your left, 195m high. The views from the trig point are excellent, but please note that it is on private land, not Access Land, so unless you obtain permission to venture to it, you need to make sure you keep the eleventh commandment (Thou shalt not get caught). The views from the bridleway, especially to Falmer Bottom, are still pretty good! Now veering just south of west, you continue forward along the excellent path to arrive, at TQ363064, at a junction with the path you began on, some 3km from TQ378058. Continue westwards, now retracing 700m to the start at TQ356064, and enjoying magnificent views ahead. To return to Woodingdean, turn left at TQ356064, retracing down the B2123 for 500m.

ROUTE 60

TQ387024-TQ356064 – Location Map E4 – OS OL11 – S

13km

**Grand Ocean, Highdole Hill, Balsdean,
Balsdean Bottom, Falmer Bottom, Castle Hill**

PT Saltdean (B start), Woodingdean (B finish)

R Saltdean, Woodingdean

This is another glorious unspoilt downland journey, incorporating fine views and some classic dry valleys that are characteristic of the Sussex Downs between Brighton and Lewes. It has the bonus of a ghost village! It's a linear route but both start and finish points are close to villages served on Brighton & Hove bus routes with frequent buses to and from them. So leave your car at home if you can.

To reach the start of the route from Saltdean, follow Longridge Avenue north-eastwards from the A259 coast road for 750m, passing the unmissable Art Deco **Grand Ocean** building, then go forward to begin the route at TQ387024, where Longridge Avenue ends and your highway becomes a bridleway. Simply continue in the same north-easterly direction, gaining height all the time as you arrive on Tenant Hill. In 1km from the start you veer sharply right, just south of east, and then continue in a generally easterly direction across more open country to reach a junction of bridleways just at the top edge of Telscombe village at TQ403031, 1km 875m from the start.

Here you turn hard left, north-westwards, for 500m, then at TQ399033 you veer right, fractionally west of north, past a reservoir that's to the left. It's then a superb high-level bridleway path proceeding north-westwards over **Highdole Hill**. If you'll forgive the alliteration, it's bridleway-ing at its brilliant best! You veer in a more westerly direction passing a beautifully-kept memorial, soon reaching a bridleway junction at TQ384052, 2km 625m from TQ399033. Go straight on here, descending on a narrow but clear path then rising to reach another bridleway junction at TQ378050, 500m from TQ384052. Turn right here, following a bridle track northwards. You veer north-westwards to meet, at TQ378058 (875m from TQ378050), a bridleway that featured in route 59 above. Unless you fancy a repeat performance of that one, don't be sucked onto it this time. Your bridleway for this route (60) veers right, northwards, at TQ378058 to arrive, in another 375m, at some isolated barns. You're here on the site of the former village of **Balsdean**. This was once a functioning village, with a Norman chapel, a manor house, cottages, farms, cricket pitch and even a lunatic asylum. However the village fell into disrepair; at the start of the Second World War it was taken over by the Ministry of Defence, the remains of the chapel being used for target practice, and the few remaining residents were evacuated. Just like at Tyneham, in Dorset, which was also evacuated during the Second World War, the villagers never returned and Balsdean is now a ghost village, the site of the chapel now marked only by a plaque. There is virtually no trace of the village left, so all you can do is what John Lennon told us to do – imagine. Look and listen for the rook and the swift, and watch beneath your feet for wild flowers such as wild mignonette and common fallow.

Pass just to right of the barns, then just beyond them, at TQ379062, you reach a bridleway junction. The continuous route turns left, north-westwards, as signed, but I recommend you detour straight on, north-eastwards, along a bridleway up another fine dry valley, **Balsdean Bottom** – a detour of 1km 500m each way. This bridleway heads north-eastwards, as stated, along the bridleway out of the valley, a stiff ascent taking you to a T-junction with the South Downs Way at TQ386075, from which there is a magnificent view to Kingston-near-Lewes and the town of Lewes. You then need to retrace to TQ379062.

Now whether you've detoured or not, follow from TQ379062 what is a delightful bridleway north-westwards along the classic and really lovely dry valley of **Falmer Bottom**, keeping Castle Hill to your right. **Castle Hill**, designated a national nature reserve, is rich in flowers, most notably orchids such as the early spider orchid and burnt orchid, and insect life, its chalk grassland supporting the country's largest colony of wart-biter grasshopper! Among the other plants you will find here are bird's-foot trefoil, yellow rattle, Nottingham catchfly, dropwort, salad burnet, yellow-wort, common centaury and small scabious, and among many butterflies on the reserve is Britain's smallest butterfly, the small blue with a wingspan of just 22mm. As you follow Falmer Bottom you might well be reminded, again, of those beautiful dry valleys in the Yorkshire Wolds. It's hard to appreciate just how close you are to Brighton and its suburbs. Keeping to the right-hand edge of the valley bottom, you veer gently right and then sharp left, reaching a gate and information board at TQ372067, 1km from TQ379062. Go through the gate and then continue straight on uphill on a clear and excellent bridleway path for 750m to a crossroads path junction at TQ367074. Turn left along what is a restricted byway, heading south-westwards over Newmarket Hill and past its very prominent mast, going forward along Drove Avenue to the end of the route at TQ356064, 1km 500m from TQ367074, where you meet Falmer Road. To reach Woodingdean and its amenities, turn left along the B2123 Falmer Road to arrive at the village centre in 500m. Frequent buses are available from here into Brighton.

ROUTE 61

TQ349101-TQ351099 – Location Map E4 – OS OL11 – S

12km 250m

Streat Hill, Plumpton Plain, Balmer Huff, Balmer Medieval Village

PT Falmer (*, B start and finish)

R Falmer

This is an uncomplicated and not too long bridleway journey that is in fact very rewarding. It is a circular route in all but name, the start and finish points just a short stroll from each other, with Falmer providing the necessary amenities at both ends of the route. However there is a substantial detour as part of this route; if you omit it, you will almost halve the length of the route.

To reach the start of this route from Falmer Station, take the north exit and follow the path under the A27 (expect here to be in the company of students, as you're right by the buildings of the University of Sussex), then bear shortly right to follow a clear metalled path parallel first with the A27, then with a slip road. Cross the junction at the top of the slip road to continue along the metalled path, going forward onto a road passing the Swan pub. Follow the road on, parallel with the A27, then veer sharp left and follow this road, Ridge Road (ignoring, for now, a right-forking bridleway), to TQ349101, where a footpath comes in from the left and you'll see a bridleway sign pointing ahead. This is the start of the route, roughly 2km from Falmer Station. Follow the lane/bridleway as directed by the sign, heading just west of north then northwards to reach the buildings of St Mary's Farm, 750m from the start.

The lane/bridleway swings sharp to the right by the farm buildings at TQ347108 – ignore the bridleway forking left at the farm. Veer right, uphill, with the lane, to reach, in 100m from the bend, an unsigned fork junction where you bear left, keeping the woods to the right. Now follow what is a really excellent bridle track steadily uphill, fractionally east of north. The views all around are magnificent. It's a long climb but never excessively steep, and eventually, at TQ352128, 2km from St Mary's Farm, you reach the South Downs Way on **Streat Hill**. Turn right along the South Downs Way, enjoying majestic views on both sides; this is your only chance on this journey to view the Wealden scenery to the north so make the most of it.

All too soon, at TQ358126, 625m from where you joined the South Downs Way, you reach a signed bridleway turning to the right, now at an area of the South Downs called **Plumpton Plain**. This is the site of a Bronze Age settlement, and there are a number of burial mounds bordering the South Downs Way on the left. Turn right onto the bridleway at TQ358126, leaving the South Downs Way and taking great care here to pass through the gate as indicated by the signage, rather than joining the track immediately beyond. Now, keeping the boundary fence to the left (and early on, having to veer right and left round the edge of vegetation), you can enjoy a quite superb march or ride on a clear green bridle track initially just west of south, then southwards, with glorious views, particularly to Firle Beacon and Mount Caburn to the south-east. You begin to descend and continue to drop until you reach the valley bottom at TQ357109, here veering south-westwards and climbing up an attractive hillside, keeping woodland to your left. At TQ353104 you reach a gate and, beyond it, a bridleway T-junction, 2km 250m after leaving the South Downs Way.

Your continuous route turns right, south-westwards, here, but if you fancy adding to your collection of trig points, I recommend you detour hard left at the junction at TQ353104 and follow the bridleway along the south-eastern edge of the wood, then through more open country north-eastwards to reach, at TQ364115 (1km 500m from the start of the detour), a junction with a bridleway very close to its junction with the South Downs Way on Balmer Down. Don't be misled by OS Explorer mapping here which appears to indicate a junction further south. Turn hard right onto the bridleway at TQ364115 which you can then follow south-westwards to the trig point at **Balmer Huff**, at TQ362107, just off the bridleway to the right, 750m from TQ364115. The views from here are fabulous, stretching to Brighton and Seaford Head. Then, another 750m down this bridleway, is the site of **Balmer Medieval Village,** surviving as earthworks that are visible as mounds and depressions just north of Balmer Farm. However far you've come, simply retrace to TQ353104.

Now, whether you've detoured or not from TQ353104, proceed south-westwards from here as stated to follow a narrowish but clear track south-westwards across Waterpit Hill, descending to arrive, at TQ351099, at a T-junction with Ridge Road where the route ends, 625m from TQ353104. You've come effectively full circle. Turn left and retrace from here via Ridge Road in order to return to Falmer Station.

ROUTE 62

TQ405101-TQ403109 – Location Map E4 – OS OL11 – M

7km 750m

Lewes, Blackcap, Mount Harry

PT Lewes (*, B start and finish)

R Lewes

This is a superb journey, for which a clear day is a must. Note that OS mapping is misleading in one or two respects, so follow my directions carefully. Your journey will be circular in all but name, and you can easily (and certainly should) start and finish in the centre of Lewes. **Lewes** is the county town of East Sussex and is a lovely place to spend a day with its wealth of interesting features. You should in particular take time out to visit the ruined Norman castle with a superb outer gatehouse added in the 14th century; the castle's museum in the adjacent Barbican House; Bull House, built in 1450 and between 1768 and 1774 the home of Thomas Paine, author of *Rights Of Man*; the splendid timber-framed Fifteenth Century Bookshop beside which is Keere Street with many fine brick and flint buildings; the church of St Michael with its twisting needle spire and 13th century tower; and the impressive Georgian White Hart Hotel. All of these features are on, or immediately off, High Street in the town centre.

To reach the start of the route from the centre of Lewes, follow High Street south-westwards, going forward, westwards, along Western Road (a continuation of High Street) past the church of St Anne and, where the road forks, forking right along Spital Road. At the end cross the A275, and it is here, at the point where a signed bridleway goes off westwards immediately beyond the A275 crossing, your route begins at TQ405101, roughly 1km from Lewes' centre. Follow this bridleway westwards, ignoring a bridleway shortly forking left, then veer north-westwards on what is a very clear and well-signed, if potentially muddy, bridleway heading fairly relentlessly uphill. In 1km 625m from the start you reach and pass extensive riding stables that are to your left, and just beyond them you kink right to reach, 1km 875m from the start, a bridleway T-junction at TQ393113. Here turn left, and follow the clear bridle track onwards and north-westwards, still rising and keeping fairly thick vegetation to your left.

At TQ384119, 1km from the T-junction, you reach a junction with a bridleway going off to your left. Continue straight on, shortly arriving on a clear green hillside, with the Mount Harry beacon, which you'll soon be visiting, up to your right. Follow the clear bridle track in the same north-westerly direction, aiming for the highest ground ahead, on which is a clump of trees known as Blackcap. You'll see your clear path forging on ahead and another forking left – ignore this left fork, but keep on in the same direction along the green path, aiming for the **Blackcap** trig point which you can see clearly ahead. Simply proceed via the path to the trig point at TQ374125, 1km 250m from TQ384119.

Blackcap stands 206m above sea level, a whopping 676 ft in old money – sounds much more impressive, doesn't it! End of grumpy old man alert. Like Wolstonbury Hill and Crown Tegleaze which we've already visited in this book (and you should do if you haven't so far), Blackcap is a classic example of a fine South Downs summit that is NOT on the South Downs Way. It supports a diverse range of plants including waxcap fungi and varieties of orchid including the bird's-nest orchid. Pause here to enjoy fantastic views which extend to Brighton, Firle Beacon and Newhaven, as well as a huge area of the Weald to the north.

Having enjoyed the view, retrace from the trig point, aiming for the **Mount Harry** beacon which you should see clearly ahead. Almost immediately after beginning your retrace, you should meet a clump of gorse, and beside it, two forking paths. You take the left fork, heading south-eastwards with the beacon still directly ahead. Follow this clear path which initially dips down; as you reach the bottom of the dip, you can see the green bridle track clearly rising to pass just to the left of the beacon. Now keep on the track as it ascends to get level with the beacon. The beacon was erected by two local parish councils to commemorate the Golden Jubilee of Queen Elizabeth II in 2002 (I wonder, who would have thought then that she would live to celebrate her Platinum Jubilee); it is the site of an earlier beacon dating back to the 16th century, being part of the defence system of the south coast, warning the local militia of invading forces. I really recommend that you leave the track and go to the beacon from which there are quite superb views to the South Downs, Lewes, Mount Caburn and the Ouse valley.

Now you have a choice. It's not clear from mapping or signage whether the bridleway is supposed to continue to follow the established track or across the open grassland, parallel with the track, eastwards from here. However, the latter is definitely recommended, and there is a reasonably clear green track over the grass. Whichever of these routes you take, you descend to arrive at a gate. Pass through the gate and now follow an obvious bridle track, still going south-eastwards. You continue to descend quite steeply, veering very gently right with the path – don't be tempted away left – then arriving at a large field with woodland to the left.

It's now very straightforward going on a grassy (sometimes muddy) bridleway path, with the ground falling quite steeply away to the left, and with open fields to your right. You veer from south-eastwards to north-eastwards, reaching a 3-way bridleway junction at TQ394115, 2km 375m from the summit of Blackcap. Take the bridleway heading hard right from here (as opposed to going left into the woods), rising to arrive almost immediately at a signed bridleway T-junction, here meeting the Greenwich Meridian Trail (see route 9). Turn right here, very shortly passing through a gate immediately beyond which is a small thicket on the left. Bear left immediately beyond the thicket to follow along the edge of it south-eastwards and then beside a fence to reach another signed bridleway T-junction at TQ395113, some 250m from TQ394115.

Turn left here down a bridleway path through vegetation and pass through a gate. Don't be tempted to go forward to the metalled road ahead, but bear round to the left to pass through another gate and go forward eastwards along a clear narrow grassy bridleway path, with a fence to the left and a large grassy area to the right. This grassy area marks the site of the Battle of Lewes in May 1264 between the forces of rebel barons led by Simon de Montfort, and the army of Henry III. When the fence veers left, DON'T veer with it but keep straight on along the fairly clear path, which then veers gently right, south-eastwards, keeping the grassy area to the right, and steadily descending. Your bridleway is a lovely path with fine views to Lewes and Mount Caburn ahead. Your path becomes firmer and you arrive at a gate, going forward to a lane, here turning left to immediately reach the A275 at TQ403109, 1km from TQ395113. This is the end of the route.

You could simply follow the A275 to the right, southwards, to meet Spital Road in 800m or so, turning left to retrace into Lewes. Alternatively at TQ403109 you could cross straight over along a metalled path, actually a bridleway. In 125m fork right along another metalled path/bridleway past Wallands Primary School, continuing along a road, going straight over Gundreda Road and on along the path beyond, going forward along Ferrers Road. At the end turn right into Prince Edward's Road and almost immediately left along Leicester Road, descending then rising to its end at a T-junction with De Montfort Road. Turn left along this road then very shortly, opposite number 55, turn right along an alleyway which leads you to Western Road, just under 1km from the end of the route. Turn left to proceed into Lewes.

ROUTE 63

TQ449024-TQ458022 – Location Map E4 – OS OL11 – S

9km 125m

Beddingham Masts, Stump Bottom, Mount Pleasant

PT Newhaven (*, B start and finish)

R Newhaven

This route, just like route 61, consists of exploration of lovely peaceful downland tracks immediately south of the South Downs Way, and, again like route 61, gives a little taste of the joys of the South Downs Way itself. It's a linear route but you can easily create effectively a circular journey by starting and finishing at Newhaven.

From the junction of the B2109/A259 in Newhaven, some 625m north-east of Newhaven Station along the A259, follow the B2109 Avis Road for 750m as far as Paradise Park to the start of your route at TQ449024, just beyond Iveagh Crescent. Here you turn right up a bridleway, a narrow path between houses, arriving at the end at a little green at TQ451027. Turn left – not hard left – northwards along

Heighton Road then just past the pub, at TQ451029, fork right along what is a restricted byway, here 500m from the start. The restricted byway heads initially north-eastwards, veering northwards uphill (becoming a bridleway), and providing increasingly good views. You descend a little, then veer north-westwards and ascend gently to arrive at the South Downs Way at TQ455060, 3km from the fork at TQ451029.

Turn right to follow the South Downs Way eastwards for 1km 250m, past the superbly sited **Beddingham Masts** as far as the Firle Bostal car park at TQ468059. Enjoy tremendous views from here, especially northwards, as you follow the ridge. At TQ468059, turn right and follow a signed bridleway, initially a farm track to Blackcap Farm and then a green path southwards, descending all the time. You drop down quite steeply and then follow the lovely **Stump Bottom** dry valley, reaching a bridleway T-junction at TQ464031, 2km 750m from the South Downs Way.

Turn half-right as signed and follow a narrow bridleway south-westwards uphill, going straight over a crossroads of bridleways at TQ461030. You arrive at a signed path crossroads at TQ460029, 500m from TQ464031. Turn left here and follow the bridleway south-eastwards for 500m onto **Mount Pleasant**, as far as a clearly signed path junction at TQ463024. (This is not to be confused with the Mount Pleasant we met in route 58 just east of Brighton!) There are really fine views from here towards Newhaven and the sea. Bear right here to follow a restricted byway south-westwards, going forward along Palmerston Road, descending to the end of the route at Palmerston Road's junction with Seaview Road and Falaise Road at TQ458022, 625m from TQ463024.

To reach Newhaven, turn left and immediately right down Mount Road to arrive in 375m at the A259. There are bus stops just here but if you wish to continue to Newhaven, 1km from here, under your own steam, turn south-westwards to follow beside the A259, passing the station then crossing the Ouse to reach the town. The centre of Newhaven isn't great, frankly, from an aesthetic viewpoint; it is however worth visiting High Street to see the 18th century Bridge Hotel. Louis Philippe, deposed in the 1848 uprising in France, stayed there after fleeing across the Channel, booking in with Queen Mary Amelie as Mr and Mrs Smith!

ROUTE 64

TQ471019-TQ473010 – Location Map E4 – OS OL25 – S

12km

Gardener's Hill, Heighton Hill, Norton Top, Bishopstone, Seaford

PT Bishopstone (*, B start and finish)

R East Blatchington

This is a splendid downland trail exploring some superb scenery between the South Downs Way and the sea. It is a linear route but can easily be turned into a circular starting from the village of Bishopstone.

To reach Bishopstone by public transport you need in the first instance to get yourself to the junction of the A259 Newhaven Road and Marine Parade, between Newhaven and Seaford, grid reference TQ469002. Frequent buses on the Brighton-Eastbourne route serve this spot, or you can travel by train to Bishopstone Station and follow Marine Parade just east of north for 250m to reach the junction. From the junction head westwards towards Newhaven beside the A259, then in 250m from the junction turn right along Bishopstone Road, arriving in Bishopstone in 1km from the A259. I describe its beautiful church at the end of the route. For now, continue predominantly northwards along Bishopstone Road for another 1km to its end at Norton, reaching a junction of lanes/paths at TQ471019. This is the start of your route. Go straight on at the junction along a bridleway heading north-westwards through a dry valley known as Poverty Bottom, the ground rising steeply to your left and more gently to your right. Already this feels very rural and a long way from the busy A259.

In 1km 500m from the start, you reach a bridleway crossroads at TQ464031. Turn right here, north-eastwards, and now, keeping the fence to your right, climb quite steeply on to **Gardener's Hill**. You now continue on a superb bridleway path, still north-eastwards, with fantastic views back to Newhaven and the sea. You cross over **Heighton Hill**, the path becoming a little less distinct, but simply follow the good signage. The path becomes clearer as you descend, keeping an area of trees to your left, and veering slightly right. At the bottom of the slope you veer very slightly left, still north-eastwards, and now ascend on an obvious path through the field; this is a very exposed section indeed. At TQ487047, 2km 750m from TQ464031, you pass through a gate. Continue in the same direction on a narrow but clear bridleway path which veers very gently left, continuing to rise. (NOTE: this path appears to take a slightly different course from that suggested on OS Explorer mapping.) You can't miss the obvious path which you continue to follow just east of north to reach the South Downs Way at TQ490054, 750m from TQ487047. The views from here are absolutely glorious; make the most of the view north from here as it's the best northward view of this route.

Having enjoyed the view, turn right to follow the South Downs Way south-eastwards downhill for 500m to reach the Bopeep Bostal car park. Adjacent to the car park turn right, away from the South Downs Way, as bridleway-signed, at TQ494051. Almost immediately you reach a signed bridleway fork. The right-hand signed fork (to Denton) no longer appears to exist as a bridleway; the left-hand fork, to High And Over, is very clear and you now follow this bridle track south-westwards. Passing above Bostal Bottom, you make excellent progress south-westwards; you veer in a more southerly direction and now enjoy a quite fantastic journey along an excellent green track with tremendous views ahead to the coast and back to the downs. Look out to your right for burial mounds including the Round Barrow named Five Lord's Burgh to your right at TQ487035.

At TQ487033 you pass the 140m-high trig point of **Norton Top** which is a little to the right of your route, and veer slightly east of south to arrive at a fork junction of bridleways at TQ489024, 2km 750m after leaving the South Downs Way. There's a thoughtfully provided seat here. You take the bridleway forking right, just west of south, and very soon you begin your crossing of Seaford golf course. The path is clear enough – simply follow the bridleway signs and blue poles. Continue just west of south over the course; at one point near the end you need to ring a bell before crossing a fairway. Nothing like a bit of hi-tech communication to enliven a bridleway bag. Go forward to reach the end of the bridleway at TQ486009, 1km 500m from TQ489024, arriving at the top end of Firle Road, East Blatchington.

Go straight on from TQ486009, along Firle Road past St John's School and College, the road veering southwards in 700m or so from where you joined it. However in 750m from where you joined Firle Road, at TQ483002, turn hard right, north-westwards, along a suburban bridleway which in 250m crosses Princess Drive, adjacent to a Co-op. Cross pretty much straight over to follow a narrowish path (not actually signed as a bridleway, although it is one) heading away north-westwards from Princess Drive, initially keeping a small green to your left. You rise and shortly emerge from the East Blatchington housing, veering a little right and soon arriving at Grand Avenue; cross straight over with the bridleway, descending to a junction with a track. Go forward along the bridle track, rising and enjoying really lovely views all round, especially to Newhaven and its surroundings.

You then begin to descend, turning sharp left at a junction with a footpath and dropping down to the road at the old and very peaceful village of **Bishopstone,** at TQ473010, 1km

250m from Princess Drive. The church of St Andrew, which you can see in front of you, is one of the finest in Sussex. Much of it pre-dates the Norman Conquest, the fine and lofty porch containing a Saxon sundial and immense Saxon corner stones. The church also boasts a beautifully moulded Norman doorway, a square 12th century font raised on three steps, a coffin lid decorated with 12th century carving, and superb windows depicting Biblical characters. TQ473010 marks the end of the route; you've come full circle. To access public transport and other local amenities, turn left, south-westwards, along Bishopstone Road, following it for 1km to reach the A259 Newhaven Road. This road is very well served by buses back to Newhaven (and, beyond, to Brighton) or on to Eastbourne; alternatively for a train back to Newhaven, or indeed down to Seaford, turn left alongside the A259 then in 250m turn right down Marine Parade which brings you to Bishopstone Station in a further 250m. **Seaford** isn't the loveliest Sussex resort but it boasts a fine Norman church and the most westerly of the so-called Martello towers, built around 1806 as a defensive measure against Napoleon's armies.

ROUTE 65

TV559991-TV558980 – Location Map E4 – OS OL25 – S

10km 675m

Friston Dencher, Jevington, Butts Brow, Willingdon Hill, East Dean

PT Friston (B start), East Dean (B finish)

R East Dean, Jevington

This superb downland journey can effectively be treated as a circular one, starting and finishing at East Dean (East Sussex), very well served by buses on the Brighton-Eastbourne route.

If you're starting your journey from East Dean, I suggest you begin at the junction where the A259 meets Gilberts

Drive, immediately adjacent to bus stops on both sides, and follow the A259 westwards towards Seaford for 800m, ascending quite steeply to reach Friston. A much safer alternative for walkers is to follow the A259 for just 125m from the Gilberts Drive turning, then turn left, south-westwards, off the A259 along Upper Street; in 200m turn right up a footpath that ascends roughly parallel with the A259 to Friston Pond. This spot is as well served by buses as East Dean so if you're not fussy about making this a circular route, you could simply hop off the bus here. We've already met Friston Pond in route 28 but if you've not got round to that one yet, it's worth pausing to view not only the charming pond but the adjacent church (briefly described in route 28) before you get going.

Anyway, to access the start of this route from Friston, head north-eastwards away from the A259 here, following the road signed for Jevington. After 200m fork right along Willingdon Road, which in 1km at TV559991, the start of the route, becomes a bridleway heading north-eastwards. This is the so-called **Friston Dencher,** a superb high-level track with really great views back to the sea. Dencher, in case you were wondering, is a contraction of "devonshiring," an old method of fertilising poor soil by burning. It has nothing to do with false teeth.

At TQ571005, 2km from the start, the bridleway turns sharply right to arrive in 150m at a T-junction of bridleways. Turn left here and continue to climb gently along the plateau but in 400m at TQ575008 you reach an unsigned fork of paths; here you need to take the left fork which continues north-eastwards as a bridleway along the plateau, arriving in 250m at a junction with the South Downs Way at TQ576010. Turn left here and now follow the South Downs Way for 1km 500m all the way down to **Jevington,** a very pretty flint village which from the plateau looks almost like a model village! We met Jevington, the birthplace of banoffee pie, in route 11, but I'm sure you won't be too sorry to find yourself back here.

On reaching the village street turn right but then (unless you're thirsty and fancy detouring 375m up the street to the Eight Bells) turn right again almost immediately, following Willingdon Lane, a metalled lane for 200m to its end at TQ564013. Go through a gate with three signed routes ahead. Take the middle one, a bridleway across the field, but as you approach the end of the field DON'T be tempted by the gateway ahead. Instead veer left (this is not signed) and make for the very far top left corner of the field to enter a wooded area. Your bridleway path is now very obvious, proceeding attractively through trees just north of east. Beyond the trees you continue on a clear track through Willingdon Bottom, the ground rising steeply to your left, then, proceeding predominantly eastwards, you rise quite steeply on an excellent track. To your left, as you ascend from Willingdon Bottom, is Combe Hill, with its abundance of plants including hawthorn, early wood-violet, cowslip, columbine and saxifrage, while butterfly spotters should look out for small tortoiseshell and brimstone.

At length you reach a track junction with the 1066 Country Walk (see route 43) at TQ579017, 1km 675m from TQ564013. Cross over this track and continue for a few metres to reach a parking area, noting the road coming in from the left. This is **Butts Brow,** a very popular spot providing tremendous views to the South Downs and Eastbourne. There's also a very impressive stone signpost here. Turn right at this point to follow a clear bridle track; don't fork left towards the mast but proceed well to the right of the mast just west of south. Beyond the mast the ground begins to rise and at TQ578013, some 500m from where you joined this bridle track, look out for, and take, a path forking right off the track you've been following. Although it's not signed, this is in fact the continuation of the bridleway.

Shortly you arrive at the 1066 Country Walk close to the plateau edge. Turn left to follow it to TQ576010, 250m from the right fork at TQ578013. You should recognise the surroundings at TQ576010; you've effectively come full circle having been here earlier. This time turn left, south-eastwards, along the South Downs Way, and in 125m at TQ577009 you reach a bridleway crossroads – the **Willingdon Hill** trig point is just to your left here. The views from here are quite exceptional, with Eastbourne clearly visible to the south-east, and Pevensey Levels and Bexhill can also be seen beyond.

At TQ577009 turn right, to head south-westwards along an excellent clear bridleway path across the plateau. In 250m you join up with a path you followed earlier, coming the other way, but in another 400m that earlier path disappears to the right; you continue resolutely south-westwards on your still excellent bridleway. At TV565995, 1km 750m from leaving the South Downs Way, you reach a gate, where you turn sharply right, then in 125m turn left through a gate with a sign saying East Dean is a mile away. Head southwards to arrive in 875m at a 3-way bridleway junction at TV563986. Ignoring the permissive bridleway heading south from here to the left of the houses, go straight on, through the gate along a narrow path between houses, shortly arriving at a road, The Link. Join this road then almost immediately turn left down Summerdown Lane (marked on OS Explorer maps as a bridleway) to arrive at a T-junction with Michel Dene Road, also marked as a bridleway. Turn left and follow the road predominantly south-westwards, all the way to reach the A259 at East Dean, where your route ends at TV558980, some 875m from TV563986.

Buses are available to Seaford and Eastbourne from here. However you should take some time to enjoy **East Dean**, the most historic part of which is on the far (coast) side of the A259. Its centrepiece is its delightful green surrounded by flint cottages, with a deli, a café and a pub all looking out onto the green and vying with each other for your custom. The church of St Simon & St Jude has walls that were probably made by the Saxons, a Norman nave, a half-Norman font described by Arthur Mee as "one of the best in Sussex," and a 17th century pulpit with canopy and 12 richly carved panels.

ROUTE 66

TV555975-TV556978 – Location Map E4 – OS OL25 – M

5km 500m

Went Hill, Flathill Bottom, Gap Bottom, Seven Sisters

PT East Dean (B start and finish)

R East Dean

This short but in places quite lung-testing route explores the superbly scenic area between East Dean and the Seven Sisters, but note that it incorporates a stretch of new bridleway that isn't yet mapped or signed. I only happened to find out about it because it was depicted on an information board! It can easily be made into a circular route by making the A259 at East Dean your start and end point.

To reach the start of the route from the A259 at East Dean which we enjoyed in route 65 above (and which is well served by Brighton-Eastbourne buses), simply follow the road Upper Street south-westwards from the A259 at TV557980, veering left past the village green and reaching a road fork at TV557977. Fork right here along Went Way (unless you want to detour to the church, described in route 65, in which case you should fork left along Lower Street then retrace to join Went Way) and follow Went Way on, almost immediately veering right, south-westwards, to reach the start of the route at TV555975, some 625m from the A259.

Go straight on along the bridleway south-westwards from TV555975, climbing steeply to reach the brow of the hill, then continue southwards over **Went Hill**, keeping to the right of the buildings. The path is indistinct at this point. Veer very gently west of south, your track becoming clearer, the views to Belle Tout lighthouse absolutely superb. Continue southwards along the track, now descending, and at TV553964, 800m after gaining the crest of the hill and some 1km 125m from the start, you reach a gate.

Pass through the gate and turn sharp right to follow the south side of the fence. Note that this right turn is NOT signed or mapped as a bridleway, nor is any of the ensuing 1km 750m or so of this route, all the way to Gap Bottom. However it is shown on local information boards as a bridleway and offers a great roller-coaster journey! You need to follow my instructions clearly, though. So if you're sitting comfortably we'll continue. In 200m or so from TV553964 you're forced away from the fence to negotiate some vegetation. Veer a little left to pick up an obvious path going down the hillside into a deep valley, curving gently right; you can see a path rising up on the far side, not that far from your trusty fence that's to the right of it. Keeping that path and fence in your sights, drop down to the valley bottom then climb steeply north-westwards, parallel with the fence that's to your right, on the clear path, reaching another patch of vegetation at the top. Stick to the clear path which again drifts away from the fence south-westwards, passing through the patch of vegetation, and descending to a gate at TV545968 at the lovely secluded valley known as **Flathill Bottom.**

Go through the gate and turn right then head steeply north-eastwards up the far side back towards the fence again, veering north-westwards to stay parallel with the fence. You should reach a footpath crossing (a footpath arrow can be seen in the fence to the right) at TV543971. Just beyond this crossing, veer half-left away from the fence to negotiate a further area of vegetation and, keeping it immediately to your right, drop down westwards on a clear path to reach the delightful **Gap Bottom** at TV539972, and arrive at a mapped bridleway.

The continuous route turns right, north-eastwards, here, along the clear bridleway path on the valley bottom, but it is definitely worth detouring left here for 375m to reach the **Seven Sisters** coast route and enjoy tremendous views to the sea and the magnificent chalk cliffs (the cliffs being the "sisters"), the legacy of geological activity between 50 and 100 million years ago. The depressions separating each "sister" are the valleys of ancient rivers, Flathill Bottom and Gap Bottom being two such valleys. The spot where, on your detour, you meet the coast path, TV537968, is itself superbly scenic, sandwiched as it is between Brass Point and Flagstaff Point, the fourth and fifth "sisters" respectively going from west to east. You'll then need to retrace to the continuous route.

Whether or not you've made the detour, head north-eastwards from TV539972 as stated, almost immediately passing a dewpond shrouded in vegetation, and veering right, following an obvious track past the buildings of Crowlink. You continue forward on a metalled road which ascends, veers left and passes through a parking area. Just beyond the parking area at TV550979, 1km 250m from joining the bridleway at Gap Bottom, you reach a gate on the right on which are bridleway and footpath signs. Bear right to pass through the gate and follow the signed bridleway, aiming for a field boundary just to your half-left in 100m. On reaching the boundary, bear left into a large open area.

The OS mapped bridleway route appears to cut diagonally north-eastwards downhill across the open area, passing just to the left edge of the trees, veering south-eastwards onto a clear track. However this path, assuming that it ever was one, appears to have lost its identity. It is preferable therefore to stick to the clear path across the hilltop along the field edge, then to bear right onto the obvious path that then descends south-eastwards to arrive at Upper Street at TV556978, the end of the route, 625m from TV550979. Turn left along Upper Street to return to the A259. Of course you may want to enjoy the amenities of East Dean before doing so, whether it's the pub, deli, café or all of the above.

ROUTE 67

TV585986 (start and finish) – Location Map E4 – OS OL25 – S

12km 125m

Warren Hill, East Hale Bottom, Birling Gap, Frost Hill, Long Down

PT A259 by Eastbourne golf club house (B start and finish)

R Birling Gap

This circular journey is a fascinating exploration of the extensive and delightfully unspoilt open downland between East Dean and Eastbourne. It is very exposed in places and not a good wet weather expedition. On the day I had planned to walk it, there were thunderstorms in the forecast; I decided to risk it and in fact it stayed hot and sunny all day, but I still wonder how I'd have coped if the weather had turned!

Your route starts at TV585986, at the bus stop (served by very frequent buses on the Eastbourne-Brighton route) by the golf clubhouse adjacent to the A259 at the top of the very steep hill coming out of Eastbourne. From the start of the route, head south-eastwards away from the A259 along the South Downs Way, in some 500m passing just to the right of the **Warren Hill** trig point. As you might expect, the views to Eastbourne and the sea are magnificent here. Very shortly beyond the trig point you pass to the right of a reservoir and here you fork right at TV588980, leaving the South Downs Way, and following a bridleway to arrive almost immediately at the B2103 road linking the A259 and Beachy Head, 750m from the start. There's a small parking area here.

Cross the road and aim for a gate just to your right (TQ587979), and having gone through the gate, head just south of west down the obvious bridleway path, with excellent views to the south-west, the Crapham Barn buildings very conspicuous ahead. Continue to descend then at the valley bottom veer gently left, southwards then south-westwards, into **East Hale Bottom**. This is really lovely going, extremely peaceful, the green vegetation delightfully complementing the stark often steep green hillsides. In 1km 750m from TQ587979, you pass (but ignore) a left fork with a sign for Beachy Head, and continue through the delightful dry valley for another 400m to reach, at TV569967, a crossroads of bridleways. Go straight over and head south-westwards for 750m to Cornish Farm. Immediately beyond the farm, TV563963, veer left for some 100m, passing a bridleway going off to your left and reaching a bridleway T-junction. Here turn left and head just east of south for 400m along a bridleway to reach a junction with a left-hand bridleway turn at TV564958.

Your continuous route bears left, eastwards, here but I recommend an out-and-back detour to Birling Gap from here. To take this, continue southwards from TV564958, crossing straight over Beachy Head Road in 150m and almost immediately (25m) beyond the road crossing, reaching a bridleway T-junction. The detour route turns right, north-westwards, here, to follow what is a most attractive partially wooded bridleway for 1km, reaching Beachy Head Road at TV556960. The **Birling Gap** complex including café, visitor centre and spectacular cliffs, is 250m along the road to the left. The Gap is the site of a glaciated dry river bed and marks the eastern end of the Seven Sisters whom we called on in route 66. In the 18th and 19th centuries the break in the cliffs here, between the Seven Sisters and Beachy Head, made it a favourite landing place for smugglers. The most dramatic feature of Birling Gap is arguably the row of coastguard cottages dating back to 1878. They look astonishingly vulnerable and who knows if they will still be there when you visit! Having visited and perhaps enjoyed refreshment at Birling Gap, now retrace all the way to TV564958.

Whether you've detoured or not, head eastwards from TV564958 as stated along a bridleway that ascends onto **Frost Hill**, your veering gently north of east and enjoying excellent views as you proceed. You arrive at a bridleway T-junction at TV575961, 1km 125m from TV564958, and here turn left. Care is needed here, as the bridleway becomes less well defined, but keep as close as you can to the fence on the right, then as you descend, maintaining the same (north-westerly) direction, follow the edge of the vegetation adjacent to (and to the left of) the fence. Shortly the way ahead becomes obvious, and you now descend, aiming for a gate. You can see the path rising on the far side of the Kiln Combe valley bottom for which you are now heading.

Accordingly, you drop steeply to the gate in Kiln Combe then rise very steeply north-westwards up the other side, following a clear path onto **Long Down**, reaching a crossroads of paths at TV572966, 500m from the bridleway junction on Frost Hill at TV575961. Having enjoyed the excellent views from here, turn right. It's now a very straightforward, easy bridleway journey over Long Down, the ground rising gradually as you go, with the views getting better all the time. In 2km from TV572966 you arrive at Beachy Head Road. Cross straight over and, having enjoyed the splendid views in all directions, head north-eastwards along a bridleway that in 125m reaches a crossroads junction with the South Downs Way at TV592972. Turn left to follow the South Downs Way north-westwards, crossing the B2103 and heading along the top (western) edge of woodland to reach TV588980, where you forked off the South Downs Way at the start. Simply retrace from here along the South Downs Way to the A259 where your route ends as it started, by the golf clubhouse at TV585986, 1km 375m or so from TV592972 where you rejoined the South Downs Way. As stated, there are frequent buses from here to Eastbourne and Brighton.

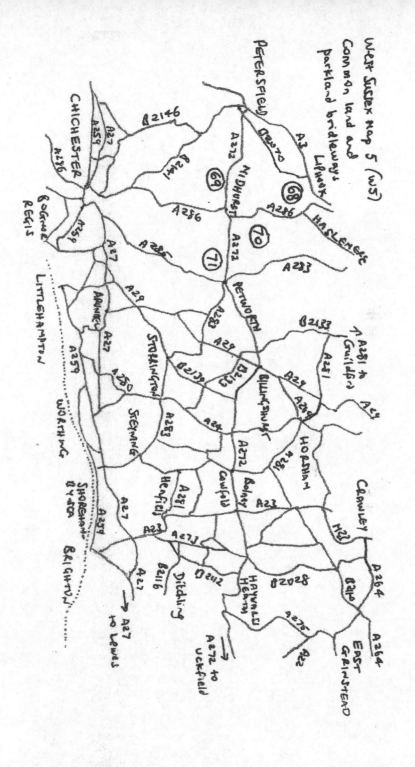

West Sussex Map 5 (w5)
Common land and
parkland bridleways,
Lifhook

East Sussex Map 5 (E5)
Common land and parkland bridleways

Part 5 – Parks and recreation - common land and parkland bridleways

S ussex enjoys a plethora of fine "open spaces" with extensive tracts of open heathland or grassland, sometimes furnished with patches of beautiful woodland, all deliciously unspoilt and a treat for the nature lover. Many bridleways pass through these areas. Here are the best of them.

ROUTE 68

SU848302-SU895316 – Location Map W5 – OS OL33 – M

8km 50m

Stanley Common, Linchmere Common, Linchmere, Marley Common

PT Liphook (*, B start), Camelsdale (B finish)

R Liphook, Camelsdale

This is a linear route but both the start and finish points link in with bus stops on the Haslemere-Liphook-Alton-Basingstoke route. It is a fiddly route in places with lots of different bridleways to follow, but there is ample reward in the form of beautiful woodland and common land.

To access the start of this route from Liphook Station, follow Midhurst Road (which crosses the railway by the bridge immediately east of the station) south-eastwards for 1km, ignoring Highfield Lane going off to the left. Then at SU848302, the start of the route, turn left, eastwards, along a signed bridleway, and in 125m veer right to head south-eastwards on along the bridleway in a dead straight line, gradually gaining height. You reach a bridleway T-junction at SU859294, 1km 375m from the start, and turn left along an excellent woodland track, just east of north. Some 250m beyond SU859294 your bridleway is signed right, forking along a path off the main track. Don't miss this! Having taken this right fork, you then need to be careful to take a bridleway fork left at the next junction in just a few metres, as signed. The path initially looks unpromising but improves, as you continue just east of north through the woods.

At SU861300, 625m from SU859294, you reach a crossroads of paths. Go straight over along a bridleway-signed path, heading due north, then in 250m at SU861302, you take a bridleway fork left. You now head in a predominantly north-westerly direction along a really smashing bridleway through the beautiful woodland of **Stanley Common**, the combination of bracken and pine quite delightful. At SU858305, 500m from the left fork, you reach a crossroads junction, going straight over; you're now on the course of the Sussex Border Path (see route 4). There now follows a lovely northward bridleway descent with woodland to your right and what looks like a practice golf hole in a field to your left, then at Lower Brookham you veer round to the right to arrive, at SU858313, at a multi-path junction, 750m from SU858305.

You continue straight on as bridleway/Sussex Border Path-signed: don't take either of the paths signed left here. In a few metres you reach a post where the Serpent Trail (see route 14) is signed left, contrary to what some OS maps suggest, but the Sussex Border Path and etched bridleway arrow point straight on. Go straight on in obedience to the Sussex Border Path signage and now enjoy a lovely climb eastwards on a narrow but clear and well signed path across the southern part of **Linchmere Common**. Look back every so often for glorious views across the woodland of Stanley Common.

Following the arrow signs, you go over a wide crossing track to a signed bridleway junction at SU862313, 375m from the multi-path junction at SU858313, temporarily here leaving the Sussex Border Path. Continue straight over in the same direction on an unpromising poorly-defined narrow path through the trees – it is actually a bridleway – but after barely 100m you reach a signed path T-junction where you meet the Sussex Border Path again! There's probably a reason why bridleway and Sussex Border Path should part company for those 100m but don't bother to put your answers on a postcard. Turn left and head eastwards along the Sussex Border Path, which is here a bridleway, to arrive at a road at the top end of **Linchmere** village at SU866314, 875m from the multi-path junction at SU858313 at Lower Brookham. You may (or may not) be interested to know that Linchmere is the north-westernmost village in Sussex!

Turn right along the road for some 350m to reach a junction with Linchmere Road that goes off left here. Your direct route turns left at this junction, SU868311, and in barely 50m forks right as bridleway/Sussex Border Path-signed. However, I recommend that, as a detour, you follow the road on for 250m beyond the left turn at SU868311 above to visit the lovely church of St Peter, Linchmere. The church is of 11th century origin and among its interesting features are a double north aisle, carved wooden cherubs (playing musical instruments) adjacent to the old organ, a bas-relief of the Seven Deadly Sins thought to date from about 1300, and a glass south door giving fantastic views to the nearby hills and woodlands.

Back on the direct route, from the left turn of that route at SU868311 referred to above, fork right in barely 50m as stated and now follow the Sussex Border Path, again here a bridleway, in a predominantly easterly direction. It is very pleasant going indeed, on good tracks some 170m above sea level. I recall following this section of Sussex Border Path one remarkably snowy early December day in 2010 and feeling very low on energy here, being revived by a bar of Fry's Turkish Delight I found buried in my rucksack and which I'd forgotten I had! A word to the wise – always have supplies of food with you on your bridleway journeyings, taking with you more than you think you'll need. Back to route 68! You enter woodland, ignoring a bridleway going off at SU878312 (1km from SU868311), but 200m east of this point, at SU880312, you reach a road/bridleway. Turn left along it, leaving the Sussex Border Path.

Be warned that things now do get rather fiddly. In 200m or so from leaving the Sussex Border Path you veer right, being joined by the Serpent Trail. Now continue east/south-eastwards with the Serpent Trail (here a bridleway), crossing straight over Marley Lane, 500m from SU880312, at SU884314. Just 75m or so east of the lane, turn right with the Serpent Trail (still a bridleway) which you now follow south-eastwards onto **Marley Common.** One of the National Trust's earliest countryside acquisitions, the common is home to Galloway cattle; birds you may see include woodlark, nightjar, Dartford warbler, nuthatch, woodcock, crossbill, meadow pipit, yellowhammer and woodpecker; in the spring there's a wealth of lovely wild flowers; and in the summer you should look out for brimstone butterflies.

In 375m from Marley Lane, at SU888313, you meet the Sussex Border Path again and now turn left, north-eastwards, following the Serpent Trail AND Sussex Border Path along the bridleway. You're now able to get properly into your stride for a bit, but in 500m at SU893315 both the name routes fork away to the right. You go straight on, steeply downhill, along the bridleway, and at SU895316, some 250m after saying farewell to the two name paths, you reach the A286, the end of this route. Buses are available from Camelsdale, 500m along the main road to the left, to Liphook and Haslemere.

ROUTE 69

SU860217-SU859215 – Location Map W5 – OS OL33 – M

7km 100m

Stedham Common, Iping Common, Trotton Common, Trotton

PT Stedham (B start and finish)
R Stedham, Trotton

This is a lovely common-land circular route with a bit of history as well. It can easily be treated as a circular route by starting and finishing at Stedham. It includes two "out and back" sections but the first is so integral to the route that I refrain from treating it as just a recommended detour!

To access the route from Stedham, served by buses from Petersfield and Midhurst, make your way to the A272 at the south end of The Street at SU861219, 250m from the village centre. Cross straight over the A272 with great care, heading on down Minsted Road for 150m to reach a bridleway heading right, just north of west, at SU860217. This is the start of your route. Turn right along the bridleway, overlapping with the signed Serpent Trail (see route 14), which is a bridleway here, You then continue in a predominantly westerly direction, staying with the Serpent Trail across Stedham Common, arriving at Elsted Road in 750m from the start. You cross this road and then continue with the Serpent Trail along a bridleway just south of west onto Iping Common. **Stedham and Iping Commons**, mostly owned by the Sussex Wildlife Trust, are among the best examples of lowland heath in Sussex, and support an amazing variety of insects and birds. The best time to visit is the summer, when the purple heather is at its most resplendent, and you may see silver-studded blue butterflies, minotaur beetles, swallows, martins, nightjars, siskins and linnets. If you visit in spring, you may be rewarded with the song of the willow warbler, stonechat or tree pipit. You need to watch the Serpent Trail signage carefully – there are so many tracks to choose from! Having followed the Serpent Trail 400m beyond Elsted Road, you reach, at SU849219, first a bridleway going off sharp right, and then the Serpent Trail veering westwards. You however continue on the bridleway south-westwards, away from the Serpent Trail and now on Fitzhall Heath. At SU846215, 400m from SU849219, you reach a bridleway crossroads.

Here turn right along a signed bridleway track that passes through trees then climbs steeply north-westwards, arriving in 375m at a T-junction with another bridleway at SU843218. Note that you will be retracing to this point from the trig point you're now heading for, so watch for helpful landmarks. Turn right at the T-junction at SU843218, and in a few metres you reach another junction of tracks, and a post with a rather confusing multiplicity of arrows! On the right, just beyond the arrows, there's a gate (A). Pass through the gate, and take the right forking bridleway; you're actually back here briefly on the route of the Serpent Trail. Follow this bridleway north-eastwards, IGNORING the signed right turn in 125m taking the Serpent Trail away, and continue through the heather to a trig point reached in 400m from the gate (A) at SU845221. The views across Iping Common, to your right, and Trotton Common, to your left, are superb. Now retrace to (A).

Here you have the option, which I highly recommend, of a visit to the church at Trotton. To do this, pass through the gate and turn right along a clear bridleway track, back on the Serpent Trail. It's lovely fast downhill going along the southern edge of the most attractive **Trotton Common**, and takes you, in 625m from the gate (A), to Terwick Lane at SU838221. To reach Trotton, some 375m away, turn right along Terwick Lane, almost immediately reaching the A272. Turn left alongside it, shortly crossing the (West Sussex) River Rother and entering **Trotton**. On your right is the splendid church of St George, dating from around 1300 and boasting two of the finest brasses in Sussex: one is that of Margaret Camoys who died in about 1310 and the other shows later members of the Camoys family, one of whom, Thomas, Lord Camoys, fought at the Battle of Agincourt.

The church also has some superb wall paintings, while visible from the churchyard is the part-16th century Trotton Place. Retrace from the church all the way to gate (A) and from there retrace to SU843218.

Back on the continuous route, from SU843218 don't retrace south-eastwards but rather join the bridleway that heads southwards from here, and descends through woodland to reach Elsted Road in 500m at SU843214. Cross straight over the road to join and then follow a bridleway heading fractionally south of east, a straight forest track, arriving in 625m at SU849213 at two parallel bridleways going off to the left in very quick succession. Turn left along either of them: the choice is yours! They are both in the shade of trees and both equally pleasant. Whichever you've gone for, at the end, in 250m, you reach Elsted Road. Turn right along the road for another 250m then at SU852217 bear right again along a bridle track heading just south of east for 750m along the south side of Stedham Common. When I walked this on a November day, it was rather badly chewed up, a combination of tree felling work and wet weather – but I guess that's the price you pay for walking in quieter months with all the children in class doing their sums. I trust when you explore it, the going will be much easier for you.

At the end you reach Minsted Road, which is the end of your route, at SU859215. To return to Stedham, turn left here up Minsted Road, crossing straight over the A272 and continuing up The Street to arrive back in the village, 400m from the end of the route. A brief description of Stedham appears in route 16. As stated, buses are available from here to Midhurst and Petersfield.

ROUTE 70

SU895258-SU891233 – Location Map W5 – OS OL33 – S

10km 825m

Henley, Verdley Wood, Bexleyhill Common, Snapelands Copse, Lodsworth, Vining Common, Grevatts, Easebourne

PT Henley (B start), Easebourne (B finish)

R Henley, Lodsworth, Easebourne

This linear route combines superb common land with fine woodland, great views and three picturesque villages. Both start and finish points are very close to bus stops on the same (Midhurst-Haslemere) bus route.

To reach the start of the route from the A286, assuming you leave the bus at the stop by the road turning leading south-eastwards to Henley (the grid reference for the junction is SU893258), follow that road south-eastwards for 200m steeply down to **Henley**'s village street. Its highlight is its 16th century Duke of Cumberland pub, magnificently situated with great views which may extend as far as Leith Hill, Surrey's highest point.

On reaching the village street turn left up that street, in 125m reaching the start of the route, SU895258. DON'T take the Serpent Trail-signed footpath just shy of this point. Having reached the start, join the restricted byway heading away to the right here, almost at once veering gently left past houses and continuing north-eastwards along a clear woodland-edge track. At SU898263, 500m from the start, you reach a path crossroads. Turn right here, and now follow a clear bridleway track through the lovely **Verdley Wood**, initially south-eastwards, then eastwards before veering south-eastwards again. Signage is very clear but be very careful to bear left with the bridleway at SU900259.

You continue to rise steadily, reaching a T-junction of tracks at SU906254, 1km 250m from SU898263. Turn left here, now overlapping with the Serpent Trail (see route 14), and follow the bridleway track for 500m uphill to its end at a road, at SU911253. Turn left to follow the road eastwards for roughly 250m, then at SU914253 fork right with the Serpent Trail, here a bridleway, heading south-eastwards across the attractive wooded **Bexleyhill Common**. The path is very unpromising at first, but soon improves. You continue south-eastwards with the Serpent Trail through woodland, passing a bridleway coming in from the left at SU918248 and going forward onto Ovis Common, reaching a bridleway fork at SU919243, roughly 1km from the road. Fork left here, keeping to the Serpent Trail, emerging from the middle of the woods and now descending along the field edge just to the right of **Snapelands Copse**. It's a lovely bridleway with tremendous views ahead.

At the bottom end of the copse you reach a path junction at SU926239, 750m from the fork at SU919243. Here you leave the Serpent Trail, veering right, just west of south, with the bridleway and passing by the Redlands Farm buildings; veer sharp left at the bottom end of the complex and descend with the bridleway to its end at SU977237 where you meet the road, 325m or so after leaving the Serpent Trail. Turn right along the road and follow it into the centre of **Lodsworth,** one of the loveliest villages in West Sussex, with a superb mix of architectural styles along its main street. Among the best are Erickers, a delightful mix of timber-framing and tile-hanging, the timber-framed Old Well House, Woodmancote, sometime home of *Winnie The Pooh* illustrator Ernest Shepard, and the impressive early 18th century Old House (formerly Dower House). The village boasts not only a delightful old pub, the Hollist Arms, but also the Lodsworth Larder, a combined general store and delicatessen, with a wonderful range of fresh produce. So enjoy a well-earned snack while helping the local economy! Church Lane, itself full of very pretty cottages, forks left away from the main street some way south of the pub (and off route) and leads down to the beautifully situated part-Norman church of St Peter, beyond which is the Manor House with 13th century features.

Follow the main street (The Street) past the pub and almost immediately beyond it, 750m after joining the road, (but before Church Lane) turn right at the road junction, passing Lodsworth House which is to your left, then turning right in 250m from The Street, up School Lane. In 125m you reach a road fork, taking the left fork here. Then in another 125m at TQ926234 fork left again off the road to join a bridleway that strikes away north-westwards from the village, passing through Vining Copse and (ignoring a footpath forking left) arriving at a signed bridleway crossroads at SU918238, by Vining Farm, now on **Vining Common**. This is some 875m from TQ926234. There's a beautifully situated bench by the signpost and the views are superb. Cross straight over, going north-westwards, reaching in 500m the buildings of **Grevatts** at SU914241. Two paths are signed to the right in close succession: you ignore the first, which is a public footpath, but take the second, bridleway-signed, heading north-westwards from Grevatts. This is simply superb going, with glorious views southwards to the South Downs escarpment and to Midhurst.

Continue along this bridleway north-westwards, soon entering delightful woodland, arriving at a road junction at SU907246, 1km from Grevatts. Follow the road going straight ahead, north-westwards, and in some 300m turn left at SU904249 along a signed restricted byway. This heads south-westwards along the edge of fine woodland with terrific views then descends through the trees, reaching a T-junction with a public way at SU895238, about 1km 500m from the road. Turn right and in 75m veer sharp left, going forward to join another (signed) restricted byway that descends south-westwards to reach the A286 at Budgenor Lodge, Easebourne at SU891233, 750m from the public way, and the end of the route.

As I indicated above, there are buses from here to Midhurst and Haslemere. However by turning left alongside the A286 and then left in 500m down the superbly-named Wheelbarrow Castle, you reach, in a further 375m, the delightful centre of **Easebourne**, also served by buses to

Midhurst. Easebourne (pronounced Ezbourne) contains a former Augustinian priory dating from 1238, the Priory church of St Mary with 11th and 12th century features, and many lovely houses of timber and distinctive local stone. The village has one particular curiosity, opposite the church, namely the Private Byepass Bridge adjacent to the main road, which was designed for horse traffic. The sign on it says "Motors Not Exceeding 2 Tons May Use It At Own Risk – Dangerous And Forbidden To All Other Traffic." Nowadays, even if the main carriageway is congested, it's hard to see what use any motorist or indeed horse-rider could make of it!

ROUTE 71

SU966188-SU896208 – Location Map W5 – OS OL10, OL33 – M

10km 175m

Duncton Common, Graffham Common, Selham Common, Ambersham Common, Little London, Heyshott Common, Midhurst

PT Heath End (B start - PB), Midhurst (B finish)

R Heath End, Midhurst

This is a hugely satisfying common-land journey. However please note it is linear in nature, served by different bus routes. Petworth or Chichester could both be used as bases if you're reliant on public transport: you could travel to the start using the Chichester-Petworth service, and travel back from Midhurst either to Chichester or Petworth.

From Heath End, served on request by prebooked buses on the Chichester-Petworth route, head westwards from the A285 at SU966188, the start of your route, along a bridleway, following the Serpent Trail (see route 14) across the picturesque **Duncton Common**. You'll be traversing a number of commons on this journey and very soon after you start you'll get a flavour of what you'll be enjoying throughout the next 10km or so. Around you is a pleasant mixture of heather, gorse, pine, rhododendron and silver birch; the commons support a great variety of bird and insect life including tree pipit, woodlark, spotted flycatcher, stonechat, nightjar and longhorn beetle, while among the thick heath vegetation you may see insectivorous sundews, adders, common lizards and sand lizards. In areas of wet heath, you may find patches of cotton grass and cross-leaved heather. On Ambersham and Heyshott Commons in particular there is a wide variety of heathland invertebrates, with many beetles, bees, wasps, flies and spiders. One species of spider that's very fond of these dry heaths is the wolf spider, which catches its prey not with a traditional spider's web but with a shot of venom.

In 750m at SU959189 you leave the Serpent Trail, forking right along a signed bridleway north-westwards for 750m in all, ascending along the edge of woodland and then proceeding through woods to reach a junction of bridleways at SU952193. Turn half-left, not hard left, along a super bridleway heading westwards for 375m on a clear woodland track to arrive at Cathanger Lane. Turn left along the lane for some 325m then at SU946191 turn right just beyond a house along a most attractive bridleway that descends north-westwards to a lake, then veers just north of west to proceed through Fitzlea Wood on the north side of pretty **Graffham Common**. Ignore a bridleway signed left at SU941196 but veer north here and continue to a T-junction of bridleways at SU941199, roughly 1km 175m beyond Cathanger Lane.

At SU941199 turn left and follow the clear bridleway track westwards for 250m to a road, crossing straight over and continuing along a lovely woodland bridleway track for 500m, initially south-westwards then veering just north of west to reach another road at SU933197. (NOTE: it is possible you may be diverted between SU938197 and SU933197 along a woodland-edge bridleway between the two road crossings to protect local wildlife. Follow signage carefully.) At SU933197 cross straight over, heading south-westwards on a bridleway through woodland, then emerge and, proceeding predominantly westwards, continue across fields, now on yet another fine common, **Selham Common**, going over a crossroads of bridleways at SU928196. Entering woodland and now veering more south-westwards, you reach a junction with the Serpent Trail at SU924195, 1km beyond the last road crossing. Taking the right fork, join the Serpent Trail (here a bridleway), heading south-westwards for some 700m to a bridleway T-junction deep in the woods at SU917192.

Turn right and continue along the Serpent Trail north-westwards as signed, descending and crossing a stream, then rising. Following the excellent Serpent Trail signage carefully, you now climb, taking care to follow the right fork at the sign at SU915194, and ascend steeply on the sandy track to the top of **Ambersham Common**, passing a trig point that's in the heather to your right. It's lovely going along an excellent bridle track. Continuing to observe the Serpent Trail signage, you follow the plateau then, as you approach the car park, turn right as Serpent Trail-signed and continue along the path to reach New Road at SU914197, 750m from SU917192. You cross straight over New Road, but then in a few metres turn left at the bridleway junction (A), being reunited in just a few steps with the Serpent Trail which has taken a mini short cut, not following a bridleway!

The continuous route turns left, south-westwards, at (A) but I do recommend you detour straight on at (A) to reach, in some 375m, the charmingly situated house at **Little London**, beyond which is a mini-descent to a gorgeous little woodland stream crossed by a bridge. It really is straight out of a Sunday teatime serial drama – without the commercial breaks. You then need to return to (A) to continue. From (A) you now head south-westwards, as stated, along a bridleway across **Heyshott Common**; this is superb going, and there's a real sense of peace and remoteness. In 750m from (A) you reach a bridleway crossroads at SU907193. Here bear sharp right, north-westwards, to follow another super path into thicker woodland; this path brings you to a bridleway T-junction at SU903201, 800m or so from SU907193. At SU903201 you turn right, now leaving the Serpent Trail but overlapping with the New Lipchis Way (see route 5). Immediately after turning right you cross a splendid red-brick bridge over the course of the old Pulborough-Petersfield railway. This opened in stages between 1859 and 1864 and closed to passengers in 1955; sadly very little of it is available for exploration, even though there are large sections, including what you see from the bridge, that could so easily be converted into a trail for walkers and riders. We live in hope.

Barely 100m beyond the bridge crossing you turn left with the New Lipchis Way, here a bridleway, and head north-westwards with it, reaching a bridleway junction at SU898206 after 750m. Leaving the New Lipchis Way you turn left here, descending quite steeply. You bear sharp right with the bridleway and follow a driveway past Costers Mill to reach Oaklands Lane at SU896208; there's actually a road junction here, of Oaklands Lane and Selham Road, some 450m from SU898206. Here your bridleway route ends. To reach Midhurst from here, cross over Oaklands Lane and follow Selham Road for 1km north-westwards to its junction with Chichester Road. Turn right along that road to access the town.

Midhurst is a lovely old town with a delightfully old-fashioned feel. Among its many highlights are the spectacular ruins of the 16th century Cowdray House, the early 15th century timber-framed Spread Eagle, the mid-16th century Market House, the very pretty ensemble of cottages around Edinburgh Square, the remains of a Norman castle above St Ann's Hill, the tiny museum in Knockhundred Row, the quaint cottages in South Street and West Street, and South Pond itself, once a breeding ground for fish and later a millpond for fulling cloth. There are also plenty of excellent pubs and eateries to refresh you after your journey. Buses are available from Midhurst to Petworth and Chichester as stated.

ROUTE 72

TQ323098 (start and finish) – Location Map E5 – OS OL11 – M

10km 900m

Stanmer Park, Stanmer Down, Stanmer

PT Upper Lodges (B start and finish, weekends and bank holidays only), Hollingbury (B start and finish, other times)

R Stanmer, Hollingbury

This is a really delightful circular exploration of the lovely open space that is Stanmer Park. If you do the complete journey you'll see Stanmer in all its aspects – parkland, downland and historic village. Please note that some of the bridleways on this circuit are permissive but in reality it's highly unlikely there'll be a problem with access at any time. Contact the relevant authority if you want to make sure!

At weekends and bank holidays buses run direct from Brighton Station to the start at the Upper Lodges car park on Ditchling Road. At other times, if you're coming up from central Brighton by bus you'll need to get yourself to the north-eastern end of Carden Avenue in the Hollingbury area of Brighton, crossing over the A27 using the bridge at TQ321095, then going over the roundabout on the far side. Just beyond the roundabout turn right then sharp left, north-eastwards along a bridleway bringing you in 175m to Ditchling Road, crossing straight over into the Upper Lodges car park at TQ323098.

From the car park at TQ323098, your starting point, head briefly eastwards along a signed bridleway then after roughly 150m at TQ325099, at a signed crossroads of paths, turn left. It's signed as a public footpath but in fact is a permissive bridleway. Now follow what is a clear wide track just west of north through the woods. There are lovely views through the trees: look out in particular for a view of Waterhall Windmill to the south-west. Throughout this journey you're in the lovely **Stanmer Park** with its rolling hills, broad expanses of grass and areas of pretty woodland. Every season brings its joys, from spring bluebells to dazzling autumn tints; I walked it in early January and it still felt vibrant and invigorating. You emerge from the trees and continue in the same direction across grassland, kinking very briefly left and then right, with Ditchling Road close by you to the left. You pass a pond at TQ323111, 1km 250m from TQ325099, and beyond it, go forward to and through the gate leading into the trees.

Now veering north-eastwards, follow the clear woodland path, ignoring tracks leading left to Ditchling Road but veering right, just south of east, at TQ327115 (500m from the pond), here joining an official bridleway! In 375m from TQ327115, at TQ330115, you reach an unsigned crossroads of tracks. Turn right at this crossroads onto a permissive bridleway, heading predominantly southwards downhill on a wide track. In roughly 200m the track veers left but you go straight on, southwards, through the gate, and follow what is a clear path downhill through very pleasant woodland. The woodland relents as your path, which can get very muddy, bottoms out, but then you enter a further patch of woodland, rising and then veering just east of south to reach a gate at the far edge of the wood, at TQ329104, 1km from TQ330115. Go through the gate and turn left. Pause here to enjoy a lovely view across this part of Stanmer Park, then follow the left-hand field edge steadily downhill to arrive, in 625m from the gate, at a T-junction with an official bridleway at TQ335101.

Here you have a choice. If you wished to keep your route short, sticking to the continuous route, turn right, south-eastwards, along the bridleway. However, if you fancy seeing more of the park and enjoying a climb onto the South Downs, there's a superb out-and-back detour available here, and I thoroughly recommend it. Turn left at TQ335101 and head very agreeably northwards through classic parkland scenery with green hillsides and, on your left, a strip of woodland known picturesquely as Granny's Belt. At this woodland strip you veer north-eastwards to reach a 4-way bridleway junction at TQ337108, 500m from TQ335101. Cross straight over at TQ337108 and follow what is a gorgeous bridleway north then north-eastwards; you begin with a fine woodland descent to a dry valley bottom then enjoy a tremendous open climb onto Bow Hill, part of **Stanmer Down**, to reach a bridleway T-junction at TQ343117, 1km 125m from the 4-way bridleway junction. Turn left here and continue uphill, northwards then north-westwards, to reach in another 1km 125m, the South Downs Way at TQ339128. The views from the ascent, and from the South Downs Way at the top, are magnificent, particularly towards the sea, but be warned that it can be incredibly blowy up there! You then retrace all the way back to TQ335101.

Whether you've detoured or not, head south-eastwards as stated from TQ335101 to reach, in 250m at TQ336098, the top end of **Stanmer's** village street. The street contains pretty flint 18th century estate cottages, and the attractive 19th century church boasts some fine timber furnishings and 16th century monuments, while in the churchyard there is a Georgian well house with donkey wheel. Stanmer's most impressive historic feature is the fine early 18th century Stanmer House, the seat of the Pelham family, with a splendid exterior consisting of ashlar blocks of Wealden sandstone. The house is described by the *Pevsner Architectural Guide* as "an exercise in a plain and gentlemanly classicism that is barely neo-Palladian." Nowadays you may be able to go into the house to take tea but remember to pull your muddy boots off first. If that's too much bother you may also get a cup of tea in the village itself where they're less fussy about things like that.

Having enjoyed the village, house and church, return to TQ336098 and now head predominantly westwards along a lane/bridleway which returns you to Upper Lodges, your starting point, in roughly 1km 250m.

ROUTE 73

TQ335194 (start and finish) – Location Map E5 – OS OL11 – E

6km 50m

Ditchling Common Country Park, West Wood, Purchase Wood

PT B2112 junction with Janes Lane (B start and finish)

R Wivelsfield, Wivelsfield Green

This is a short easy circular route, but can be lengthened should you wish to detour onto the very picturesque Ditchling Common. It incorporates some permissive sections, for which permission could in theory be withdrawn; check with the relevant authority if you want to make sure of the position.

Your route starts close to the junction of Janes Lane and the B2112 at TQ335194; there are bus stops/shelters on both sides of the road here, served by regular buses on the Crawley-Brighton route. You'll notice between the two bus shelters a metalled approach road on the far side of the B2112 from Janes Lane, leading to St George's Park retirement complex. Follow this approach road very briefly, but almost immediately you reach a crossing path; this is in fact a bridleway, and is the start of this route. Turn right here, south-westwards, to follow the bridleway through the trees past the retirement complex, crossing another metalled approach road in some 200m. Go straight over along the path through grass, keeping a white fence to your left. The fence ends as you arrive in further woodland and immediately beyond the end of the fence you need to veer sharp left up a bridleway path running uphill, keeping the edge of the wood immediately to the left; ignore a parallel path that's to your right.

After a gentle climb you approach another building complex, predominantly brick-built, that's to your left; just before getting level with it look out for a metalled gate, also to your left. Don't pass through the gate, and don't go straight on either, but veer gently right here along the clear path. Continuing to ascend gently through the trees in the same general direction as before the gate, you reach a path T-junction. Turn left to immediately arrive at a crossroads junction with a metalled lane; cross straight over and immediately fork right, south-eastwards, along a green-arrow-signed path. Don't be misled by the colour: I assure you this is the bridleway route and I assume the green signage denotes an overlapping nature trail. If I'm wrong, well, I believe this could be the only bridleway in Sussex that is green arrow-signed. But ours is not to reason why. Don't trouble to let me know if you find any others!

Now things get less fiddly. Follow this excellent path through the trees, reaching a gate with a metalled kissing gate adjoining it: straight ahead, there's an area of open grassland and, beyond, really lovely views to the South Downs. As the crow flies, Ditchling Beacon is less than 6km away. You've arrived at **Ditchling Common Country Park**, a most popular spot for walkers and picnickers. Signage is poor here: DON'T go through the kissing gate, but kink left and right to continue along a wide path in the same south-easterly direction at the edge of the trees, keeping the open grassland immediately to the right. The views are, and continue to be, absolutely superb. You then descend through thicker woodland along a clear but often muddy path, emerging to enjoy further good views of the country park and the Downs.

At TQ338181, 1km 500m from the start, you get level with a car park that's to your right, with a pond to your left. At this point your bridleway veers left, and an unsigned path goes off to the right. By bearing right along this path you're able to embark on a detour along a permissive bridleway which enables you to see more of Ditchling Common and perhaps, if you're on foot, venture into its interior if that does not sound over-dramatic or pretentious – we're talking cosy East Sussex here, not the African bush! If you wish to detour, turn right as stated along a stony path which soon widens and becomes grassy. You pass alongside the car park, keeping it close by to your left. Just before it ends, you reach a crossing track. Go straight over it, following the arrow-signed path on, but almost immediately, by a litter bin, another path forks left. Join this one, your soon being reassured by a post with a horseshoe depicted on it. Now follow the path heading westwards, keeping a road, Folders Lane East, close by and parallel with you to your left. As you follow the path you soon reach a grassy area to your right, and across it you can see the pond which lies in the heart of the country park. There is a superb diversity of flora and fauna across the common, with its variety of habitats including grassland, woodland and pond. Spring brings with it an abundance of bluebells; trees include mature oak and willow; other plants to be found here include a profusion of bracken as well as adder's tongue fern, petty whin, meadow thistle, heath bedstraw, tormentil, betony, and varieties of orchid. The common/ country park boasts many butterflies, including the green and purple hairstreak, while varieties of bat, including Bechstein's and barbastelle, both threatened species, have also been seen across the common. A nature trail, for walkers only, is in fact signed from the car park. The permissive bridleway path heads westwards as far as the junction between Folders Lane East and the busy B2112 and then turns sharply northwards to proceed adjacent to that road. However the traffic noise does spoil things a bit as one heads northwards; I recommend in fact that you stick to the path as far as the Folders Lane/B2112 junction then retrace the same way, using the east-west route (500m end-to-end) as your launching pad for further exploration of the common/country park, depending on how much time you have. Complete your detour by returning to TQ338181.

From TQ338181, as stated, your bridleway veers left, more starkly south-eastwards. You go straight over a driveway, passing a signboard for THE HOLT and THE HOLE, and shortly go straight over a metalled industrial estate approach road. The going gets quite muddy as you proceed on through the trees to arrive at the end of the bridleway at Folders Lane East, at TQ340179, some 250m from TQ338181. Turn left alongside the road, in 125m reaching a junction. Don't bear right along Spatham Lane, but continue briefly eastwards, along Middleton Common Lane. Almost immediately, however, in barely 50m at TQ341178, turn left as bridleway-signed, now on the Sussex Border Path (SBP) spur route (see route 4). Now follow this bridleway initially just east of north, arriving in 375m at a bridleway fork junction at TQ343182. Here you take the bridleway forking left, just west of north, staying with the (signed) SBP. You then veer northwards and continue along the edge of most attractive woodland, including **West Wood** and then **Purchase Wood**. Some stretches of the SBP can be a little uninspiring, but this section is one of the more enjoyable, certainly of the spur route if not the whole route, with lovely views from the woodland edge across adjacent fields. However it can be exceedingly muddy at times. There are also numerous places where there is more than one path available, but fear not: the way forward, northwards, is always clear with occasional bridleway signs to reassure you. Near the end you find yourself proceeding through the middle of woodland and, as you approach a large house to the right, paths do diverge significantly. You need the one going closer to the house, going forward along a driveway and arriving at a T-junction at a road at TQ345199, 1km 750m from TQ343182.

Here the SBP goes off to the right, along Eastern Road; should you wish to sample the amenities of Wivelsfield Green, you too should bear right along Eastern Road then at its end in 500m turn right along Green Road, following it for 500m into the village centre. However the continuous route turns left at TQ345199 along a bridleway that is initially a metalled road. The road ends beside a splendid timber-framed house, Jack O Clubs, that's to your right. Immediately beyond the end of the road, you reach two forking paths. There's a slightly misleading sign here but you need the left path, a bridleway which then heads south-westwards through the trees to arrive within a stone's throw of the B2112 in 500m from TQ345199. Ignore a bridleway signed to the right, leading to the roadside (this features later in this book as one of the shortest bridleways in Sussex!) but continue straight on as bridleway-signed, keeping the B2112 a short distance to your right. This bridleway isn't in fact shown on recent OS Explorer maps. Keep parallel with the B2112 along the bridleway continuing south-westwards, arriving back at the start point, the St George's Park approach road, at TQ335194, in a further 500m. Your route ends here. Bear right along the approach road to almost immediately reach the bus stops by the Janes Lane junction, for buses towards Crawley and Brighton.

ROUTE 74

TQ491289-TQ507304 – Location Map E5 – OS 135 – M

6km 875m

Ashdown Forest

PT Crow & Gate (B start), Crowborough (B finish)

R Crow & Gate, Crowborough

This is a linear route but both start and finish points are very close to stops on the same (Brighton-Tunbridge Wells) bus route. Your route starts right by the A26 at TQ491289 conveniently close to the Crow & Gate pub between Heron's Ghyll and Crowborough (buses stop just by the pub); the actual starting point is some 375m west of the pub, where a signed bridleway, also the Vanguard Way (see route 24), goes off northwards from the A26. You now follow this bridleway, almost immediately veering north-westwards and now striking out very enjoyably across **Ashdown Forest.**

The word "forest" here is misleading, as the landscape making up Ashdown Forest is extremely open and in many areas wholly devoid of trees. Rather than a forest, it is a tract of sandy heathland, dominated by heather, bracken and scrub as opposed to woodland. It's made up of the lowest strata that lie under the huge dome of chalk with which Sussex was once covered; as a result of earth movements and erosion, the crest of the dome has been worn away, the sands of this area exposed as the ancient core. The area was used for trackways in prehistoric times, and in Roman times it was a thoroughfare from London to the South Downs. From Norman times onwards, commoners exercised rights over the land which included the collection of wood for fuel, and in due course ironmasters cut down forest trees to heat their forges. The resultant legacy of all this is a largely open tract of land, with sandy soil and a multitude of tracks; ironically a good deal of tree planting has taken place in the last century to give relief for the supposed barrenness of the land!

With its great views, its sandy soil which drains exceptionally well and so is easy to walk on, and its multiplicity of routes across it, Ashdown Forest is extremely popular with visitors. There's an exceptional variety of bird life, including Dartford warbler, stonechat, meadow pipit, skylark, yellowhammer, goldcrest, woodlark and reed bunting; fallow deer and roe deer are plentiful; the forest supports 34 species of butterfly; trees include oak, Scots pine, alder, silver birch and hazel; and among plants you may find are bell heather, dwarf gorse, heath-spotted orchid, and, in wetter areas of the forest, sphagnum moss, bog asphodel and marsh gentian. A glance at the map reveals there are very few signed bridleways on Ashdown Forest, which may surprise you, but bear in mind that much of the Forest is designated as Access Land and thus available for exploration without specific signage to tell you so. In fact as part of a policy to minimise manmade structures in the Forest, signage of any kind on the Ashdown Forest tracks is extremely sparing; I made the mistake of relying too much on signage when I walked the Ashdown Forest section of the Vanguard Way and found myself so disorientated in places that I half expected to find myself back where I'd started the previous day, on the windswept down platform of Newhaven Harbour Station.

Anyway, your bridleway follows what is an obvious track through the heart of the Forest, until, 2km 250m from the start, you get to TQ474300, just short of a large clump of trees marked on maps as Kings Standing Clump, with a bridleway signposted right. Turn right here as bridleway-signed, descending, then veer sharp left with the bridleway, and follow it north-westwards to reach the B2188 at TQ473303, 250m or so from TQ474300. Turn right alongside the B2188 for 750m, then at TQ475309, by the buildings of Deerswood Farm, turn right as bridleway-signed.

You now follow a clear bridleway track that will bring you all the way into Crowborough. Initially you descend, enjoying fine views across Ashdown Forest to your right, heading south-eastwards and passing through delightful unspoilt woodland, veering right after 1km. The descent seems to go on forever, but as you reach and pass Old Mill Farm, 1km 250m from Deerswood Farm, your path bottoms out and you veer left, north-eastwards. You now begin what will be a long steady climb in a predominantly north-eastward direction, initially through woodland then emerging from the wood and ascending steadily to Home Farm. Despite your nearness to Crowborough this still all feels very remote and peaceful.

At Home Farm at TQ495305, roughly 1km from Old Mill Farm, you reach a junction of tracks. Turn right here, just south of east, along a farm lane that is a continuation of your bridleway. In 1km from Home Farm your lane veers gently left, just north of east, and enters Crowborough. Continue along the same lane, going forward along what is Warren Road, rising steadily and arriving at TQ507304 (1km 375m from Home Farm) with Rannoch Road going off to your left and Fielden Lane and Melfort Road going off to your right. This is the end of the route. To reach the centre of Crowborough, with its bus connections, go straight on along Warren Road for 375m to its end at Beacon Road, turning left along Beacon Road (A26) for another 750m.

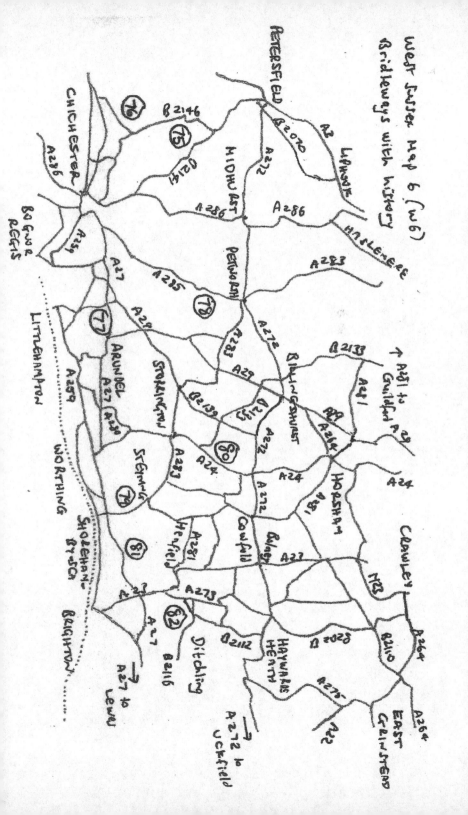

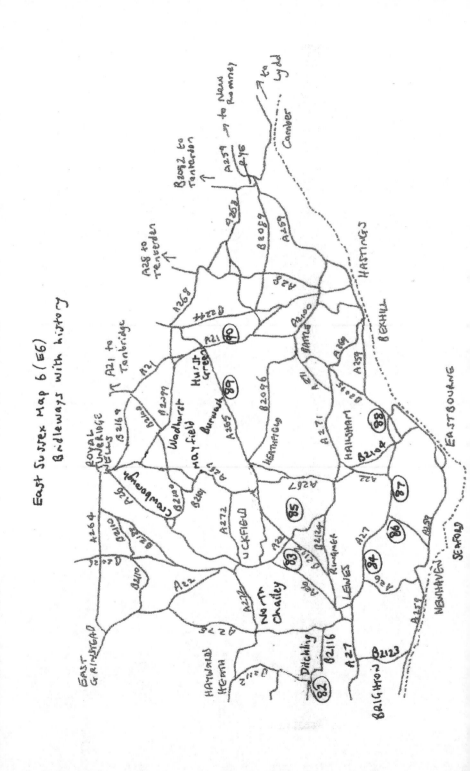

East Sussex Map 6 (E6)
Bridleways with history

Part 6 – Bridleways with history

When I say "history" I use the word in its broadest sense to include not only fine architecture but prehistoric monuments and relics from our industrial past. It's all here: country houses, a deserted medieval village, a camera obscura, a Roman road, follies, quaint Norman churches, priory ruins and more besides. And they're all easily accessible thanks to our wonderful network of bridleways. Note that some of the historical features are at the start and/or finish of the bridleway route in question rather than actually on the route itself.

ROUTE 75

SU778146 (start and finish) – Location Map W6 – OS OL8 – E

6km 950m

Bevis's Thumb, Telegraph Hill, Up Marden, Compton

PT Compton (B start and finish)

R Compton

This is an immensely rewarding circular route with lots of history. To access the start of this route from the square in the centre of the pretty village of Compton, served by buses on the Petersfield-Chichester service, head south-eastwards along School Lane leading away from the square. You arrive, in 250m from the square, at a junction of bridleways, SU778146, where the route starts. At the bridleway junction you turn hard left as signed to follow a bridleway that proceeds north-eastwards for 1km 250m along the edge of delightful woodland, finally reaching a junction with a road, Long Lane, and another bridleway at SU787155. At this junction is a Neolithic long barrow or burial mound known as **Bevis's Thumb**. The burial mound is an elongated barrow, and indeed at 60m in length it's one of the largest earthen long barrows in the south-east of England. As to how it got its name, legend has it that Bevis worked as a warden at Arundel Castle (where you can still find Bevis's Tower) and every week ate an ox washed down with two hogsheads of beer; he was said to be so tall that he could walk from Southampton to the Isle of Wight without getting his head wet. According to legend, Bevis threw his sword from the parapet of Arundel Castle to mark the spot where he should be buried, and the sword landed here.

At the junction, turn hard right onto a bridleway that proceeds south-westwards on an obvious track heading up onto **Telegraph Hill** – there are really fine views as you gain height – and at SU781146, roughly 1km 125m from Bevis's Thumb, you reach a crossroads of paths. Take the bridleway going left here and now head just south of east, dropping downhill quite steeply. At the bottom of the dip you veer eastwards and now rise, the views improving as you gain height. Just to the right at SU795141, roughly 1km 500m from the path crossroads at SU781146, you'll find the completely unrestored 13th century church of St Michael, **Up Marden**, the epitome of the remote country church with its thick walls, white or cream plaster work, brick floor, box pews and wooden benches. The *Pevsner Architectural Guide* describes it as boasting "one of the loveliest (church) interiors in England…a visible loving testimony of the faith of successive generations."

Having visited the church – whatever your faith you will be truly inspired by it – retrace all the way back to SU781146. Here turn left, just west of south. Continue along the bridleway for 750m to SU780139, turning right at the bridleway junction here and then in 200m turning right again at SU778140. Now head northwards for 625m along what is a most attractive bridleway, with fine views to the valley below to your left; this bridleway takes you back to the start at SU778146, and you turn left to retrace along School Lane to **Compton**. This very pretty village boasts many lovely houses of flint and brick, with its focal point being its square containing village store/café, pub and

Millennium wellhead. Among the finest buildings in the village are its church of St Mary, with its late 12th century north arcade and chancel arch, the early 18th century grey-brick vicarage, and the more modern timber-framed Farndens and Old Manor House.

ROUTE 76

SU782094-SU768129 – Location Map W6 – OS OL8 – E

6km

Lordington House, Racton Tower, Stansted Park, Stansted House, Stansted Forest, West Marden

PT Walderton (B start), West Marden (B finish)

R Walderton, Stansted, West Marden

This is a generally easy and undemanding route, much of it in the beautiful Stansted Park. It's a linear route but both start and finish points are close to bus stops on the same (Chichester-Petersfield) bus route.

To access the route from the edge of Walderton, specifically from the fork turning off the B2146 north-eastwards signed Stoughton 1 mile (grid ref SU787105 – there is a bus stop here on the Chichester-Petersfield route), follow the B2146 south-westwards from that fork junction. As you follow the B2146 south-westwards, you pass the driveway leading to the impressive buildings of **Lordington House.** This L-shaped house dates back to 1623 but was remodelled in the early 18th century and updated in 1895 for Admiral Sir Phipps Hornby. Its mix of flint and brick is described in the *Pevsner Architectural Guide* as having a "very mellow and attractive effect." The interior, which sadly is not accessible to the public, boasts a superb staircase with depictions of heraldic beasts, dragons, bears and lions.

Some 375m beyond the house entrance road, and 1km 250m from the Walderton/Stoughton turning referred to above, you reach a fork junction of the B2146 and B2147.

Fork right with the B2147 Westbourne road and then almost immediately, at SU782094, the start of the route, turn right, north-westwards, along a restricted byway. You ascend and in some 500m after leaving the road, you reach the really splendid brick-built **Racton Tower**, a so-called folly, constructed in 1770 to a design by Henry Keene for the 2nd Earl of Halifax in an outlying part of his Stansted Park estate. It's described in the *Pevsner Architectural Guide* as "like most follies, perhaps best seen from a distance, but also strange and moving up close...mock sinister rather than truly sinister." It is its unexpectedness and incongruity, in this otherwise unremarkable landscape, which makes it special, and the views from the far side of the tower are extremely good, extending to the Isle of Wight on a clear day.

Continue just north of west along the restricted byway path through the trees, descending to arrive, roughly 625m from Racton Tower, at a signed restricted byway going off right at SU771097. This is actually a comparatively recent route, not marked as a right of way on some OS maps. Turn right to follow it northwards for 1km through lovely woodland, reaching a path junction at its end, at SU771107. Turn left here to proceed fractionally south of west along a bridleway, now following the course of the Monarch's Way (see route 6) through the splendidly maintained **Stansted Park.**

In roughly 1km 125m from SU771107, at SU760105, you reach a driveway on the left which gives access to **Stansted House.** The original building here was a Royal hunting lodge which in 1686 was replaced by a house designed by William Talman and extended in the late 18th century, the grounds having been laid out in the early 18th century. In 1724 Daniel Defoe commented on his ability to see from the west end of the house right down to the town and harbour of Portsmouth and ships at Spithead; the avenue to the west, laid out in the early 18th century and replanted in 1820, is said to be one of the best in England. The house was very badly damaged by fire in 1900 and largely rebuilt by Arthur Blomfield in 1903, although parts of the earlier construction remain. The drawing room retains a distinctly 18th century feel, there are paintings by Joshua Reynolds, the servants' quarters vividly reproduce the running of a great house in the early part of the last century, and the walled gardens feature restored Victorian glasshouses. There's a delightful chapel, built between 1812 and 1815 and boasting a superb little chancel with a window filled with painted glass of Jewish motifs. And there's also a fiendish maze if you've the time and the patience. You'll need a good deal of both!

Returning via the driveway to the bridleway, follow the bridleway on westwards for 150m or so, and then at SU759105 turn right, off the Monarch's Way, along a bridleway heading just east of north. This is a quite delightful well-defined bridleway along the edge of woodland, then through woods along the eastern fringes of **Stansted Forest**, passing stretches of wood mapped as Forest Hanger, Rosamond's Hill and Wythy Piece. Continuing in the same general direction, just east of north, and ignoring crossing/ forking tracks and footpaths, you gradually gain height, and, roughly 1km 625m from SU759105 where you joined this bridleway, you emerge from the woodland on top of a plateau. Staying on the bridleway, you can then enjoy a very attractive and straightforward 975m field journey on the plateau past Lodge Farm to arrive at the end of the route at SU768129, at the junction with Oldhouse Lane.

To get down to West Marden, cyclists and horse-riders need to turn left along the lane for 250m to meet the Forestside-West Marden road, turning right along this road for some 750m to reach the village. Walkers can simply cross Oldhouse Lane onto a public footpath which cuts down to the Forestside-West Marden road, thus saving about 250m overall! **West Marden**, with its pretty flint-built cottages and picturesque 16th century farmhouse, is actually the biggest of four villages known as the Mardens, the others being East Marden, Up Marden and North Marden. By following the main village street to its end, you reach a T-junction with the B2146 where buses are available on the Chichester-Petersfield route.

ROUTE 77

SU965062 (start and finish) – Location Map W6 – OS OL10 – M

15km 600m

Slindon, North Wood, Stane Street, Gumber Corner, "Bridle Road To Bignor," Walberton

PT Walberton (B start and finish)

R Walberton, Slindon

This circular route incorporates lots of different aspects of history: an old Roman road, some splendid architecture and a nod to a World War 2 politician who gave his name to a pie! It also offers some fine woodland and downland scenery.

To reach the start of this route from the nearest convenient public transport at Walberton (served by buses from Barnham which is on the rail network), proceed to Walberton's village green, follow West Walberton Lane north-westwards away from the green then in some 200m from the green turn right up Copse Lane at SU965062. This is the start of your bridleway route. Follow the bridleway northwards – in spring there are particularly impressive bluebells in the woods adjoining the bridleway here – and cross, with great care, over the A27. I well recall crossing the A27 here on a warm sunny Easter Monday in the early afternoon; ordinarily it would have been very busy but this was in the middle of the first lockdown and there wasn't a car in sight. All very surreal!

Beyond the A27 crossing, continue northwards along the bridleway, ignoring a right-hand bridleway turn at SU965074 and going forward to cross the A29, roughly 1km 375m from the start of Copse Lane. Continue straight on along the bridleway beyond the A29 to arrive in 375m at **Slindon**, meeting roads coming in from the left and the right at SU965079. Slindon is a very pretty village, its architectural highlights being the flint-built 16th century Slindon College (the site of an older palace of the archbishops of Canterbury) and the partly 11th century flint church of St Mary. Although it has been heavily restored, the church retains one feature of great interest, namely the only wooden effigy in Sussex, that of a reclining Tudor knight believed to be Anthony St Ledger of Binsted who died in 1539. It's described in the *Pevsner Architectural Guide* as "admirably modelled, alert and inquiring and individual." Just over the road from the church, in the grounds of Church House, is a thatched railway carriage!

Go forward from SU965079 straight up the main street (School Hill), turning left in 200m up Church Hill (passing the church and the railway carriage) and then, in 450m, left at the T-junction at the end to join Top Road. Now follow this road for 1km 250m, passing Slindon College and, veering sharp left, continuing downhill to reach SU950085, where a bridleway turns right off the road. Follow this bridleway which heads just west of north, rising gently but most pleasantly and passing round the edge of Nore Wood, veering north-eastwards. At SU951102 take care to turn left with the bridleway (rather than straight on with the footpath) and head fractionally west of north for 250m downhill to a bridleway T-junction at SU951105, here 2km from leaving the road.

Turn right at the T-junction at SU951105 and head eastwards for 400m through the middle of woodland, ignoring a bridleway soon forking right, arriving at a bridleway crossroads at SU955105. Turn left here and now head north-westwards on a dead straight bridleway for 1km. You're now in **North Wood,** some of the loveliest woodland in Sussex, and as you proceed you will see areas of recently planted trees to your right. At SU952114 you reach a multi-track junction. Turn right (not hard right) as Monarch's Way-signed and now follow the Monarch's Way (see route 6) north-eastwards. This bridleway follows the course of the old **Stane Street** Roman road constructed in about 70 AD by the Romans to link London and Chichester. Just as you might expect, it's dead straight so you would have to be a genius to lose your way here! As you proceed, the views become increasingly impressive, with particularly good views to Halnaker Windmill and the sea.

At the very top of the rise, at SU967126, having followed Stane Street for 2km from SU952114, you reach an area of trees and a path crossroads. Here turn right, eastwards, along the signed Monarch's Way (here a bridleway) for 150m through the woods, emerging at **Gumber Corner**, a bridleway junction, at SU969126, with brilliant views to the coast. Here leave the Monarch's Way, turning right and now proceeding on a superb bridleway track just east of south on a woodland edge. Ignoring turnings-off you simply stick to this track which in just under 1km from Gumber Corner emerges from the woods and proceeds decisively downhill, veering just west of south. This is an absolutely exhilarating journey, with a lovely open feel, magnificent views and the going very clear and straightforward. It's what bridleway exploring is all about!

You continue to descend, then, ironically, begin to climb gently, and some 3km 500m from Gumber Corner, at SU965092, you reach a path junction on the edge of woodland; note the lovely **"BRIDLE ROAD TO BIGNOR"** sign at this spot, pointing back the way you've come. It has the feel of an old-fashioned road sign and seems rather out of place here, but that just adds to its charm. Continuing in the same direction, just west of south, you now ascend into the woodland with the bridleway. Enjoying superb views on emerging from the woods, you now head southwards along Mill Lane to arrive, at SU965085, (some 700m from the BRIDLE ROAD TO BIGNOR sign) at a junction with Baycombe Lane on the edge of Slindon. Go forward southwards along Baycombe Lane and at the end turn left down School Hill.

As you descend School Hill you reach a road fork at SU965079 where you were earlier, 600m from your arrival at Baycombe Lane; you've come full circle. The very popular Forge shop and tearoom is reached by forking left here and you'll see it shortly on your right. However to proceed to Walberton you now retrace from earlier, taking the bridleway running between the two road forks at SU965079, heading just east of south to reach the A29 in 375m. Cross and continue as bridleway-signed, initially just west of south (ignoring a bridleway turning left at SU965074), then head southwards to reach the A27. Cross straight over this busy dual carriageway with immense care then continue down Copse Lane southwards, veering south-west then south again to meet West Walberton Lane at SU965062, about 1km 375m from the A29 crossing.

Your bridleway route ends here, but before heading home you should visit Walberton. To do this, turn left along West Walberton Lane then left again at the green along The Street to arrive at Walberton village centre, some 500m from the bottom of Copse Lane. **Walberton** itself is a pretty village whose church of St Mary boasts 12th century nave arcades (and older nave walls), and an early 12th century font described in the *Pevsner Architectural Guide* as "crude but powerful." One other feature of interest in the church is a window dedicated to Lord Woolton, Minister of Food during the Second World War; he gave his name to a special wartime concoction known as a Woolton Pie, a pastry dish filled with vegetables!

ROUTE 78

SU960171-TQ007176 – Location Map W6 – OS OL10 – S

18km 425m

Duncton Mill, Burton Park, Barlavington Hanger, Sutton, Bignor, Hospital Copse, Decoy Copse, Lord's Piece, Coates, Fittleworth

PT Duncton (B start - PB), Fittleworth (B finish)

R Duncton, Sutton, Bignor Roman Villa, Fittleworth

This is a strenuous but massively rewarding route, with lots of history and great scenery as well. Note that it is a linear route with different bus routes serving the start and end points of your journey, but you could use Petworth, served by buses on both these routes, as your base; buses are available to Petworth from the nearest railhead at Pulborough.

Your journey starts at Duncton, an unremarkable village on the A285 Chichester-Petworth road (and served by prebooked buses on the Chichester-Petworth service), but boasting a fine pub, the Cricketers, situated just south of the start point down the A285. At one time the pub was owned by the cricketer James Dean who played over 100 times for Sussex over 25 years in the 19th century, and who gave the pub its present name; it was previously called The Swan. From the starting point at SU960171, just north of the pub, you head eastwards from the A285 along a bridleway, Dye House Lane, here overlapping with the West Sussex Literary Trail (see route 5). In 375m you veer right, south-eastwards, then more gently left, south-westwards, proceeding past ponds and going forward to **Duncton Mill**, an early 19th century watermill and pond, the waters of which provide excellent fishing for rainbow trout and brown trout. Pause to note all the large fish in the pond to your right!

Immediately beyond the mill, at SU964165 (875m from the start) you reach a signed bridleway junction. This is a superb spot: looking to your right you can enjoy a mini-gorge with stream running through it, and in spring there are magnificent flowering shrubs dotted over the hillside. It is quite reminiscent of the Yorkshire Dales! At this junction you turn left, eastwards. In 300m at SU967165 the continuous bridleway route goes straight on but a bridleway goes off to the left, and with this left-turning bridleway comes the opportunity for a detour to **Burton Park**, 1km 125m each way. To undertake this detour, take this left bridleway turn, northwards, descending along the edge of Fountain Copse to a pond, then rising and joining a driveway, taking you past the house at Burton Park which dates from 1831, as far as the stunning church of St Richard. It boasts a Norman nave and chancel and, described in the *Pevsner*

Architectural Guide as "a lovable, unrestored building, one of the mellowest in Sussex," contains a superb range of memorials for such a small church including effigies and brasses, many to the Goring family and their descendants. You then need to retrace to SU967165 to be reunited with the main route.

Whether you've detoured or not, you now continue for 125m south-eastwards from SU967165 to reach Folly Lane which you cross more or less straight over as bridleway-signed. The bridleway beyond Folly Lane heads steeply uphill, south-westwards, soon entering the gorgeous woodlands of **Barlavington Hanger** and continuing to climb. These woodlands contain many species of interesting plants; there is a particular abundance of the bird's-nest orchid and the nettle-leaved bellflower. After some 750m from Folly Lane, you veer south-eastwards and now follow a woodland edge, veering southwards and descending. The masts of Glatting Beacon, which you're heading for, still seem a long way off from here! At SU964152, 1km 375m from Folly Lane, you pass a bridleway coming in from your left and, just 50m beyond that, cross a signed public way and now climb again. At the top of the rise, the bridleway follows a delightful course through a small cutting. There's then a further descent, your bridleway veering just east of south then south-westwards to a thicket with another bridleway coming in from the left here at SU962140, roughly 1km 250m from the public way crossing.

Turn hard left onto this bridleway, heading north-eastwards and steeply downhill through the woodland of Glatting Hanger, then at the foot of the hill you proceed beside a stream – or, quite possibly, through it, following periods of rain! At SU971146, 1km 125m from SU962140, you reach the end of the bridleway but carry on in the same direction along Glatting Lane. Ignore a right turn in 250m but continue just west of north along the road, which becomes Folly Lane, for another 500m to SU970154. Turn right here onto a really delightful signed bridleway that heads in a generally easterly direction for 875m, with superb views to the downs to your right, arriving in the main village street of **Sutton**. The street boasts several pretty cottages of sandstone, brick, flint and timber; there's also (at the time of writing) a popular pub, the 18th century stone and brick built White Horse, and the impressively large church of St John the Baptist, which boasts an 11th century nave, late 12th century aisle, 13th century marble font and a west tower that may date back to the start of the 14th century. Houses in the village of note include the Old Rectory which dates back to the early 14th century, and the 17th century Beck Hall.

On reaching The Street at SU980155 (the church immediately to your left here) your route bears right, south-westwards, down this road. At the T-junction at the end, turn left, eastwards, until at SU983151 (700m from SU980155) the road bends sharply right. The continuous route forks left, north-eastwards, along a bridleway here, but I recommend you detour right with the road to visit **Bignor** with its Roman villa. The villa's existence was discovered in July 1811 when a ploughman struck a large stone thought to have been a piscina. Beginning as a simple farmstead about 190 AD, it developed into a palatial governor's house with 65 rooms which formed a complete square around a central courtyard. It boasts one of the longest mosaics on display in Britain at 24 metres, the mosaic floors depicting the seasons and the heads of legendary figures. To reach it, follow the road southwards from SU983151 for 500m, then turn left at a fork junction (A) along a road past the part-Norman church of the Holy Cross and the magnificent 15th century thatched and timber-framed Yeoman's House. The road veers to the right to reach a T-junction in 375m from (A). Turn left here to reach the villa entrance in another 250m. Then retrace to SU983151.

Whether you've detoured or not, turn north-eastwards, as stated, at SU983151 up a bridleway that takes you through the very pleasant **Hospital Copse** and **Decoy Copse**. The bridleway has a good firm surface and you will feel as though you're following the course of a disused railway track! In 1km 500m after joining this bridleway, turn left at SU991163, heading northwards along another bridleway, reaching a bridleway T-junction in some 250m. Turn left, westwards, along a very pleasant woodland bridleway which in 500m arrives at a T-junction with the Serpent Trail (see route 14) at SU985165. Turn right to follow the Serpent Trail, which is here a bridleway, north-eastwards, crossing a road after 750m and continuing north-eastwards over the delightful area of common known as **Lord's Piece**, veering eastwards in 450m from the road crossing and proceeding over Sutton Common.

At SU996173, 625m from the road crossing, you reach a junction with a (very short!) bridleway going off to the left; the continuous route goes straight on eastwards along the bridleway here, but by turning left along the short bridleway and going forward along the road, Coates Lane, you'll reach, in 500m from the start of the detour, the very pretty church of St Agatha, **Coates**. I do recommend this detour: the *Pevsner Architectural Guide* says the church makes "an enchanting sight from the south, for all the world like a toy." It boasts a number of Norman features including its walls and chancel arch, and a 12th century font. The nearby 17th century Coates Manor is particularly photogenic, and is described by Pevsner as being one of the best preserved small manor houses of this period in West Sussex.

Whether you decide to detour or not, the continuous route heads eastwards, as stated, from SU996173, reaching in 250m a junction of bridleways at SU999173. Bear left, still of course on the Serpent Trail, and proceed north-eastwards for 875m along a very pleasant woodland bridle track across Coates Common, and then a farm lane, to the B2138 road at TQ007176. The route ends here. To proceed to the village of **Fittleworth** bear left along the B2138 for 1km 250m past (or maybe detouring into) the Swan pub, then, as you arrive in Fittleworth, turn right up School Lane which takes you in some 400m to the A283 at TQ012193 from which there are buses to Midhurst, Petworth and Pulborough. If you've time before your bus, it's worth detouring left, north-westwards, up the A283, to the bend, and here turn right onto Bedham

Lane where there are some lovely houses especially a delicious (and apparently nameless) pink thatched timber-framed cottage. The nearby church of St Mary, Fittleworth, boasts an Early English tower and chancel, and an early 15th century octagonal font.

ROUTE 79

TQ197093-TQ207059 – Location Map W6 – OS OL11, OL10 – M

10km 425m

Botolphs, Coombes, Steep Down, Lancing Ring, Lancing College Chapel, Shoreham-by-Sea

PT A283 South Downs Way crossing (B start), Shoreham-by-Sea (*, B finish)

R Shoreham-by-Sea

This is a magnificent route, the highlights of which are a stunning viewpoint and some very contrasting but fascinating churches. It is a linear route but Shoreham-by-Sea makes a convenient base if you're relying on public transport.

The route starts at the South Downs Way crossing of the A283 at TQ197093, where there's a bus stop with regular services from Shoreham and Steyning. From here, proceed as South Downs Way-signed beside the A283 briefly southwards from the bus stop then by the water point turn sharp right, almost immediately crossing the River Adur with the South Downs Way and going westwards with it, beside then away from the river, to reach Annington Road at **Botolphs**. Turn left, leaving the South Downs Way, and follow the road to shortly reach the part-Saxon church of St Botolph, just over 500m from the A283. It's definitely worth stopping to view the church, the nave and chancel arch of which date back to around 1080, and the tower of which is 13th century. The church also contains some wall paintings of various dates.

From the church continue south along the road (which becomes Coombes Road) to arrive at **Coombes**, 1km from Botolphs Church, at TQ192083; from here, take a bridleway that heads right, south-westwards from Coombes Road, to pass, in some 250m, Coombes' tiny Norman church. It boasts an 11th century nave and a chancel dating back to 1200, as well as a tower bell dating from 1150 that is the oldest surviving tower bell in Sussex. The church's finest feature is its collection of wall paintings that date back to around 1100, including depictions of the infancy of Christ and many other figures. Adjacent to the church there's a working farm, sometimes open to visitors. Your bridleway passes just to the left of the church and farm complex, then immediately beyond the church it veers sharply left, south-eastwards, through the trees, climbing steeply. On emerging from the trees you then reach a path junction at TQ191080, 375m from the road, and here you veer sharp right, westwards, with the bridleway.

You now follow the bridleway, initially veering just north of west then, below Coombehead Wood, just south of west, proceeding very pleasantly indeed across open rolling countryside with excellent views. (Some OS maps suggest a slightly sharper bridleway bend at Coombehead Wood – the bridleway has been rerouted very slightly here.) At TQ168080, 2km 500m from TQ191080, you reach a path crossroads. Turn left here, then almost immediately fork right as bridleway-signed, climbing steeply southwards to reach the trig point of **Steep Down**, 375m from TQ168080. Steep Down is one of the finest viewpoints away from the South Downs Way in West Sussex, giving quite magnificent views to the coast as far west as Bognor Regis, as well as the Adur valley, the Weald and the South Downs escarpment.

Veering south-eastwards with the bridleway, you descend in 750m from the trig point to a T-junction at TQ174071, turning left and then in roughly 75m reaching another T-junction, this time with a restricted byway. Turn right here, and proceed along the restricted byway uphill, south-eastwards, enjoying magnificent views to the Adur valley. Rise to an area of woodland, part of the **Lancing Ring** Nature Reserve. The Reserve is notable for its chalk grassland, supporting butterflies, adders and common lizards; the dewpond is a habitat for dragonflies and newts; and flowers in the deciduous woodland include the early purple orchid. Keep along the path through the Reserve, reaching a car park and a fork junction of paths at TQ183063, 1km 250m after joining the restricted byway; take the left bridleway fork, proceeding just south of east along the bridleway and descending to Hoe Court Farm.

Beyond the farm you carry on along the bridleway eastwards, and drop down, keeping **Lancing College Chapel** to the left. At length, 1km 500m from TQ183063, you reach Lancing College Drive, effectively the chapel approach road, at TQ197062. Turn left and follow the drive for 500m up the road, to visit the chapel, a hugely prominent landmark across a wide area. The chapel was begun in 1868 and built in early 14th century English Gothic style using Sussex sandstone; it boasts an internal height of some 28m and its foundations are in places over 21m deep. Its outstanding features are its painted ceiling, the 1978 stained-glass Rose Window at its west end, and, above the High Altar, massive tapestries, completed in 1933 and once the biggest in the country. Some contrast from the tiny intimate churches of Botolphs and Coombes! There is an overwhelming sense of spaciousness and grandeur; one of my proudest moments as an amateur musician was when, as part of a charity hymnathon in aid of Friends of Sussex Hospices, a hymn tune I had composed was belted out by an organ scholar on the Chapel organ. Sadly I think only two or three people were listening!

Retrace now to the bridleway at TQ197062 and continue eastwards from there along what is a bridleway section of Lancing College Drive for 250m, arriving, at TQ200061, at a junction with Coombes Road. Don't turn left into Coombes Road but go straight on to arrive, in another 100m, at the A27. Cross the A27 at the traffic lights just here, and more or less immediately opposite join and follow Old Shoreham

Road eastwards, the road taking you to the Old Shoreham bridge crossing of the River Adur; curiously, the crossing (though not the section of road preceding it) is designated as a bridleway. Go straight over the bridge to meet the riverside path at what is the very start of the Downs Link. Here, at TQ207059, your route ends, 750m from the A27 crossing. In front of you, across the A283, is the church of St Nicholas, Old Shoreham; see route 1 for a little more about the church and indeed the bridge you've just crossed.

Although there are buses to Shoreham town centre from the A283 just beyond the bridge crossing, it's easy enough to reach Shoreham under your own steam, by turning right to follow the riverside path for 1km or so to reach the A259 coast road by the Ropetackle centre. Turn left here to immediately arrive at Shoreham's main street, the station just a few minutes away. **Shoreham-by-Sea** is and has for centuries been an important port at the mouth of the Adur. Architecturally the two outstanding buildings are firstly the 12th century church of St Mary de Haura with its magnificent choirstalls and 25m tower, and secondly Marlipins, a Norman building with an exterior of chequerboard flint and Caen stone, a most unusual example of a surviving secular non-military Norman construction.

ROUTE 80

TQ121182-TQ107231 – Location Map W6 – OS OL10, OL34 – E

10km 825m

Knepp Wildland, Shipley, Coolham Advance Landing Ground Airfield, Blue Idol

PT Ashington (B start), Coolham (B finish)

R Ashington, Coolham

This route boasts a lovely mix of both fascinating history and natural beauty, but for those of you reliant on public transport it is logistically not hugely straightforward. It's a linear journey that is served by different bus routes, but you should be aware that most buses serving Coolham, at the end of the route, only run a couple of days a week. If you're going to try to rely on these buses, Worthing is a logical base.

To access this route from Ashington, served by buses from Worthing and Horsham, leave the bus at the roundabout at the very north end of the village at TQ133166. Then follow the B2133 Billingshurst Road away from the roundabout northwards, veering north-westwards, to reach the start of the route at TQ121182, 2km 125m from the roundabout. Turn right to join the bridleway at this point, heading north-eastwards, initially along a clear farm lane which passes straight through the Bowford Farm complex where at the time of writing alpacas were reared.

Continue north-eastwards as bridleway-signed beyond the complex along a delightful clear track, arriving at a gate where a sign indicates the bridleway veering to the right. Now, staying in the trees, you keep the fence (and field beyond) to your right initially but you veer gently left, keeping close to the left edge of the trees. Then, observing signage, continue in the same direction through the trees. You pass the entrance to the Blonks Farm complex which is to your right, and at TQ133194, 1km 750m from the start, you reach a metalled lane, Hooklands Lane.

Turn right along the lane for 150m, then left along a good bridleway path, heading just east of north. You're now entering the **Knepp Wildland** area. Knepp Wildland is the first major lowland rewilding project in England, consisting of 1400 hectares of farmland in the grounds of Knepp Castle (some way off route and not accessible by bridleway). The land supports many rare species including turtle dove, barbastelle bat, glow-worm and grass-snake, and is a major nesting site for nightingales; it's also home to the first beavers living in the wild in Sussex for 400 years. Look out on the right for a ladder leading up to an observation point among the treetops, providing a superb view of the surrounding countryside. You should definitely make the climb! Continue along the obvious bridleway (here Penbridge Lane), veering more decisively north-eastwards to reach another lane, Countryman Lane, at TQ141213, 2km 125m from Hooklands Lane.

Turn right along Countryman Lane, then in 50m bear left as signed, northwards, along a pretty bridleway path which in 500m passes the magnificent **Shipley** windmill. This is a smock mill built in 1879, the last and biggest smock mill to be erected in Sussex; also known as King's Mill, it is arguably the most impressive windmill in Sussex. The writer Hilaire Belloc, famous for his *Cautionary Tales*, purchased the mill in 1906 and owned it until his death in 1953. Continue beyond the windmill for some 50m to a T-junction with School Lane at TQ143219.

The continuous route turns left, westwards, along this road but I recommend you turn right at TQ143219 along School Lane then in 125m bear right again along Red Lane to reach, in a further 125m, Shipley's beautiful church of St Mary. It was built for the Knights Templar who were given the site between 1129 and 1140, meaning that the church was the order's earliest surviving church in England. It is noteworthy for its huge tower arches, a fine pointed arch of decorated local sandstone, and the 17th century alabaster monument to Sir Thomas Caryll and his wife. There is also a tablet on the south wall commemorating the composer John Ireland who lived in the village of Washington, not too far away, and is buried in Shipley churchyard. Then retrace to TQ143219.

Whether you've detoured or not, head westwards, as stated, from TQ143219 along School Lane. Keep going for 250m from TQ143219, then at TQ141220 fork left, westwards, along a signed bridleway that takes you down to cross the infant River Adur, which will mature to become one of the principal Sussex rivers; you'll see (or will have seen) it in all its pomp at the end of route 79 above. Having veered left to cross the river you then veer right, to reach a road, Smithers Hill Lane, at TQ135220, 500m from the start of the bridleway. Cross straight over and head just north of west on a clear bridleway, ignoring a bridleway going off left in 500m or so at TQ131222. You're now skirting the **Coolham Advance Landing Ground Airfield**. This was one of seven Advance Landing Ground airfields built in Kent and Sussex in 1943/1944 to ensure Allied superiority in the D-day invasion in June 1944; as you proceed, you'll notice to your left a line of beautifully maintained memorials to those who served here. Close by to your right is the pond of St Julians, effectively the western source of the Adur.

Veering gently right and then left, you continue along the bridleway to arrive at the B2139 just south of Coolham, reaching the road at TQ119226, roughly 1km 800m from the Smithers Hill Lane crossing. Note the large memorial close to the road hereabouts: the memorial honours all who served at Coolham Airfield during the Second World War and in particular those members of the RAF and Polish Air Force who were based at the airfield and who perished in that conflict.

If you were pushed for time, you could opt to call it a day here, turning right to reach the centre of Coolham, at the junction of the B2139 with the A272, just 125m to the right up the road from the end of the bridleway. However the full route turns left at TQ119226, following the B2139 for 1km just west of south to reach a crossroads junction at TQ117217. Turn right here along Sproutes Lane, in 400m reaching the buildings of Sproutes and a junction with three paths. Go straight on, north-westwards, along a bridleway, first a farm track then field-edge paths, to reach a bridleway T-junction in 750m at TQ107222.

Turn right here, northwards, here overlapping with the West Sussex Literary Trail (see route 5) and in 1km at TQ107231 you reach the end of the route at the so-called **Blue Idol**. This is a superb timber-framed Elizabethan farmhouse, part of which was converted into a Quaker meeting house in 1691. William Penn, the founder of the state of Pennsylvania, who had campaigned for the establishment of a Quaker meeting house locally, used to walk here from nearby Warminghurst to worship while his family travelled by ox-drawn coach! The unusual name for the house is thought to be derived from the fact that when during the 19th century it was not in use, therefore idle, it was colour-washed in blue and therefore known as the "blue idle meeting house." It is however in use today as a Quaker meeting house and in recent years has been restored, the impressiveness of its exterior complemented splendidly by its attractive gardens which make an ideal picnic spot.

To return to civilisation, simply continue northwards up the lane with the West Sussex Literary Trail for 375m to reach the A272. Cyclists may find it easier to turn left and cycle along the A272 into Billingshurst, whilst walkers, to get to Coolham for buses to Horsham (well served by rail) or Storrington (where buses are available to the railway stations of Pulborough and Worthing), should turn right beside the A272, following it (pavement mercifully provided) for 1km 500m to arrive in the village. As stated in the preamble to this route, most buses from Coolham only run a couple of days a week – so if you pick the wrong day, that's an awful lot of Su Doku puzzles you'll have time to complete.

ROUTE 81

TQ242079-TQ257070 – Location Map W6 – OS OL11 – S

11km 50m

Perching Hill, Fulking, Fulking Escarpment, Foredown Tower

PT Mile Oak (B start), Portslade (B finish)

R Mile Oak, Fulking, Portslade

This route has a wonderfully remote, peaceful feel, despite its proximity to the Brighton & Hove conurbation, and contains three pieces of interesting history as well as great scenery. It's a linear route but both start and finish points are very close to bus stops on routes from central Brighton, and you can create a circle if you don't mind a walk or ride on some suburban roads.

To access the start from Mile Oak, situated to the north-west of Portslade and well served by buses from Brighton, simply continue on along Mile Oak Road, the main road through Mile Oak village. Follow it north-westwards beyond the houses and under the A27 bridge (some 625m from the centre of Mile Oak), going forward beyond the bridge along the same road past Mile Oak Farm, where refreshments may be available. As you pass the farm complex (100m beyond the bridge), continuing on the same road, you reach and pass the start of the route at TQ242079, now on a mapped restricted byway.

Keep straight on, ignoring a path forking right at TQ240081 and also ignoring one coming in from the left in another 50m, and continue on north-westwards. Now follow the obvious well-signed track predominantly north-westwards, the surroundings becoming much more rural and remote. At TQ235093, roughly 1km 625m from the start, you go through a gate and enter Access Land. Immediately beyond the gate a rather indistinct track forks left. Ignore this but head north-eastwards on what is a permissive bridleway. It's unavailable for riders for just a few days each year, so you may want to check ahead if you wish to ride it! This is a superb bridleway that veers northwards then north-eastwards again on to **Perching Hill** and its very isolated barn at TQ241103. It's a wonderfully secluded spot, and it's hard to believe that there was a village here in medieval times. Not only was there a medieval settlement, now deserted; there was an adjacent area containing associated cultivation terraces, situated on a north-west facing slope of a chalk downland hill. Three stepped, levelled terraces, roughly 90m long and up to about 18m wide, edged by banks up to around 3m high, are to be found on the site, and contain evidence of at least eight buildings, representing the main dwelling houses and outbuildings of the settlement. Green-glazed pottery sherds dating back to medieval times were found here during the 1950's.

You then veer northwards again and ascend to reach the South Downs Way at TQ242109, 1km 750m from the gate at which you entered Access Land. Here, at TQ242109, turn right to head eastwards along the South Downs Way for 500m to TQ247109. Here you fork left along a bridleway which heads north-eastwards away from the South Downs Way, down the hillside. This is spectacular – for the best views you should climb onto the parallel ridge and enjoy looking down to Fulking below and a vast area of Wealden countryside beyond.

In some 375m at TQ249111 you reach two path signposts very close together, with a multiplicity of footpath and bridleway options! There are bridleways here heading hard right and more gently right. Make a note of the one heading hard right (B2) as you'll be returning to this very spot and following that bridleway later. (If you wish to cut out the descent to Fulking skip to the asterisked point below.) For access to Fulking you need, from TQ249111, to take the bridleway heading more gently right (B1) and then zigzagging sharp left and sharp right before veering left again, down to Poynings Road at TQ251115, 625m from TQ249111.

Turn left along the road just south of west for 225m then as the road bends right, at TQ249114, continue straight on, just south of west, along a bridleway which takes you in 250m to **Fulking**'s village street (The Street). You come out right by the very popular Shepherd & Dog Inn, while beside the road beyond is a very attractive stream bubbling from a Victorian brick-built shelter. The stream was utilised by means of a reservoir with hydraulic ram (in the pub garden), and on the village street you'll see various paraphernalia connected with water supply including a water trough said to be in honour of John Ruskin, a brick drinking fountain, and hand pumps. At one time the stream was a sheepwash, where shepherds would dip their flocks. Hence the well-known Christmas carol, "While shepherds washed their flocks by night." Having enjoyed your time in the Shepherd & Dog, retrace via the bridleway to TQ249114, road to TQ251115 and then the zigzagging bridleway to TQ249111.*

Now follow the bridleway referred to above as B2 south-eastwards up the hillside, the views getting better with each step. You arrive in 500m from TQ249111 at a multi-fingered path post at TQ254107: go straight on up the hillside for 50m or so to reach the South Downs Way. Turn right to follow the South Downs Way very briefly, but in roughly 75m fork left to join the spur route of the Sussex Border Path (see route 4) heading south-westwards on a bridleway, away from the South Downs Way. Follow the Sussex Border Path south-westwards over Fulking Hill **(Fulking Escarpment)**, the views from the plateau quite magnificent, then veer gently just east of south and descend, your bridleway evolving into a restricted byway. You stick to the Sussex Border Path until TQ249091 where the Sussex Border Path strikes away to the right, 1km 750m from the South Downs Way. You however continue just east of south along a clear restricted byway, the going very easy; there are tremendous views from here to the coast.

You pass a trig point on the hillside known as Mount Zion and continue down to reach the A27, 1km 625m from leaving the Sussex Border Path. Bear right at the path

T-junction to negotiate the road by a bridge, then continue beyond the bridge along the restricted byway, Foredown Road, passing the **Foredown Tower**. The tower was built in 1909 as a water tower of the Foredown Isolation Hospital; it closed in 1988 and now houses a camera obscura, one of just two operational camera obscuras in south-east England. For the purpose, it's been given a pyramid roof and glazed clerestory above the water tank, and remains a very conspicuous landmark. The restricted byway, and your route, officially ends at TQ257070, 600m from the A27 crossing, but simply carry on along Foredown Road to reach, 125m from the end of the route, a T-junction with Fox Way on the edge of Portslade. Buses are available here towards central Portslade and Brighton. To get back to Mile Oak, turn right along Fox Way which almost immediately veers right, north-westwards, then veers south-westwards and becomes Chalky Road, descending to a T-junction with Mile Oak Road. Turn right to arrive almost immediately in the centre of Mile Oak, roughly 1km 750m from the end of the route.

ROUTE 82

TQ322138–TQ336151 – Location Maps W6 and E6 – OS OL11 – S

13km 725m

Keymer Post, Chattri Memorial, Lower Standean, North Bottom, Ditchling Beacon, Westmeston, Streat, Ditchling

PT Hassocks (* start and finish)

R Ditchling Beacon (occasional), Ditchling

This route, one of the more strenuous bridleway routes in this book, explores some lovely downland scenery in the Ditchling area, with a fair bit of history too. It can effectively be treated as a circular route by beginning and ending in Ditchling. If you're reliant on public transport, please note that buses to and from Ditchling aren't hugely frequent, but it is a not unmanageable 2km 500m each way from the nearest railway station at Hassocks to Ditchling.

To access the start of the route from the centre of Ditchling, the meeting of the B2116 with the B2112 High Street and South Street, head southwards down South Street then as the B2112 veers sharply right in 125m, go straight on, southwards, along Beacon Road for 1km 250m to a T-junction with Underhill Lane. Turn right here along this lane until in 375m you reach a bridleway bearing left, southwards, away from Underhill Lane at TQ322138. This point is the start of your route. Overlapping now with the Sussex Border Path spur route (see route 4), follow this bridleway, Burnhouse Bostal (a bostal, as I mentioned in route 10, being a small road leading up a very steep hill), which soon veers south-westwards and climbs extremely steeply to reach the South Downs Way in 1km 250m. Turn right to arrive, in 100m, at a junction of paths marked by an impressive signpost named **Keymer Post**. Pause to enjoy the glorious views from this spot, then turn left here to follow the Sussex Border Path south-westwards, away from the South Downs Way. It's a very clear obvious bridleway track with superb views towards Wolstonbury Hill and Pyecombe.

In roughly 1km 250m after leaving the South Downs Way you reach a bridleway crossroads junction at TQ309117. Mark this carefully as you'll be returning to it! Continue straight on south-westwards along the Sussex Border Path for 1km to reach, on the left, the **Chattri Memorial**. Unveiled in February 1921 by Edward, Prince of Wales, it is dedicated to Indian soldiers who fought on the Western Front during World War 1. The setting is wonderfully atmospheric and the views glorious; you may want to carry on a bit further along the Sussex Border Path for further great views. Then retrace to the bridleway crossroads at TQ309117 and turn right.

Now, follow a wide bridle track initially south-eastwards, away from the Sussex Border Path. In a few metres this track bends sharply left and then sharply right, descending towards the cosily sited buildings and farming paraphernalia at **Lower Standean**. The surroundings really are delightfully rural, unspoilt and redolent of a different age. Shortly before reaching the buildings you cross a newly-signed junction of paths, some 625m from TQ309117, and then 75m further down, at TQ314115, you turn hard left to join what is signed as a "licensed bridleway" (do check if you want to make sure permission hasn't been withdrawn when you make your visit!) which soon passes through a gate and then heads clearly north-eastwards, uphill, round the edge of the Lower Standean buildings. Fine views quickly open out in all directions.

At the top of the hill you go through another gate and then veer south-eastwards, descending very pleasantly to a signed bridleway junction at TQ318115, 450m from TQ314115. Now from TQ318115 turn left to head north-eastwards on the bridleway along the lovely **North Bottom**, a wide and most attractive dry valley. You need to be careful to switch sides of the fence as signed, so that you then keep the fence to your left. You rise very gradually, following a not terribly distinct track across the grass, and woodland starts to make incursions on both sides as you veer more eastwards. You then reach a field boundary beyond which the character of your bridleway changes completely, as you rise quite steeply, heading north-eastwards again, along a clear but narrow path through rough grass. Ignore a bridleway going off to the right at TQ328121 but continue uphill, enjoying superb views now to the west.

At TQ329123, immediately beyond a gate, you reach a signed bridleway junction, 1km 375m from TQ318115. Turn right, eastwards, for 150m then at TQ331123 turn sharp left, just east of north, along a field-edge bridleway path, enjoying quite breathtaking views to the east. Firle Beacon is especially conspicuous. At TQ332131, 750m from the sharp left turn, you arrive at a gate. Go through it and turn left, and in a few metres you'll reach the **Ditchling Beacon** trig point, the highest ground in East Sussex. You will also have met this notable historic landmark on your South Downs journey in route 8.

Having enjoyed the views, veer right and drop down a few metres to arrive back at the South Downs Way. Turn right along the South Downs Way until you reach a car park (where you may be lucky enough to find an ice-cream van), with Ditchling Road immediately beyond, some 150m from where you joined the South Downs Way. Cross the road and continue very briefly along the South Downs Way eastwards, but in barely 50m fork left along a bridleway that initially proceeds parallel with the South Downs Way then in 250m or so strikes out away from it, heading eastwards while the South Downs Way veers south-eastwards. In some 675m from the road crossing, your bridleway, Westmeston Bostal, bends very sharply left, north-westwards, descending steeply. Veering northwards with the bridleway you drop right down to the foot of the downs and reach the B2116 at **Westmeston** at TQ338136, roughly 1km from the sharp left bend. Turn right along the B2116, immediately passing the fine flint church of St Martin which boasts a font and wall paintings that date back to the 12th century.

Follow the B2116 eastwards beyond the church for 375m then at TQ342136 turn left along a bridleway heading north-eastwards, arriving at a bridleway crossroads in the trees 875m from TQ342136 at TQ345145. Here you turn right to follow a bridleway initially eastwards then north-eastwards along the top edge of Middleton Plantation to arrive at Streat Lane at TQ350146, 625m from the bridleway crossroads. Turn left down Streat Lane to arrive in 500m at the village of **Streat**. Here you'll find two features of interest. The first is the church which boasts a 12th century nave and 13th century chancel, as well as a cast-iron monument slab to the Gott family, this being the largest iron grave-slab in the country; there are other fine monuments including two large elegant tablets to William and Mary Dobell in multi-coloured marble. The church enjoys a beautiful setting with views to the South Downs and to a V-shaped line of trees including beech, fir and lime, planted here in honour of Queen Victoria's Golden Jubilee. The second feature of interest in Streat is the flint-built Streat Place which was rebuilt in around 1620, the probably Jacobean front being described in the *Pevsner Architectural Guide* as "monumental."

From just by the church in Streat head left, westwards, away from Streat Lane along a bridleway, which in roughly 375m reaches a bridleway T-junction. Turn left to arrive, in no more than 125m, at a path junction at Hayleigh Farm; turn right here to follow a bridleway heading unerringly westwards for 1km, enjoying superb views to the South Downs escarpment. You arrive at a road, Spatham Lane, at TQ336151, and this junction marks the end of the route. To return to Ditchling, riders need to turn left down Spatham Lane for some 250m to reach the B2116 Lewes Road, then right along Lewes Road for 1km to arrive at the village centre. Walkers, from the end of the route, have the option of crossing straight over along a public footpath then going forward along a road, East End Lane, to arrive at Ditchling High Street, just north of the B2116/B2112 road junction, in 1km.

Ditchling itself is a most attractive village with a number of features of interest. These include the church of St Margaret, with both Norman and Early English features, the nave dating back to the 12th century; the new and excellent museum of Art and Craft; the magnificent timber-framed Wings Place on West Street; on the High Street, the lovely Conds Cottage, sometime home of the writer Esther Meynell; and, next door, Sopers, the home of the sculptor Eric Gill for a time. Gill's work includes a sundial commemorating the coronation of George V, which sits in the churchyard. Also on the High Street is the 17th century timber-framed No.5, adjacent to which is the 16th century Bank House. On North End, effectively the continuation of High Street, there are two 15th century timber-framed hall houses, Forge Cottage and Forge House. By heading left along Boddingtons Lane off High Street and going forward along Lodge Hill Lane, you reach, in 1km from High Street, the delightful Oldland windmill, a post mill consisting of an octagonal brick round-house with a weatherboarded structure above it; it dates back to about 1700 but has recently been handsomely restored.

ROUTE 83

TQ459164-TQ485128 – Location Map E6 – OS OL25 – M

9km 175m

Moatpark Farm, Bentley House, Laughton Common, Laughton Level, Laughton Place

PT Rose Hill (B start), Laughton (B finish)

R Rose Hill, Bentley House (if open), Laughton

This is a lovely undemanding journey through an unspoilt and unsung piece of the Low Weald in East Sussex with a number of features of historic interest. It is a linear route; if you're reliant on public transport you may wish to base yourself in Lewes, catching a bus to the start point at Rose Hill on the Brighton-Lewes-Tunbridge Wells route and then returning to Lewes by bus from Laughton on the Hailsham-Lewes route.

Buses on the Lewes-Uckfield route serve Rose Hill, as stated, and indeed there's a bus stop right by the start point, TQ459164, where a bridleway heads away just south of east from the A26. Take this bridleway, a clear track through Plashett Wood, emerging from the woods just shy of the beautiful brick buildings of **Moatpark Farm**, 750m from the start. The farm dates from the 18ᵗʰ century, built on the site of what was Plashett deer park. Veer right, south-eastwards, along the bridleway as it crosses the meadow then ascends along a lovely woodland-edge path with really good views back the way you've come. You then follow the bridleway on through the woods to arrive at a road, Harvey's Lane, 750m from Moatpark Farm.

Turn left along the lane and in 850m reach a sharp left bend, where there's the public entrance to the fine buildings of **Bentley House**. The fine Palladian house was built in the 18th century as a farmhouse but then was extensively added to in Palladian style in the 1960's and 1970's. It has boasted a magnificent collection of wildfowl and a display of vintage cars and motorbikes while the grounds contain mixed woodland that has been dotted with sculptures. At the time of writing, however, the house has been closed to the public and it's unclear when it may reopen.

Just before the house entrance and bend in the road, your continuous route turns right off the road along a signed bridleway. You almost immediately veer left with the bridleway and then shortly sharp right to follow a most attractive path south-eastwards alongside the grounds of Bentley House. You pass through an area of woodland that incorporates an adventure park, and in fact a permissive bridleway route (not shown on OS Explorer maps) is clearly signed round the edge of the park if you want to avoid groups of adventurers and don't fancy becoming one yourself! Beyond this area of woodland you continue in the same direction, veering gently right and then proceeding in a straight line all the way to the B2192 at Shortgate, 1km 750m from the Bentley House entrance.

Cross the B2192 and turn left beside the road for 300m to TQ492150 where the road bends left. Here turn right along the signed restricted byway – don't make the mistake of joining the immediately adjacent public footpath. In 150m you bend sharply right, south-westwards, arriving in 375m at a path junction at TQ492145. Go straight on along what is a lovely woodland restricted byway heading south-westwards but veering gently left, southwards. You're now on **Laughton Common**, a charming unspoilt stretch of the Low Weald. You continue southwards through the very pretty Longfield Wood, with its extensive lakes among the trees, following the path all the way to its end at the B2124 at TQ486132, 1km 500m from TQ492145.

Turn right beside the B2124 for 500m to where a metalled lane, Cow Lane, comes in from the left. Bear left along this road for 250m to reach a restricted byway heading right, away from it, at TQ485128; turn right onto this restricted byway to follow what is a clear farm lane heading south-westwards. You now find yourself in an extraordinary landscape, as you pass through the **Laughton Level** with its many ditches, no roads, and precious few houses or trees, but providing magnificent views to the South Downs and Mount Caburn. After 625m you kink left and then right, passing farm buildings, then continue south-westwards, now heading for your objective, Laughton Place.

Though the restricted byway officially ends at TQ483118, 1km from the road, there seems no reason why you couldn't, or shouldn't, continue along the farm lane to get a better view of the remarkable tower of Laughton Place to your left. **Laughton Place**, the only major house in Sussex with extensive use of terracotta decoration, was the home of the Pelham family, one of the most noteworthy families in Sussex, from 1401, and in 1534 the tower was rebuilt by Sir William Pelham. The Pelhams (whom we also meet in route 85 below) left in 1594, and the red and black brick tower is all that remains. Not only is it an extraordinary and photogenic structure, but its setting, surrounded by a moat and in the middle of nowhere, is remarkable. When I walked here in early March 2020 it was a wet and grey afternoon, and Covid was about to do its worst, but somehow the gloom added to the atmosphere and the sense of being in a different world.

However close to Laughton Place you've chosen to go, simply retrace via the restricted byway to Cow Lane, at TQ485128. Your bridleway route ends here. For Laughton, turn right along Cow Lane, veering sharp left after 375m and reaching the B2124 in a further 375m. Turn right to follow the B2124 for 1km 250m into Laughton, where there's a pub, and from where, as stated, there are buses to Lewes on the Hailsham-Ringmer-Lewes route. Bus drivers on this route will apparently (though I've personally not tested this!) be prepared to stop in rural areas where there is no bus stop, providing it's safe to do this, so you may not have to walk all the way to Laughton if you don't want to. Riders, you may prefer to turn left onto Cow Lane at the end of the bridleway route; having reached the B2124 in 250m you then have a 3km 750m ride to Ringmer, considerably close to Lewes than Laughton.

ROUTE 84

TQ483080 (start and finish) – Location Map E6 – OS OL25 – S

9km 425m

Firle, Firle Place, Firle Beacon, Charleston Farmhouse, Firle Tower

PT A27 at Firle (B start and finish)

R Firle, Charleston

This is a straightforward circular route with lots of history and a fair bit of legwork too! From the bus stop by the A27 just north-east of Firle (served by infrequent buses between Lewes and Eastbourne) which is the start of this route at TQ483080, follow the bridleway-signed lane south-westwards from the A27, past the hamlet of Heighton Street, to the lane's end at TQ477069, 1km 375m from the start. To your right as you proceed are the house and grounds of Firle Place, about which more below. Bear right at the end along a byway for 200m to TQ475068.

The continuous route turns hard left here, just east of south, but I recommend you detour some 750m each way in order to visit the pretty village of **Firle;** to do this, continue straight on along the byway fractionally north of west, then veer sharply right, going forward along a small stretch of bridleway into the village. Its two outstanding features are its church and stately home, Firle Place. The 13th century church of St Peter boasts a heavily buttressed 13th century tower, some very fine brasses, and a stained-glass window by John Piper entitled *Homage to William Blake's Book Of Job*. **Firle Place** is believed to have been built around 1530 by Sir John Gage, who was sometime Constable of the Tower of London, and who presided over the execution of Lady Jane Grey in 1554. There is a Gage chapel in the church containing three splendid alabaster monuments including one to Sir John. The house itself has a lovely drawing room; Keith Spence calls the drawing room a "perfect period piece," stating that "gilt Ionic columns, portraits and furniture form a harmonious unity." The house's Great Hall, meanwhile, boasts the huge van Dyck portrait of the Count of Nassau and his family, as well as two beautiful tapestries. Having enjoyed both the house and the village, you'll then need to retrace to TQ475068 to progress.

Now, whether you've detoured or not, head just east of south from TQ475068 as stated along a bridleway which ascends along the east side of Firle Plantation then veers left, south-eastwards, and heads very steeply up to reach the South Downs Way in 1km 250m from TQ475068. Be warned that this is a really stiff climb! Once you've reached the South Downs Way you bear left onto it, and it's then just 300m to **Firle Beacon**, one of the great viewpoints and most photogenic features on the national trail. The views are quite astonishing in all directions: particularly impressive is a wonderful view of a long strip of coastline. A clear day is a must!

Beyond Firle Beacon, continue south-eastwards along the South Downs Way for a further 750m to arrive at a bridleway junction at TQ490054. To locate this, you need to be well over to the northern edge of the escarpment; it is easily missed otherwise. Now from this junction leave the

South Downs Way to follow what is a dramatic bridleway northwards off the ridge, descending quickly. You veer right, north-eastwards, to cross the byway you briefly followed earlier, then head more gently north-eastwards to pass Tilton Farm, veering north-westwards to a junction of tracks at TQ493069, roughly 1km 675m after leaving the South Downs Way. Here, at TQ493069, turn left along a bridleway.

In 250m this bridleway reaches **Charleston Farmhouse**; it's most unusual for a building of such historic importance to be accessible only by bridleway! The farmhouse dates from the 16th century and was modernised around 1800. In 1916 it was adopted as the country retreat of the artists Vanessa Bell and Duncan Grant, and for many decades endured as the hub of the so-called Bloomsbury Group of artists, writers and intellectuals including not only Bell and Grant but Virginia Woolf and David Garnett, while notable personalities entertained here included T.S. Eliot, E.M. Forster and Maynard Keynes. Duncan Grant continued to live at Charleston until his death in 1978 at the age of 93. The house has recently been restored to re-enact the atmosphere of the house as it was in the 1950's. It's a fascinating place to look round, as is the garden, and refreshments are available.

Beyond the farmhouse continue westwards on the bridleway along what is a field-edge path, kinking left and right and proceeding along a right-hand field edge, then, maintaining your westward direction, go forward through a field, and ascend through two further fields to reach the edge of a patch of woodland. At the top, look carefully to the right to see the circular castellated structure known as **Firle Tower**, poking through the trees. It was built around 1820; it's unclear whether it was built as a folly or for a purpose, but it was used by the gamekeeper for signalling to a similar structure at Plashett Park some 8km away. Nowadays they'd probably just use Whatsapp. Much less fun.

Continue round the bottom (south) edge of the wood and veer right, north-westwards, onto and along a clear section of bridleway descending diagonally through a field, passing a house and arriving at the bridleway lane you followed at the start, at TQ478072, 1km 250m from Charleston. After enjoying the views across to Firle Place which lies more or less straight ahead of you as you look westwards from the lane, turn right along the lane and retrace for 875m past Heighton Street, back to the start/end of the route at the A27 at TQ483080.

ROUTE 85

TQ525162-TQ576123 – Location Map E6 – OS OL25 – E

7km 725m

East Hoathly, Chiddingly, Farley Farmhouse, Hellingly, Horselunges Manor

PT East Hoathly (B start), Hellingly (B finish)

R East Hoathly, Chiddingly, Farley Farm, Lower Horsebridge

This is a lovely Low Weald journey with some fine historic features. It is a linear journey, the start served by buses on the Eastbourne-Polegate-Uckfield route, the end point served by buses on the Heathfield-Hellingly-Polegate-Eastbourne route. So Polegate, which has a railway station, is a good location to base yourself if you're reliant on public transport.

East Hoathly is a very pretty place to start your journey, with a number of attractive late Georgian cottages, and an impressive mid-19th century building, the Gate House on Waldron Road at the north end of the village. The church is chiefly 19th century but it has a fine squat tower, built by the Pelham family in the 15th century. This church, as well as that at Chiddingly (which we'll visit later on on this route) and Laughton Place (which we visited in route 83), contains the Pelham family badge, a belt buckle known as the Pelham Buckle. Inside the church is a memorial to E.T.

Kemp who was killed in the Indian mutiny. The church has some 100 figures painted in its windows and mosaics of four archangels in the sanctuary wall.

From the centre of the village of East Hoathly, make your way north-eastwards up High Street past the Kings Head pub, then just beyond the pub turn right, south-eastwards, along Mill Lane, the lane in 125m becoming a bridleway at TQ525162 (the start of the route), going forward along a track continuing south-eastwards, downhill. After 500m or so from the start you veer sharp left and then right along a woodland edge, continuing south-eastwards across an attractive meadow to reach Graywood Lane, some 825m from the start. Now overlapping with the Wealdway (see route 13), cross straight over Graywood Lane and continue south-eastwards along a most attractive bridleway path through further meadows, arriving in 1km 250m from the lane at Frith's Farm and continuing along a farm lane to reach Highlands Lane. Turn left along the lane to reach the pretty village of **Chiddingly,** 875m from Frith's Farm. The village has a delightful 1930's feel, with its olde-worlde inn sign on the brick-built Six Bells, and the sadly now defunct village store which has retained its old signs. Your continuous route, leaving the Wealdway, turns right, south-westwards, in the centre of the village along The Street, but I recommend your going straight on along Church Lane to reach the church in roughly 125m. The church has another Pelham tower (see above) and 40m high octagonal stone spire dating from the 15th century, early 14th century nave arches, 18th century box pews, 18th century canopied pulpit, and superb alabaster 16th and 17th century memorial effigies to the Jefferay family; Sir John Jefferay was Lord Chief Baron of the Exchequer under Elizabeth I.

However, as stated the continuous route heads south-westwards away from the village along The Street. It then veers left, eastwards, to arrive in the village of Muddles Green, reaching a junction with Burgh Hill Road just past Chiddingly Primary School, the junction 1km 125m from Chiddingly. Continue eastwards from that junction along the road through Muddles Green, and in roughly 125m from the junction, to your right, is a very useful shop/café as well as a gallery. Then a little further on, also to your right, you reach the splendid **Farley Farmhouse**. The farmhouse was rebuilt in 1760 and from 1949 was home to the British surrealist painter Roland Penrose and his wife Lee Miller; the house, which has been kept largely as it was during their time here, contains examples of Penrose's work and also a tile painted by Picasso (himself a guest here). The garden is filled with sculpture, and the gallery you passed just before holds regular art exhibitions. Trivia fact: after World War 2 Lee Miller bathed in a home owned by Hitler, and was photographed in the bath with a portrait of Hitler beside the bath and her wartime combat boots on the floor in front of it.

Almost opposite the farmhouse, the road forks; ignore the left fork, Scraper's Hill, but rather take the right fork, Rosemount, following it south-eastwards beyond Farley Farm to reach the T-junction with Thunders Hill at TQ552131. This is 750m from the Burgh Hill Road junction. Go more or less straight over to join a signed bridleway, heading south-eastwards; you pass Pekes Farm, taking care to bear half-right with the bridleway (away from the farm driveway) as signed, and continue very pleasantly along an excellent track south-eastwards, passing an attractive pond. The surroundings aren't spectacular but it's extremely peaceful and unspoilt countryside.

You arrive in the vicinity of Perryland Farm, reaching a track coming in from the right. Follow it on briefly towards the farm but very soon you're signed away from it onto a much rougher parallel bridleway path which goes forward along a right-hand field edge, veering eastwards. A footpath comes in from the left at TQ568124, 1km 750m from Thunders Hill; here you veer south-eastwards again and follow what is a much clearer bridleway lane. In 400m from TQ568124, at TQ572121, you reach a gate to your left. According to OS maps, this is a bridleway junction. Your bridleway turns left to pass through the gate, then follows the left-hand field edge round, reaching a footbridge; go over the bridge and as arrow-signed, bear half-right aiming for another gate. Proceed across the field to this gate, 500m from TQ572121. The gate, at TQ576123, marks the end of the route, beside the busy A267.

To reach Hellingly, cross over the A267 with care, turn right and, again carefully, proceed for 100m or so alongside the road down to a junction with the B2104. Turn left down the B2104 then in 125m bear hard left beside Hellingly Primary School along a minor road into **Hellingly,** some 625m from the end of the route. Hellingly boasts two features of interest: the first, on the main street, is the late 12th century church of St Peter & St Paul which has a battlemented Victorian tower and a particularly fine Early English chancel, as well as a late 13th century north chapel, 14th century aisles and chancel arch, and a fine brass to a Lady with horned headdress dating back to around 1440. It's believed the churchyard dates back to the 8th century as it's in the form of a circular mound that was typical in the early days of Saxon Christianity. Adjoining the churchyard there are some particularly lovely tile-hung cottages.

The second feature of interest in Hellingly is **Horselunges Manor**. You reach this by continuing along the road, Station Road, and crossing the Cuckmere River. Walkers can then immediately bear right, southwards, along the Wealdway, while riders need to turn right along a driveway 125m further as Station Road veers gently left. Either way in 125m you very shortly reach the quite magnificent timber-framed Horselunges Manor. Substantially restored in around 1925, it actually dates from 1475, being built on an older site; its bizarre name is a corruption of the names of two owners of a previous house here, Herst and Lyngyver. Sadly the house is not open to the public but you can marvel at the exterior of the house, the moat that guards it, and its superb setting. As stated, buses run from the centre of Hellingly to Polegate.

ROUTE 86

TQ524048-TQ525044 – Location Map E6 – OS OL25 – S

17km 125m (longer route), 11km 125m (shorter route)

Berwick Church, Green Way, The Comp, High And Over, Rathfinny, Alfriston

PT Berwick (* start and finish), Alfriston Road (by A27)(B start and finish)

R Berwick, Alfriston

This strenuous route could qualify as a downland bridleway route but it has some splendid historical features, namely Berwick Church and the beautiful historic village of Alfriston, so history wins! It is effectively a circular route, served by the so-called "Bloomsbury Route" Lewes-Eastbourne bus service. Buses aren't hugely frequent so the other possibility is to use the train, starting and finishing at Berwick Station.

To reach the start of the route from Berwick Station, simply follow Station Road southwards from the station, all the way to the A27, a distance of 1km 500m. Cross the A27 with care (there is a pedestrian crossing) to join Alfriston Road. Just as you enter Alfriston Road there is a bus stop on the Bloomsbury Route – that's where you need to leave the bus if you're using it! Now follow Alfriston Road southwards, towards Alfriston, for 475m to reach the start of the route almost exactly opposite Drusillas – a very popular children's zoo park – at TQ524048. Turn off Alfriston Road here, westwards, along a signed bridleway which follows a grassy path. You veer just north of west and cross more or less straight over the Vanguard Way (see route 24) at TQ519049, but you should detour the very short distance to the right here to visit the sensational **Church Of St Michael & All Angels, Berwick**. This contains 12th century arches and a chancel rebuilt in the 13th century, but its main attraction is its stunning array of paintings around the church, the work of Duncan Grant, Vanessa Bell and Quentin Bell in 1942/43. Of course we met Duncan Grant and Vanessa Bell and their Bloomsbury Group associates at Charleston in route 84. The paintings, the initiative for which had come from Bishop George Bell, are quintessentially English and have been described by Sir Charles Reilly (who recommended Grant to the Bishop to do the job) as "stepping out of foggy England into Italy." They include the *Annunciation* and the *Nativity* by Vanessa Bell, *Christ In Glory* and *Four Seasons* by Duncan Grant, and the *Sacraments* and the *Wise And Foolish Virgins* by Quentin Bell. The view southwards from just outside the church towards Alfriston is really excellent.

Having visited the church, continue along the signed bridleway westwards from the Vanguard Way crossing, just north of west, reaching a T-junction with a bridle track at TQ517050, 750m from the start. Here turn left and follow the track south-westwards for 375m, reaching a junction with a byway at TQ514047. Turn right along it but then almost immediately bear left, south-westwards, along what at first is a narrow dirt bridle track. You pass below a steep-sided hill which is to your left, then your bridleway path widens into a fine green track heading gently uphill to a path junction (unsigned) at TQ507043, 875m from TQ514047. Fork left here along another clear green track, actually a bridleway, ascending and bringing you in 150m to another path junction at TQ505043. Turn hard left here, south-eastwards, soon being reassured by a bridleway sign and ascending a narrow but clear path, veering gently south-westwards as you near the top. It is tough going, but the views just get better with each step, and the view from the top of the ridge is absolutely magnificent.

On reaching the top of the ridge, 250m or so from TQ505043, bear very briefly right and you'll see a pathway between fences, going away to your left, gently downhill. Follow this pathway which in 100m at TQ506039 reaches the South Downs Way, clearly signed. Turn right along the South Downs Way north-westwards and follow it for 800m to a signed path junction at TQ499045. Having enjoyed your final, wonderful northward views, turn left down the clearly signed bridleway, heading resolutely south-westwards. This, **Green Way,** is a superb track and this is good fast going. At the foot of the hill you meet a bridleway joining you from the left; continuing south-westwards, now ascend along a much narrower potentially muddy path – ironic after losing so much height! At the top of the rise, at TQ489024, 2km 250m from the South Downs Way, you reach a junction of bridleways. There's a useful seat here.

Now it's decision time. The continuous route takes the left of two forking bridleway paths (ie NOT the right-hand one with the seat beside it!) then almost immediately you fork left again (A), steeply downhill to reach in 450m a junction of bridleways at TQ492021 where you turn left. However rather than forking left at the second fork (A) you could choose to stick to the main (right-forking) path known as **The Comp** in order to detour to the impressive High And Over viewpoint. It's a good clear bridleway path through the trees and there are nice views through the trees to the left, the ground falling away here steeply. Maintaining its height, your path heads south-eastwards, veering eastwards across Cradle Hill then descending to reach Alfriston Road at TQ510012, 3km from (A). By turning right here and following the road uphill for 400m or so you reach a car park, trig point and viewpoint known as **High And Over**, with quite sensational views to the Cuckmere valley and magnificent downland and woodland landscapes beyond. On the hillside below you is the early 20th century carved white horse of which you can get a better view by following the South Downs Way east of Alfriston (see route 11 above). Now retrace down Alfriston Road to return to the bridleway you followed to get here, and then retrace all the way along that bridleway, but this time follow The Comp only as far as TQ493017, 2km 250m from Alfriston Road. Here you fork right along a signed bridleway that descends to reach, in 400m, TQ492021, turning right here. You're now reunited with the main route.

Whether or not you've detoured, follow the bridleway from TQ492021 eastwards, very soon kinking right then left, and now head north-eastwards uphill on a clear field-edge path, crossing from the right-hand field edge to left-hand field edge as you ascend. You'll note a very distinct shield-shaped motif on the path signage hereabouts, signifying the Rathfinny Trail; the attractive **Rathfinny** vineyards, established in 2010, are to the right as you ascend, but the estate's wine tasting room is sadly some way off your route! At TQ499026, 1km from TQ492021, you reach the top of the rise and are signed sharp right. You now enjoy a glorious ridge journey, with superb views towards the Comp, Cradle Hill, and High And Over to the south-east. All too soon, at TQ504024, 500m from TQ499026, you're signed along a left fork away from the ridge, and now undertake a long, steady descent on a clear bridleway, heading predominantly north-eastwards and arriving at the road at the south end of Alfriston at TQ519028, 1km 500m from TQ504024. The popular Deans Place Hotel is opposite.

Turn left to follow the road, High Street, into **Alfriston.** The High Street boasts many fine examples of tile-hanging, flint, weatherboarding, brick and timber. The 15th century Star Inn on the left, described in the *Pevsner Architectural Guide* as one of the best timber-framed houses of East Sussex, has ceiling timbers decorated with carved animals, and on the street corner beside it is a large red lion, the figurehead of a 17th century Dutch ship, pilfered from a wreck off the Sussex coast. Other fine buildings on or around the High Street are the 15th century Old Farmhouse and Steamer Cottages, the late 15th century George Inn, and the 16th century Manor House. By turning right off High Street down an alley by the former Congregational Chapel, you reach a green at the top end of which is the splendid 14th century parish church of St Andrew, symmetrically cruciform and known as the Cathedral of the Downs. It is described by Arthur Mee as "very handsome" with its lofty concave piers, a reredos sculpture of Christ calling the fishermen, and a splendid east window filled with depictions of saints, while Mee is much amused by the depiction of a "merry monk" on the canopy of a tomb by the chancel, the monk keeping company with a dog tucking its head between its legs. Across the green from the church is the thatched timber-framed 14th century Clergy House, a Wealden yeoman's house which was the first purchase of the National Trust for the princely sum of ten pounds. When the floor was relaid in the last century, the job was done with lumps of chalk rammed down and sealed with sour milk!

In 500m or so from Deans Place Hotel you reach Waterloo Square, the small (and actually triangular) square in the village centre; beyond this square fork left up West Street. In 125m fork right up Sloe Lane, which shortly becomes a bridleway heading northwards past Winton Street Farm then veering eastwards to arrive back at Alfriston Road at Berwick Court, at TQ525044, 1km 500m from joining Sloe Lane. This, TQ525044, is the end of the route, but by turning left along Alfriston Road you reach, in just 375m, the start of the route at Drusillas. For public transport connections, it's 475m onwards up Alfriston Road for the bus, and another 1km 500m beyond that (via the A27 crossing) back to Berwick Station. There's actually a pub right by the station which is useful if you find you've a wait for your train.

ROUTE 87

TQ544043-TQ543040 – Location Map E6 – OS OL25 – M

5km 575m

Wilmington, Folkington, Long Man Of Wilmington

PT Wilmington (B start and finish)

R Wilmington

This is effectively a circular route, your being able to close the circle simply by following the road for 375m at the end! It's one of the shortest routes in the book, but don't underestimate it.

Wilmington, where you start and finish, is served by bus from Lewes and Eastbourne. To reach the start of this route from the A27 at Wilmington, where buses stop, follow Wilmington's main street just west of south for 625m, reaching the church at the top of the rise. **Wilmington** is a very pretty village of brick, timber, flint and thatch, with two outstanding features. The first is the ruin of a Benedictine priory originally founded not long after the Norman conquest, the earliest remains today dating back to around 1225. In fact it fell into decay prior to the Dissolution and became a farmhouse; the surviving buildings of the priory include sections of hall, gatehouse and enclosed courtyard. The second feature of interest is the part-Norman and part-Gothic parish church of St Mary & St Peter, boasting a plain Norman font, ancient and now faded wall paintings, fine Jacobean pulpit complete with sounding board, and a small window behind the organ depicting a bee, butterflies and moths. The church was connected to the priory by a cloister. In the churchyard there is a magnificent yew tree, its limbs held together by chains and supported by uprights made of timber.

Your route in fact starts directly opposite the church, a restricted byway heading away south-east from the road here (The Street) at TQ544043. Follow this restricted byway for 250m to TQ547042 where you reach a gate. Fork left off the main path, along a signed bridleway across the field. The bridleway is undefined through the field; you need to head uphill and then at the top of the rise drop downhill, aiming for the bottom left-hand end of the field. As you get near you see a gate in the corner. Pass through the gate and now the going along the bridleway gets very easy. Follow a firm green path eastwards along the bottom edge of the field, then at the corner at TQ555043 (875m from TQ547042), turn 90 degrees to the right as signed, ascend and then turn sharp left to follow the top right-hand edge of the field ahead. Go forward along a most attractive woodland path which emerges at **Folkington** at TQ559039, at a road corner, 625m from the 90-degree right turn as stated. Turn right up the road (Folkington Road) past the delightfully situated church of St Peter. Dating from the 13th century, it contains 18th century box pews and pulpit; there's no chancel arch but there are two monuments in the chancel, dating from the end of the 17th and start of the 18th century. In the churchyard there's a slate headstone for the famous cookery writer Elizabeth David. The manor house, opposite the church, was built in Tudor style in 1843-44.

Just past the church, at TQ559038, 125m from TQ559039, turn right to join the Wealdway (see route 13), following a most attractive restricted byway just north of west along a woodland edge. At TQ551040, 1km from where you joined the Wealdway, you reach a signed junction at the Holt, the Wealdway pointing left. Though the continuous route here bears left, south-westwards, I recommend you detour straight on for another 250m or so along the restricted byway to enjoy a splendid view as the trees recede, with Arlington Reservoir a particularly attractive feature in the middle distance. Retrace to TQ551040 to continue. Whether or not you've detoured, now head south-westwards as stated from TQ551040 along the Wealdway, and enjoy a really superb bridleway journey along the hillside, with great views northwards and westwards.

At TQ543035, 1km from TQ551040, you reach a junction of bridleways. Your continuous route turns right, northwards, here, but first you should look to the left (south) to get a close-up view to the **Long Man Of Wilmington**. This is one of the most iconic and photogenic sights in Sussex. Carved into the side of Windover Hill, it is a simple outline of a human figure, almost 70m high, holding what appears to be a staff in each hand. Its origin is a mystery: some theories date it back to ancient times, given that Roman coins found nearby bear a figure with similar stance. However others suggest it's of Saxon origin or possibly represents a medieval pilgrim, while the authors of the most recent *Pevsner Architectural Guide*, spoilsports, assert that "it is probably not of very great antiquity," the earliest reference to it apparently being in an 18th century manuscript. Arthur Mee much more romantically describes it as "one of the most remarkable pieces of ancient craftsmanship anywhere in the world." I recommend you then continue just north of west along the bridleway to enjoy lovely views as you contour the hillside, arriving in 350m at a bridleway junction at TQ539036, then retracing to TQ543035.

Having admired the Long Man, taken the further detour (if desired) and retraced, you head northwards as stated along the bridleway from the bridleway junction at TQ543035. Follow the bridleway down towards the road – ironically the views of the Long Man are better as you get further away from him! At TQ543040, 500m from TQ543035, you reach the road. Your route ends here. To return to Wilmington, turn right to follow the road, keeping the impressive priory ruins to your left; in 375m from the end of the route you reach Wilmington Church having come full circle from the start. Retrace along The Street from here to the A27 for buses.

ROUTE 88

TQ645049-TQ649121 – Location Map E6 – OS 124 – M

11km 150m

Pevensey, Pevensey Levels, Herstmonceux, Science Centre, Plantation Wood, Windmill Hill

PT Pevensey (*, B start), Windmill Hill (B finish)

R Pevensey, Herstmonceux, Windmill Hill

This could equally well qualify as a waterside route but its history is so good I have decided to keep it here! It's a linear route and I suggest that if reliant on public transport you use Eastbourne as a base; from there you can get a train or bus to Pevensey, and then catch a bus from Windmill Hill back to Eastbourne at the end.

Before you start, do spend time in **Pevensey** and in particular make sure you visit the castle. This was the Roman fort Anderida, started around the end of the third century AD. Following the Norman invasion the fort was developed substantially by William the Conqueror's half-brother, Robert, Count of Mortain. Subsequently it was passed to a succession of royal favourites but was constantly on the verge of ruin and following its use as a state prison in the 15th century – James I of Scotland was a prisoner here – it fell out of use under the Tudors, and a survey of 1573 reported it to be totally ruined. But it has been used for defensive purposes since: a gun emplacement was established here in anticipation of an invasion by the Spanish Armada, and a command and observation post was set up here during World War 2. There are two other buildings of interest in Pevensey. The first is the church of St Nicolas, built between 1205 and 1216, with a Norman font of Caen stone and a nave dating back to 1210; the church is regarded as a splendid example of Early English architecture. The other is the Court House and Gaol in the High Street. It's believed that the building served as such from Tudor times, and indeed it remained in use as such until 1886. It is now a fascinating museum. Another eye-catching building in the High Street is the timber-framed and tile-hung Mint House, of 16th century origin. But don't expect to be able to stock up on Kendal Mint Cake.

Having enjoyed Pevensey, make your way to TQ645049, where a bridleway is signed northwards away from the B2191 Westham-Pevensey road. If you're coming at it from the village centre, head south-westwards along the High Street (B2191) then veer sharply right and left round the castle precinct and you reach the bridleway almost immediately beyond the left bend, the bridleway heading off to the right. This is your starting point. (If you're approaching from Pevensey & Westham station, follow the B2191 High Street northwards from the station, veering north-eastwards and reaching the start on your left some 800m from the station.)

Now head northwards from TQ645049 along the bridleway, crossing over the A27 with care then, some 425m from the start, veering north-westwards and keeping a channel, Pevensey Haven, to your right. You're embarking on a traverse of **Pevensey Levels**, a massive contrast to the downland and woodland exploration elsewhere in this book. Also known as Pevensey Marshes, the Pevensey Levels boast a huge variety of bird life across the flat fields with the abundance of drainage ditches. Birds you might see include wigeon, teal, short-eared owl, peregrine, hen harrier, lapwing, redshank, sedge warbler, reed warbler, yellow wagtail, marsh harrier, wheatear, cuckoo or whinchat; look out for the fen raft spider in ditches, and, around your feet, plants such as flowering rush, arrowhead and great spearwort. Looking northwards you should identify the distinctive domes of the Science Centre which you'll be visiting later on this route. They still seem quite a way off!

Continuing on the obvious path, which follows the 1066 Country Walk (see route 43), you follow a generally north-westerly direction, veering northwards and reaching a road at Bridge Farm, Rickney at TQ627069, 3km 250m from the start. Turn right onto the road, immediately reaching a road T-junction; turn right, crossing the channel and then immediately turn left, just east of north, as bridleway/1066 Country Walk-signed, the channel (here named Yotham) now immediately to your left. Continue in a north-easterly direction along the bank, veering gently left and then proceeding predominantly northwards, the trusty channel (here named Hurst Haven) still to your left. Finally at TQ633095, 3km from Rickney, just before the channel veers sharply left (if you veer left with it, you've overshot!) your bridleway veers right, away from the channel, just north of east. Your marker, as it were, is a conspicuous line of bushes at right-angles to the bank. Follow the bridleway across the grass to a gate, then follow a winding but clear track, predominantly eastwards enjoying fine views to the domes.

At TQ642097, roughly 1km from leaving the channel, you turn left along a clear bridle track that takes you uphill, north-eastwards, then veering north-westwards past the buildings of Church Farm, to arrive at the bottom of Church Road in 450m or so from TQ642097. You almost immediately bear right, eastwards, here, TQ643101, but you really should detour the very short distance up the road to visit the impressive church of All Saints, **Herstmonceux.** The church is chiefly 13th century, though there is Norman work in the nave, but its chief feature of interest is a pair of memorial effigies between the chancel and north chapel, thought to represent Thomas, Lord Dacre, and his son Sir Thomas Fiennes. They are armoured without swords, but with a bull and lion at their feet. The chapel's east window has panels depicting Christ, the Virgin Mary and St Luke, while a window in the chancel depicts the Virgin and St John in a variety of colours. Meanwhile, a splendid brass on the chancel floor shows Sir William Fiennes, who is also depicted in full armour, and from whom Thomas, Lord Dacre is descended.

Whether or not you've detoured up to the church, head eastwards as stated, still with the 1066 Country Walk, here a bridleway, looking to your left for fine views to Herstmonceux Castle. It was originally built in 1440 by Sir Roger Fiennes (you can't move in Herstmonceux for Fiennes-es!), who himself became Lord Dacre. The castle was one of England's first and largest brick buildings; with its original battlements and turrets still remaining, and its round towers 26m high, it's one of the most photogenic castles in Sussex. It fell into ruin but was restored by Colonel Claude Lowther and then Sir Paul Latham roughly a century ago. The grounds contain a lake that's full of waterlilies and populated by dragonflies and kingfishers, and there's also a walled garden with rhododendrons and azaleas. If you wish to visit the castle you'll have to use the entrance off Wartling Road which you'll reach shortly.

You then ascend through woodland, a nice contrast to the exposed Pevensey Levels, to arrive at Wartling Road at TQ654103, 1km 125m from TQ643101. Turn left here, northwards, alongside Wartling Road to arrive almost at once at the entrance road for the castle and **Science Centre**. The centre stands on the site of what was the Royal Greenwich Observatory which had moved here from London in 1957 owing to atmospheric and light pollution, though the same problems led to the evacuation of the Observatory from here in 1990; happily, however, it was reborn as the Science Centre in 2004. The Centre has an excellent telescope used by the astronomer Patrick Moore in 1994 to observe a collision between a comet and Jupiter, and also houses numerous hands-on scientific and educational exhibits. Its most iconic aspect is its domes, which, as I mentioned, can be seen from some way away; completed between 1953 and 1958, they were designed for telescopes that were equatorially mounted – that is, tilted parallel to the Earth's axis of rotation.

Having visited these attractions, continue northwards beside Wartling Road initially, but almost immediately you're able to join a new (not shown on even the latest OS Explorer map), parallel bridleway just to the left of the road. This continues for 450m or so to reach a bridleway junction at TQ654107. Here turn left, just north of west, along a really delightful bridleway through **Plantation Wood**, past a large lake that's to your left. You then veer right, north-westwards, along the right-hand edge of further woodland, reaching a bridleway junction at TQ648110. Go straight on here, uphill, north-westwards, to a bridleway T-junction with Comphurst Lane at TQ646116, 1km 375m from TQ654107. Turn right, north-eastwards, up the lane, to arrive in 500m at the end of the route at TQ649121, at the A271, **Windmill Hill**. Before catching your bus towards Eastbourne or Hastings, you should head left (westwards) for 200m or so beside the A271 to view a most impressive windmill which gives the village its name. A post mill, it was built around 1814 and was – and is – the tallest and largest post mill in Sussex. It ceased to work by wind in 1893 and became derelict, but it has benefited from a significant restoration project. In 2014 a grant was given for the restoration of the machinery and sweeps to enable it to grind flour, and in November 2015 the refitted sweeps turned again for the first time for 120 years.

ROUTE 89

TQ671238 (start and finish) – Location Map E6 – OS 136, 124 – S

12km 750m

Burwash, Brightling Follies, Purchase Wood, Brightling, Bateman's

PT Burwash (B start and finish)

R Burwash

This is a long circular expedition with a lot of up-and-down work and a fair bit of road travel but it is immensely enjoyable, with some fine woodland as well as the "history" of Bateman's, which you should allow time to explore, and sight of five of the so-called Brightling Follies.

Your route starts from Bateman's, the home of Rudyard Kipling. I suggest you actually use the nearby village of **Burwash** (reachable by bus on the Uckfield-Etchingham service, which doesn't run at weekends), as your base, as it has plenty of history of its own. Spread along a ridge between the River Rother and the River Dudwell, it was a significant centre of the iron industry three centuries ago when the Weald was the country's principal source of iron ore. The High Street consists of an almost unbroken line of brick-faced old shops and cottages, a number of which date back to the 18th century or earlier, with a row of pollarded trees on its north side. Arguably the finest houses on the High Street are the late 17th century Rampyndene, a superb house of brick and timber; Mount House, adjacent to Rampyndene, timber-framed and dating back to the early 16th century; the Corn Stores, a medieval hall house; Chateaubriand, part of a late 15th century hall house; and Burghurst with its Georgian exterior, but actually the remnant of a 14th century Wealden house. The church of St Bartholomew, at the east end of the High Street, has a Norman west tower with twin bell openings, a very broad Early English chancel, and a 14th century iron tomb slab set into a wall at the end of the south aisle, the slab claimed to be one of the oldest of its kind in the county.

To reach the start of the route from the centre of Burwash, head along the High Street and turn right just before the church down School Hill. Then immediately before the Dudwell river bridge, 750m from the church, turn right along Bateman's Lane and follow it for 750m to reach a very sharp right-hand road bend, with the Bateman's building immediately opposite. Here, at TQ671238, your route begins in the form of a bridleway heading left. I'll describe Bateman's on our return to it.

Accordingly, then, bear left at TQ671238 as bridleway-signed, fractionally west of south, following a lane that then goes forward through the Park Farm complex. Beyond the complex, follow the signage carefully as you leave the more obvious path and, still heading just west of south, take a narrower path, a bridleway in the shade of trees, climbing quite steeply. You enter High Wood, following a clear track and ascending to a T-junction of tracks at TQ668229. Turn left and then almost immediately right, going forward to another track junction at the edge of the wood. Don't go on into the woods but turn left, southwards, with the bridleway, following the eastern edge of the woods then veering right, south-westwards, along what is a clear track that then dips to a road, Willingford Lane, at TQ665222, 1km 750m from the start.

There now follows an unavoidably long road section of just over 2km, but it is certainly not unpleasant. Turn left, south-eastwards, along the road uphill, in 1km 125m passing a splendid obelisk which is to your left. This is one of the so-called **Brightling Follies**, the work of a local MP John Fuller, known as Mad Jack Fuller, who was born in 1757 and lived at nearby Brightling Park. In Parliament he was known as the Hippopotamus on account of his size. He was however nobody's fool: he founded the Fullerian Professorships of Chemistry, the first holder of which was the scientist Michael Faraday. He was also an amateur astronomer and a collector of Turner paintings – he persuaded Turner to visit Sussex – and he bought Bodiam Castle, historically one of the finest castles in Sussex, when it was in danger of demolition, actually saving it from destruction. He also comes into the world of literature, for Charles Lamb mentions him as Ursa Major in one of his essays. Fuller, though, is far more famous for his six extraordinary constructions or follies in and around the village of Brightling. All of them are still standing today and you will see four others beside the obelisk on this route. The obelisk, 20m high, is known as the Brightling Needle and marks one of the highest points of East Sussex away from the South Downs, at 197m.

In 250m beyond the obelisk, you reach a crossroads. Here turn right, southwards, along the road towards Woods Corner, in 250m passing a second folly, the so-called Observatory. Designed by Sir Robert Smirke, built of ashlar between 1810 and 1818, and boasting a lead dome, it originally housed a camera obscura but is now a private house. Some 400m further along the road beyond that, at TQ670203, a signed bridleway goes off to the left. Turn left here to follow this really lovely bridleway south-eastwards through **Purchase Wood**, following a dead straight line. This is some of the finest and easiest woodland journeying in East Sussex, as you proceed resolutely downhill. In 625m you veer sharp right; having done so, you almost immediately turn hard left, south-eastwards, with the bridleway, not being seduced by the more obvious-looking track that heads south-westwards. Continue south-eastwards into Mainsbrook Wood; don't be led astray either by a track that forks right, but rather veer left, eastwards along the track that stays close to the left-hand (northern) edge of the woods. This is still really unspoilt enjoyable going.

At TQ687195 you reach a T-junction of bridle tracks, 2km from the point at which you left the road. Here turn left, heading just west of north along a clear track, from which you get a good view, on the hillside to your left, of a third folly, the very photogenic Classical temple or rotunda, also dating back to around 1810. Believed to have been designed by Sir Robert Smirke, it incorporates a Tuscan colonnade and dome. The rotunda is situated in the grounds of Brightling Park, Fuller's home, and I rather naughtily trespassed into the park grounds to view it very early one Saturday in June. I got my just deserts when thanks to the morning mist I lost my bearings altogether on my descent and was relieved to make it back to Camp Four with my oxygen supplies still holding up.

Having passed the rotunda you veer right and then left with the bridleway, climbing to reach a road at TQ687206, 1km 125m from TQ687195. By looking just north of east here you may see, half-hidden in the woods, another of

Fuller's follies, a tapering circular stone tower, 10.7m high. It's been suggested that this is actually the work of another John Fuller known as John Fuller The Second. It is however only accessible by public footpath which begins just down the road to your right. Your continuous route turns left at TQ687206 and follows the road north-westwards for 500m into the hilltop village of **Brightling.** You ignore a right-hand turn and go forward to a very sharp right bend and then a very sharp left bend by the church. In the churchyard is a 7.6m high pyramid built in 1810 and known as the Mausoleum. Again it was designed by Sir Robert Smirke, based on the Roman tomb to Caius Cestius. Mad Jack Fuller, who died in 1834, was buried beneath it; he is said to have been buried wearing a top hat, seated and holding a bottle of claret! The church itself, dedicated to St Thomas Becket, dates back to the 13th century, and contains an 18th century gallery, fragments of wall paintings going back to the 16th century, and some 15th/16th century memorial brasses. Brightling Park, the home of Mad Jack Fuller, stands to the south-west of the church.

Having negotiated the right and left bends with the road, you then follow the road along the ridge just south of west for 875m, enjoying glorious views across the Weald to your right. At TQ676209 you turn right off the road as bridleway-signed. At the very start the bridleway path is unclear but head northwards and almost at once you'll pick up a track which then veers right and dives into Rounden Wood. It's then very straightforward going, descending on a clear track north-eastwards. You cross the conveyor line linking Brightling gypsum mine (owned by British Gypsum), just 375m to the north-west of here, with the main Robertsbridge-Battle rail line. It is a remarkable and arguably incongruous thing to find in such a remote and otherwise unspoilt location although it has to be said that the conveyor is more of a curiosity than an eyesore and there is a certain beauty and uniqueness about it.

You then continue on through Beak's Wood to arrive at a bridleway T-junction at TQ688223, 1km 750m from leaving the road. Here you turn left along a charming woodland bridleway heading uphill, north-westwards, into and through the Perryman's Farm complex to reach a road, Fontridge Lane, in 750m at TQ681226. Turn left along the road, reaching a road T-junction in 200m where you turn right along King's Hill Road. After 375m from the right turn, at TQ678229, you turn left, north-westwards, along a signed bridleway that heads through open fields then descends through Park Wood and out the other side. OS Explorer mapping is misleading here; the bridleway doesn't veer sharp left as the map suggests, but veers much more gently left to arrive at a signed bridleway T-junction at a gate at TQ670234, 1km from TQ678229. You've now come full circle; turn right along the bridleway to arrive back at the start, by Bateman's, in some 400m.

Bateman's, a handsome stone mansion with towering chimneys and fine mullioned windows, was originally built by a lawyer, William Langham, in 1634 but is best known for being the home of Rudyard Kipling, who purchased it in 1902 and whose home it was until his death in 1936. Subsequently it was acquired by the National Trust. During Kipling's time here he wrote such works as *Puck Of Pook's Hill* and *If*. His study has been left just as it was when he was alive. Upstream from the house there's a fine weatherboarded watermill, while nearby is the water-drive turbine which Kipling had installed in 1902 to light Bateman's with electricity. The garden was largely planned by Kipling, paid for by funds from his 1907 Nobel Prize for Literature. To return to Burwash turn right to retrace along Bateman's Lane to the T-junction by the Dudwell river bridge then turn left up School Hill to arrive at the main road by the church.

ROUTE 90

TQ741236-TQ740225 – Location Map E6 – OS 124 – E

9km 375m (longer route), 5km (shorter route)

Kent & East Sussex Railway, Salehurst, Robertsbridge Abbey, Wellhead Wood, Maynards Wood, Robertsbridge

PT Robertsbridge (*, B start and finish)

R Robertsbridge, Salehurst

This is just a lovely easy flexible bridleway route with which to end our exploration of the best bridleway routes in Sussex. Attractive woodland, fine views, two very pretty villages, lots of history – it has it all. It can easily be treated as a circular route, starting and finishing at Robertsbridge which is served by rail.

To reach the start of this route from Robertsbridge Station, head eastwards along Station Road for 450m or so to a T-junction with High Street, turning left and immediately right along Fair Lane which reaches in 250m a bridge crossing of the A21. Cross the bridge, the lane here at TQ741236 becoming a bridleway, thus marking the start of your route. Having crossed the A21, bear left with the bridleway for 125m (parallel with the A21) dropping down to a continuation of Fair Lane and turning right to follow it. For now your route ceases to be a bridleway, but at Redlands, 375m from the right turn, the lane becomes a bridleway, proceeding very pleasantly eastwards in the Rother valley. In 500m from Redlands at TQ751238 you reach a bridleway junction, turning left here along a bridleway heading northwards. In 125m or so you cross Church Bridge over the river Rother; further east it will broaden to become one of the widest as well as one of the longest rivers in East Sussex.

Just beyond Church Bridge you cross the course of the old railway linking Robertsbridge, on the Charing Cross-Hastings line, and Headcorn, on the Charing Cross-Ashford line. The section of line between Robertsbridge and

Tenterden via Bodiam, Northiam and Rolvenden opened in March 1903, the extension to Headcorn opening in May 1905. From the early 1930's onwards the line, known as the **Kent & East Sussex Railway**, was running at a loss, and closed to passengers in January 1954. However first the section between Rolvenden and Tenterden, and then the section between Bodiam (just east of here) and Rolvenden, reopened as a preserved steam railway, an immensely popular tourist attraction. It is hoped that the section between Robertsbridge and Bodiam will reopen one day. For now, all you can do is stand on this picturesque spot and try and imagine the railway as it was. The crossing just beyond Church Bridge was the site of Salehurst Halt, a station on the Robertsbridge-Bodiam section, but there was never a station building here.

Continue on along the bridleway, veering north-westwards then westwards with the track to arrive in the very pretty village of **Salehurst,** 500m from the bridleway junction at TQ751238. It is dominated by its largely 13th century church of St Mary the Virgin, the tower thought to date back to the early 13th century. The church contains a remarkable late 12th century font, carved with salamanders running round the foot, and an early 14th century north chapel containing a number of memorial cartouches to members of the Peckham family. In the chancel is a stone with five crosses, once the altar stone of the now ruined Robertsbridge Abbey which we'll meet shortly. Other buildings of note in Salehurst include Parsonage Farmhouse, the medieval rectory still containing some 15th century features; the timber-framed 17th century Goodgrooms; and the brick-built Church Farmhouse which conceals a 15th century Wealden hall house. The name Salehurst, incidentally, literally means "willow wood" and the area has indeed been famous for its cricket bat willows.

Now retrace the 500m to the bridleway junction at TQ751238 and turn left, eastwards, to continue, your bridleway soon passing the remains of the Cistercian **Robertsbridge Abbey** that are to your left. The abbey, the only Cistercian house in Sussex, was founded towards the end of the 12th century but was dissolved in 1538 and is now a ruin: most of what is left has been incorporated into a private dwelling, Abbey House, although in the garden there are fragments of the abbey walls including the ruins of a refectory and dormitory undercroft. In 375m from TQ751238 you veer sharp right and then left with the bridleway to reach, at TQ756237 (625m from TQ751238), some buildings on your right. DON'T go straight on along the footpath here, but turn right, just east of south, along a continuation of the bridleway, which skirts the west side of the buildings. The OS mapping could be misleading here, but your route simply follows the obvious track, turning right at a T-junction of tracks and shortly (250m from TQ756237) reaching a bridleway junction at TQ757235.

You now have a choice. For a shorter journey, go straight on, shortly veering right, south-westwards, along the bridle track and ascending in the trees close to the woodland edge, then descending along the woodland edge to another bridleway junction at TQ753232, 500m from TQ757235.

However, you could choose to take a longer route at TQ757235, but be warned there is an unavoidable road slog for 1km on what is quite a busy B road, the B2244. Should you decide on the longer route, turn left, eastwards, at TQ757235 along a delightful bridleway that begins in open country but soon enters Wellhead Wood and climbs steeply, then exits and, with lovely views ahead, follows a field edge down to the buildings of Eyelids. Veer left round the left-hand edge of the complex, and then go forward to join the driveway leading down to the B2244 at TQ771235, 1km 375m from TQ757235. Turn right, southwards, alongside the road for 1km, exercising great caution, particularly if on foot or horseback; there's no pavement and there's a fair bit of traffic. Now you need to be careful! The old OS-mapped bridleway junction at TQ771223 has been re-routed; watch instead, at TQ771225 (prior to the supposed mapped junction), for a signed bridleway path forking right from the road. You take this path and rise, proceeding roughly parallel with the road, then veer right as bridleway-signed, heading westwards and rejoining the OS-mapped bridleway. Now things get a lot better as you follow what is an excellent bridle track westwards through **Wellhead Wood**. You remain within the woodland initially, but then veer right, north-westwards, emerging from the wood and following the right-hand field edge, keeping the wood immediately to your right. The surroundings and the views here are absolutely lovely. You descend quite steeply with the bridleway, veering sharp left, westwards, arriving at TQ753232 and being reunited with the shorter route, 2km 500m from TQ771225.

Now, whichever route you've taken, head south-westwards from TQ753232 for 250m along an obvious bridle track which skirts Salehurst Park Farm and reaches a T-junction of tracks at TQ751231. Here turn left along a bridle track which veers right to reach a path crossroads; go straight over and continue along a clear bridleway heading south-westwards. This is again quite superb, with really smashing views across unspoilt countryside to your left, and a really nice green path providing a veritable carpet for the feet – or wheels! You ascend to skirt **Maynards Wood** then, passing a pond, continue south-westwards to reach a metalled road at TQ740225, the end of the route, 1km 375m from TQ751231.

To return to Robertsbridge, turn right along the road which in 125m reaches the A21. Turn right to follow beside it for some 450m – fortunately a parallel path is available – then fork left along John's Cross Road (it being unclear what John is cross about) to arrive in 500m back in the centre of Robertsbridge. You need to turn left along Station Road to return to the station, but before you catch your train you should spend some time in **Robertsbridge**. It contains several old houses, many of them half-timbered; there is a particularly fine 18th century coaching inn (the timber-framed and tile-hung George Inn), while other houses of note on the High Street include Rose Bank, a Wealden house dating back to around 1400, and the Seven Stars, of similar age. In Northbridge Street is the fine Monks House, another Wealden hall house dating back to around 1400, and off this street is the former Robertsbridge Mill, one of the largest watermills in Sussex. You might also want to check out the United Reformed Church on the High Street to see if Nikolaus Pevsner was justified in calling it "truly horrible!"

Part 7 – More bridleways – the best, wackiest and worst of the rest

In this final Part I take a somewhat more irreverent look at a variety of other Sussex bridleways, all of them notable in some way, some of them well worth visiting and enjoying, some well worth avoiding. As this Part goes on, you'll note an increasing emphasis towards the unusual and the offbeat, both in the best and worst senses. Please note that some of the routes described may be a fair distance from the nearest public transport.

Anyway, I start with one that I hope will go down extremely well in every sense!

The wine lovers' bridleway

Generally speaking, walking and alcohol don't mix: trying to quench a mid-walk thirst with a couple of pints or a glass or two of wine is unlikely to do you a huge amount of good. But there's one bridleway route in Sussex which is absolutely made for the oenophile – the route from West Chiltington to Nyetimber vineyards. So here it is! It starts and indeed finishes at **TQ085181** (OS OL10) and the there-and-back route comes in at 3km 400m, to which you can add 950m if you detour to West Chiltington.

To access this route from Little Hill, West Chiltington Common, served by buses from Pulborough, follow Little Hill north-eastwards from its junction with The Common. At the road junction in 250m bear left along Mill Road past West Chiltington's very elegant street sign and also fine windmill, a smock mill dating from around 1800 and now part of a private dwelling, with two surviving sails; opposite the mill is the fine 17th century Friar's House. Just a few metres north of the windmill is a road junction, and immediately beyond that junction is the start of the bridleway route at TQ085181. Follow the bridleway which heads uphill just east of north for 550m as far as a bridleway T-junction at TQ086186.

The continuous route bears left here, just north of west, but if you wish to visit West Chiltington, take the bridleway going right, bearing right at the T-junction of paths in 250m and then, in 100m, left along the road for 125m, bearing right at the crossroads into the very pretty village centre. The village's chief highlight is the church of St Mary, one of the most interesting and attractive in West Sussex. It boasts nave and chancel walls dating back to the 11th century; a large number of wall paintings some of which date back to the 12th century, depicting a number of subjects including scenes of Christ's Passion and warning to Sabbath-breakers; and an unusually long squint to the chancel through a thickened chancel wall. Retrace the same way to TQ086186.

Now, whether you've detoured or not, head just north of west from TQ086186 as stated along the bridleway, enjoying fine views, reaching a path junction in 150m. Here take care to turn right with the bridleway, and in 225m you reach another path junction in delightful surroundings. This time you turn left with the bridleway and head westwards, descending and in 125m passing but ignoring a bridleway going off at TQ085189. You then veer right to reach a bridleway lane at Lower Jordans, here meeting the West Sussex Literary Trail (see route 5). Turn right up the lane, just east of north then northwards to arrive, at a junction of tracks at **TQ084195,** at Nyetimber Vineyard, some 650m from the bridleway you passed at TQ085189. Nyetimber was the first producer of English sparkling wine to exclusively grow three celebrated grape varieties, Pinot Noir, Pinot Meunier and Chardonnay; the first vines were planted in 1988 and Nyetimber wines are now reputed to be among the finest sparkling wines in the country. There are regular open days and tours so make sure you plan to do this bridleway route when they are happening and you can enjoy them. Return exactly the same way.

The great, straight bridleway

The straightest bridleway in Sussex also happens to be a very good one. Situated a little to the west of Worthing in West Sussex, it starts at **TQ111026** and ends at **TQ097025** (OS OL10); it is just 1km 375m long.

The start of your route is immediately west of the roundabout junction of Sea Lane and Ilex Way in Goring, at TQ111026; regular buses from the centre of Worthing ply the A259 immediately east of the roundabout. From the start, you follow Ilex Way, going forward along Ilex Avenue, fractionally south of west, in a dead straight line, on what is a signed bridleway. That's all there is to it! The avenue, considered to be one of the best of its kind in the world, was planted around 1840 by the Lyon family who lived at Goring Hall, which immediately adjoins the avenue on the left. The original Goring Hall was also built around 1840 but following a fire in 1888 it was rebuilt in 1892 and is now a hospital; the avenue was originally intended to facilitate access to the hall from the east and west. There's a fine variety of wildlife and bird life to be enjoyed in the avenue, including woodpecker, tawny owl, stag beetle, harvest mouse, vole, weasel and many kinds of butterfly, while plants include speedwell and winter heliotrope. The bridleway ends, all too soon, at TQ097025, after 1km 375m, at another Sea Lane, this time in Ferring. Turn right up Sea Lane and after 250m bear left at the T-junction to reach, in a further 250m, the centre of Ferring with buses available towards Worthing and Littlehampton.

Eight Sunday leisurely bridleway strolls

All of these are, even if you undertake a there-and-back journey, 3km 250m or less in length. They may lack the pzazz of the routes described in Parts 1 to 6 above, but they give a delightful taste of the joys of bridleway exploration and may tempt you to try one or more of the longer routes in future. I anticipate you would want to walk them rather than ride them (hence the heading) but the choice is yours. Please note that you may need to rely on a car to access at least some of these routes.

TQ063164-TQ055160 (OS OL10) provides a charming bridleway stroll of 750m each way across the lovely wildlife haven of Wiggonholt Common, which also boasts a popular Visitor Centre on the edge of Pulborough Brooks Nature Reserve. The bridleway starts at the A283 between Pulborough and Cootham (both locations boasting pubs), heading westwards from TQ063164 and veering south-westwards to end at Greatham Lane. The areas bordering both your bridleway and the adjacent Visitor Centre are exceedingly rich in flora and fauna: among birds you may see are the peregrine falcon, barn owl, lapwing and nightingale, and you should look out for dragonflies and damselflies as well as tiger beetles and minotaur beetles.

Next up, here's a 750m-each-way stroll with a bridleway starting point at **TQ072193** (OS OL10) just north of Nutbourne. If you're coming up from the ivy-clad Rising Sun Inn in the very pretty Nutbourne village centre, head northwards then north-westwards along Nutbourne Lane (stated on some maps to be Nutbourne Road!), arriving at the starting point in some 600m from the pub, at TQ072193 as stated. Turn left here along a bridleway heading westwards, offering fabulous views to the South Downs. I suggest you go as far as a very sharp right-hand bend at **TQ065193**, 750m from TQ072193, then retrace.

TQ103175 (OS OL10) just west of Thakeham, is the start point for a lovely bridleway amble (800m each way) to a great view of the South Downs. If you're coming up from the White Lion (sadly closed at the time of writing) in the pretty village of Thakeham, head north-westwards uphill from the pub along the village street to reach the B2139. Turn right onto the road then as it bends right in some 125m, you reach the starting point, as stated at TQ103175. Here turn left along a bridleway/farm road. In some 50m you kink left and right with the bridleway, initially passing through woodland then veering north-westwards and emerging, 250m from the start, to follow a track from which there are lovely views to the South Downs. I suggest you go as far as a sharp right bend at **TQ098181**, 500m from the woodland, then retrace.

TQ314070 (OS OL11) provides the launching pad for this 1km 500m-each-way stroll, heading off Ditchling Road in the outskirts of Brighton, with pubs and cafes not far away. A signed bridleway sets off north-eastwards from Ditchling Road at TQ314070 just opposite Beacon Close (itself just north of Osborne Road). It proceeds very pleasantly through woodland, forking left after 250m and arriving at the Hollingbury golf course approach road in just under 1km from the start. Turn right along the approach road and then in a few metres turn left up a signed permissive bridleway through the trees, this path bringing you out onto the golf course. There are lots of paths that can then take you to the elevated ground beyond the course, this highest ground being around the trig point on the Iron Age Hollingbury Castle fortification, just 500m or so beyond the golf course approach road (the grid reference of the trig point being **TQ321079**). A permissive bridleway follows the castle wall round, offering stunning views to Brighton and along the coast. Simply retrace to Ditchling Road, remembering the paths you took on your way up!

TQ466347 (OS 135) at Upper Hartfield, on the B2110 between Forest Row and Hartfield, is the start point for an easy, 1km 125m-each way, bridleway stroll with a great objective. Head south-eastwards from here along the bridleway lane, then in 750m at a bridleway junction veer right, south, along the bridleway to reach, in 375m, one of the most iconic spots in Sussex, namely Poohsticks Bridge, at **TQ470338**. This of course was the creation of Winnie the Pooh, or more properly Pooh's inventor A.A. Milne, though the bridge itself was effectively rebuilt in 1999. Choose a day when the flow of water under the bridge is neither too sluggish nor too hectic, and let the games begin! Then return the same way; the drinks are on the winner at the Gallipot Inn, Gallipot Street, 500m or so north-eastwards up the B2110 towards Hartfield.

TQ526067 (OS OL25) is the starting point for a 1km 625m-each-way journey from Berwick to Selmeston and back, a perfect Sunday post-lunch or summer evening stroll – and you're blessed with a pub at both ends! If you're coming from Berwick Station, head very briefly south of the level crossing but almost immediately, just opposite the Berwick Arms pub, turn right, westwards, at TQ526067 along a signed bridleway, part of the Vanguard Way (see route 24). You start with a field crossing and then enjoy a superb straight green path stretching ahead with tremendous views to Windover Hill to the left and Firle Beacon in front of you. The Vanguard Way leaves you but you continue just north of west on a good clear path which arrives at its western end at TQ509069 by Selmeston's pretty flint church, rebuilt in the 19th century. It has unusual brasses and in the churchyard you'll find the grave of Stanley Mockford who was the inventor of the 'Mayday' distress call. In the church there's some fine stained glass, including the window of Annunciation by Charles Kempe. The churchyard is a delightful spot especially in early spring with its profusion of daffodils and snowdrops. If you've worked up a thirst you could turn left, south-westwards, onto The Street here to reach, in 500m or so, the A27 where you'll find the Barley Mow pub. Otherwise simply retrace to Berwick.

If, having returned to the Berwick Arms or the station, you fancy a little more exercise, there's another, 1km 250m-each-way, excursion you could do, still on OS OL25, as follows. From Berwick Station, continue up the road north of the level crossing for 625m then at TQ527074 turn right off the road along a signed bridleway, almost immediately reaching a bridleway junction. Turn left here and now follow the signed bridleway which takes you past a parking/refreshment area and on north-eastwards round the edge of Arlington Reservoir. Vegetation often obstructs the view to the water but where it relents, there are some excellent viewpoints with Windover Hill making a very splendid backcloth. The reservoir, which opened in the 1960's, not only provides water to the nearby area but is a nature reserve with over 170 recorded species of bird including migrating osprey and egret, and you may also see the great-crested grebe, swallow, mallard, cormorant and pied wagtail. Ironically there is a footpath (NOT a bridleway) considerably closer to the water's edge, and with a much firmer surface! I recommend you stick to the bridleway until the footpath comes up to join you at **TQ533078**, 625m or so from the start of the bridleway. Here walkers could turn hard right to follow the footpath down to the water's edge. Whether you choose to do that or not, retrace to Berwick Station the same way.

Let's move further east for our final Sunday stroll. On the B2096 Heathfield-Battle road, there's the White Hart at Netherfield (OS 124). By working westwards from there for just under 1km 500m and then turning right at TQ696191 at the Darwell Hole crossroads along a road towards Brightling you reach, in 375m up this road, a bridleway crossroads at **TQ695195**. Here you have a choice of routes – you can do either or both. You can turn left to follow a bridleway through the very charming Prinkle Wood which is designated Access Land, taking the left fork after 125m to proceed through the trees for up to another 500m or so, as far as the B2096 at **TQ691191** should you so wish. Instead, or as well, at TQ695195, you can turn right along a bridleway heading north-eastwards through Darwell Wood. Spectacular displays of wild garlic and bluebells carpet the woodland in the spring, while you should listen out for the songs of birds such as siskin, crossbill, buzzard, nightjar and sparrowhawk, as well as the knocking of green woodpeckers. I suggest you turn back after 1km where the main path executes a hairpin bend at **TQ698204.**

Slightly more than a Sunday bridleway stroll – but only slightly!

If you want a slightly more demanding Sunday afternoon expedition, here are half a dozen great "out-and-back" bridleway routes which can fit in nicely with a Sunday pub meal. Again I anticipate you would want to walk rather than ride (hence the heading) but the choice is yours. Please note that, again, you may need to rely on a car to access at least some of these six routes.

The first is a lovely gentle 2km 250m-each-way journey with a pub at the start – ideal! – and a most interesting historical feature at the end. To reach the start of the route from the Kings Arms on the A286 just south of Fernhurst (OS OL33) served by buses to Haslemere and Midhurst, you need to follow beside the A286 northwards for 375m to **SU895274** where the route begins in the form of a bridleway here heading off to the west. Unfortunately the stretch of road needed to get from the pub to this point is particularly unpleasant with lots of traffic and barely adequate verges. If you're able to be dropped at the start of the route, so much the better! From the start of the route you head westwards away from the A286 along the bridleway through lush green meadows and along the north edge of Whitter's Copse, then enter the wood. You go across a footpath crossroads then veer briefly south-westwards before veering sharp right (1km from the start), now heading north-westwards, your predominant direction of travel for the rest of this bridleway route. There's a steep descent to a footbridge and an equally sharp ascent the other side, and your clear bridleway then continues through the glorious coniferous woodland of Turner's Copse. There's another steep descent to a footbridge, with hefty vegetation on both sides, beyond which you go over another footpath crossing and, emerging from the woods, now go forward as bridleway-signed along a right-hand field edge. You enter further woodland and veer right, descending (in 1km 250m from the sharp right turn referred to above) to the beautiful Furnace Pond (**SU879282**), legacy of an ironworks that was situated here and which flourished in the 17th and 18th centuries using local ore, charcoal and water power. There are remnants of the old workings to the right, while the pond is to your left. Retrace from here to the A286.

The second route, just over 2km each way, starts at **SU941261** (OS OL33). To get there from the village of Lurgashall, with its Noah's Ark pub, make your way to the crossroads at the south end of the green and join Mill Lane, the road heading south (not south-west), almost immediately passing the Greengates turning to the left. Follow the road for 1km to arrive at the start of the route, SU941261, where a bridleway heads off to the right, heading south-westwards. You soon pass the delightful Mill Pond, with weir, and Mill Farm, where you may be greeted by farm animals, then head south-westwards on a lovely well-defined path with gorgeous hedgerows and beautiful views to Bexleyhill Common ahead. I suggest you follow it all the way to its end, where the bridleway meets the Lickfold-Lodsworth road, 2km from the start, at **SU927246**. Simply retrace to SU941261. Either before or after doing this journey it's worth spending time in Lurgashall; its church is part 11th century and boasts a 16th century timber gallery, and there are some most attractive cottages round the green including the part-16th century Malthouse.

The third route nicely links two attractions close to Petworth (OS OL11 and OL33). There is just over 3km of bridleway travel but if you walk/ride all the way from the A272 at SU966216, the round trip works out at just under 5km. I suggest that to access this route you work eastwards from the pretty village of Tillington. Its part-Norman church of All Hallows boasts an early 19th century tower, arcades that date back to around 1200, and a monument to William Mitford in four different shades of marble. The village also has a fine stone-built Manor House dating back to around 1600 and an early 19th century rectory, not to mention its Horse Guards Inn. From Tillington, proceed eastwards then south-eastwards beside the A272 for 500m from the village centre – a path is provided. To your left is Petworth

Park, itself well worth exploring. The park consists of 700 acres of beautiful parkland, ponds and woodland including ancient oaks, and accommodates the largest herd of fallow deer in the country. One particular feature of interest in the park is the woodland garden, known as the Pleasure Ground, and believed to be one of the finest achievements of Capability Brown. Whether you've detoured into the park or not, you will, in 500m as stated along the A272 from Tillington, reach SU966216. Here you turn right, heading southwards along a track known as Hungers Lane, a public way as opposed to a bridleway. It proceeds very pleasantly southwards between trees and becomes a sunken lane, evolving into a bridleway at **SU966208** (the start of the bridleway travelling) and descending to a bridleway junction with Rotherbridge Lane at SU966203, 1km 250m from the A272 and 500m from SU966208. Go straight over Rotherbridge Lane, and very shortly there's a lovely footbridge crossing of the West Sussex River Rother, the river looking particularly impressive here; the West Sussex Rother is arguably the finest river in West Sussex which doesn't flow into the sea, it being a tributary of the River Arun. Continue south-eastwards along a charming lane past Kilsham Cottages, rising and then descending, noting another lovely Rother bridge crossing on the left with the course of the old Pulborough-Petersfield railway visible to the right. You reach the A285 at **SU969192**, 1km 150m from SU966203, but by turning left very briefly beside the A285 you reach the fascinating Coultershaw heritage site which contains an old waterwheel and 18th century Beam Pump. Its setting beside the River Rother is quite charming. En route to and from the heritage site you pass the Badgers pub and, adjacent to the pub, a road leading to Petworth's former railway station, now beautifully restored as a hotel. Simply now retrace all the way to Tillington.

The fourth route under this heading takes you from the sprawl of Angmering (OS OL10) up to one of the best viewpoints in Sussex, and from the start of the route it's only just over 2km each way. If you're coming from Angmering village centre, head eastwards along the High Street for some 625m, at which point you reach a very sharp right bend; don't take the bend but go straight on eastwards along a quieter road for a further 150m. You then, at **TQ076043,** the start of the route, fork sharp left as bridleway-signed, almost immediately crossing over the A280 and then veering sharp right with the bridleway, heading southwards for 150m before veering left, eastwards. Now follow the bridleway steadily uphill (passing just to the south of a derelict post mill), reaching a signed bridleway junction at TQ089042, roughly 1km 500m from the start. Go straight on as bridleway-signed, onto Highdown Hill, heading eastwards; it's a clear and excellent track, the views getting better all the time. You pass a signed public footpath going off hard right and then veer left to reach, at **TQ094043** (625m from TQ089042), a 4-way junction, with bridleways signed straight on and right, and a public footpath signed left. If walking, you may wish to detour left for 150m or so up the footpath to the trig point and site of a Bronze Age hillfort, which was refortified in the 3rd century AD. The views from the trig point on a clear day are sensational, extending as far as Selsey Bill, perhaps beyond to the Isle of Wight, to the west, and Beachy Head to the east. Alternatively or as well, you could detour from TQ094043 along the bridleway signed right, just south of east along the top of the ridge; this brings you in some 250m to an area of trees in which you'll find the so-called Miller's Tomb, the tomb of the 18th century eccentric miller John Olliver, whose mill once stood on the hill. He had a strange preoccupation with death: his coffin was kept under his bed and he had his tomb made 30 years before he died. However far you've chosen to go, retrace the same way.

TQ626209 (OS 124) just north of Punnett's Town on the B2096 Heathfield-Battle road is the start of a delightful restricted byway leading all the way to the A265 Heathfield-Burwash road. To reach it from Punnett's Town (roughly 2km to the east of Cade Street, also on the B2096 and boasting the Half Moon Inn), follow North Street heading northwards from the B2096 at TQ625204, for 625m to arrive at the start. Your restricted byway heads just west of north from here through the lovely Twenty Acre Wood, with superb views ahead, plunging down to a footbridge crossing of the River Dudwell. You then rise most picturesquely along the edge of Milkhurst Wood, keeping Tottingworth Park to your left, to reach the end of the restricted byway at the A265 at **TQ620229,** 2km from the start. Return exactly the same way.

TQ761159 (OS 124) just east of Battle, is the start of a charming bridleway (maximum 2km each way) heading eastwards off Marley Lane (which links Battle and the A21) into the very attractive Great Wood, following the 1066 Country Walk (see route 43) in a dead straight line. You couldn't get lost if you tried! The woodland is predominantly coniferous and supports a variety of common butterflies, dragonflies and damselflies, as well as badgers and deer, while birds you may see (and/or hear) include the nightjar, tree pipit and crossbill. The bridleway then does veer south-eastwards to emerge from the wood after just under 2km at **TQ779156;** simply retrace from however far you've decided to stroll, back to Marley Lane. By turning left along Marley Lane on return and following it for 1km, you arrive at the historic town of Battle, best known of course for its abbey and for being the site of the Battle of Hastings.

Three moments of unexpected bridleway bliss

Heading south-westwards along the bridleway from **SU891302** to **SU893299** just north of Fernhurst (OS OL33) you may think, well, it's pleasant but nothing special. Then in some 450m you veer left, south-eastwards, to suddenly and unexpectedly reach, at **SU891297,** an absolutely fantastic viewpoint, the panorama extending across West Sussex as far as Devil's Dyke. The area is known as Marley Heights – you certainly hit the heights here.

The bridleway between **TQ060273** and **TQ077280** from Newpound Common to Okehurst, west of Billingshurst

(OS OL34), is pleasant but unremarkable. However, in the middle, at **TQ068276,** is the crossing of the Wey & Arun Canal at the delectable red-brick Loves Bridge, restored by the Wey & Arun Canal Trust in the 1970's. It really is a place where time seems to have stood still.

The bridleway running north-eastwards from **TQ423294** to **TQ438299** (as re-routed) (OS 135), near Chelwood Gate just south of Forest Row, starts as a pleasant woodland track and then towards its end provides an airy journey across one of the many exposed sections of Ashdown Forest. But what a surprise awaits in the middle. After proceeding for 550m or so along the woodland track you arrive at **TQ429295**, at a delightful stepping-stones crossing of a stream, particularly impressive at times of wet weather; if you don't want to risk getting your feet wet, use the delicious little footbridge nearby. A great place to picnic and, since we're in Winnie the Pooh country, a perfect base for some heffalump hunting.

Good bridleway walk(s) NOT spoiled

A number of bridleways in Sussex cross golf courses. At the far north-west corner of West Sussex there's a section of bridleway, from **SU834294- SU834292**, right beside a short hole at Liphook Golf Club (OS OL33), which we met back in route 14. Next up, **TQ074162-TQ078169**, a 750m bridleway (OS OL10) crosses the delightful West Sussex Golf Club. As for Brighton & Hove, see above for a suggestion for a Sunday stroll that visits Hollingbury golf course starting at **TQ314070**. In East Sussex, a bridleway running from **TQ453393** north-eastwards to **TQ460400** for 1km (OS 135), crosses the most picturesque course of Holtye Golf Club. Route 64 (OS OL25) above includes a traverse of part of Seaford golf course between **TQ489024** and **TQ486009**.

And lastly, a bridleway running from **TQ509295** south to **TQ509289** for some 625m (OS 135), provides an excellent view of a number of holes of the outward nine of Crowborough Beacon Golf Club.

Not only are all of these routes wonderfully scenic, with mixtures of heather and pine, but you can enjoy watching the golfers, congratulating them on their good shots, and consoling them when they fluff one by reminding them that the pros make it all look too easy on the telly!

Bluebell bridleway bonanza

There are lots of bridleways that pass through bluebell woods but I have a soft spot for one in particular. To reach it you need to head northwards from Hartfield (visited in route 13 above) alongside the B2026. After roughly 1km 500m from Hartfield at **TQ479375** (OS 135) turn left along the bridleway which skirts the grounds of Bolebrook Castle. In 375m you swing sharp right, then veer sharp left in 125m and sharp right again in 50m, passing the very fine buildings of Bolebrook, rebuilt in the 16th century but the original 14th century gatehouse remains. You then follow what is an excellent bridleway north-westwards into woodland with quite stunning displays of bluebells and at one point a delightful stream crossing. You emerge from the woods momentarily before diving into the equally beautiful Coomb Wood, which I suggest you follow to its end at **TQ470385**, roughly 1km from the second sharp right turn referred to above. In good weather and with the bluebells in bloom, it is sheer heaven. Retrace to Hartfield the same way.

Spring simplicity

You may remember I wrote this in my introduction to this book.

'This was my diary entry for a walk across unremarkable countryside between Henfield and Hickstead on 13th May 2019: "Just perfect…nice clear wide track, beautiful spring flowers, the shade of trees, birdsong, and attractive countryside beyond."'

Well, if you want to follow in my footsteps...the walk I did (but it can of course be ridden) starts just south of Wineham, near Henfield, at **TQ237193** (OS OL11). Follow the bridleway, here Gratten Lane, heading eastwards from Wineham Lane, past the buildings of Wyndham Farm. In some 450m from the start, veer sharply right with the bridleway then in 125m veer left with the bridleway by Great Wapses Farm. Simply then continue eastwards for another 1km 375m from the left bend, along the track to its end at Twineham Lane by Herrings Farm at **TQ255191**.

Bridleways with nice names...

TQ108159-TQ110171 just south of Thakeham (OS OL10) is called Strawberry Lane, and it is actually a delightful bridleway with attractive views and, in Thakeham, a pretty village at its northern end.

TQ111082-TQ119068 on the side of West Hill above High Salvington (OS OL10), actually a restricted byway, rejoices in the lovely name Honeysuckle Lane. Incidentally, a bridleway leading south-eastwards off Honeysuckle Lane at TQ114075 leads to the mast on West Hill from which there are fine views towards Cissbury Ring, and by continuing to the end of this bridleway at TQ121069 then going straight on you reach the photogenic High Salvington Windmill, roughly 1km 250m from TQ114075.

TQ123353-TQ127363 just north of Rowhook (OS OL34) is called Honey Lane but sadly it is a good deal less enjoyable and often unclear on the ground.

... and bridleways with odd names

A bridleway going from **TQ163149** to **TQ163163** between Ashington and Steyning (OS OL10) is none-too-elegantly named Spithandle Lane. It is in fact a very picturesque woodland route and worth exploring.

And of course we met Earwig Lane in route 22!

A new bridleway for a new road

For non-motorists it's always a sad day when a piece of unspoilt countryside is split in two by a new road, and that was indeed what happened when, in order to relieve chronic congestion on the A259 south of Combe Haven (OS 124) between Bexhill and Hastings, a new road (A2690) was built along the northern edge of the Combe Haven wetlands to absorb much of the traffic. But hats off to the planners; with the new road has come a very fine new shared-use route running alongside the road, but never so close as to make the traffic noise intrusive. Starting just west of Actons Farm at **TQ750103** it runs all the way from there alongside the A2690, often curling and undulating, to its end at **TQ773109**, a distance of 3km. There are fine views across Combe Haven to the south throughout.

Three seafaring bridleways

Just two OS-mapped bridleways in the whole of Sussex touch the sea shore without a coast road or cliff face in the way.

The first of these, marked on maps as Berrybarn Lane, **SZ780981-SZ778975,** (OS OL8) is the most direct and convenient walking route from the centre of West Wittering to the sea. The second makes a link between West Preston, just east of Littlehampton, and the seafront; its grid reference is **TQ063025-TQ061014** (OS OL10). I wonder how many of those who have followed their respective lengths of 600m and 1km realise that as they head for the beach clutching their buckets, spades and inflatable dolphins, they've been doing their own bits of bridleway bagging.

As well as these, there's a section of permissive bridleway which reaches the seashore at **SZ822951**, between Bracklesham and Selsey (OS OL8). It really is well worth following. Here's how.

Make your way initially to the Clappers Lane turning off the B2198 just north of Bracklesham. There is a bus stop at this turning, served by frequent buses from Chichester. Follow Clappers Lane eastwards and in 750m you reach a road fork just shy of Earnley's charming part-13th century church. Fork right, keeping the church to your left, and veer right with the road, heading southwards past the very sorry-looking buildings of the former Earnley Concourse. Shortly beyond these buildings, and some 375m from the road fork, you reach the car park at **SZ816966** on the right, and a track signed as public footpath and permissive bridleway going away to your left. This is the start of your route. Follow the public footpath/permissive bridleway heading eastwards from the road, then in some 200m veer right with the track and continue along a winding but very clear track, predominantly south-eastwards, keeping a channel to your left. You can enjoy beautiful views ahead to Medmerry Nature Reserve and northwards to the downland beyond Chichester. Look out for a variety of birds in and around the fields including dunnock, skylark, yellowhammer and stonechat.

In 1km or so from the start, at SZ827964, you reach a signed T-junction of footpath/permissive bridleway tracks. Turn right and follow, for 1km 250m, what is a superb wide track that strikes out south-westwards then veers southwards and proceeds past a farm complex and then, on your right, the so-called Stilt Pools, home to the avocet in spring and the teal in winter. The track veers right and ascends, passing just to the right of a huge accumulation of rocks that form part of the Medmerry sea defences between the Witterings and Selsey. Climb to the end of the track to be faced, suddenly, with the sea itself, with tremendous views to the Isle of Wight and Portsmouth, as well as the great bank of shingle to your right separating you from Bracklesham and the Witterings. There is a sign here, SZ822951, indicating you have just been following a public bridleway (rather than a permissive one) but this has to be an error given other signage and the fact that it is not designated as a public bridleway on rights of way maps. The sign is actually very conspicuous and can be seen for much of the way back to SZ827964! Before turning round you should go a few steps to your left, south-eastwards, to enjoy views to Selsey as well as the astonishingly impressive new sea defences which have been very effective and blend superbly with the landscape. Retrace the same way to the car park.

The bridleway M25

I think I would not be unfair in suggesting that Burgess Hill is not the most picturesque town in Sussex. However, the town is perhaps unique in Sussex in having a bridleway that follows round the perimeter of its entire southern half. And just as the M25 provides a means of avoiding the through traveller having to grapple with London traffic, so does a chain of bridleways provide a through traveller with the means of avoiding Burgess Hill. It isn't the most beautiful bridleway route in Sussex, but it is far from the most ugly; in fact it's surprisingly very rewarding. So here it is. It starts at **TQ291199** and ends at **TQ327196** (OS OL11) and is 6km 225m long.

To access the start of this route from the centre of Burgess Hill (sadly of little historical interest and arguably best known for its brickworks), I suggest you get the town circular bus service from the town centre at Church Road to the stop nearest the far end of West Street, then from the far end of West Street continue westwards along Gatehouse Lane. If no bus is available, it's a 750m trek westwards from the B2036 London Road (which cuts right through the town north to south) along West Street which then leads straight on into Gatehouse Lane.

Now whether you've got to Gatehouse Lane under your own steam or not, follow it westwards from West Street, then north-westwards, cross the A273 Jane Murray Way (625m from the end of West Street) and continue along the lane for some 300m beyond the A273 crossing to Gatehouse Farm where the route starts at TQ291199.

Turn left to follow the signed bridleway south-eastwards from Gatehouse Lane; this is Pangdean Lane, a really delightful woodland track. In 250m at TQ292196, turn off Pangdean Lane onto a left-forking bridleway which heads very pleasantly south-eastwards, crossing Malthouse Lane at TQ294194, and now route finding is extremely easy as, sticking with the bridleway, you stay parallel with the A273 Burgess Hill bypass. The noise of the traffic on this road is evident but not greatly intrusive and the bridleway itself is a very good track with a number of fascinating sculptures beside it, as well as one particularly impressive stream crossing which you can either bridge or, if you're feeling brave, ford. There are also excellent information boards detailing wildlife you may see on your journey.

Finally at TQ306179, 2km 500m from the start of the forking bridleway at TQ292196, you have to cross the A273; having done so you immediately veer right, just west of south, to follow the bridleway parallel with it, then in 125m at TQ306178 bear left, just south of east, along a bridleway that proceeds to the railway, the main London-Brighton line in fact. There's a lovely pond just before the railway crossing on the left. You duly cross over the railway and at the path junction just beyond the crossing, at TQ312177, 500m from the A273, you bear left, north-eastwards, parallel with the railway along an excellent bridleway track, arriving in 375m from TQ312177 at another path junction at TQ314180.

The bridleway forks right here, just north of east, away from the railway, and arrives in another 375m at Keymer Road; turn left up this road and in 75m or so, arrive at a road junction of Keymer Road and Folders Lane. Cross and take the bridleway heading half-right between these two roads, heading north-eastwards – there's a suburban feel to it but it's still pleasantly leafy. Staying with the bridleway, in 900m you cross the railway (the Lewes branch off the main London-Brighton line) and in 250m beyond the railway you cross a road, Kings Way, continuing north-eastwards beyond the road for 375m to a T-junction of bridleways at TQ330192. Turn left, northwards, reaching a bridleway fork in 125m; this is a delightfully rural spot, despite the proximity of Burgess Hill. Here turn left (not hard left) along a bridleway that heads very attractively north-westwards, just east of a suburb of Burgess Hill ominously known as World's End!

In 375m from the fork the bridleway ends, and your route ends, at TQ327196, at a junction with Manor Road. To reach Wivelsfield Station, on the London-Brighton line (the vicinity is also well served by buses), turn right along this road to its end in 625m at Janes Lane; turn left along Janes Lane, and at its end in 200m, turn left and immediately right along Leylands Road to reach the station in 125m. Well done – you are now officially an expert on the perimeter of the southern half of Burgess Hill. Maybe one day you'll be able to walk round the perimeter of all of it. Who knows!

Chichester's Lake District bridleway

The bridleway route on OS map OL8, heading south-eastwards from **SU869035,** reaching in 1km a bridleway T-junction at SU875028 and then turning left to reach, in just over another 1km, **SU878039,** passes an astonishing 9 named lakes. Were it not for the nearby industrial estates and caravan park, and the absence of mountain backcloths, and the incessant traffic noise from the A27 Chichester bypass, and the often very busy Vinnetrow Road, you might think you were in the heart of Cumbria....

Let's shop!...the retail bridleway

The bridleway **TQ270387-TQ261384** is ideal for killing two birds with one stone – it goes through a retail park in the outskirts of Crawley (OS OL34) so you can do some bridleway bagging and catch up on your shopping at the same time.

The bridleway with a bit of – almost – everything (but not retail therapy)

Some bridleways just consist of one kind of surface, eg a driveway, or farm lane, or woodland track. But the one heading south from Icklesham (OS 124) at **TQ877162** has everything. It begins with a straightforward farm lane where only a genius could go wrong. In 500m at Knockbridge Farm it becomes a firm grassy path, keeping a pond below to the right. You then have a steep descent along an enclosed path to reach the valley floor. There's now no track at all and you need to pick your way through the rough grass, aiming for a bridge crossing of a stream. Beyond the bridge crossing you continue southwards up the hillside but still with no path, arriving at a woodland edge. You then enter Pannel Wood and now follow a clearly defined dirt track through the trees, going forward onto a clear firmer track, climbing to a junction with Pannel Lane where the bridleway ends at **TQ876147**. There – at least five types of bridleway surface for the price of one, across just 1km 500m!

Get out the crampons – steep bridleways

There is one particularly steep section of bridleway that we've already explored – the climb from Amberley to Rackham Hill on the South Downs Way which we visited in route 6 starting at **TQ034125** and only properly relenting at **TQ043125.**

However, there are two further contenders for the title of steepest bridleway in Sussex. The first is the bridleway from **SU935165** to **SU934161,** at Graffham Down (OS OL10). It is near vertical in places and the surface is rough. Great for abseilers and tobogganers coming down – not so good for bikes, hooves or knees in either direction.

The other contender for steepness is **TQ510034-TQ515034,** a bridleway heading eastwards off the South Downs Way just west of Alfriston (OS OL25). Again this is near vertical although the surface is a lot better than the Graffham Down candidate.

Are we nearly there yet – the longest bridleway

It's difficult to assess what the longest bridleway in Sussex is because you could effectively create a giant bridleway route from a network of bridleways, uninterrupted by road crossings. However, the section of South Downs Way between the B2141 crossing just below South Harting, and the A286 crossing just south of Cocking, could be said to be technically the longest bridleway/restricted byway stretch, providing a direct link between these highways without any intervening road junction whatsoever. This stretch is some 11km 625m long and forms part of route 4 above.

Blink and you'll miss them – the shortest bridleways

In contrast to the above, there are a number of ridiculously short bridleways. Here's a selection.

SU977044 This bridleway between Barnham and Yapton (OS OL10) sets off from Lake Lane by straightaway crossing a railway line. Then, according to OS mapping, it stops immediately the line has been crossed. You can carry on from there along what is Maypole Lane to the Maypole pub, and indeed on to North End Road, but you're no longer on a bridleway.

TQ030184 This bridleway adjoins the White Hart at Stopham, near Pulborough (OS OL10), running from the pub to the main road. Not really sufficient to walk off the ploughman's lunch!

TQ109096 This bridleway, just north-west of Findon (OS OL10), appears in route 52 and provides a link between a bridleway and restricted byway running parallel but extremely close, with no natural obstruction between them. If you're wanting to transfer from one of these longer parallel ones to another, you would need to be extremely conscientious to seek to identify and follow this link route.

TQ175112 In Steyning (OS OL11), this is a partially-covered alleyway providing a convenient short cut from the

High Street to the police station. Most helpful for enforcers of law and order wanting to swiftly convey miscreants into the nick from the town's main thoroughfare.

TQ339198 Just west of Wivelsfield (OL11), this bridleway leads off a rather longer one that goes from Wivelsfield to Ditchling Common Country Park; the "tiddler" simply links that longer one with the B2112, a few metres distant.

TQ408101 – a classic over-before-it's begun bridleway just west of Lewes town centre (OS OL11).

Never Eat Shredded Wheat – extreme bridleways

The most **northerly** piece of bridleway in Sussex is Church Lane at **TQ302410-TQ304410**, a frankly unexciting bridleway (made even less pleasant thanks to noise from the nearby M25 and planes arriving at or leaving nearby Gatwick) heading west to east from Peeks Brook Lane to the M25, just east of Gatwick Airport (OS 146). Once over the M25 it heads further north, but by then it has shifted into Surrey. Surrey is welcome to it, some might say.

The most **easterly** piece of bridleway in Sussex is a dead heat between two pieces of bridleway, each coming up from Camber (OS 125) and meeting at TR011202, just over the border into Kent. One piece of bridleway crosses the border at **TR009202**, the other at **TR009203**. The surroundings, on the fringes of Romney Marsh, are remote and inhospitable and indeed have a post-apocalyptic feel – see the very last entry in this Part which actually includes this "most easterly" segment.

The most **southerly** piece of bridleway in Sussex is, according to the OS Explorer maps, officially at **TV565956**, at the south-eastern end of a bridleway that's come from Birling Gap and here reaches the Birling Gap-Beachy Head coast road (OS OL25). A right turn along this road from the bridleway brings you in just 150m to the South Downs Way coastal route and some of the most spectacular cliff scenery in Sussex.

However, there's a signed permissive bridleway, not marked on OS Explorer maps, which ends at SZ834941, just west of Selsey (OS OL8). Just before it ends, at **SZ838940**, it reaches a point that is the furthest south that any bridleway, public or permissive, reaches in Sussex. This is a most undistinguished spot, and merits a separate mention later in this Part.

The most **westerly** piece of bridleway in Sussex again has two contenders (both OS OL8). There is **SU745165**, part of a section of the Sussex Border Path (see route 4) which moves here from Hampshire into West Sussex in charming woodlands between Chalton and Ladyholt Park. However this is right on the border, and when the section of bridleway does strike out into West Sussex it is further east than the other contender. That is **SU748088**, on a section of the Sussex Border Path between Emsworth Common Road and Woodberry Lane, and clearly in West Sussex.

The bridleway with an identity crisis

A section of path from **TQ459029** to **TQ460029** is signposted at its bottom end, at the top of Cantercrow Hill above Newhaven (OS OL11), as a bridleway. At its top end, though, it's signposted as a public footpath. While on the latest OS Explorer map, it's not marked as either a bridleway or a footpath!

Feel the bridleway width – or lack of it

The section of bridleway **SU919243-SU918238** between Henley and Lodsworth (OS OL33) begins deceptively easily as a clear track. However just as you congratulate yourself on the progress you're making, you're suddenly directed away left. You think this must be a mistake – but no, the signage is correct and you are being led down an exceedingly steep very narrow path which seems to be screaming at you "This must be wrong!" In fact it is very definitely correct. The path itself is not only narrow but spectacularly uneven, inviting twisted ankles and/or buckled wheels. Fortunately, it does improve...eventually.

The section of restricted byway **TQ611190-TQ608209** between Warbleton and Heathfield (OS OL25), starts comfortably enough, on a stony but wide track. Before long it narrows dramatically, the ground so uneven that you cyclists may find yourselves, as I found myself, pushing your machine, having to reach beyond Health & Safety recommended height to grasp the handlebars, your bike having to follow ground that feels like several feet higher than you are. The scenery thereabouts is nothing special and the reward is not in the aesthetic qualities of the surroundings but in getting to the other end and finding your bike is still in good working order.

The bridleway service interruption ...

Two bridleway/restricted byway routes, **TQ266164-TQ272164,** and **TQ269149-TQ273141,** have been split rudely in half by the building of the A23 between Hickstead and Pyecombe (OS OL11). In both cases, it is impossible to cross the A23 in order to get from one half to the other. You'll have to turn back and find a way round. It may be good for the souls, but it's not so good for the soles.

The bridleways that die...

A number of bridleways stop and continue as public footpaths, barred to cyclists and horse-riders, or simply reach a dead end, barred to everyone. Just south of Ashcombe Bottom (OS OL11) the OS Explorer map shows a bridleway heading south from **TQ376112** but after 400m or so, at **TQ376108,** it stops. Well, in fact an unmapped bridleway does take over – how many poor baggers have been deterred from accessing or following it because the map suggests it's a dead end? D'oh! The restricted byway starting at **TQ585203** at the south end of Heathfield (OS OL25) heads innocuously just east of south for 500m to

TQ587198 then stops, the only way forward being on an admittedly generous choice of 3 public footpaths. Fine if you're a walker, but not if you aren't. Similarly, a pleasant piece of bridleway heading south-westwards for 750m from **TQ691280** just south of Ticehurst (OS 136) leads to a choice of 3 public footpaths at **TQ687273**. Well, again, 3 is better than one – unless you're a cyclist or horse-rider. From **TQ864190** a steady bridleway descent from Udimore (OS 125) followed by a pretty bridleway meadow crossing reaches an impressive bridge in just over 1km and at this point there's 2 footpaths to choose from at **TQ861179** – nothing else. At **TQ443347** just east of Forest Row (OS 135), a restricted byway begins but at **TQ445347** is demoted to a public footpath in 200m, and this time there's no choice of footpath – there's just the one. **TQ161297-TQ153293** goes one better. It begins conveniently and happily enough, at Tower Hill just south of Horsham (OS OL34). It heads just north of west then south-west through Parthings and attractive countryside – then reaches a bank above the A24 and...stops. In this instance there is absolutely no way forward; it can't even be said that the A24 has interrupted continuity with a bridleway on the far side. There's no public footpath continuation. That really is all, folks.

...And the bridleway that dies twice...

The bridleway that heads eastwards from **TQ039216** from just east of Pallingham Bridge (OS OL34) proceeds harmlessly enough, soon crossing a road and heading north-eastwards to arrive at a bridleway fork junction at **TQ045218**. So far so good. Except not just one, but both forking routes simply stop within 100-125m, and there is no way further forward, for walkers or riders, in either case. As Dick Dastardly was wont to say in *Wacky Races*, double drat!

... And the most disappointing ending to a bridleway

The permissive bridleway between Earnley, near Bracklesham, and Selsey that starts at **SZ816966** (OS OL8) has much to recommend it, and indeed the early part of it is incorporated into a recommended route earlier in this Part. But as it nears its end, it finds itself sandwiched between an (inaccessible) embankment to the right, blotting out what would be lovely sea views, and a seemingly endless sprawl of chalets to the left, being part of a caravan park to the west of Selsey. The permissive bridleway finally lingers to a close at a gate at **SZ834941**; to make further progress you then have to go through the gate and into this sprawl of chalets, hoping you will somehow emerge somewhere in Selsey before nightfall.

Three mapmakers' bridleway aberrations?

On OS OL11 a bridleway heading north-east from Rottingdean at **TQ371025** seems, according to that map, to come to an abrupt end at **TQ375028**, although in fact this is a proper, through bridleway route which goes forward to meet a road at **TQ378030**.

There's a similar gap on OS OL25 on the bridleway **TQ535036-TQ539036** – but there is fact no break in the bridleway at TQ537035 notwithstanding what the map says.

And at **TQ527073**, off the Berwick-Upper Dicker road just north-east of Berwick Station, there is, according to OS OL25, a bridleway heading south-eastwards for 50m then stopping in the middle of nowhere. There's certainly no signage and no path here. Had the cartographer had a particularly good lunch?

What's the point?...Part 1: the waste-of-time bridleway

At **SZ849978** at Keynor, just south-west of Sidlesham (OS OL8) a bridleway strikes out southwards from Keynor Lane. After 900m of heading southwards, it turns sharply left, eastwards, and in 375m it turns sharply left again, northwards, to return in 800m to...Keynor Lane, 250m eastwards of where you left it, at **SZ852977** – without one single feature of interest in the 2km 75m you have covered; it's just a mish-mash of nurseries, houses and businesses. So that's half an hour of your life you're not going to get back...

What's the point?...Part 2: the waste-of-space bridleway

At **SU849213**, just south-west of Stedham (OS OL33) a bridleway begins, heading north-eastwards for 250m to **SU850215**. So what? Well, barely 25m to the right of this bridleway, another bridleway does exactly the same thing, running almost exactly parallel with the first. As Alexander Armstrong is wont to say, welcome to Pointless.

The plane noisy bridleways

Three bridleways, **TQ235393-TQ229402, TQ264399-TQ270392, and TQ275402-TQ285397** share the unwelcome distinction of having the greatest volume of aircraft noise of any Sussex bridleway routes, all of them bordering Gatwick Airport (OS OL34 and OS 146). The third of these qualifies for a separate mention as possibly the least agreeable bridleway in Sussex. The most northerly bridleway in Sussex, mentioned above, **TQ302410-TQ304410,** offers an equally unpleasant cocktail of aircraft noise and the roar of traffic on the M25.

Dullest bridleways

Alas, many bridleways which used to provide rights of way through countryside now find themselves hemmed in by new residential and/or industrial development. Yet still they remain marked on maps as bridleways and still they can be negotiated -if you are really that keen to negotiate them. Here's a selection of these rather sad suburban routes:

SZ957998-SZ963996 – through anonymous housing development in Felpham (OS OL10)

TQ155043-TQ157043 – through a small segment of East Worthing (OS OL10)

TQ186332-TQ186331 – a no more likeable morsel of suburban Horsham (OS OL34)

TQ253351-TQ253354 – a slice of suburban Crawley (OS OL34) for your delectation – or maybe not.

TQ259067-TQ260067 – an unlovely piece of residential Portslade (OS OL11)

TQ323202-TQ323203 – passing through a residential area of Wivelsfield (OS OL11), this could live quite happily in the "Blink and you'll miss them" category – and frankly you won't have missed much

TQ331250-TQ328249 – in the suburbs of Haywards Heath (OS 135). Cyclists are spared this one as they're prohibited!

TQ408103 – a forgettable soupcon of Lewes (OS OL11)

TQ527303-TQ526301 – a spectacularly ordinary portion of suburban Crowborough (OS 135)

Glorious bridleway mud

It's difficult to nominate a "muddiest bridleway" as the amount of mud will depend on the weather conditions at the time, but the narrow bridleway just north-west of West Chiltington (OS OL10) between **TQ084195** and **TQ081196** was, when I tackled it, quite astonishingly muddy across its entire 300m length.

A piece of bridleway you can't actually get to

You couldn't make it up. What was obviously once a continuous bridleway between **TQ549379** and **TQ550381** between Groombridge and Langton Green (OS 135) is broken up by the Spa Valley Railway, with no means of crossing it. At least the southern "segment" is easily accessible and followable, give or take fairly generous quantities of undergrowth. But the northern "segment" can only legally be reached by working back from the far northern end of it; to access it requires you to follow a section of Kent bridleway – itself completely impenetrable! There is therefore no legitimate means of accessing the northern segment of this bridleway route.

Is this the least agreeable bridleway in Sussex?

The bridleway in question, 1km 125m long, is **TQ275402-TQ285397**. This (starting on OS 146 and continuing on OS OL134) leads due south from TQ275402, very close to Gatwick Airport and its attendant plane noise and fumes. As I reached the start of the route I was told by some official at one of the adjoining complexes that I had no right to be there. Bowled over by this effusive welcome, and able to appease the official only by walking smartly off on my way, off I duly went. The bridleway, proceeding southwards, passes grim industrial buildings on either side, heading in determined fashion for the noise of the A23. As you reach the A23 there's a tantalising choice: to detour left to follow a bridleway alongside its northern edge until it peters out after 125m, meaning you're forced to backtrack, or to press on with the continuous route. So no choice at all really. The continuous route crosses the A23 and then heads south-eastwards along a track leading to an industrial estate and ending at a mini-roundabout. Add the aircraft noise, and you have one of the least pleasant bridleway experiences possibly in the whole country, not just in Sussex.

And finally...the post-apocalypse bridleway

Route 45 above is a fine circular route north-west of Camber towards Rye, across the southern edges of Romney Marsh, which I would highly recommend. There is a much more formidable circular route of 8km 400m or so that can be followed starting from **TQ983182,** off the A259 between Camber and Jury's Gap, roughly 1km 750m east of the centre of Camber (OS 125). It is a surreal experience which you will love – or hate – or maybe a bit of both.

You shouldn't expect any assistance with signage to get you on your way, so read carefully on. Your route begins with a section of bridleway proceeding north-eastwards away from the A259 (as stated, at TQ983182) going parallel with and immediately to the right of a metalled lane... leading to a sewage works. There's no actual path, but I don't suppose you'll be shot if you stick to the lane. In any case you need all the help you can get on this one. Just before the works, 500m from the start, a bridleway sign does condescend to direct you to the right, then you veer left to continue north-eastwards for another 2km, keeping a water channel, delightfully (not) named Jury's Gut Sewer, to your right. Your bridleway arrives at TR005195 where you're unable to continue with the channel, being forced to veer left. It is the fact of having no choice that could explain total lack of signage here. In 100m or so you reach a junction with a track onto which you turn right, proceeding north-eastwards with the bridleway on this – I have to say – excellent track to reach, in 800m, a T-junction with another bridle track at TR011202. You have just slipped into Kent.

Here turn hard left along this other bridle track, slipping out of Kent as unremarkably as you slipped into it. In 500m you veer right and in another 250m you reach another bridleway T-junction at TR004205. This really is the most surreal spot; it is wild, windswept, featureless and puts you in mind of a godforsaken corner of a Soviet satellite country in the Cold War or the kind of landscape that makes up a post-apocalyptic world in a low-budget science-fiction movie. The presence of a line of electricity pylons to the right, stretching as far as the eye can see, enhances the general doom-laden atmosphere.

You turn left, south-westwards, at this T-junction (TR004205), and looking at the OS map, you're entitled to feel optimistic that the track will return you comfortably to Camber. As you proceed along an excellent bridle track, you may feel even more optimistic still. But oh dear: in 1km 250m or so, at TQ993200, your bridle track literally dies, with no signage. It's left to you to blunder through featureless grass in the same direction, like some wretched survivor of a nuclear blast in aforementioned low-budget science-fiction movie, aiming for a grassy embankment ahead, the embankment guarded by another channel of water. If you're fortunate enough to have found said embankment in roughly 350m from TQ993200 at TQ988199 – well, allegedly – you turn left, south-westwards, to follow it for 1km 500m, to a gate at TQ975193. These fifteen hundred metres are often very rough and the grass beneath your feet is liable to turn your ankle over if it takes a dislike to you. If you find yourself attempting to cycle or take a horse along this stretch of alleged bridleway – *bonne chance*, as the French would say. Del Boy in *Only Fools And Horses* would doubtless have an even better way of putting it.

In fact, though, the worst is now over and for the last bit you're overlapping with route 45 which is a much better way of exploring Romney Marsh. You pass through the gate and carry on for another 150m, then bear sharp left, just east of south, for 250m to reach a T-junction of bridleways at an entrance to a caravan park. Turning right, westwards, here, you follow the bridleway for 500m, turning left to reach the centre of Camber in another 250m at **TQ967188.** Here your route ends. It's great to be back in civilisation. That is, assuming you are, and that you're not still blundering your way around the marshes with only sheep to ask the way.

SECTION 3

CONFESSIONS OF A DAFT BAGGER

Please forgive this section of the book. It is very personal and might seem a little self-indulgent. If it comes over that way, I am sorry. But in explaining why I set myself the task of following every bridleway in Sussex, and how I managed to successfully complete it, I hope I may inspire you to create, and strive to achieve, your own walking/riding ambitions, just as I have done. And in relating how I survived the interruption of the task by the Covid lockdowns, I hope you will see how good things and good lessons can come out of even the most unpromising situations.

Walking, completism, and me

My love for walking goes back to my late teens and at that time was focussed very much on walking in the parts of Kent and East Sussex around Tunbridge Wells. My roots were in fact in that area: my dad had grown up in nearby Tonbridge, and my maternal grandma and grandfather had had their family home between Wadhurst and Mark Cross, just over the border from Kent in East Sussex and only a short distance from Tunbridge Wells. It was there that my mum and her brother spent what was a very happy childhood, despite the intervention and the hardships of the Second World War. It followed that although I spent my childhood firstly in Hampshire and then in south-west Surrey, I got to know a great deal about the Tunbridge Wells area (though more East Sussex as opposed to Kent), not only from my parents' recollections but through frequent family visits to the area. All of the local place names resonated with me when I saw them on maps or road signs: Wadhurst, Mark Cross, Cousley Wood, Frant, Rotherfield,

Tidebrook, Mayfield, Lamberhurst, Ticehurst and many more. Having left school and started working in London I decided I wanted to go out on foot – with a little help from the buses and good old British Rail – and find out more about all these places, and the surrounding countryside, for myself. By this time my maternal grandma had a flat in Tunbridge Wells, and, living alone as she did, she was always very happy to have me to stay. So it was that many a Friday night in the late 1970's and early 1980's would find me, after a train journey from London to Tunbridge Wells, ensconced in my grandma's living room, ahead of a weekend's exploration in the locality, guidebook and map on one arm of my chair and a cup of tea and plateful of my grandma's finest lardy cake within easy reach. Then, on Saturday morning, replete from the gloriously cholesterol-rich fried breakfast which my grandma would unfailingly have cooked for me, and with my guidebook and map now in hand, I'd be setting off to follow the first of the routes I'd planned out for the weekend. And the more I explored, the greater became my attachment to it, an attachment which has continued to this day.

Of course, to be a good explorer you need to be a good map-reader, and I was never a great map-reader in them early days. I would set out into that Kent or East Sussex (but usually East Sussex) countryside with the best of intentions, namely to follow what were stated on maps to be public footpaths, and so enhance my knowledge and enjoyment of the area. But I was always going to be just one ambiguous or non-existent piece of signage away from disappearing off the radar and into walkers' oblivion, and I lacked the navigational skills necessary to steer me away from the abyss. Usually I would, by pure luck, find a way to a road or a legitimate path, but often at the cost of having to endure the indignity of surmounting locked gates, and/or limbo dancing under any number of barbed-wire or electric fences, consequently returning to civilisation with aching and bruised limbs and sporting torn and spectacularly mud-splattered clothing. Worse than that was being shouted at by a local resident or landowner whose attention had been drawn to my antics, the questions "Are you lost" or "Can I help you" being polite, albeit far from subtle, codes for "What the hell are you doing here." I recall one Saturday I was out walking near Mayfield and, lacking a rucksack, was using my work briefcase as my substitute backpack. As I blundered around in a forest, seemingly miles from the nearest legitimate route, carrying my work briefcase, I was accosted and asked if I was conducting a tree survey! These toe-curling experiences at least partially explain why, when I see a bridleway or footpath sign has been blown or knocked down, I am anxious to put it back up again somehow, or even create and install my own. I wouldn't want my all-too-frequent youthful misfortunes visited on others.

Fortunately, my map-reading improved with experience and, as time went on, if I came home with soil-encrusted clothes and footwear it was increasingly likely to be because of the state of the paths I was correctly following rather than plain unmitigated incompetence or misadventure. Not that my new-found confidence in navigation prevented me from encountering other hazards. These included (but weren't necessarily limited to) getting soaked during periods of wet weather (or at the other extreme, getting seriously dehydrated on hot days), wearing shoes and socks that became mobile blister factories, and being subjected to the attentions of over-friendly canines. I've never had anything against dogs but I resented, and still do resent, their owners thinking that I will like it when they (the dogs, rather than the owners) bound up to me and plaster their muddy paws all over me, their owners' assertions that "He's only being friendly...he won't hurt you" being the standard reaction to my palpable discomfiture. However, the bad experiences were vastly outweighed by the good ones. I loved my walks across the Weald and the South Downs and the contrasts they presented to the noise and fumes of London. I loved the varying scenery, whether downland, woodland or waterside. I also loved my creature comforts which I felt my efforts deserved. To me the perfect complement to a long Sussex walk was (and still is) a cup of tea and slice of cake in a cosy Sussex café…or failing that, Greggs or McDonald's. Even now I look back fondly on the bank holiday at the end of May in 1979 when after a lung-testing tramp across the heart of the Sussex Weald, I reached the ridgetop village of Burwash, and enjoyed a bottomless pot of tea and slice of millionaire's shortbread for the princely sum of 32p.

As my confidence in my walking abilities increased, I got to love walking in wilder parts of the country. I well remember sitting in my grandma's flat reading the excellent (and sadly long out of print) Penguin publication, *The Walker's Handbook* by H.D. Westacott, and this inspired me to be more adventurous in my walking destinations. My walking CV is summarised in the introduction to this book and from it you'll notice the "completism" inherent in the tasks I have sought to accomplish: all the national trails, the entire south coast, and the highest point of each country in the UK. I have always been something of a completist – that is to say, wanting to obtain complete collections of certain things. So, for instance, being a fan of sitcom, I've striven to get hold of complete sets of my favourite sitcoms on DVD. As someone who enjoys a memory challenge, I didn't just want to learn and perform by heart a selection of Gilbert & Sullivan operas or a few of the books of the Bible; I wanted to perform (and in fact was to succeed in performing) all the works of Gilbert & Sullivan and the entire New Testament. The same goes for walking. I found it wasn't enough for me just to want to walk the odd national trail, the odd section of coastline or the odd peak. I wanted "the set;" all the national trails, the whole south coast, the highest point of each country in the UK. Some might say that even these "sets" are fairly modest, and of course compared with some walking "sets," eg walking each continent from top to bottom, or walking the banks of the ten longest rivers in the world, they are indeed modest. I don't profess to be a super-walker, if there is such a thing! But the principle is the same. There are still lots of walking "sets" which have not necessarily been attempted but which are well worth building up, are within the capability of ordinary mortals, and will provide great enjoyment and great memories to boot (pun kind of intended).

The bridleway project is born

In June 2018 I had just completed walks along all – there I go again – the major long-distance routes of Sussex (my book on these walks being published in autumn 2018 as *The Great Walks Of Sussex*), so my walking engagements diary, so to speak, was empty. I was looking for a new challenge: something which combined my love for walking not just in East Sussex but also in West Sussex (where, since the age of 28, I had become a permanent resident) and indulged my desire to build up another "set" of something. With those considerations in mind, I hit upon the idea of seeking to walk the entire network of bridleways (including restricted byways – all references to bridleways in this chapter include restricted byways) in Sussex, not just the bridleways I thought were the best or most accessible.

What was, and is, so special about bridleways? I hope the introduction to this book has answered that for you, but in summary, bridleways really are win-win. They provide a great means of safe and largely congenial exploration of the countryside, the routes being generally well signed and defined, and at the same time lacking the noise and fumes of motor traffic which can blight minor as well as major roads. I did wonder about attempting to walk all the public footpaths in Sussex, but a look at the mapping told me that to walk every single footpath in East and West Sussex (including Brighton & Hove) was a step – or rather, what felt like several million steps – too far. I felt that bagging all the bridleways was neither too modest nor too ridiculous; furthermore, I did think that my explorations could form the basis of a guide that had the potential to be enjoyed by cyclists and horse-riders as well as walkers. In fact, in the course of my research, I was to end up walking rather than cycling virtually all of the bridleways, but as a matter of personal choice. As a rule, if I'm out exploring the countryside, I do prefer to walk rather than cycle, for two principal reasons: walking gives more time to appreciate the surrounding scenery and landmarks, and avoids the risk of an expedition being spoilt by mechanical failure.

With any big challenge like this, knowing how and where to start is the hardest part. But in a sense I had already started, in that I had already covered many of the bridleways, almost all on foot. Before my fieldwork began, I carefully identified the many bridleways I would not need to walk because I had already done them. These included the entire routes of the South Downs Way, Downs Link, Worth Way and Forest Way, each (as you'll have seen in routes 1-13 in this book) consisting of bridleways through their entire length. They also included the bridleway sections of other great trails in Sussex that comprised the Vanguard Way, Wealdway, Serpent Trail, and more besides. But that still left a great many bridleways to cover, including a sizeable proportion that were a long way from the nearest public transport; train and/or bus travel were necessarily to be the default means of my accessing the bridleways from home, given that more often than not I would have no car available to me. I genuinely had no idea how long the task would take me, especially as I had other commitments which meant I couldn't simply swan off whenever I wanted. I set myself a very rough target of two and a half years from start to completion, though I could not possibly have foreseen what it was that would serve to frustrate that timescale. I knew the task wouldn't be easy. I had visions of having to travel for several hours either by car or by train and possibly bus, just for the privilege of bagging one or two bridleways that might each be only a few hundred metres in length, and then undertaking several more hours' travel home after bagging them. I also foresaw my OCD getting the better of me, my conscience protesting that I may not have walked the whole of a particular bridleway; or, shock horror, I may have cut a couple of corners; or, worse still, I may have gone off on the wrong track entirely – meaning I might feel constrained to repeat part or all of a day's bagging activity. Many are the times that I've engaged in walking exploration that has caused me to doubt my own fitness to remain in the community. Was this, I asked myself, the walking project that would finally push me over the edge, and/or attract the attentions of mental health care professionals? Of course I wouldn't know until I tried.

The bug bites

My first official bridleway bagging expedition was June 22nd 2018 and it got off to a surreal start: I was waiting for my train at Barnham Station but so absorbed was I in my route-planning for the day that I failed to notice my train come in and then leave without me. But the next one wasn't too far behind and I opened my account with a vigorous day's exploration of a number of bridleways between Pulborough and Billingshurst, enjoying great downland views, flirting with the Wey & Arun Canal, and fighting my way through vegetation which looked as though it had last been cleared when Nottingham Forest were champions of Europe. The day saw my first encounter with what I termed a spider's web – a large concentration of short bridleways interlinking with each other. I'd get to meet many more spider's webs in the months that followed! As I meticulously ensured each of these bridleways in this first spider's web was done, I realised my OCD was kicking in already, and this was only day one.

I hoped obviously for good weather to bless my passage during my first few bagging weeks, but I suppose it was a case of being careful what I wished for. These weeks coincided with a sustained period of hot sunshine where every surface, even surfaces you just knew would turn into mudbaths after a ten-minute rain shower, assumed a granite hardness, and the normally lush green hillsides south of the South Downs between Cocking and Amberley, an area where many of my initial explorations were focussed, turned an unappetising parched brown. Suddenly woodland bridleways took on a special refreshing quality, the rich verdancy of both the evergreen and deciduous trees seemingly unaffected by the successive days of scorching heat, and providing welcome shade from the burning sun. I well remember doing a talk on the Great Trails of Sussex, as part of the 2018 Festival of Chichester, during this time, and advising my listeners to go and enjoy the woodlands while the heat lasted, saying the weather would turn again soon enough. There was almost an element of wishful thinking there. But I was right: two and a half weeks after that talk I just made it back from a long bagging morning when a thunderstorm broke, and less than two weeks after that I found myself following a succession of bridleways beside an area of lakes on the southern outskirts of Chichester, in absolutely bucketing rain. Yes, my initiation period had begun and I had had my baptism by way of fire (well, heat anyway) and water. And once I'd ticked a few off my list, I became suitably motivated to keep wanting to tick more still off the list, if for no other reason than to justify the effort put in so far. The bridleway bug had well and truly bitten, and it proved to be a particularly persistent bug that was always sharpening his teeth ready to bite me some more. And of course there was to be no respite from the accompanying OCD: I was finding myself, as I warmed to the task, checking and double-checking my completion of each and every bridleway, cursing when I realised that I had missed a "tiddler" which I would then need to return to complete another day, and adjusting my future plans when another bridleway, which I'd previously missed, popped up on a map where I least expected it.

I allowed myself a reasonably "soft" start, devoting the opening weeks of the task to tackling bridleways close by my home city of Chichester. I then decided to take each OS map sheet in turn and, between the middle of August 2018 and early September 2019, worked my way through all the West Sussex bridleways on firstly the OS Explorer map sheet for Crawley & Horsham (OL34), then what was left on the Chichester map sheet (OL8), followed by Arundel & Pulborough (OL10), Brighton & Hove (OL11), Ashdown Forest (135) and finally Haslemere & Petersfield (OL33). My final piece of West Sussex bridleway bagging, or so I thought, was on 6th September 2019, in the company of my choir friend Dirk, walking from the A286 just south of Fernhurst, to Fernhurst Furnace Pond. This route incidentally appears in Part 7 of the central section of this book. I think Dirk felt quite honoured to be joining me to celebrate my achievement; unfortunately, however, I subsequently discovered I'd failed to visit, and follow, one tiny piece of bridleway near Elsted, just south-west of Midhurst. I didn't have the heart to tell him about my oversight! I then ploughed on into Brighton & Hove and East Sussex, covering the rest of the bridleways on the Brighton & Hove Explorer map sheet (OL11) and getting going on those on the Eastbourne & Beachy Head sheet (OL25). Indeed I was still going strong in March 2020, hopeful of completing the task by the end of that year, when my timetable was overtaken by events.

Bagging ups and downs

So what was it like to be a daft bagger? Well, here goes: most of what I've written under this heading in fact applies to my experiences throughout the course of my bagging, right through to completion in late 2021, though many of my "bagging lessons" were necessarily learned earlier rather than later in the process.

Between June 2018 to March 2020 I enjoyed a bagging period that was uninterrupted by any acts of God or *force majeure* – aside from the occasional postponement of a bagging day when the forecast was particularly bad. I almost always went out for day trips rather than staying overnight, setting out not too early (it was and is always much cheaper by train after 9am) and relying on the rail and bus network to get me to my "bags" and then, after

I'd walked 18-24km a day on average, to get me home again in one piece. As I've said, public transport, rather than the car, proved to be the default means of accessing the bridleways. This was not only for all the right green reasons but because my long-suffering wife Sue never loved getting in our vehicle the day after one of my bags-by-car and having to fumigate the area into which my mud-and-manure-splattered coat and backpack had been hurled the previous evening – especially if I'd eaten a McDonald's takeaway in the car as well. It has to be said that integral to the whole bagging experience was indeed some nice food or drink at the start and end, whether it was a Morrisons deep-filled mince pie to set me off on my way to the first bag of January 2019, the more than occasional pre-bag fried egg crusty from Baps n Buns in Barnham (whose station, being my home station, tended to be the launching pad for many of my adventures) or a McDonald's McMuffin and hash brown, and at the end of the day, celebration in the form of a Sainsbury's jam doughnut, a Greggs iced Belgian bun, or (sorry Sue) a take-out Big Mac and fries. After my conquest of Black Down (forming the basis of route 17) I visited Costa in Haslemere at about 4pm and was given coffee for free…because I was the first customer of the day who'd said "Please!"

As far as conditions went, I found myself walking in everything from searing heat to drenching rain, one moment having to dodge the puddles and only a bag or two later observing the sorry dried-up state of downland dewponds. Although dry sunny days should have been the best, there were many occasions when warm sunshine was accompanied by an obstinate soupy murk which hung over the horizon and robbed me of the views I'd worked so hard to enjoy. I would always rather walk in cloudy but clear conditions than sunny hazy ones. I didn't like to postpone a bagging expedition because the weather forecast was bad, but sometimes it made sense, particularly if thunder and lightning were in the mix. One Monday in August 2019 I was caught in a wholly unexpected thundery downpour but actually got quite philosophical, reflecting that if I was fatally struck by a bolt of lightning I would have been taken while doing something I really enjoyed – and you can't ask for a better way to go than that. I never minded the rain too much by itself, but I never got to love the mud that persistent rain inevitably generated. It would not only inevitably slow me down, but would also cling to me, meaning that when I got home I found I'd brought what seemed like half of Sussex home with me and within seconds of closing the front door behind me I'd succeeded in depositing it across every carpet in the house. One of the joys of exploring over such a sustained period was that I got to see the Sussex landscape in every season, from the exuberant fresh greenery of spring to the glorious colours of autumn, from soft late afternoon summer sunshine to crisp tangy mornings in the depths of winter. There were remarkable temperature extremes within just one month: on 5th November 2018 I explored an assortment of bridleways between Plaistow and Kirdford with just one layer of clothing, but my 20th November exploration, just 15 days later, of paths off the South Downs Way west of Cocking required three layers, plus scarf, hat and gloves. Then on 8th February 2019 I faced wintry squalls for my exploration of bridleways around Sullington, but just two and a half weeks later, during my voyage of bridleway discovery between Arundel and Patching, I experienced the warmest February day on record in this country, the thermometer in London, a mere 80km away, reaching 21.2 degrees Celsius! In the spring of 2019 I walked across bone-dry dusty fields which would have made ideal pictorial fodder for a journalist wanting to illustrate the effects of drought conditions on the rural Sussex landscape, then on two successive bags the following month, so-called flaming June, I was almost washed away by persistent rain and resultant flash flooding – my fingers still hadn't thawed out hours later. A spell of exceedingly wet weather in January and February 2020 meant that some bridleways turned into ponds and I was wading into them having no idea how much of my body was about to be submerged. But just a few months later I was walking in temperatures exceeding 30 degrees Celsius. I've included a few paragraphs elsewhere in this book on clothing and equipment, but one thing is certain and that is you need to be dressed ready for anything. Nowhere is this truer than in relation to footwear. I have bagged in all sorts: walking boots, trainers, Converses and wellies. I can even now hear you seasoned walkers emitting sniffs of disapproval at the thought of anyone going for a long walk in wellies, but providing they're properly broken in, and worn with a decent pair of thick socks, there's nothing to beat them when it's muddy and wet underfoot. As for the trousers/shorts debate (if there is such a thing), I've discovered the hard way that even if you flatter yourself that you've got lovely legs and consequently you want to show them off to the world at large, shorts really aren't great if you find yourself, as I frequently did, walking through patches of thistles or nettles, and even less great if, as I did, you sustain a tick bite that then gives you cellulitis and compels you to attend A & E or minor injuries unit and get placed on a course of antibiotics.

I had to accept that some bagging days would be more productive than others. I might be exploring an area that was very rich in bridleways, and where I could bag lots in just a few hours, but next time round it might be that there were only a handful of bridleways I could realistically get to bag in a single session. As I had foreseen, there were indeed instances of my having to walk several kilometres just to bag a bridleway that might only be a couple of hundred metres along a residential lane; in one or two cases I did actually take my bike with me to eat up those kilometres. Some contrast to what I've already referred to as the spider's web – a huge concentration of bridleways within a small radius. I sometimes wondered why so many bridleways were felt necessary within a tiny area, but mine was not to reason why: mine was to check them out, walk them, and if necessary walk them again in order to get to the start of the next portion of bridleway. Sometimes it became a bit like a game in a children's comic, as I endeavoured to see how many bridleways I could walk without having to retrace along them. I'm sure I ended up retracing along far more than I probably needed to. There were however many "spur" or dead end routes where there was no realistic option but to follow them and then retrace them. Sod's law dictated that most spur routes involved a near vertical descent that made me wish I'd invested time and money in a crash course in abseiling; having got to the bottom end of the spur I'd then be reaching in vain for crampons, ice axes and bottled oxygen for the climb back up. Some spur routes were the clear result of road building, the A24 and A23 both responsible for breaking up what should otherwise have been through routes and effectively creating spur routes by default. Other spur routes, where the bridleway just simply came to an abrupt end, seemed plain daft, with no obvious explanation for them, and I've given examples of such routes elsewhere in the book. But spur route or no spur route, the completist in me compelled me firstly to seek to do them all, then, as I did them. to carefully record when I did them. This meant ticking boxes in my notebook to confirm I'd presented myself, eticket and passport in my hand, at the start of a given bridleway and had not unfastened my seat belt and re-opened the plane doors until I had touched down right at the very end of it. I sometimes even felt constrained to repeat a bridleway if the relevant notebook entry wasn't sufficiently clear. Yes, my OCD kept nagging me, like a rapacious mosquito, and I had yet to find a suitable repellent. But I never got to question my sanity or ask myself if there was any point. And the reward for my labours was that I was able to build up an impressive knowledge of and love for the Sussex landscape and Sussex wildlife in all their aspects – and that, after all, was what this project was really all about.

I do tend to be a bit greedy when I go off walking, maybe wanting to cover more distance than is sensible or reasonable within a day, and that was certainly the case with my baggery. Perhaps there were days when I would have been better advised to cut my explorations short, reminding myself that it would all still be there next time. That said, I always tried to be sensible, not only stocking up with a good breakfast before starting the day's walk, but having a goodly supply of picnic and snack food. I came to see the thermos as one of the best inventions of all time, providing a guaranteed hot drink when I knew the nearest café was likely to be many kilometres away. I couldn't always guarantee I'd find a seat on which to enjoy my coffee, though, and many was the occasion when I was forced to crouch down on a patch of grass, wincing as my backside made contact with the cold often wet vegetation. Sod's law dictated, of course, that I'd then pass a seat within five minutes of hauling my protesting limbs back up again and resuming my walk.

I thought you might be amused by an account of a typical bagging day for me, and accordingly, here's my bridleway diary entry for October 5th 2018 – the thoughts of a daft bagger indeed. To save time, I had my bike with me throughout. The entry has everything: a packed programme, great scenery, consternation at the thought of missing even the smallest bridleway route...and an apparent eagerness to help line the pockets of the owners of Pret A Manger.

"I got the 9.03 (from Barnham) to Horsham, with bike, and after an early Pret elevenses I set off, zooming to Cowfold in just 35 minutes. At 10.55 I was starting my first of 11 bridleways today, basically sweeping up everything in the bottom-right portion of the Crawley & Horsham map. I began with a nice gentle path in the shade of trees off Wineham Lane, then forged on along the A272 to capture one going south-west of Butlers Farm at Ansty. I then headed down Bishopstone Road, doing an out-and-back past a pond, then headed along number 4 with bike through trees to reach Cuckfield Road. Number 5 was done partially with bike, a pleasant field-edge path with good downland views, crossing the B2036 and actually crossing onto the next map. I did a similar cross-over bridleway walk a bit further north, at Harvest Hill. From there I returned to the A272 at Ansty and did a quick out-and-back from

Deaks Lane to Butlers Farm, the dullest one of the day, then carried on up Deaks Lane to do a super out-and-back walk through woodland past a real 'dream house' to the A272 near Cuckfield. I then carried on up Deaks Lane and past Slough Green to do number 9 with bike, a short enclosed track, very pleasant, then came number 10 which I thought would be my last, linking a farm lane with the High Weald Landscape Trail north of Cuckfield – lovely ridge views and woodland tracks. I set off back to Horsham but remembered just in time that there may be one off Broxmead Lane, and indeed there was – thankfully just a 25-minute round trip for a 3-minute bridleway. Would have been annoying to miss it. I then zoomed back to Horsham, getting there just after 4, and enjoyed a Pret treat, completing the crossword quite easily."

It does seem that on that particular day, all went as planned, save the oversight near the end which was remedied with no damage done. That hiccup certainly didn't deter or discourage me: my diary records that I was out bagging again three days later.

And, to be fair, things mostly did go to plan as I built up my supply of bags. But there were the occasional setbacks. I had a couple of nasty falls, the second of these consisting of a Lionel Blair-esque routine combined with a spectacular nose-dive to the ground, after catching my foot on an exposed flint on Balmer Down in January 2020. Having just turned 60, I felt exceedingly fortunate that I was able to get straight up and walk away without having broken a bone. Meanwhile in November 2019 near the charming village of Streat I found myself a hapless and involuntary swimmer in a bath of mud, mud, glorious mud, fortunately encountering no hippopotami as I endeavoured to haul myself out. And an even worse calamity befell me on 28 September 2018 when I found on arrival in Horsham after a long day's walk that Sainsbury's were out of jam doughnuts. I still have nightmares about that today.

Being at the mercy of public transport always brought its own risks of getting stranded and being condemned to watch even *Newsnight* on catch-up, but that said I can't actually ever recall a scheduled bus failing to turn up on one of my bagging trips. Just like my dad before me, I used to feel, and still do feel, a little sad climbing into a bus on which I found I was the only passenger, wondering how long it would be before the under-usage of that particular route caused it to fall victim to whatever the bus equivalent is to the Beeching axe. The effect of Covid on the local economy certainly won't have helped matters. I don't see myself as a Greta Thunberg – my grey hair is a bit of a giveaway – but our bus network is precious and a very necessary means of keeping private car usage in check. It's better by bus – better for all of us. I did drive to some of my bagging start points, but always feared damaging my vehicle on poorly surfaced minor roads, or, stuck for somewhere to park, upsetting somebody by leaving my car somewhere I should not have. One morning I did return from a bagging expedition, reached by car, to find a (very polite) note on my windscreen pointing out I'd been obstructing a vehicle turning area. It wasn't exactly running off with the Crown Jewels or blowing up the Houses of Parliament but I didn't like to feel I'd besmirched the reputation of the walking fraternity in the eyes of the local populace.

The biggest headache for me, though, as an ever maturing bagger was uncertainty about the correctness of where I was walking, notwithstanding my increased confidence in my navigational abilities. I've mentioned in my introduction how there is often a major discrepancy between the map and the ground – between what the OS Explorer OL8 says in the comfort of your own front room during a *Coronation Street* ad break, and what you see once you've laced up your walking boots or trainers and been decanted from the nearest bus. You hope that the signage will be in place and will reflect what the Ordnance Survey tell you. But sometimes I was left scratching my head when I expected to see a sign and it was either absent, or stated the path to be a footpath rather than a bridleway, or appeared to be pointing the wrong way, or it was unclear which side of a fence it was supposed to be pointing, or what I thought was the way ahead was barred by either natural or man-made obstructions. Indeed some bridleways, like John Cleese's parrot, had very clearly ceased to be, rung down the curtain and joined the choir invisible, their demise evidenced by impenetrable and terminal blockage. I often wondered if the bridleway had ever actually existed at all or whether the map-maker had had a funny five minutes. Regardless as to whether it had or hadn't existed in the past, the sorry state of a mapped bridleway often left it impossible to tell whether it was still a right of way, thereby giving me licence to attempt to fight my way onto it and along it, or whether it was now an ex-bridleway and I would be trespassing if I attempted to follow it. Simply the lack of a signpost, or the fact that embarking on the route required negotiation of vegetation that would dwarf even the cellophane flowers of yellow and green in the Beatles' *Lucy In The Sky With Diamonds*, couldn't by itself conclusively prove the bridleway wasn't there any more, assuming indeed it ever had been there in the first place; but equally the presence of a signpost wasn't conclusive either. I well remember being challenged by a landowner when I was attempting to follow a mapped but frequently obstructed bridleway route at Hammerwood near East Grinstead, and being told that it had ceased to be a right of way years ago – despite the fact that at the southern end it was signed as a bridleway.

Conversely, on occasion I would discover a new or re-routed bridleway, sometimes a proper public bridleway and sometimes designated a permissive bridleway, the course of which didn't appear on my not-always-so-trusty maps, but with clear evidence for its existence in the form of standard bridleway signage, or its appearance on a local information board. What should I do – attempt to follow it and trust it to emerge somewhere recognisable; put it on the list for a future expedition; or cop out altogether and say that because it's not on the OS map it's actually either an optical illusion or the sign is there by mistake. The trouble is, as I've made clear in the introduction to this book, OS maps are only as accurate as the information fed to them and the OS cannot pretend to have the last word on accuracy and authenticity as far as the bridleway network is concerned. So, yes, once I found what was ostensibly a new bridleway, however I got to hear about it, the completist in me constrained me to follow it whatever the maps said or didn't say. I did occasionally come across alternative bridle routes which had clearly been created by landowners as sensible expedients. We've met one such, in route 83 – a permissive route clearly designed to avoid an adventure park. I found another, near Selham, which had been created to protect wildlife through an area of woodland at certain, particularly sensitive, times of year (see route 71). One more, between Partridge Green and Dial Post, was called a "voluntary bridleway," designed to divert walkers away from a house where there lived dogs that presumably couldn't be trusted not to extend the paw or (more likely) teeth of welcome to passers-by. The result was the same in every case: extra miles were consumed and any chance of making Greggs before they ran out of iced Belgian buns disappeared round the U-bend.

The other big bugbear I found myself facing was sections of bridleway that were signed as shut for essential maintenance or improvement work, which might be work on the bridleway itself, or tree-felling, or in one case a dirty great hole in a bridge supposedly carrying a bridleway across a river. There was no easy way of foreseeing these closures, or the possibility that a closure advertised as lasting a particular period of time may be extended. Knowing that my day's plans could be hopelessly upset by such a closure, I would often take the risk that I could get through okay, and mostly I got away with it. One particular bridle route I took near Liphook was advertised as being closed owing to a broken plank bridge. I took a chance and when I got to the bridge I found it was so narrow I was able to jump over it – and I can assure you I certainly had never won any long jump events on my school sports days. I didn't always get away with it; on one occasion I followed a "closed" bridleway just south-east of Crawley and I was shouted at by a man working on it. Consequently I was forced to speed from the scene of the crime, then spend the rest of the walk nervously watching the sky for police helicopters.

But it would be wrong to dwell too much on the negatives of my bagging. Most of the time I was loving it and many were the times I stepped off the train at my home station, Barnham, at the end of a day's exploration, and, like a priest announcing parish notices at the end of Mass, found myself declaiming to anyone who cared to listen, where and when the next bag was to be.

Throughout the autumn of 2019 and into the winter of 2019-20, I kept chipping away at the bridleways in Brighton & Hove and in East Sussex, confident I would have the job done in late 2020 as originally hoped. The winter was exceedingly wet: on 13th February 2020, a Thursday, I completed a particularly challenging bag in the vicinity of Wivelsfield and Ditchling Common, where for two of the bridleways I was wading through flood water that reached almost to the top of my wellies. I followed that up eight days later with a succession of rather muddy scrambles up and down bridleways linking the South Downs between Ditchling and Blackcap with the villages immediately to the north of the escarpment. I managed two bags on successive days in the following week, but on the second of those, again I wondered if I should have invested in some anglers' wading boots before heading out of the house. I was however philosophical. The wet winter would mean there should be no water supply or drought issues in spring and summer, and the days were steadily getting that bit longer. I looked forward to long spring and summer days, travelling further eastwards into East Sussex and enjoying the mix of Wealden and downland scenery with which my bridleway bagging would surely reward me. Conditions, I decided as I spent a subsequent Sunday morning scraping mud off the sides of my wellies for the umpteenth time, could only get better.

Except conditions were getting much, much worse.

Covid strikes

As February 2020 ended and March 2020 began, there were now very real fears about the spread of the coronavirus and what needed to be done to stop it. We were forced to accept that this was no longer just a media scare story or just another elf and safety issue, but a potentially major health crisis capable of affecting every one of us. It wasn't merely another flu virus; it could, we were told, be very serious, make people very ill, and actually have life-threatening consequences for those with a range of underlying health issues.

It was already dominating the news headlines as I went out bagging on Wednesday 4 March, a grey damp day which saw me following bridleways in the vicinity of Laughton between Lewes and Hailsham. As I followed a bridleway southwards towards Laughton Place, rain had begun. Low cloud hung over Laughton Level and the Low Weald as well as the nearby Cliffe Hill, and there was a sense of gloom and foreboding in the atmosphere. My subconscious must have guessed what was coming, for I found myself upping the bagging pace, completing further bags on Friday 6th, Monday 9th and Wednesday 11th March, all in the Alfriston area. The news was getting daily more concerning. On Saturday 14th March, on which in the company of my journalist friend Phil I followed the Downs Link all the way from Shoreham to Bramley, near Guildford, the entire professional football programme was cancelled. Then after a perversely glorious bag on the Monday 16th March around Friston Forest and Wilmington, I felt constrained to write in my diary the next day that "thanks to the coronavirus, normal life in this country has effectively come to a halt." Yet still it was not forbidden, at that stage, to go out walking as I had been, and thus it was that next day, Wednesday 18th March, I tackled a mish-mash of bridleways between Berwick, near Alfriston, and

Hailsham, mostly along farm tracks that boasted not only soggy bottoms but soggy everything else. On the face of it, things were functioning – trains and buses were running, cars were on the roads, shops were open, and I'd enjoyed my Baps n Buns breakfast before getting going. I rather liked being given this false impression that things were as they should be. And of course this is what walking can do. It takes you into a landscape where nothing may have changed for hundreds or even thousands of years. It puts you in touch with timeless. It asks you to forget the temporal concerns of the present, but rather to consider the values of eternity. Some might say that it's an unhealthy escape, a state of denial, a sense of hiding from reality. I prefer to see it as placing the troubles of our world into perspective and reminding ourselves of the essential changelessness of so much that surrounds us, and of what will still be here long after we have gone.

Which was why it was such a shock to be propelled back into the urgency of the moment, and having caught the 4.17pm train from Polegate and then the 5.02pm from Brighton, to learn that schools and colleges were shutting from Friday and that panic-buying was already setting in in anticipation of our not being allowed to get out to the shops. The days that followed were surreal, with many stores, eateries, pubs and businesses opting to shut down, albeit without any specific government decree forcing that to happen.

Despite the speculation I still trusted that any restrictions on our movement would not be so great as to bring an end to my baggery. Ominously, though, a friend of mine who was a doctor was quite sure that we would be made to stay at home in order to prevent the spread. I clung to the hope that I might just manage one more bag before the shutters came down, but that was snatched away on the following Monday 23rd March when Boris Johnson, the Prime Minister, announced that we must now stay at home save for only a handful of reasons. One of these reasons, yes, was for the purpose of exercise, but although no maximum exercise period appeared to have been prescribed, I did not feel, in all conscience, able to continue to venture from the western half of West Sussex into East Sussex (where all the remaining bags on my "to do" list were situated) to undertake it.

At that time, of course, nobody had any means of knowing how long these restrictions could or would last. I was faced with the possibility that I might never get to finish the East Sussex bridleways. I decided to split the project in two, reassuring myself that I had at least completed the bridleways in West Sussex so could say that my completist yearnings had in one sense been satisfied. Like everyone else, I got on with other things within the rules. I got to know very well the footpaths in our neighbourhood, and as March gave way to April, and April to May, I came to appreciate, as I'd never properly appreciated before, the variety of spring flowers, colours and birdsong – the birds continued to sing exuberantly and joyfully throughout the lockdown! It was a very valuable lesson, which I carried into my bags when able to resume operations – to enjoy what's in front of you, not to take any of it for granted, and not to try to do too much. I learnt to realise that no two walks are ever the same, even if you're following exactly the same route and in the same direction. There will always be something new to see or experience.

That said, I did miss the bagging excursions I'd come to take for granted as part of my weekly round. My hunger to start exploring again and pick up where I left off was always there, just below the surface, and, like the lure of forbidden fruit, the prospect of new discovery seemed that much more enticing for my being kept from it. We are so fortunate in this country to have free access to some of the most beautiful scenery in the world. Perhaps it is easy to forget how fortunate we are. The network of bridleways, well maintained and for the most part well signed, is very much part of this package of access. It was a wise writer indeed who wrote "Don't it always seem to go that you don't know what you've got till it's gone." I am sure I wasn't the only one who only seemed to appreciate the value of free access to the countryside when that access was curbed so fundamentally.

Writing this now, with lockdowns hopefully now no more than a memory, I realise what important lessons the bridleway explorer could learn from those weeks in the spring of 2020. Make the most of what the countryside offers, love it for its sense of changelessness and permanence, and don't treat lightly the ability to access it.

Project restart...stop...re-restart

Gradually the restrictions lifted, and by July it was possible to go off and explore again. I began with three bagging expeditions using the car, all in the Uckfield and Heathfield areas of East Sussex, back on the Eastbourne and Beachy Head and Ashdown Forest Explorer maps. I could tell how well I was progressing across East Sussex by the sight, during one of these expeditions, of a very splendid converted oasthouse, a type of building more closely associated with Kent. On 5th August I did my first bag using public transport since restrictions were eased, enjoying a splendid array of bridle routes in the Friston and East Dean areas, and I then had three days and two nights based in Eastbourne, soaking up the many bridle routes between Beachy Head and East Dean, and across Friston Forest. I chose probably the three hottest days of the year to get these done; on the morning on which I undertook my Friston Forest bag I got through five full water bottles, a carton of takeaway coffee and a thermos coffee, and over the three days, thanks to the Eat Out To Help Out scheme, I cleaned the Hikers' Rest café at East Dean out of salmon and cream cheese sandwiches. Further trips to Eastbourne and East Dean followed later in August, before my focus shifted back to the Uckfield area in early September, and then later in September and October I concentrated on bridleways in the Forest Row and East Grinstead areas.

But now the Covid storm clouds were gathering again. As I completed, on October 19th , a bag in the Holtye area, necessitating a not-so-good dollop of walking beside the busy A264, I heard that Wales was going back into lockdown. It seemed only a matter of time before we followed suit, and indeed a fresh stay-at-home order was issued to take effect from 5th November. I decided to get in with one last hurrah three days before that, following a charming web of bridleways in the Herstmonceux Castle/ Science Centre area (now making inroads into the Hastings & Bexhill Explorer map 124), then resolved to put any further bagging on hold till April when, one hoped, the countryside would be back open again. In fact apart from a respite in the first half of December, stay at home was to be the order of the day right through the winter. So once more it was a case of enjoying and appreciating the paths in my home area, and being grateful for simply being out in the crisp January and February air.

Although restrictions were lifted at the end of March 2021 I was only too aware how easily the situation could deteriorate again, so I resumed bagging operations in the knowledge that it might be stop-start right through to the finish. But in fact I was able to enjoy an uninterrupted bagging period right through to the completion of the task at the end of August and start of September, my final two bagging expeditions consisting of explorations of an often surreal network of bridle routes around Camber on the fringes of Romney Marsh, right at the south-eastern end of East Sussex. Like everyone else I was coping with the new normal, which meant face coverings on trains and buses: it was certainly good to remove my covering once the train or bus had plonked me down at the start of my day's activity. Before the lockdowns I had completed all the downland bridleways and the majority of routes remaining to be done, in the eastern half of East Sussex and consequently the furthest away from my home near Arundel, were of the woodland and waterside variety. I worked my way through the Hastings & Bexhill map, leaving me just a few bridleways to cover on the High Weald sheet (136) and Romney Marsh, Rye and Winchelsea

(125) and the job would be done. Conditions were as varied as they had been pre-lockdown, from pouring rain as I set out from Stonegate Station to explore the bridle route to the ominous-sounding Wreckery Bridge, to 30-degree heat as I worked my way round the western fringes of Bewl Water. Spring saw the annual bluebell carpets, the riot of cow parsley, the fragrance of wild garlic, the dazzling apple and cherry blossoms and the chirruping of the skylark, while summer hummed with busy bees and darting dragonflies. I followed more dirt tracks, more driveways, more field-edge paths, more suburban roads. I kept pushing myself to do more than was probably good for my sanity and my OCD often demanded mobile phone evidence to confirm completion of the shorter, blink-and-you'll-miss-them routes. The Ordnance Survey continued to keep me on my toes, inviting me to follow bridleways which seemingly no longer existed, and testing my navigational skills as I attempted to tackle bridleways which had apparently come into existence but of which the OS, Manuel-like, would claim "I know nothing." I continued to hone my psychic skills in working out where a route went in the absence of clear and unambiguous signage. As for the inner man, Baps n Buns continued to fortify me before I set out, and Greggs or Sainsbury's in Hastings became my go-to spot for the last iced Belgian bun or jam doughnut of the day. The long light evenings spent sitting on trains bringing me home from Hastings towards Chichester would see me looking out across the Pevensey Levels and the Weald, reliving my day's conquests, and loving the delicate pink evening skies that signalled an enforced end to another busy and productive time in the countryside. And my diary entries were just as breathless as that one on 5th October 2018 had been. But I shan't bore you with any more extracts!

In short, it was business as usual, and continued to be business as usual through to the conclusion of the task at the end of summer. It was with a sense of real satisfaction that on Monday 6th September 2021 I relaxed on the train heading from Eastbourne towards Lewes, looking up at the sun as it set over Mount Caburn, knowing that the sun was also setting on my bagging activity. I knew I would discover one or two rogue bridleways that had slipped through my net, and sure enough I did, but these turned out to be easily manageable and easily completed.

And as a consequence I can now say that I have walked all the mapped bridleways in Sussex and, I trust, all the unmapped ones as well. It's not quite an achievement on the scale of climbing Everest, or walking round the world. But I suspect it's unique. And as I've found, it's been well worth doing, and is well worth doing; it's not only immensely rewarding but eminently achievable. If this book encourages you either to follow in my footsteps, or create your very own "set" of walking or riding routes, I will be absolutely thrilled.

Now what can I strive to complete next?

AUTHOR'S ACKNOWLEDGEMENTS

I would like to thank Michael Walsh for another absolutely superb job in preparing my book for printing. He has, as always, been a model of politeness, kindliness, patience and efficiency. And may I thank my wife Sue and daughter Jenny for their constant love and support in what has been a tough year for them both.

BIBLIOGRAPHY AND SUGGESTIONS FOR FURTHER READING

Pevsner Architectural Guide – Sussex: East With Brighton & Hove – by Nicholas Antram and Nikolaus Pevsner – Yale University Press 2013

Pevsner Architectural Guide – Sussex: West – by Elizabeth Williamson, Tim Hudson, Jeremy Musson and Ian Nairn – Yale University Press 2019

Unto The Hills – by Patrick Coulcher – Book Guild 2001

The King's England – Sussex – by Arthur Mee – Hodder & Stoughton 1964

The Companion Guide To Kent And Sussex – by Keith Spence – Companion Guides 1999

Curious Sussex – by Mary Delorme – Robert Hale 1987

Walking The Disused Railways Of Sussex And Surrey – by David Bathurst – SB Publications 2010

The Great Walks Of Sussex – by David Bathurst – Walk & Write Publications – 2018

ABOUT FRIENDS OF SUSSEX HOSPICES

Friends of Sussex Hospices is a registered charity run entirely by volunteers. It raises funds, through a variety of activities, to support the running costs of the 12 hospice care providers that serve the adults and children of Sussex. All proceeds of sale of this book will be donated to them

THEMATIC INDEX

Rather than providing a straight A to Z index of features described or alluded to in Parts 1 to 7 of the central section of this book, I have decided to index the features under theme. This will, I believe, make it easier for you to locate sights and locations that are of particular interest to you in the course of your bridleway exploration.

Rivers/Bodies Of Water

Natural Phenomena

Hilltops/Viewpoints

Long-Distance Trails/Green Roads

Historic Mills (see also under Historic Villages)

Visitor Attractions